A TURN TO EMPIRE

A TURN TO EMPIRE

THE RISE OF IMPERIAL LIBERALISM IN BRITAIN AND FRANCE

Jennifer Pitts

PRINCETON UNIVERSITY PRESS   PRINCETON AND OXFORD

Published by Princeton University Press, 41 William Street,
Princeton, New Jersey 08540
In the United Kingdom: Princeton University Press,
3 Market Place, Woodstock, Oxfordshire OX20 1SY

Library of Congress Cataloging-in-Publication Data

Pitts, Jennifer, 1970–
A turn to empire : the rise of imperial liberalism in Britain and France / Jennifer Pitts.
p. cm.
Includes bibliographical references and index.
ISBN 0-691-11558-3 (cloth : alk. paper)
1. Imperialism—History—18th century. 2. Imperialism—History—19th century.
3. Great Britain—Colonies—History—18th century. 4. Great Britain—Colonies—History—19th century. 5. France—Colonies—History—18th century. 6. France—Colonies—History—19th century. 7. Political science—Great Britain—History.
8. Political science—France—History. 9. Liberalism—History—18th century.
10. Liberalism—History—19th century. I. Title.

JC359.P54 2005
325′.341′01—dc22   2004059366

British Cataloging-in-Publication Data is available

This book has been composed in Sabon.

Printed on acid-free paper. ∞

pup.princeton.edu

Printed in the United States of America

10 9 8 7 6 5 4 3 2 1

For my parents

Contents

Acknowledgments

I HAVE INCURRED many debts to people and institutions during the years that went into this book, and it is a great pleasure to acknowledge them here. I am thankful for the generous funding that enabled the initial research for this book, from the Jacob K. Javits Fellowship Program of the United States Department of Education and the Charlotte W. Newcombe Fellowship of the Woodrow Wilson Foundation. The Minda de Gunzburg Center for European Studies at Harvard University provided an unparalleled research environment and scholarly community at a crucial stage in my graduate work.

I presented earlier versions of much of this book at conferences and colloquiums, and I benefited greatly from the thoughtful comments and searching questions from the audiences: at Harvard, the graduate student conference on "Europe and Empire" at the Center for European Studies, and the political theory workshop; at Yale, the Department of Political Science and the political theory workshop; the departments of Political Science at the New School for Social Research and the University of Chicago; the UCLA Clark Library and Center for 17th and 18th Century Studies; the New York–area chapter of the Conference for the Study of Political Thought; the conference "The Legacies of Colonization and Decolonization in Europe and the Americas" at the Centre National de la Recherche Scientifique in Paris; the conference "Towards Cosmopolitan Citizenship?" at the Convento do Arràbida, Portugal, sponsored by the Fundaçao Oriente; and Annual Meetings of the American Political Science Association, the International Society for Eighteenth Century Studies, and the International Society for the Study of European Ideas. I am grateful to John Roemer for inviting me to present work to his seminar in New York, and to members of the seminar for their keen questions and insights.

A version of chapter 4 was published in *Political Theory* 31, no. 2 (2003). Several passages, mostly in chapter 7, were first published in the *Journal of Political Philosophy* 8, no. 3 (2000) and in my introduction to Alexis de Tocqueville, *Writings on Empire and Slavery* (Johns Hopkins University Press, 2001). I thank Sage Publications, Blackwell Publishers, and Johns Hopkins University Press for permission to reprint these.

Richard Tuck's enthusiasm for the history of political thought has been compelling and infectious, and his engagement with this project has been instrumental in shaping it from the very start. Stanley Hoffmann's moral seriousness and his love for French thought set inspiring, if unreachable, standards, and I am particularly thankful for his guidance on the French chapters. Pratap Mehta has asked many of the toughest and most important questions, which I will spend years trying to answer; I am deeply grateful for his wise guidance, his example of imaginative and engaged scholarship, and his friendship. David Armitage and Cheryl Welch both read the entire manuscript twice and offered innumerable apt and thoughtful suggestions for its improvement; their tremendous generosity with their time and ideas, and the example of their own work, have provided particular inspiration during my revision of the manuscript. My debt to all of them is immeasurable, and I can only hope that the book's remaining flaws do not mask all I have learned from them.

From the earliest stages of this project I have benefited from the camaraderie and constructive criticism of my fellow graduate students, now colleagues: Arash Abizadeh, Danielle Allen, Benjamin Berger, Peter Cannavò, Jim Fuerst, Nancy Kokaz, Sharon Krause, Karuna Mantena, Jason Neidleman, and especially Christopher Brooke and Michaele Ferguson of the memorable 6 Marie. Gary Bass kept my attention on politics. Samantha Power's passion for ideas and the world helped me keep the project in perspective. I owe particular gratitude to Patchen Markell and Andy Sabl for their acute questions and painstaking comments on countless drafts and for conversations about political theory that have taught me as much as any. With imagination and empathy, Peter Berkowitz, Jill Frank, and Bonnie Honig grasped my most inchoate thoughts and helped me develop them. Istvan Hont offered insights about the eighteenth century and set a standard of historical scholarship I cannot hope to meet. I thank the wonderful staff at Harvard's Center for European Studies, and especially Lisa Eschenbach, for support throughout my years at the Center, and Tom Ertman, Daniel Goldhagen, and Susan Pedersen for conversations and advice during the writing of the dissertation that served as the basis for this book.

I found a rich and congenial intellectual home at Yale, in the political science department, in the Directed Studies program, and at the Whitney Humanities Center; I acknowledge with gratitude the generous research funding provided through the Junior Faculty Fellowship and the Ethics, Politics, and Economics program's John K. Castle fund. I am grateful to John Roemer, Ian Shapiro, Rogers Smith, Steven Smith, Norma Thompson, and Robert Wokler for their suggestions and support, to Seyla Benhabib for her careful reading of the entire manuscript and her advice on honing the book's argument, and to an extraordinarily vibrant and supportive group of junior faculty for friendship and intellectual fellowship: especially to Vicky Murillo, Pauline Jones Luong, and Anna Grzymala-Busse. Winifred Amaturo sharpened the language of several chapters. David Bromwich's thoughtful and extensive comments on a number of chapters deepened my understanding of some crucial matters. Matthias Risse and Ala Alryyes, over many conversations, helped me articulate key points. Most of all, I am indebted to John McCormick for his unstinting encouragement and his always apt advice.

Princeton University and the University Center for Human Values provided a welcoming and conducive environment for the final months of revision, for which I am grateful to friends and colleagues there, especially Stephen Macedo.

Michael Suarez, S.J., has been a scholarly model, an unfailing source of ideas historical and professional, and a priceless friend. Melvin Richter offered expert and judicious guidance from a very early stage. George Kateb has been generous with his support and ideas, and his characteristically incisive comments improved my treatment of Mill. I am grateful to Fred Rosen for his kind welcome at the Bentham Project, to Luke O'Sullivan for his generous assistance in navigating the collection and deciphering manuscripts, and to Luke O'Sullivan and Catherine Pease-Watkin for their readiness to share by email texts that had been edited but not yet published. Bentham continues to be well cared for by his friends.

I am especially obliged to the friends, colleagues, and teachers who have commented on portions of the manuscript and with whom I have had valuable conversations about its themes: Arash Abizadeh, Sunil Agnani, Ala Alryyes, Winifred Amaturo, David Armitage, Gary Bass, Seyla Benhabib, Richard Bourke, David Bromwich, Benjamin Berger, Erik Bleich, Richard Bourke, Christopher Brooke, Aurelian Craiutu, James Der Derian, Stéphane Dufoix, Roxanne Euben, John Ferejohn, Michaele Ferguson, Bill Foltz, Robert Forster, Caroline Fox Elkins, Jill Frank, Mokhtar Ghambou, Robert Goodin, Ryan Hanley, Stanley Hoffmann, Bonnie Honig, Istvan Hont, David Johnston, George Kateb, Christine Korsgaard, Sharon Krause, Jacob Levy, James Livesey, Ian Malcolm, Karuna Mantena, Harvey Mansfield, Patchen Markell, Kirstie McClure, John McCormick, Pratap Mehta, Uday Mehta, Joseph Miller, Sankar Muthu, Anthony Pagden, Bhikhu Parekh, David Plotke, Samantha Power, Melvin Richter, Patrick Riley, Mathias Risse, John Roemer, Fred Rosen, Nancy Rosenblum, Alan Ryan, Andy Sabl, Naomi Schor, Ian Shapiro, Stephen Skowronek, Rogers Smith, Steven Smith, Sarah Song, Michael Suarez, Richard Tuck, Georgios Varouxakis, Gauri Viswanathan, Patrick Weil, Cheryl Welch, Robert Wokler, and Bernard Yack.

At Princeton University Press, I am indebted to my production editor Sara Lerner and to Sophia Efthimiatou for shepherding the manuscript through production, and to Richard Isomaki for scrupulous copyediting, and to Thomas Broughton-Willett for preparing the index. Ian Malcolm has been an author's dream editor: insightful, attentive, and forbearing. I am greatly and happily in his debt.

My extended family—my brother, John Pitts; Lynn Freed and Jessica Gamsu; and my family-in-law, Jeya and S. P. Muthuchidambaram, Uma Muthu, and Phoebe and John Vlahoplus—know how much I appreciate their unquestioning support.

For ten years, Sankar Muthu has been my most treasured companion and critic. He has read countless drafts with sensitivity and keen intelligence, and has intervened with ideas and energy when mine were depleted. His love and intellectual comradeship enrich my life and my work more than even he realizes.

My greatest and most inexpressible debt is to my parents, Lawrence and Mary Pitts, whose energy awes me and whose unconditional enthusiasm for my projects sustains me. This book is dedicated to them.

Abbreviations

Jeremy Bentham

RRR *Rights, Representation, and Reform: Nonsense upon Stilts and Other Writings on the French Revolution.* Edited by Philip Schofield, Catherine Pease-Watkin, and Cyprian Blamires. Oxford: Clarendon Press, 2002.

WJB *Works of Jeremy Bentham.* Edited by John Bowring. 11 vols. London: Simpkin, Marshall, 1843.

Edmund Burke

WS *Writings and Speeches of Edmund Burke.* General editor, Paul Langford. Textual editor for the writings, William B. Todd. 9 vols. Oxford: Oxford University Press, 1981–.

James Mill

HBI *The History of British India.* 5th ed. Edited by H. H. Wilson. 6 vols. London: James Madden, 1858; reprint New York: Chelsea House, 1968.

John Stuart Mill

CW *Collected Works.* Edited by John M. Robson and R. F. McRae. 33 vols. Toronto: University of Toronto Press, 1963–.

Adam Smith

EPS *Essays on Philosophical Subjects.* Edited by W.P.D. Wrightman and J. C. Bryce. Indianapolis: Liberty Fund, 1980.

LJ *Lectures on Jurisprudence.* Edited by Ronald L. Meek, D. D. Raphael, and Peter G. Stein. Indianapolis: Liberty Fund, 1982.

TMS *The Theory of Moral Sentiments.* Edited by D. D. Raphael and A. L. Macfie. Indianapolis: Liberty Press, 1982.

WN *An Inquiry into the Nature and Causes of the Wealth of Nations.* Edited by R. H. Campbell, A. S. Skinner, and W. B. Todd. 2 vols. Indianapolis: Liberty Press, 1976.

Alexis de Tocqueville

OC *Oeuvres complètes.* Edited by J.-P. Mayer. 18 vols. Paris: Gallimard, 1958–98.

A TURN TO EMPIRE

One

Introduction

In the closing years of the eighteenth century, a critical challenge to European imperial conquest and rule was launched by many of the most innovative thinkers of the day, including Adam Smith, Bentham, Burke, Kant, Diderot, and Condorcet. They drew on a strikingly wide range of ideas to criticize European conquests and rule over peoples across the globe: among others, the rights of humanity and the injustice of foreign despotism, the economic wisdom of free trade and foolishness of conquest, the corruption of natural man by a degenerate civilization, the hypocrisy required for self-governing republics to rule over powerless and voiceless subjects, and the impossibility of sustaining freedom at home while exercising tyranny abroad. European explorers, wrote Denis Diderot in 1780,

> arrive in a region of the New World unoccupied by anyone from the Old World, and immediately bury a small strip of metal on which they have engraved these words: *This country belongs to us*. And why does it belong to you? . . . You have no right to the natural products of the country where you land, and you claim a right over your fellow men. Instead of recognizing this man as a brother, you only see him as a slave, a beast of burden. Oh my fellow citizens![1]

While Diderot's criticism of empire was among the most radical and thoroughgoing, skepticism about both particular imperial ventures and the general project of unlimited European expansion was, by the 1780s, widespread among intellectuals. Just fifty years later, however, we find no prominent political thinkers in Europe questioning the justice of European empires.[2] Indeed, nineteenth-century liberals, including most prominently Alexis de Tocqueville and John Stuart Mill, turned decisively from the earlier thinkers' skepticism about empire and supported the expansion and consolidation of European rule over non-European subjects. "Despotism," wrote Mill, "is a legitimate mode of government in dealing with barbarians, provided the end be their improvement, and the means justified by actually effecting that end."[3] Mill and Tocqueville were joined in their support for empire by many of their liberal contemporaries as well as by other political thinkers of their age, including Hegel and even Marx to some degree. But while both British and French liberals in the nineteenth century undertook to advocate and justify imperial rule, they did so in divergent ways that reflected their countries' different degrees of international power and reputation—Britain was secure, dominant, and culturally confident, while France, which had lost much of its earlier empire by the end of the Seven Years' War, was politically unstable at home and had not yet regained power abroad—and that also reflected the somewhat different courses taken by liberalism in each country.

This book examines several important moments in the development of a strand of British and French political thought that appeared, by the 1780s, to hold the promise of a critical approach to European expansion, and its displacement by an imperial liberalism that by the 1830s provided some of the most insistent and well-developed arguments in favor of the conquest of non-European peoples and territories.[4] This sea change in opinions on empire accompanied an increasingly exclusive conception among European thinkers of national community and political capacity. The liberal turn to empire in this period was also accompanied by the eclipse of nuanced and pluralist theories of progress as they gave way to more contemptuous notions of "backwardness" and a cruder dichotomy between barbarity and civilization.[5]

The historical and theoretical questions addressed in this inquiry include the following: What were some of the theoretical underpinnings of the criticism of empire we find expressed in the late eighteenth century, and what changes accompanied the decline of such critiques and the emergence of new justifications of empire? What intellectual dispositions have been conducive to skepticism about empire, and what beliefs and modes of moral judgment have led to the conviction that the conquest and despotic rule of other peoples is justified? How did discourses surrounding the conceptions of progress and nation change in ways that led to support for imperial rule?

This book considers the thought of British and French political thinkers of the late eighteenth to mid-nineteenth century, paying particular attention to figures—Burke, J. S. Mill, and Tocqueville—who were not only political philosophers of the first order but also active in the politics and administration of the British and French empires. Edmund Burke viewed his sustained condemnation of British actions in India as the most important political work of his life.[6] John Stuart Mill worked from the age of seventeen for the British East India Company; he rose quickly to one of its most influential posts; and he fought for the Company's continued rule there, resigning only after the Company lost its battle to maintain control over Indian affairs when Parliament assumed direct rule over India in 1858. Alexis de Tocqueville established himself, early in his parliamentary career, as the Chamber of Deputies' expert on Algeria and as a prominent defender of French conquest and settlement there. The work of all these thinkers combined engagement in concrete debates over imperial conquest and governance with broader philosophical reflections: on the nature of Europe's relations to the non-European world, on the duties of powerful countries toward more vulnerable societies, on the relationship between responsible representative government at home and despotic rule abroad. This study also addresses thinkers—Smith and Bentham—who, although not legislators or colonial administrators, followed the progress of their countries' empires closely and critically.[7]

Liberalism, Pluralism, and Empire

The thinkers considered here, for all the great differences in their thought, can be said to have shared a commitment to the values of equal human dignity, freedom, the rule of law, and accountable, representative government. They were universalists in the sense that they adhered to the principles that all human beings are naturally equal and that certain fundamental moral principles are universally valid. All eschewed both biological racism and the relativism that regards cultures as mutually incomprehensible or founded on irreconcilable values. As we shall see, their different universalisms—their different negotiations of the tension between a belief in human unity and a recognition of cultural, social, and political variation—had remarkably different implications as they responded to the political questions surrounding the imperial expansion of European states.

Because of the shared political and philosophical commitments among the central thinkers considered in this book, all might be regarded as members of a liberal tradition, broadly conceived. To be sure, "liberalism" emerged as a self-conscious tradition only in the nineteenth century and is thus anachronistic as a description of earlier thinkers' self-understanding. While Tocqueville, Bentham, J. S. Mill, and Constant explicitly described themselves as liberals, Burke and Smith would not have recognized liberalism as a tradition or category of political thought.[8] Still, while it is impossible and probably counterproductive to attempt anything like a definitive or narrow definition of the term, liberalism has been usefully evoked to describe overlapping strands of thought long prior to the term's invention at the turn of the nineteenth century.[9] Cheryl Welch's definition of liberalism, following early-nineteenth-century usage—in which liberalism "connote[s] a commitment to certain individual rights (specifically equality before the law, freedom of the press, and religious freedom), opposition to the policies of the mercantilist state, opposition to monarchical power if not to monarchical government, and a certain expansiveness of social sympathies"—captures well the range of commitments shared by the thinkers considered here.[10] While some might dispute an application of the last phrase to Burke's thought (a question addressed in chapter 3), this definition suits these thinkers remarkably well.

The question "what happens when liberalism encounters the world?" is more central to liberal thought than was long appreciated, as recent scholarship has begun to suggest.[11] There has been considerable disagreement in the literature and in popular understandings of the tradition about what the "liberal" position on empire has been, and about what the implications of liberal thought are for international justice more broadly. Some have claimed that liberalism has always contained an imperialist core: that a liberal insistence on progress and establishing the rule of law has led liberals over and over again to support imperialist projects. In this view, nineteenth-century Britain and the French *mission civilisatrice* serve as typical examples of the imperialist logic of liberal political thought.[12] Others suggest that liberalism is inherently anti-imperialist, given its commitment to human equality and self-government: in this account, otherwise liberal thinkers who support empire merely reveal an illiberal side or smuggle illiberal ideas into their arguments. Jeremy Bentham himself used this argument polemically when he wrote to the Spanish people that if they maintained their domination over their New World possessions, "in vain would you continue your claim to the title of liberals."[13]

The first view cannot explain the many thinkers widely considered liberals who strongly opposed European imperialism, particularly in the eighteenth century. The second disregards the fact that many of the staple concepts of liberal political thought have indeed been mobilized in favor of the European imperial enterprise, and that European liberalism was forged alongside, and deeply affected by, imperial expansion. Liberals—in different times and under diverse circumstances in the history of the liberal tradition—have been among imperialism's most prominent defenders and its sharpest critics. No explanation that rests on some set of basic theoretical assumptions in the liberal tradition can possibly explain such flexibility on the question of empire: liberalism does not lead ineluctably either to imperialism or anti-imperialism. Rather, we must investigate the pressures and anxieties of certain historical moments to understand how thinkers whom we understand to exist within a broad but identifiable tradition could have disagreed so thoroughly about one of the most important political developments of the late eighteenth and nineteenth centuries: the expansion of European colonial empires.

While I want to insist that there is no logical necessity that liberalism be a tradition critical of empire, I also suggest that, if liberalism can be said to rest on a commitment to human dignity and equality, the support for empire among so many nineteenth-century liberals poses a theoretical problem that requires explanation. This is not to say that support for empire is ipso facto illiberal. Rather, the endorsement of radically different political standards for different people implied by imperialism requires theoretical justifications that form an often unexpected and indeed uncomfortable element in liberal thought in the nineteenth century.[14] Nor should we believe that there is simply a gap between liberal theory and liberal practice, or that liberal practice, under political pressure, found itself unable to live up to its theory. Rather, this book examines the articulation of liberalism as a practice. Liberal theory has been constituted by its engagement in politics, and it is an important if often overlooked historical fact that the creation and consolidation of empires was central to that process.

The issue of empire draws out aspects of thinkers' theories in surprising and productive ways. It focuses our attention on certain blind spots or incisive moments that are not always apparent in their views on domestic politics. Writings on imperial politics allow us to answer more fully, for instance, who are the objects of a thinker's exclusions. John Stuart Mill was attuned to a degree remarkable for a man of his day to the ways in which European society and laws infantilized women, treating them as wards incapable of bearing adult responsibility. At the same time, he accepted with little question the view that Indians were similarly immature and incapable of self-government. In contrast, Burke is often considered the oligarchic thinker par excellence. As I argue in chapter 3, however, Burke's writings on international and imperial politics draw our attention to his powerful opposition to oppression by the few over the many and his own self-understanding as a reformer in the service of the vulnerable and excluded. These works suggest that what appears to be Burke's remarkable indifference to the sufferings of the French people under the ancien régime may be itself a blind spot in his thought, rather than an indication of broader and deeper commitments to aristocratic rule at any cost, as it is often taken to be.

This book asks how thinkers' views about cultural diversity, progress, and nationality affected their moral and political judgments regarding non-Europeans. I suggest that a strong conviction of the rationality of all people and the fundamental reasonableness of all societies was essential for robust resistance to imperial expansion and rule. Simple belief in human moral equality proved to be inadequate for genuine respect for unfamiliar people and insistence on humane and egalitarian relations with them. Condorcet, for instance, argued that European conquests had been cruel and wrong; but, believing non-Europeans to be, on the whole, backward and incapable of self-government or self-improvement, he hoped for a pacific settlement of Europeans throughout the world, leading to a partnership of unequals in which kind Europeans would take trusting savages into their care and tutelage. Although Condorcet's language, passionately critical of European depredations abroad, bore considerable resemblance to that of his more robustly critical contemporaries, his brand of what we might call a nonpluralist anti-imperialism proved to be a fragile construct.

A central concern of this book, then, is how the thinkers under study analyzed and judged unfamiliar societies. Did their views of moral judgment speak to the difficulty of understanding unfamiliar others in different social contexts, or address the biases that beset moral and cultural judgment? How critical were they about their sources of information on non-European societies, especially when invoking them to demonstrate "backwardness"? Did they regard personal observation of such societies as important for proper judgment? Many Scottish Enlightenment thinkers, for instance, drew attention to the dangers of basing theoretical and political judgments on sources that were notoriously biased and unreliable. Tocqueville insisted on seeing Algeria for himself; he altered his views about what was practicable and appropriate for French Algeria as a result of his journeys, and forbore from writing about India because of his inability to travel there. James Mill, in contrast, boasted that his writing about India was the more impartial and well informed because he had not been distracted by the arbitrary observations that are the lot of a traveler and had instead confined himself to a thorough canvassing of the (English-language) literature on India.

Not merely the philosophical arguments, but also the rhetorical practice of these thinkers illustrates the difficulty of engaging in moral reasoning about strangers, of extending the limits of moral norms. Burke's parliamentary speeches draw explicit attention to this problem of appealing to an audience in familiar moral language, when one is discussing people whom it hardly understands, and for whom it has little sympathy. How does a thinker not only develop a nuanced and respectful understanding of an unfamiliar society for him or herself, but also articulate this understanding for the larger society? Arguments about the audience's hypocrisy play a crucial role in this process of attempting to expand the scope of moral norms, for hypocrisy appears to be a failure to expand that scope, an unwillingness to apply such norms to strangers. Burke, Bentham, and Constant all drew upon accusations of hypocrisy in an effort to prompt their audiences into a more respectful and equitable frame of mind. Also on the level of rhetoric, I want to suggest that the thinkers most critical of empire are those most inclined to use irony and humor in their arguments. The confidence—even self-righteousness—of imperial liberalism requires a kind of presumption incompatible with the sharply ironic, self-critical stance so characteristic of the eighteenth-century thinkers considered here. We encounter an earnestness in J. S. Mill or a grand high-mindedness in Tocqueville that is quite foreign to the style of Bentham or Burke.[15]

Scope and Summary

I begin, in chapter 2, with a discussion of Adam Smith's theories of progress and moral judgment, arguing that he developed resources for cross-cultural respect that nineteenth-century theorists of progress would fail to maintain. As a theorist of development, Smith combined, on the one hand, a belief in universal moral principles and the possibility of moral progress, and on the other hand, a posture of respect for precommercial and non-European societies. Smith approached the radically different moral and political commitments and practices to be observed in precommercial societies, then, with the thought that they were the result not of the ignorance or distorted values of their members, but rather of a familiar process of judgment employed in very different circumstances.

Chapter 3 discusses Burke's critique of the British empire in India and Ireland. Burke, whose understanding of moral judgment and societal development shared important features with Smith's, produced a singularly scathing indictment of British imperial practice in both hemispheres. In his works on India and Ireland, Burke analyzed with remarkable sensitivity the forms of political and moral exclusion that characterized Britain's relations with its colonial subjects. Burke perceived that British actions in the world were governed by a restricted notion of moral and political community that led to contempt for imperial subjects and a willingness to suspend ordinary British moral and political norms. There is considerable irony in the fact that while the late eighteenth century is known for defenses of the rights of man, perhaps the most notorious opponent of this formulation also sustained what may have been the most dedicated and impassioned advocacy on behalf of a remote people suffering at the hands of a European state. Attention to Burke's writings on India and Ireland is indispensable for a proper understanding not only of what lay behind his suspicion of the revolutionary "rights of man" but also of the possibilities generated by his own response to vulnerable groups. These writings reveal the pluralism and tolerance that underlay Burke's well-known hostility to grand ideologies and sweeping reforms based on abstract principle. While none of Burke's contemporaries matched either the breadth or the direct political involvement of his fight against imperial injustices, I argue that Burke's achievement was not that of a uniquely sensitive and eccentric figure. Rather he shared with others, including Smith and Bentham, a critical posture toward European claims of cultural and political superiority, a skepticism about whether political change could or should be imposed by an imperial power on very different societies, and a concern about the dangers that exercising despotic power abroad posed to political liberties at home.

As I argue in chapter 4, Bentham, whose utilitarian theory would be exploited by subsequent generations as the theoretical bulwark of the British government in India, himself insisted on the injustice, corruption, and presumptuousness of the European effort to rule distant subjects whose interests were best known to the people themselves. Bentham's writings on empire betray none of the enthusiasm for "progressive" despotism over backward subjects that would come to dominate the writings of his self-designated successors.

With James Mill and J. S. Mill, among others, British utilitarians abandoned Bentham's remarkably egalitarian and emancipatory posture toward empire. The common assumption of a continuous tradition of utilitarian imperialism not only distorts Bentham's own theoretical and political enterprise and leads to misreadings of some of his writings; it also fails to recognize the novelty of the Mills' thinking on empire. It was only when cruder theories of progress and "barbarity" had become dominant; only when a narrower conception of nationality began to take root; only when both the British state and the East India Company perceived a need to solidify their rule with an appropriately "progressive" ideology, that Benthamite utilitarianism was transformed into the imperialist doctrine it is widely understood to have been.[16]

As in Britain, late-eighteenth-century France evinced a growing moral and political disapproval of empire. Its most potent exponent was probably Diderot, but we find this critical posture to varying degrees in other thinkers, such as Diderot's coauthors of the *Encyclopédie* and the *Histoire des deux Indes*; Condorcet; and, in the early years of the next century, Benjamin Constant.[17] In chapters 6 and 7, I discuss the shift in liberal views on empire in France that is, perhaps, best captured by a contrast between the writings of Constant on the "spirit of conquest" and those of Tocqueville on the French empire in Algeria and the West Indies. I argue that although Constant shared with Tocqueville many concerns typical of nineteenth-century French liberals—above all the desire to build a cohesive liberal society in the wake of the Revolution and the empire—Constant was suspicious of imperial conquest in ways that his liberal heirs were not.

Tocqueville, the most prominent and highly respected of the liberal advocates of empire in mid-nineteenth-century France, believed that conquest of Algeria would contribute to the foundation and perpetuation of the liberal order he sought for France, by providing a grand collective political project for an apathetic public as well as a laboratory for the municipal self-government he had admired in America. I examine the ways in which Tocqueville overcame earlier liberal concerns about the dangers or injustices of empire and came to believe that his liberalism might demand, or at least be materially assisted by, empire.

Tocqueville's enthusiasm for empire is in some ways so unexpected that it has escaped some readers altogether. Isaiah Berlin, for instance, seems simply to have extrapolated from the elements of pluralism in *Democracy in America* to argue that "Tocqueville believes in the exercise of rights even in immature communities . . . for otherwise men will never learn to stand and respect reciprocal liberties. Hence his opposition to paternalism and colonialism, every form of rule by outsiders no matter how benevolent."[18] Such a claim suggests that to ignore Tocqueville's writings on empire is to misunderstand quite profoundly the implications of his writings on Western democracies. Moreover, Tocqueville's writings on Algeria should not be dismissed as merely an oversight or blind spot in the career of an otherwise enlightened liberal pluralist. For these works demonstrate particularly forcefully the degree to which a concern to place the modern democratic nation on a secure footing drew nineteenth-century French liberals into an exclusionary and violent international politics that so many of their predecessors would have seen as a betrayal of liberal humanitarianism.

This book focuses on treatments of European imperial expansion into territories with substantial indigenous populations, relations with whom were regarded as a central question of imperial policy. For Britain and France during the period in question, these were predominantly non-European populations in Asia and North Africa. I consider treatments of Ireland as well, because the British colonization of Ireland was seen by many, including Burke and Mill, to pose questions very much like those Britain faced in non-European colonies such as India. For Burke, these were problems of the political and moral exclusion of populations the British settlers considered inferior, and he regularly drew connections between his own efforts on behalf of Irish Catholics and Indians, two excluded and, as he said, "oppressed" peoples. For Mill, Ireland and India posed similar problems and questions about how best to govern a backward society, though only in the case of Ireland did he acknowledge Britain's complicity in that alleged backwardness.

I discuss only briefly these thinkers' treatments of the North American settlement colonies, although Smith, Burke, and Bentham all participated actively in debates about the fate of the American colonies, before and during the American War of Independence. Certainly the American conflict and eventually the loss of most of the New World settler colonies affected the views of Smith, Burke, and Bentham about imperial rule in other parts of the world. Their exposure to and involvement in the debates surrounding independence of American colonies (and in Bentham's case, Spain's South American colonies as well) inflected their attitudes toward other imperial matters. In particular, the American crises made all three thinkers wary of imperial overreach and conscious of the many problems involved in ruling at great distances over people whose interests are different from—and often opaque to—those in the metropole who seek to control their fates.

Smith believed either independence or complete political incorporation was the only just policy regarding the American colonies (see chapter 2). Burke, who acted as agent for the colony of New York, was sympathetic to the colonies' demands. Although he pleaded for an accommodative policy that would reconcile the colonies to the imperial structure, he accepted the Americans' bid for independence when it became clear that Britain would not adopt such a policy of conciliation. Bentham alone of the three was initially hostile to the demands of the American colonists, primarily because he objected to the natural rights language in which they were so often couched by both colonists themselves and their British supporters such as Richard Price.[19] But he too soon came to believe that, for reasons of both justice and prudence, European states ought to emancipate their settler colonies. By the late 1780s, Bentham had become an enthusiastic supporter both of American independence and of the American system of government, though he remained famously hostile to natural rights arguments and was quoted at the end of his life arguing that he had opposed American independence because of the bad arguments offered in its support, instead of "the only good one, viz. the impossibility of good government at such a distance, and the advantage of separation to the interest and happiness of both parties."[20]

At this time, the central problems in America were considered to be relations with settlers very much like the metropole's population in their social and political culture, members of the metropole's community of moral and political concern.[21] The problem of relations with Amerindians was less central to debates surrounding imperial policy in America by the late eighteenth century, although a few British observers did hold that American settlers could not be trusted to deal justly with the indigenous population, and that the continuation of the imperial relationship was justified as a means of protecting Native Americans from rapacious settlers. In contrast to this relative neglect of the question of Native Americans in the larger debate over the colonies' status in the 1760s and 1770s, the question of relations with and rule over a "subordinate" population was central to debates in the settler colonies of Ireland and later French Algeria. How to treat distinct indigenous populations—whether conceived of as inferior, or vulnerable, or wrongly excluded—remained central to British and French understandings of the political dilemmas of these colonies as well as nonsettlement territories such as India.

While a thorough treatment of these thinkers' views on the struggle with the American colonies is beyond the scope of this book, then, I consider how their arguments about such settler colonies contributed to their views about British and French rule over indigenous populations in colonized territories. Similarly, Tocqueville's travels along the American frontier, and his understanding of relations between European settlers and Amerindians, bore in important ways on his analysis of French imperial policy in Algeria. Tocqueville's hope that Algiers might prove to be a "Cincinnati on the soil of Africa"—an economic dynamo with traditions of local self-government and self-reliance—illustrates the way in which he drew lessons from America not only for French democracy but also for the French Empire.

The turn to empire among liberal thinkers in Britain and France during the early decades of the nineteenth century was characterized by certain shared theoretical features, most prominently an increasingly secure belief that Europe's progressive civilization granted Europeans the authority to suspend, in their relations with non-European societies, the moral and political standards they believed applied among themselves. Still, Smith, Burke, Bentham, and Constant, despite certain affinities in their distaste for empire, differed in their particular diagnoses of the problems associated with European imperial expansion. Likewise, Mill and Tocqueville, though they were prominently identified with the justification and exercise of imperial power in their respective countries, disagreed—explicitly, as we will see—about what sort of empire could be justified, and how. Much of the theoretical discussion of the earlier thinkers' criticism of empire and the eclipse of that criticism among their successors, then, must be particular to each thinker and is carried out chapter by chapter. Still, certain features of the changing political, economic, and intellectual landscapes provide an important backdrop to these theoretical developments, and I address these in brief in the following section.

Historical Contexts

Political Developments in the British and French Empires

The transformation in political thought that I describe in this study took place alongside great changes in the British and French empires as well as domestic political upheavals. From the Seven Years' War through the end of the American War of Independence, Britain's imperial energies increasingly shifted from the settler colonies of the New World toward Asia and the rule of largely non-European subjects.[22] Britain's great military successes throughout the Seven Years' War—in Canada, the West Indies, Africa, and South India—led the British public to regard their state as a territorial as well as a maritime power and to see their empire, for the first time, as truly global. At the same time, the loss of the preponderance of the British colonial settler populations meant that the British Empire could no longer be regarded as almost exclusively European and "free."[23] As David Armitage and Kathleen Wilson have recently shown, these developments of the second half of the eighteenth century challenged the long-held British belief that their empire, unlike those of the Portuguese and Spanish, or even the French and the Dutch, was one of commerce and not conquest: that it was characterized by, and responsible for spreading, free British institutions and political practices.[24] This image was, of course, always to a considerable degree an illusion, particularly in its assumption that North America was essentially vacant land whose acquisition did not require conquest of indigenous peoples but rather purchase from them or merely settlement alongside them. Still, as long as the majority of colonial subjects could be seen to be fellow Europeans, who still shared the metropole's history and political culture, and were closely linked by commercial and family connections to residents of the mother country, the British Empire could be envisaged as "Protestant, commercial, maritime, and free," in Armitage's words.[25] If colonists lacked formal representation equivalent to that enjoyed by some Britons, they had considerable political autonomy through colonial assemblies, and, crucially, they were recognized to have political standing; they enjoyed inclusion in the British circle of moral and political recognition. By the late eighteenth century, with the loss of the American colonies and the expansion of the empire in India through a series of military campaigns sustained over several decades, the fantasy of the peaceful trading empire extending British freedom abroad became ever harder to sustain. Although many continued to labor under the illusion of the free and peaceful empire of trade and settlement, more astute observers had become deeply troubled by British imperial despotism, by both its injustices to foreign peoples and the dangers it posed to liberty at home.[26]

Britain's nonsettlement colonies, primarily in India, underwent profound administrative changes at the end of the eighteenth century. Until that time, trading companies with minimal parliamentary oversight were, both nominally and in practice, largely responsible not only for trade and diplomatic relations with Asian states, but also for the acquisition and control of territory and the deployment of military forces. In the late eighteenth century, the British East India Company still considered itself primarily a trading company, though in acquiring territory and considerable military capacity it had begun the transformation to a governing body, a transformation that Smith, Burke, and others considered not just bad for trade but more importantly dangerous to the Company's Asian subjects. Beginning in the 1760s, the East India Company's debts and increasing territorial reach occasioned a protracted struggle between Parliament and the Company over the Company's status, duties, and privileges.[27] By 1833 the Company had lost its commercial privileges and become entirely a governing body, essentially the sovereign of an enormous territory. Its civil service had become regularized and professionalized with the eclipse of older patronage networks and the foundation of Haileybury College, where Company servants were trained in languages and administration. The Company remained the official ruler of India until 1859, when its administrative apparatus was folded into the state; this paved the way for Queen Victoria's acquisition of the title Empress of India in the 1870s.

Better preparation of Company servants for work in India in the nineteenth century did not lead to greater esteem for Indian civilization. Indeed, at the higher levels of administration, admiration for the achievements of Indian culture was far more widespread in the eighteenth century, even among Britons working for the expansion of the empire. Prominent among eighteenth-century colonial administrators were Orientalist admirers of Indian civilization such as Sir William Jones, a pioneer of the European study of Sanskrit and Indian literatures.[28] Even Warren Hastings, who invoked Asian traditions of arbitrary government as justification for his own despotic rule, professed respect for Indian civilization, learned several Indian languages, and collected antiquities.[29] Eighteenth-century Europeans were also less disposed to missionary activity in Asia than their successors. The greater influence of Evangelical missionaries on imperial politics in the nineteenth century meant that colonial administrators were more willing to intervene in Indian religious and cultural life than they had been. As Evangelical missionaries increased their activities in India and became important sources of information about Indian society, the missionaries' own conviction in the superiority of Christian Europe over non-Christian societies came more and more to inflect British attitudes toward India, even outside Evangelical circles.[30] Both increased power and new disdain for Indian civilization meant new widespread efforts to intervene in Indian cultural practices and newly determined attempts to transform them.

France, in contrast, had lost much of its territory in both North America and Asia to Britain and later to America. After the burst of expansionist fervor under Napoleon, and in the wake of his defeat, the French public and political leadership under the Bourbon restoration were widely hostile toward expansion. By the time the French conquered the city of Algiers in 1830, however, French political leaders had come to believe that Britain's growing empire was a major source of its international power and had to be imitated if France was to remain a significant power. Empire was by no means a fait accompli: supporters of empire during this period, Tocqueville most notably, believed that they must actively advocate conquest or squander France's opportunity to be a significant international power. The argument that critique was unthinkable in the nineteenth century, whereas it had been conceivable in the eighteenth, cannot hold. For many in the eighteenth century, including Adam Smith, already believed that no European country could be persuaded to give up its colonies, in which so much honor and self-respect were invested. And critics of empire survived throughout the nineteenth century, even if their voices were muted and their influence negligible. Indeed, Smith's arguments themselves remained prominent among those critics who remained: political economy continued to generate arguments against conquest and imperial rule and bolstered the moral critique.[31]

The erosion of absolutist or ancien régime powers and the partial emergence of the democratic nation-state produced pressures and anxieties for liberal thinkers of the period that may have facilitated a turn to empire. Tocqueville believed that the vicissitudes of French politics in his day required a dramatic solution, and he turned to the conquest of Algeria as a possible solution to political problems that seemed intractable to any purely internal response. J. S. Mill developed a restrictive, normative understanding of nationhood that required *both* the bonds of fellow-feeling forged by a common political culture *and* the capacity for self-government that was peculiar to a small group of European nations. The narrowness of his definition of nationality reflected his belief that nationhood was an arduous achievement: if this was true for Britain, how much more so, on his account of progress, for backward peoples. At the same time as the development of democracy produced profound anxieties for liberal thinkers such as Tocqueville, it also meant that they had a commitment to their state's political order that their ancien régime predecessors such as Diderot did not have. They were not, it seems, prepared to be as scathingly critical as those earlier thinkers about a political order whose precariousness seemed so worrisome and whose potential for progress so hopeful.

Civilizational Confidence

One of the most striking contrasts between the views of the eighteenth-century thinkers I consider here, and those of their nineteenth-century successors, might be described as the dramatically increased sense of cultural or civilizational confidence exhibited by thinkers across the spectrum of nineteenth-century political thought, from conservatives to liberals and radicals. While Europeans in the late eighteenth century undoubtedly were becoming increasingly secure in their sense of superiority—intellectual, moral, political, economic, and technological—over the rest of the world, we find among a number of eighteenth-century thinkers a continued sense of the fragility of their own civilization's achievements, persistent doubts about the justice of European political and social orders, and respect for the achievements, and the rationality, of other societies.[32] Although most European thinkers of this period believed Europe had indeed made economic and political progress beyond other societies, many doubted whether Europeans were sufficiently responsible for or knowledgeable about the causes of their progress to presume to govern "backward" societies, especially by force. In the nineteenth century, a number of factors, from the end of the ancien régime in France and the extension of suffrage in Britain, to the abolition of the slave trade and eventually of slavery in European colonies, to the economic and technological breakthroughs of the industrial revolution, lent a conviction even to radical social critics such as J. S. Mill that European (or at least British and French) political culture was unimpeachably superior to those of the rest of the world's societies.

The earlier view that Europeans were in no position to spread their political cultures and institutions was articulated particularly powerfully among those who had experienced the injustice of autocratic regimes within Europe, including Germans such as Kant and Herder and French critics of the ancien régime such as Diderot.[33] Their antipathy toward their own regimes led them to regard the violence of imperial expansion as a form of injustice characteristic of European politics in their day. As I discuss below, none of the British thinkers considered here doubted so thoroughly the justice of the British political order at home, although Bentham regarded British laws and institutions as to a great extent absurd and unjust. While James Mill and other utilitarian radicals followed Bentham in this disdain for British legal obfuscations, they judged Indian society (the particular object of their interest) to be so far behind Britain in political and civilizational advancement that even arbitrary and unaccountable rule by the British was preferable to any sort of local government. John Stuart Mill, more reconciled to the prevailing political order in Britain than his father, was all the more confident that a British despotism was the best government to which backward societies could aspire, and also that such a despotism could be exercised knowledgeably and benignly to induce progress in such societies.

Critics of empire in the eighteenth century regarded European imperial expansion as bound up with, and to some extent analogous to, the horrors of the slave trade and slavery. As P. J. Marshall has shown, British reformers in the 1770s and 1780s—notably Burke and William Wilberforce (like Raynal and Diderot in France)—fought slavery in the West Indies and British injustices in India as twin evils.[34] Similarly, Hugh Mulligan, the author of a 1788 work entitled *Poems Chiefly on Slavery and Oppression* and dedicated to Wilberforce, linked British oppression of West Indian slaves with British depredations in India, Ireland, and Africa in a series of four dialogues in verse. He complemented the poems with copious footnotes citing Raynal's *Histoire des deux Indes*, other works that charged East India Company servants with exacerbating the famine in Bengal by price gouging, and still others arguing for free trade with Ireland.[35] It is striking that this marriage of "humanitarian" causes had fallen apart by the end of the eighteenth century. Whereas the opposition to slavery spread in the early decades of the next century beyond the coterie of reformers and intellectuals that had first led the movement, to be taken up by much wider circles, evangelical and otherwise, such unqualified criticism of British actions in India faded by the late 1790s. Marshall argues that while both "slavery and the East India company appeared to have won reprieves in the 1790s," when Britain was preoccupied with Jacobinism and then Napoleon in France, opposition to slavery soon regained its former vigor, while "many sections of British opinion . . . were coming not merely to acquiesce in what was being done in India but to express positive enthusiasm for it."[36] By the 1830s, liberals such as J. S. Mill and Tocqueville could take for granted that slavery was an evil to be eradicated; but they abandoned the skeptical posture toward *imperial* expansion that had characterized the foremost critics of slavery of the earlier generation.

The contrast with the fate of the antislavery movement highlights one important reason that criticism of British imperial expansion faded after the 1790s. Justification of British imperial rule from that point, through much of the nineteenth century, began to rest primarily on arguments that Britain brought (and was alone capable of bringing) good government to India. The outstanding violence and corruption of British actions in India during the previous decades—military campaigns against formidable Indian enemies, the vast private fortunes gained—gave way to more subtle forms of oppression such as onerous taxation and export policies, policies that were justified as part of a system of improvement in which the benefits of secure property and the rule of law were said to replace despotic indigenous governments. Civil servants trained at Haileybury College in administration and Indian languages, and regarded as impartial professionals, were replacing the rapacious "boys" Burke had disparaged as partly responsible for the violence and disorder of the Company in India. And, as Marshall notes, reports from India were also becoming uniformly positive about Company rule by the turn of the nineteenth century in a way that they had not been earlier, when dissenters had sent damning reports back to England about Company servants' crimes.[37] Thus, while Burke could insist on "the Evils which arose from a System of sacrificing the Being of that Country [India] to the Advantage of this,"[38] nineteenth-century European observers were not prepared to believe that the colonial system either intended to or actually did sacrifice Indian interests to British. Indeed, many (including both James and John Stuart Mill) held that British rule in India was in fact costly to Britain, but that it was nonetheless justified by the great benefits it conferred on its Indian subjects.

Moreover, the abolition of the slave trade and then slavery removed one of the most glaring injustices of eighteenth-century European politics and society from the sights of reformers. Radicals no longer could—or needed to—point to slavery as evidence of barbarousness or injustice of the European political order. On the contrary, after the abolition of slavery in British colonies in 1838 and French colonies in 1848, the persistence of slave-trading in Africa, rather than indicting European imperial activities, seemed to vindicate them, as both religious and secular reformers called for Britain to penetrate areas of West Africa where the slave trade persisted and abolish it there as well.[39] Tocqueville, as I argue in chapter 7, regarded the abolition of slavery in the French West Indies as essential for keeping the islands within the empire.

Economic Development and Industrialization

The far greater cultural confidence of mid-nineteenth-century Europeans, especially Britons, compared with their predecessors of a few generations earlier can also be attributed to the extraordinary surge in economic and technological development of the first decades of the nineteenth century. That surge itself was probably due in good measure to British exploitation of colonial resources, particularly slavery and the almost limitless land in the New World. Conversely, the stagnation attributed to the Indian economy by nineteenth-century Britons was due in part to the effects of British rule itself. Thus when nineteenth-century Britons contrasted their own progressive society with backward India, they were observing, on both sides of the comparison, phenomena that had not existed before 1790 and that were partly the consequences of colonial rule.

While many in eighteenth-century Europe asserted Europe's economic superiority over other "civilized" societies, particularly China and India, it was still possible to argue that the opulence and refinement of Chinese and Indian manufactures, and the greater well-being of their poorest subjects compared with those in Europe, demonstrated that those societies were Europe's equals in prosperity.[40] Kenneth Pomeranz's painstaking comparisons of economic data in the eighteenth century suggest that standards of living, mortality and fertility rates, quality of manufactures, and technological innovativeness were comparable in the most economically advanced areas of Asia (the Yangzi valley, parts of Japan, and Bengal) and Europe (England and the Netherlands). Pomeranz has argued that it was not until the last decades of the eighteenth century that some western European economies became decisively more productive than those in parts of China, Japan, or India. He also demonstrates that Europe's surge in productivity was probably due in large part to serendipities rather than to long-standing patterns of superior economic arrangements.[41] Although a portrait of Asian societies as stagnant was beginning to emerge, when eighteenth-century Europeans compared their own society with those of China or India, it did not seem obvious to them, as it did to French and British observers several generations later, that their own societies were dramatically more progressive, wealthier, or superior or more enlightened in their social and political practices.

Moreover, colonial rule itself was probably crucial for Britain's rapid economic development in the nineteenth century, primarily by easing land constraints shared across Eurasia and providing voracious demand for European manufactured goods. Colonial expansion violated many principles of Smith's economic theory: it diverted capital away from where it would "naturally" be invested; it effectively taxed the majority of the nation not involved in the colonial trade for the benefit of a few, and it imposed great military expenses on the metropolitan citizenry. While Smith believed the benefits of global trade could be had without the costs of imperial rule (whether over European settlers or non-European populations), the new economic analyses synthesized by Pomeranz suggest that the violence and coercion of European colonial rule were essential to Europe's vast economic growth in the decades after Smith's death, which was denied to countries like China that continued to follow the path of trade alone.

It is likely, too, that parts of nineteenth-century India were indeed "backward" compared with what they had been before the spread of British power in India. When nineteenth-century British observers of India claimed that Indian society was marked by economic stagnation, and cultural traditionalism, they described phenomena that were in some measure true thanks to their own exploitative rule. D. A. Washbrook has detailed the ways in which British rule in the early decades of the nineteenth century caused deurbanization and deindustrialization in many parts of India. British rule—including misgovernment and the imposition of a trading regime favorable to British industrial interests—contributed to the destruction of a vibrant and high-quality manufacturing economy, the emergence of an "increasingly agrarian and peasant-based" Indian society, and the onset of a decades-long economic depression.[42] Although some British observers recognized the role of British rule in these pernicious developments, particularly regarding the East India Company's disruptive efforts to fix property rights, the widespread assumption was that Indian culture was responsible for the society's backwardness and British rule was the country's main hope for enlightenment and advancement.

In cultural respects, as well, British rule may well have helped cause Indian society to become more "traditional" than it had been: the caste system became more rigid, and its effects penetrated areas of Indian society and religion where it had not been influential; revivalist Hindu and

Muslim movements developed in reaction to the threat of Christian proselytizing, "making Indian society more overtly 'religious' and 'sectarian' than prior to British rule."[43] As Washbrook argues,

> The predominant effects which [British rule in India] had (both intended and unintended) were less to transport British civilization to the East than to construct there a society founded on the perpetuation of "Oriental" difference, as Edward Said has put it. India became a subordinate agricultural colony under the dominance of metropolitan, industrial Britain; its basic cultural institutions were disempowered and "fixed" in unchanging traditional forms; its "civil society" was subjected to the suzerainty of a military despotic state. British rule before the Mutiny may be credited with having fundamentally changed Indian society. But this change moved against the anticipations of "modernization" and left it with a vast legacy of "backwardness" subsequently to undo. (399)

While Indian backwardness was invoked as justification for civilizing British rule by liberal supporters of the empire, then, that rule more probably created, exacerbated, or entrenched aspects of Indian society that the British considered backward.

Race and Human Difference

Changing perceptions of race and new forms of racism also contributed to the dramatic shift in European perceptions of many non-European societies, even among those, such as Mill and Tocqueville, who reviled theories of biological differences among races. Many scholars have noted the transition from a belief in human uniformity to one in heterogeneity that occurred around the end of the eighteenth through the first decades of the nineteenth century. Roxann Wheeler has argued that by 1770s the "ubiquitous commitment to human similarity was beginning to show some weak spots" and that by the 1790s the shift away from biological universalism was widespread. Nancy Stepan notes that a new consensus took hold in the mid-nineteenth century, when Britain saw "a change from an emphasis on the fundamental physical and moral homogeneity of man, despite superficial differences, to an emphasis on the essential heterogeneity of mankind, despite superficial similarities."[44] While all the thinkers considered in this book were explicitly committed to a belief in human equality and biological uniformity, the intellectual context of an increasing insistence on the depth of differences among human groups as the nineteenth century progressed is reflected in the development of their views on non-European peoples and on empire.

Smith, Burke, and Bentham shared their era's presumption of human uniformity, and in their reflections on cultural difference, all three always insisted on the equal rationality of all human beings, as I argue in chapters

2 through 4. By the mid-nineteenth century, in contrast, European discourse reflected a pervasive assumption that human groups are characterized by deep differences in temperament and ability. Such a notion inflects the work of Tocqueville and J. S. Mill, even though both of them rejected biological theories of human difference. Tocqueville argued heatedly against the racist theories of his friend and disciple Gobineau, calling them "false and pernicious."[45] Mill likewise criticized the nineteenth-century penchant for biological explanations of human difference—a tendency he tellingly compared to the tendency of "primitive peoples" to attribute to divine intervention whatever they cannot explain.[46] The racism of Mill's contemporaries also should be taken into account when we consider his effort to prosecute Governor Eyre of Jamaica, as I argue in chapter 5. Mill was contending with virulent racism among Eyre's British defenders, including such prominent and eloquent writers as Carlyle and Ruskin. Mill's insistence, in that context, on the importance of securing justice for Britain's black and white subjects alike represents a striking commitment to the moral equality of different races.

And yet Mill's own writing is shot through with the language of human heterogeneity in a way that has affinities with racialist discourse, and he himself insisted that "I never intended to deny the influence of races" (*CW* 15:691). As Georgios Varouxakis has noted, although Mill explicitly rejected biological determinism and racial explanations, his "tacit assumptions and his use of language" often suggest a relation between physical or biological factors and human character.[47] Many of his statements about "national" character betray both an untheorized and blunt categorization of human groups and a suggestion of physical determinism: "The most envious of all mankind are the Orientals. . . . Next to Orientals in envy, as in activity, are some of the Southern Europeans. . . . With the French, who are essentially a southern people . . ."[48] Although Mill regarded biological explanations as lazy and crude, he considered the identification of the "character" of different human groups—and the ranking of those groups on a scale of advancement—an essential element of sociological analysis. As we will see, he considered Bentham's neglect of such categories and hierarchies one of the most important failings of Bentham's thought.

Theorists of progress came to hold that progress was a matter of increasing rationality and cognitive capacity, so that members of societies regarded as being at "earlier" stages of development came to be described not simply as rational human beings acting within different contexts of social organization but rather as themselves cognitively limited: mired in error or enslaved to superstition, incapable of the abstract thought necessary for abiding by contracts or treaties, "untrustworthy" and lacking in "character," and incapable of participating in their own governance not simply because of illiteracy or lack of education but because of deeply rooted (if often vaguely described) civilizational deficiencies.[49] As a result of these features of nineteenth-century philosophies of history and theories of progress, the very idea of linear development or progress has been described as imperialist in character. And yet Adam Smith's theory of history and his broader moral and political theory show that there were eighteenth-century understandings of historical progress that could be developmental while resisting any implication that non-Europeans ought to be excluded from ordinary standards of political respect, inclusion, or reciprocity.

All the thinkers considered here, then, can be described as universalists who negotiated in different ways the tensions between universalistic moral commitments and a recognition of particularity. All were universalists in the sense that they were committed to the idea of human uniformity and human moral equality and rejected theories of polygenesis and the biological racism that was gaining currency throughout this period.[50] Still, their universalism took different forms with radically different implications for international politics and cross-cultural judgment. Burke and Mill would likely have agreed that the British Empire, in Burke's words, should be "united on one common bottom of equality and justice."[51] But they developed significantly different understandings of how that equality might function in practice, given the undeniable differences between European societies and their colonial subjects. In the universalist vision informing the imperial liberalism that arose in the first half of the nineteenth century, Europe stood at the pinnacle of a universal history, a vantage point that was thought to grant Europeans the knowledge and moral authority necessary to impose progress on less advanced societies, using violence and coercion when these were deemed necessary by appropriately informed and well-intentioned colonial authorities. This progressivist universalism justified European imperial rule as a benefit to backward subjects, authorized the abrogation of sovereignty of many indigenous states, and licensed increasingly interventionist policies in colonized societies' systems of education, law, property, and religion. With the development of this strand of imperialist liberal thought, a more tolerant and pluralist universalism was eclipsed, one premised on the equal rationality of all human beings and the belief that standards of morality and justice that governed relations within Europe also obligated Europeans in their dealings with other societies.

Part One

CRITICS OF EMPIRE

Two

Adam Smith on Societal Development and Colonial Rule

ADAM SMITH WAS ONE of the eighteenth century's most innovative and sophisticated theorists of societal development, one who believed that while commercial society was by no means perfect, it made possible material comfort, improvement of laws and government, and refinement of manners unavailable in earlier stages of society. At the same time, Smith articulated a moral and social theory that was broad-minded in its analysis of unfamiliar societies and practices and careful to avoid presumptions of European cultural or moral superiority. Smith managed, that is, to sustain a difficult balance between a belief that the rise of modern society constituted improvement, and a respectful posture toward non-European societies he regarded as being in earlier stages of development. Many contemporaneous and subsequent theorists shared Smith's analytic framework, using a combination of anthropological evidence and conjecture to trace the development of society through stages identified by their mode of subsistence. And yet Smith's theory is unusual in its refusal to rank societies or deprecate members of less "polished" societies, and Smith did not draw on it to support civilizing European rule over other societies, as theorists of progress, almost without exception, did in the nineteenth century.

Despite Smith's own nonjudgmental approach to non-European societies, it is unsurprising that his theory of development may have left an ambivalent legacy: that the categories and historical arguments he introduced were deployed by others to justify civilizing imperial rule. Since at least the late seventeenth century Europeans had sought explanations for the emergence of modern states and commercial activity, for the diversity of societies about which ethnographic information was increasingly prolific, and for the apparent similarities between Europe's own past and some contemporary societies (such as indigenous Americans or nomadic Arabs). Smith drew on and greatly developed suggestions in Montesquieu to produce a theory that seemed to be able to explain much of the diversity in laws, manners, and forms of government among nations by showing their congruence with modes of subsistence arranged along a historical trajectory.[1] Smith's analysis suggests that a good deal of human cultural diversity can be accounted for in terms of such a scale of development, and it places European commercial societies at the position of greatest development: such elements of his thought could be drawn upon in order to argue, as Smith himself did not, that divergence from European practices or norms indicates inferiority, backwardness, or ignorance.[2] In many other hands, developmental theories undergirded a European chauvinism very unlike Smith's tolerant impartiality, and were used to justify the colonial conquests he abhorred.

How did Smith theorize societal development without making the kinds of moral judgments about the superiority or inferiority of entire peoples that can be found in varying degrees in contemporaneous and, usually in a more pronounced manner, in later theories of progress? Understanding the sources of Smith's tolerant approach to cross-cultural judgment serves both to correct mistaken assertions that have been made about Scottish conjectural history as a whole, and to indicate the broader intellectual disposition that animates Smith's political thought, including his hostility toward European colonization. As I will argue, a theory of progress need not imply a pejorative assessment of less "advanced" peoples or support for European colonial expansion. Smith's most important philosophical differences with his successors, particularly those in the nineteenth century, lie in his complex account of historical change and in his distinctive moral psychology and moral philosophy.

Some of the central features of Smith's theory of societal development were shared by other Scottish conjectural historians, although of all the Scottish historians he was the most consistently respectful of precommercial societies as well as the most consistently skeptical about European claims to superiority and the expansion of European political power around the globe. While Smith regarded commercial society as an improvement over earlier forms, he was at the same time conscious that such a view could be an all too easy self-deception. "The over-weening conceit which the greater part of men have of their own abilities, is an antient evil remarked by the philosophers and moralists of all ages. Their absurd presumption in their own good fortune, has been less taken notice of. It is, however, if possible, still more universal."[3] He noted that all societies from the rudest to the most polished are biased in favor of their own way of life and apt to believe that every quality or ideal habitual among themselves represents the "golden mean of that particular talent or virtue."[4] Smith's attention to the temptations of civilizational self-satisfaction was shared by several of his Scottish contemporaries, notably Adam Ferguson, William Robertson, and James Dunbar, all of whom were in fact more explicit than Smith about the attendant dangers for the victims of European imperial expansion. Ferguson (as a self-conscious Highlander who celebrated the virtues he saw as characteristic of "savage" societies) was particularly attuned to the easy and false superiority of "civilized"

Europeans who took it for granted that their own values ought to serve as a standard for all other societies. "No nation," he wrote, "is so unfortunate as to think itself inferior to the rest of mankind: few are even willing to put up with the claim of equality." Even when people seem to offer a reasoned argument for the superiority of their own practices, he argued, they are often deluded by partiality, deeming their own characteristic practices praiseworthy even when they are harmful, senseless, or unjust: Ferguson pointed to conquest as one such practice on which nations foolishly and wrongly pride themselves.[5] Robertson, too, remarked on the "mutual contempt" that nations at different stages of development had for one another, and the injustices this contempt had led Europeans to commit in India.[6] And Dunbar criticized Europeans for their tendency to set themselves apart from the rest of humanity, arguing that "[a]ccording to this theory, the oppression or extermination of a meaner race, will no longer be so shocking to humanity. Their distresses will not call upon us so loudly for relief. And public morality, and the laws of nations, will be confined to a few regions peopled with this more exalted species of mankind."[7]

This wariness of European complacency and self-congratulation largely disappeared among later theorists of progress who took it for granted that Europe was in every way advanced in comparison to the despotic and benighted East and the savage New World. If Smith's theory of development gave later thinkers some of the terms and tools of analysis with which to advance such ideas, those thinkers were nonetheless doing an injustice to Smith's approach. Given that Smith's account of development remained unpublished for over a century and was transmitted only through his students' use of the ideas he introduced in lectures, it is perhaps unsurprising, though disappointing, that the tolerance and skepticism of his approach were to a great degree lost in subsequent decades.

The Causes and Complexity of Development in Smith's Thought

In his lectures on jurisprudence at Glasgow University, given in the 1750s and 1760s, Smith offered what was perhaps the most complex account in the eighteenth century of human societal development through four stages characterized by their mode of subsistence: hunting, pastoral (herding), agricultural, and commercial.[8] From the late 1750s onward, many other Scottish thinkers produced accounts of societal development based on something like Smith's four stages, with various emphases and varying degrees of sophistication.[9] Smith never published a complete account of his historical theory, though he drew on it in the *Theory of Moral Sentiments* (1759) and at greater length in *Wealth of Nations* (1776). Although he announced at the end of the *Theory of Moral Sentiments* his intention to publish a work on jurisprudence, no such text ever appeared, and papers relating to it may have been burned before Smith died.[10] While Smith was not the first to *publish* a stadial account, then, his lectures on jurisprudence were probably delivered several years before the first stadial theories were published in Scotland. His account was almost certainly highly original, rather than derivative of any other such theories, and also itself likely exercised great influence over many of the others through his Glasgow lectures.[11]

Although he was probably making similar arguments in lectures as much as a decade earlier, Smith's historical theory is preserved most thoroughly in two sets of notes taken by students during lectures he offered in the academic years 1762–63 and 1763–64.[12] While the notes from the 1762–63 lectures, published for the first time in 1978, are remarkably complete and appear to capture the argument and its illustrations in great detail, we cannot place the same confidence in the particular language that we might in a published text. Because Smith's arguments about development remained unpublished until the first, less detailed, set of student lecture notes appeared in 1896, his account was unavailable to those outside his immediate circle (including James and John Stuart Mill, discussed in chapter 5, who were influenced by Smith's successors). Indeed, some of the nuances of Smith's approach may well have been lost on those who heard the lectures and incorporated his approach in their own writings, such as his student and later colleague John Millar. Smith's theory of history and approach to cross-cultural judgments, informed by his moral philosophy, achieve a degree of subtlety unmatched in other accounts. That his insights were to some degree lost may be due to the absence of a text from which later theorists of societal development could learn. What follows is by no means a complete discussion of Smith's stadial history, but rather an effort to draw out those features of the theory that made it compatible with a nontriumphalist account of history and a treatment of non-European societies that was neither condescending nor dismissive.[13]

Smith emphasizes material factors in his taxonomy of societies, characterizing each stage by the dominant mode of subsistence and tracing the more complex forms of property, social relations, laws, and institutions that developed with each new stage. His stadial history seeks in part to explain the ways in which social and legal arrangements stem from, and are rational responses to, a society's mode of subsistence.[14] Smith's narrative describes a "natural" progress from one stage to the next, driven, among other factors, by the pressures of population growth and universal human capacities and desires, such as the desire to better one's condition and the "disposition to truck, barter, and exchange."[15] According to Smith, these forces lead to the emergence of more efficient means of providing sustenance and comfort, from the domestication of animals, to the development of agriculture and the increasingly complex division of labor. These produce an increase in the general well-being of a society's members, and an improvement in the quality of their arts and manufactures, from "rude" to "polished."[16] The improvement of "arts and manufactures," then, is itself part of the "natural," that is, the normal and usual material evolution of agricultural and commercial societies.[17] An early (1755) manuscript nicely captures Smith's confidence in the naturalness and universality of progress: "Little else is requisite to carry a state to the highest degree of opulence from the lowest barbarism, but peace, easy taxes, and a tolerable administration of justice; all the rest being brought about by the natural course of things."[18]

While the role of economic factors in the definition of each stage has led some scholars to describe Smith's history as "materialist," recent scholarship has questioned the degree to which Smith's and other stadial theories privileged material factors as the predominant causes of social change.[19] Critics of the materialist reading of Smith have argued that it mischaracterizes his theory as monocausal, determinist, and apolitical, and leaves little scope for the "science of a statesman or legislator" he sought to advance.[20] Smith certainly recognizes a complex range of factors as potential causes of development, including accident and better or worse political arrangements. He neither dismisses the importance of normative and other noneconomic factors in historical development, nor suggests that human motivations stem primarily, much less exclusively, from economic interests.[21] Nonetheless, Smith stresses physical and material factors as the basis for many laws and institutions, especially in his narratives of early stages.[22] He also turns first to environmental and material explanations for a society's level of development and seeks to explain the diversity of developmental stages around the world without suggesting that more advanced societies are so because they are abler or more rational.[23] For this reason, Smith's account is usefully distinguished from those, like Condorcet's, that regard historical change as caused fundamentally by new ideas or development as a process of the gradual elimination of error.[24] Because Condorcet portrays progress as the discarding of error and ignorance, he tends, unlike Smith, to assume that societies at "earlier" stages of development have less rational laws and practices, and that cultural diversity is something that will, and should, be eradicated by the spread of reason and civilization through (peaceful) colonization.

In addition to explaining many customs as reasonable responses to circumstance, Smith argues that certain steps of societal development and certain institutions develop naturally, unless the harshness of the climate or other inconveniences of their surroundings prevent a people from developing beyond a certain stage. Societies, he argues, progress more or less quickly as a result of many environmental and material factors beyond obvious qualities of climate: the defensibility of their land, or access to effective means of transport to distant markets, especially navigable rivers, abundant in Europe, India, and parts of China, but not in Africa or the Americas.[25] Such environmental factors explain why the peoples of "Tartary" and Arabia remained nomads governed by chieftains, for instance, when the ancient Greeks, who inhabited land that could more readily be cultivated and defended, developed republican government (*LJ* B.31). Smith's account suggests that those who assume a population must be inferior if it lives "primitively" on good soil have probably misjudged other less obvious factors.[26]

Smith's discussions of the development of popular participation in Roman government, the end of slavery in western Europe, and the decline of the power of clergy and nobility in the late feudal period, all illustrate his recourse to the material grounds of political developments, even in more advanced societies. While he approves of all these events, his partly material or physical explanations enable Smith to avoid the self-congratulatory note common in discussions attributing such developments to Europeans' special understanding of the values of freedom or political equality. Instead, Smith ascribes the Roman people's acquisition of political power to "the improvements of arts and manufactures," which enabled Roman nobles to spend their wealth on "domestic luxury" rather than using it to support dependents. Freed from personal dependence on the powerful, the people refused to vote for them and demanded their own leaders (*LJ* B.36). Material factors by no means *determine* such an outcome: Smith is sensitive to the place of political action by both groups and individuals such as the tribunes and to the role of noneconomic motives such as pride (the plebeians, he wrote, resisted the rise of the tribunes, "because they thought it disagreeable to have their equals so far above them"). And yet the crucial role played by material factors that were not, from the actors' perspective, obviously connected to the political situation means that no human agents can take primary credit for bringing about the beneficial development.

Similarly, Smith notes that slavery is a common, indeed almost universal, phenomenon, especially in early stages of society, thanks to human beings' love of domination and the fact that the initial weakness of government makes it impossible for society as a whole to ban the practice (*LJ* A.iii.116–17). While he writes that it has been abolished only in a "corner of Europe," he attributes this abolition to the self-interested actions of two sets of political actors that, in Europe, happened to have developed considerable power.[27] Both the clergy and the kings had interests in increasing their own power at the expense of the nobility's, and

Smith argues that the abolition of slavery depended on the power of those groups.[28] While their power in society was not itself a mark of moral or political progress (indeed, the power of the clergy was in many ways destructive of good government, he argues), in the case of slavery it secured a great political good. In one version of the lectures on jurisprudence, Smith makes a particularly direct claim that interests, rather than the progress of moral ideas, led to Europe's abolition of slavery: "It was not abolished by humanity or the improvement of manners—but as the slaves were armed by their lords and so dangerous to the king, the king abolished slavery." [29] Other thinkers, then, would argue that political and civil freedoms in Europe sprang from a particularly morally advanced culture. Smith claims only that a peculiar conjunction of events, not themselves evidence of moral or even political advancement, conspired to liberate the laboring population, through agents for whom the advancement of freedom was not an object.

Moreover, far from assuming that morals or laws necessarily improved with economic conditions, Smith notes that the historical career of slavery offers one example of an inverse correlation between material improvement and the virtues of humanity and benevolence.[30] Slaves are far better treated in simple societies, which are relatively egalitarian, and under monarchs, who have reason to protect their weakest subjects and curb the power of feudal lords, than they are under republics. "The more society is improved," Smith writes,

> the greater is the misery of a slavish condition; they are treated much better in the rude periods of mankind than in the more improved. Opulence and refinement tend greatly to increase their misery. The more arbitrary the government is in like manner the slaves are in the better condition, and the freer the people the more miserable are the slaves; in a democracy they are more miserable than in any other. The greater the freedom of the free, the more intollerable is the slavery of the slaves. (*LJ* A.iii.111)

As with the emergence of modern "benevolence," Smith's argument is that varying treatment of slaves results not from differences in their masters' moral perspicacity, but from a change in situation. Increased opulence, he proposes, enables people to behave with greater sympathy for most others around them. But it means greater misery for slaves, because wealthy masters who live at a greater remove from their slaves are better able to ignore their condition. Here, as elsewhere, by undermining the notion that laws and morals necessarily become better, more just, or more rational alongside the "progress of improvement," Smith avoids the self-congratulation such assumptions produced in later thinkers.

In his treatment of the decline of the power of the Catholic Church in Europe, Smith calls even more explicit attention to the idea that human reason alone is not responsible for some of the most important developments in the progress of freedom and well-being.

> The constitution of the church of Rome may be considered as the most formidable combination that ever was formed against the authority and security of civil government, as well as against the liberty, reason, and happiness of mankind. . . . Had this constitution been attacked by no other enemies but the feeble efforts of human reason, it must have endured forever. But that immense and well-built fabric, which all the wisdom and virtue of man could never have shaken, much less have overturned, was by the natural course of things, first weakened, and afterwards in part destroyed. (*WN* V.i.g.24)

Clergymen's power, just like that of the ancient Roman nobility and later the European feudal nobility, was weakened as they began to spend their revenue on new manufactured goods, instead of on maintaining dependents.[31] Their desire for ever greater income to spend on luxury goods led them to grant leases to their tenants, making those tenants "in a great measure independent of them." (*WN* V.i.g.25) Those involved were not conscious of the factors that led to developments such as the weakening of the clergy and the feudal nobility, and they could not have achieved them through deliberate action. Such developments thus could not be attributed to superior European understanding, for instance to a triumph over superstition or an emerging consciousness of human equality. This account suggests that Europeans could not derive moral authority from such developments, that they could not point to them as evidence that they alone had perceived certain moral and political truths while other societies remained mired in ignorance or error.

For Smith, development through the four stages is at once a natural process and one pervaded with contingency and the unpredicted consequences of myriad individual actions. Smith did not regard Europe's development as the result of a uniquely progressive culture. Rather, he believed, on the one hand, that the transition from hunting to commercial societies was natural and presumptively universal, and on the other that the fact Europe had advanced farthest was accidental and fortuitous.[32] Moreover, on Smith's view Europe's history was in many respects not a model of pure natural development at all. On the contrary: he regarded the history of European society as "unnatural and retrograde," thanks to the interventions of the powerful, such as feudal lords, and of misguided legislators, such as those who created the mercantilist system at the behest of merchants.[33]

As these examples—the extension of Roman political participation, the abolition of serfdom, and the decline of the Catholic Church in Europe—illustrate, Smith's attention to the many unintended consequences of human action led him to resist the thought that commercial and civil society in Europe granted Europeans authority to bring about progress elsewhere.[34] First, as we have seen, Smith believed that many beneficial developments, such as the extension of civic and political freedoms, resulted from actions taken for quite other reasons. Moreover, Smith reminds us, to live under a good system is not necessarily to understand how it evolved, or even exactly how it works: even if Europeans benefited from a fortunate set of circumstances to produce relatively free and effective governments, they might not be in a position to export those institutions. The unintended consequences Smith identified often involve the beneficial social results of individual actions, as in the paradigmatic case of the market's invisible hand. But he recognized too the ways in which well-meaning but inept interventions can disrupt societies.

Smith's attention to unanticipated results of social actions should not lead us to read him as either apolitical or antirationalist: as one who envisioned a "science of the legislator," he believed laws and social orders are amenable to analysis and improvement.[35] Still, his appreciation for the intricacy of social phenomena made him wary of the presumptuous theorist who would impose his vision on a society, heedless of its complexity and of the habits and prejudices of its members. Smith's criticism of such imposers of system eloquently indicts those who, confident in the superiority of their own political understanding, seek to mold a society for its own good, yet without a textured understanding of the society or a sufficiently chastened view of what is possible for a well-intentioned political actor to effect. The "man of system," Smith writes,

> is apt to be very wise in his own conceit; and is often so enamoured with the supposed beauty of his own ideal plan of government, that he cannot suffer the smallest deviation from any part of it. He goes on to establish it completely and in all its parts, without any regard either to the great interests, or to the strong prejudices which may oppose it. He seems to imagine that he can arrange the different members of a great society with as much ease as the hand arranges the different pieces upon a chess-board. (*TMS* VI.ii.2.17)

Efforts to impose radical societal change, Smith suggests, are likely to be ineffective or even dangerous. Smith's attention to the unforeseen consequences of human action produces a tempered approach to politics without putting a halt to political action or efforts toward improvement and reform. Several commentators have noted the "ironic dimension" that the idea of unanticipated consequences lends to Smith's understanding of human motivation.[36] If, as moral and political agents, we understand the moral order or logic of society to be partly opaque to us, we will be more tempered in our efforts to deploy great power, and especially violence, for distant and uncertain ends. The potentially conservative or traditionalist implications of the idea of unintended consequences have often been remarked; less well noted are its critical implications for colonial enterprises and cross-cultural interactions. Smith's view of historical development as at once universal or natural, and also shot through with contingency, indicates that the use of despotic power for the purpose of inducing progress in a backward society is both unnecessary and presumptuous. Smith's theory suggests such ambitions rest on false confidence about what we can know about and do in the world.[37]

Progress, Rationality, and the Early Social Stages

An important consequence of Smith's attention to material causes of development and to the role of chance and unintended consequences in historical development is an avoidance of disdainful or belittling characterizations of societies in the early stages of development. Smith's care in this regard distinguishes him from many other conjectural historians who described members of the most "primitive" hunting societies as ignorant, outside the course of human progress, or even, as Kames suggested, possibly of another species altogether.[38]

In his pioneering study of stadial theories, Ronald Meek used the phrase "ignoble savage" to describe the views of savage societies among Scottish and French historians of the 1750s (he sees Rousseau as "the only real exception") on the grounds that they believed contemporary European society was superior to earlier hunter-gatherer or pastoral forms.[39] While Smith undoubtedly believed that the development of modern commercial societies was largely a story of progress, to suggest that he therefore regarded nomadic societies as ignoble is misleading— for he accorded them and their customs and values, as he understood them, a striking degree of moral respect. Although Smith sometimes uses the adjectives *savage* and *barbarous* as terms of opprobrium (especially in the *Theory of Moral Sentiments*), he generally does so outside the context of any historical theory.[40] In his discussions of "savage" and "barbarian" societies, he far more frequently uses the terms analytically, as descriptions of early stages of society, rather than evaluatively, as terms of moral rank or status.[41]

Smith analyzes hunting societies much as he does later stages, treating their practices with a comparable interpretive generosity, and describing their members as reasonable. As we will see, he implies throughout his discussions of hunting societies that their members make moral judgments in the same manner as all other people do, through an exercise of sympathy and an effort to imagine how an impartial spectator might judge their motives, emotions, or actions. Indigenous Americans are Smith's primary example of savage societies; while he also alludes at several points to Europe's own savage or hunting stage, he had access to little evidence that might support detailed analysis of this stage of Europe's history.

Contrary to what other interpreters have suggested, Smith incorporated even the earliest stage of society, the savage or hunting stage, into his universal history of progress.[42] To suggest that Smith portrays pastoral societies as the first dynamic stage, or that he excludes hunting societies, especially Americans, or relegates them to permanent savagery is to overstate the divide between hunting and pastoral societies in his account. He proposes that hunting society naturally evolves into pastoral society through the gradual taming of animals. To be sure, Smith argues that the step between the hunting and pastoral stages "is of all others the greatest in the progression of society," given that pasturage is the "age where government properly first commences."[43] Hunting societies, Smith argues, do not extend property beyond immediate possession because there is nothing one can own that is worth the trouble of protecting in this way. Since he regarded inequalities of property as the origin of government, Smith believed hunting societies could not be said to have proper government at all.[44] Still, while such societies might be simpler in their organization, their laws less precise and their manners less refined than those of more advanced societies, they are not, in his account, generically different from the other three stages, or set apart from the course of history.

For Smith, progress is a matter of experience—the formation of certain habits, the development of new needs and forms of interaction—which leads to increasingly complex and regularized rules and institutions. The rules and customs of simpler societies are based on similar social calculations, but ones that are less precise due to less diverse experiences, fewer interactions with strangers, and less differentiation among various members of society. Smith argues, for instance, that the savage tendency to equate foreigners with enemies results from the absence of trade relations among hunting peoples and a lack of experience with strangers outside war: not from their simplicity or innate ferocity. He suggests that the experience of more familiar social relations with foreigners leads hunting peoples to behave much like members of later stages: "Two savage neighbouring nations who are in alliance will treat the members of each other with some considerable humanity." (*LJ* A.v.92–93) The manners and customs characteristic of hunting society arise from natural and reasonable human responses to circumstance; given different experiences, savages would judge and behave like others.

Smith maintains that members of societies of all stages of development make moral judgments by the same process. Moreover, while he considers aspects of civilized life to make possible more refined or subtle moral judgments, he suggests the virtues valued by commercial societies are not always superior in a universal sense, but rather that societies' values reasonably differ according to their situation.[45] (He also occasionally points out judgments and practices among savage societies that are superior to those of more advanced societies, observing, for instance, that women are more respected as "rational creatures" in North American Indian societies than anywhere else and are consulted on questions of war "and in every important undertaking" [*LJ* B.105]) Smith questioned the inevitability of the superiority of civilized values not because he feared, as Adam Ferguson did, that civilized society produced a weakening of the individual, a loss of primitive virtues of courage or self-reliance, leaving its members effeminate, enervated, and dependent. Instead, Smith's understanding of the social context of moral judgments led him to surmise that societies' diverse values reflect and fit their situations.[46]

Smith notes, for instance, that while there is less "sympathy or indulgence for . . . weakness" in savage than civilized societies, in both cases people make moral judgments by the same mechanisms. They develop judgments about what is proper, right, or virtuous through the operations of sympathy and by attempting to discern how an impartial spectator would judge their actions. (I discuss the role of the impartial spectator in Smith's moral theory below.) People acting in a given society know what they can expect of a spectator in their society, and they adjust their own judgments and actions accordingly.[47] A savage will rein in his emotions, knowing that his spectators' arduous lives keep them from entering into sympathy for exuberant passions; consequently, he will come to see hardiness and self-control as great virtues. In contrast, a member of civilized society, aware that those who witness his actions can afford to be indulgent about violent expressions of passion, will permit himself such displays and will come to value deep feeling and tender-heartedness.

In both of these cases, the actor judges his own actions by comparing his view of himself with the view he thinks others will take; actors in societies at all stages are concerned to avoid the contempt of those around them—and, it would seem, to be both praised and praiseworthy. Smith reasons that members of savage nations in Asia, Africa, and America, who have been described by European observers as having "habits of falsehood and dissimulation," acquire such habits as a result of their circumstances: required to exercise great self-command, they are "impenetrable" and able to conceal the truth even under torture.[48] The very different values that emerge from similar processes in various societies suggest, then, not that savages lack a capacity for moral judgment, but that, because of the situated way in which all people make moral judgments, they are bound—and indeed right—to cherish values different from those of commercial society.

The idea that societal development involved an improvement in cognitive faculties was proposed by other Scottish conjectural historians and was common in nineteenth-century theories of progress.[49] It is largely absent from Smith's account, however, and the result is a less condescending, less dehumanizing account of savages. He held instead that humans beings in different situations apply the same faculties to their particular problems and tend to produce solutions of roughly equivalent rationality: as I suggest below, less rational or natural practices were not, for Smith, closely correlated to a society's stage of development. To be sure, most thinkers at this time maintained that all humans beings have the same nature and capabilities: until the end of the century, arguments for biological difference among human groups remained relatively rare.[50] Even so, theories of development such as those of Robertson, Millar, and at times Ferguson, emphasized savages' weakness of understanding or inability to think abstractly. Millar, characteristically, described societal development as a "natural progress from ignorance to knowledge." Ferguson, although he was particularly alert to Europeans' easy assumptions about the inferiority of other peoples, wrote of a "weakness in the genius of [Africa's] people."[51] Pocock has argued that that in Smith, too, "the narrative shows the mind as itself developing."[52] If Smith's occasional use of terms such as *ignorance* might suggest as much, however, his analysis of societies in early stages repeatedly undercuts the idea that societal development is characterized by increased cognitive capacity.

Unlike many other theorists of progress, for instance, Smith almost never likened "savages" to children or described the savage state as the "infancy" of society. A rare instance of such usage occurs in the early and fragmentary essay titled "History of Astronomy," where Smith describes the "impotence of mind" displayed by people in "savage ages" and writes that a "child caresses the fruit that is agreeable, as it beats the stone that hurts it. The notions of a savage are not very different."[53] I have not found another such instance, and it seems possible that Smith thought better of this analogy and chose not to use it in later works, whether publications or lectures. Notably, when Smith mentions a child who beats a stone in the *Theory of Moral Sentiments*, he compares him to a dog and a choleric man, but abandons the reference to the savage. The equation of savages with children, common among other developmental thinkers, tends to suggest an explanation for the simplicity or "rudeness" of savage society at the level of the individual cognitive incapacities. Smith, in contrast, did not attribute societal development to enhanced mental capacities on the part of individual members of a society; his are resolutely complex explanations at the level of social interaction.

Similarly, Smith did not regard savages as incapable of forming the abstract ideas necessary to the institution of property; he argued that they simply had not yet experienced the needs that would lead them to institute extended property rights. In discussing the development of property as an institution, Smith does assert that people "at first . . . conceived" of property as immediate possession only.[54] Yet according to Smith this is not because of their limited imagination but because, like members of other societies, hunters employ a spectator method to determine rightful possession. This method, applied to the goods valued in hunting societies—namely wild game—produces an idea of legitimate possession as being direct possession only. Smith's narrative of the "progress" by which this notion of property, natural to hunting societies, gradually gave way to one that recognized ownership even when an owner was absent did not rely on changes in the very mental structures and capacities of the people involved, but rather in the emergence of new kinds of valuable possessions thanks to the natural development of a new mode of subsistence. Smith's theory of the history of property is one of structural societal change, not individual cognitive advancement.

Smith's account of a property dispute in an indigenous Canadian society, drawn from the Jesuit missionary Charlevoix, exemplifies his approach to hunting societies and his ideas about how their members might conceive property rights and moral obligations, and how they might make moral judgments. He describes a case in which members of a hunting society recognize direct possession alone as legally authoritative but are also able to imagine and acknowledge more extended forms of property. He tells of a woman of a Canadian hunting society who left a string of wampum, which was clearly precious to her, in the field of another woman, who then took it. When the first woman appealed to one of the chief men of the village, he told her that "in strict law" she no longer had a right to the wampum (Smith describes the chief as using the language of law, although he has held that government strictly speaking does not arise until the pastoral stage). The chief added, however, that the second woman ought to give back the beads, or she would risk a scandalous reputation for avarice; recognizing the force of his argument, it seems, she returned the beads to their rightful owner (in equity if not in law). The anecdote, as Smith has told it, neatly suggests that although a certain institution of property, even the simplest form of direct possession, may be appropriate to a given stage of society, there is no reason to assume that the society's members are therefore incapable of imagining more abstract forms of property. The story also suggests a possible mechanism for the evolution of abstract property rights, in people's natural moral reactions to new situations, and in the exercise of an equity that, it seems, is accessible to members of any society.[55]

Smith discusses the evolution of contracts in similar terms, showing that oral and then written contracts emerge only in later stages of society not because individuals in earlier stages are incapable of understanding contractual obligations, but rather because the material and social conditions for securing obligation do not obtain.[56] For Smith, what makes a contract binding lies not in the intention of the promiser in making a promise, but rather in the relation between the promiser and the person promised to: the obligation to fulfill a promise stems from "the reasonable expectation produced by a promise."[57] If an impartial spectator—as always, someone taking account of the social circumstances—judged the nonperformance of a promise or contract worthy of resentment, then it would constitute a breach of obligation.[58] One reason contracts emerge only in later stages is the "difficulty and inconvenience of obtaining a trial" in early, typically egalitarian societies, which convene the whole body of the people for trials. Such societies, Smith proposes, would naturally reserve judicial proceedings for cases that severely disrupt the social order, such as murder and robbery (*LJ* A.ii.62). Societal adjudication of *nonviolent* breaches of contract must await the development of a more extensive judicial system, which itself requires an expansion of government that occurs only in wealthy pastoral or agricultural societies. Smith notes that societies in early stages, if they do not recognize contracts, certainly acknowledge related values such as a "sense of honor or veracity," and they often have analogous means of providing the clarity necessary to make promises binding.[59] Smith thus sought to show that all human beings employ the same faculties in responding to certain persistent dilemmas of social interaction, and that the complexity of the solutions they develop will depend not on individual capacities but on a range of material and social factors. This complex social explanation stands in stark contrast to the increasingly widespread assumption that the absence of formal contracts in early stages of society indicated an incapacity on the part of "savages," as individuals, to conceive of obligation in sufficiently abstract terms, as in J. S. Mill's claim (discussed in chapter 5) that "barbarians will not reciprocate. They cannot be depended on for observing any rules. Their minds are not capable of so great an effort."[60]

Smith's analysis of more "advanced" non-European societies, such as China and India, was, similarly, strikingly nonjudgmental about those societies' apparent cultural and developmental differences from Europe. Smith did not believe, as many later British writers would, that certain, particularly Asian, cultures threw up barriers to progress, that some peoples' passivity in the face of their laws, customs, religions, or taboos made them less amenable to progress, or less capable of initiating development from within.[61] Nor did he claim that some peoples were inherently more "progressive" than others. While Smith did not agree with those who held that China and India were far less advanced than Europe economically, he did attempt to explain why China had appeared to plateau at a certain (high) level of economic and political development.[62] In this sense Smith shared the widespread eighteenth-century view that Chinese society, and its level of economic development, had changed little in many centuries.[63]

Smith's explanation for Chinese "stagnation," however, does not rest on the widespread notion that Chinese despotism stifled creativity by imposing an inflexible legal structure and bureaucratic hierarchy. Rather, he points to certain ill-advised laws, most notably China's prohibition of foreign commerce, that he suggests have prevented further expansion. He does not suggest that this stationariness was a permanent condition of the nation; that it stemmed from a peculiarly Chinese or Eastern immobility; or, finally, that immobility was a quality characteristic of Chinese individuals. As a recent analysis sums up the eighteenth-century European verdict of Chinese stagnation, "Stagnant societies must be made up of stagnant individuals."[64] And yet Smith, with his resolutely social and political explanations of development, resisted this assumption, as well as closely related claims that members of "backward" societies are deficient as individuals and therefore in need of governors more able or energetic than they.[65]

Only recently have European and American economic historians such as Kenneth Pomeranz begun to challenge the view that Chinese economic and political development was largely stagnant during the centuries Smith and his contemporaries analyzed, and to argue instead that China was technologically innovative to much the same degree as Europe throughout most of the eighteenth century. Although Smith did not suggest such a line of argument in his analysis of China (accepting instead the interpretation of China as stagnant), Pomeranz's historical arguments resemble Smith's in important respects: in their attention to contingency and unintended consequences, their insistence that Chinese culture was not peculiarly immobile, and their tendency to analyze particular inventions and developments rather than assuming that societal change is a unitary phenomenon.[66] Smith was not alone in making such arguments, but he was writing at a time when the early enthusiasm for Chinese social, political, economic arrangements (especially among Jesuit observers of the seventeenth century, and their readers such as Leibniz and Wolff) was being eclipsed by a new confidence among Europeans that deficiencies deeply rooted in Chinese and Indian culture—uncritical enslavement to tradition and conventional social hierarchies, and a horror of innovation—marked these societies not only as inferior to European social arrangements but also as incapable of generating change or progress internally, without European intervention.[67]

Moral Progress and Commercial Society

Smith professed worries about some deleterious moral and intellectual consequences of commercial society.[68] His most striking portraits of mental debility, for instance, occur in his discussion of civilized societies, where, he asserts, division of labor tends to leave "mutilated and deformed" the minds of laborers confined to repetitive, uninteresting tasks.[69] Smith notes that members of earlier stages of society enjoy varied occupations and occasions for the exercise of their faculties, so that in them "[i]nvention is kept alive, and the mind is not suffered to fall into that drowsy stupidity" of Europe's laboring poor.[70] Still, he held that commercial society engenders not only unimaginably greater material wealth for entire populations (including the poorest and most oppressed in commercial societies), but also possibilities for moral improvement. First, because commercial society produces opulence and leisure, it allows greater concern for the welfare of others than is possible in poorer and rougher societies.[71] Second, commercial society, in which interactions frequently occur among strangers who cannot rely on one another's benevolence to temper their selfishness, must then rest on the establishment and continual refinement of rules of social engagement unnecessary in simple societies.

Third, commercial society and free government were most hospitable to the development of what Smith called natural justice. In the final paragraphs of the *Theory of Moral Sentiments*, in one of his strongest articulations of an idea of universally valid principles of justice, Smith argued that while no actual society's laws could be said to embody natural justice, the laws of well-governed commercial societies were likely to approximate it most closely. It is in this strongly universalist passage that Smith suggests that laws in primitive societies are cruder and less apt, not just simpler, and that they are cruder because people's "natural sentiments of justice" themselves are unrefined.

> In some countries, the rudeness and barbarism of the people hinder the natural sentiments of justice from arriving at that accuracy and precision which, in more civilized nations, they naturally attain to. Their laws are, like their manners, gross and rude and undistinguishing.[72]

Good jurisprudence depends on both manners and government: both the absence of fine distinctions of justice in primitive societies, and the active disruption of the progress of jurisprudence by despotic governments, can be said to be responsible for a society's poor standards of jurisprudence. It is worth noting, however, that Smith calls attention to the deficiencies not of such people's moral judgments generally, but specifically of their laws and manners. The sentiments of justice are, for Smith, a special sub-category of moral sentiments, distinct from "all the other social virtues" (*TMS* II.ii.1.5). Because justice involves particularly complex considerations of social utility and depends upon enforcement by government, Smith conceives of this aspect of morality as a natural attainment of more advanced societies.

Smith was certainly prepared—even as an outside observer of a culture—to judge some practices unreasonable or immoral: he understood jurisprudence, after all, as an attempt "to shew the foundation of the different systems of government in different countries and to shew how far they are founded in reason." He did not suggest, however, that more complex societies necessarily had more rational customs. Thus, when Smith criticizes certain stages of the institution of property, his target is not the primitiveness of such social arrangements, but rather their unfairness, their ineffectiveness, or their inappropriateness to other institutions of the society. For example, he deems feudal laws granting lords property over all game on their land not only tyrannical but also contrary to "what is most agreeable to reason." Smith argues that these egregiously inequitable laws persisted only because the extreme powerlessness—indeed enslavement—of the peasantry under feudalism made possible such a tyrannical exercise of power and "encroachment . . . on the rights of the lower rank of people" (*LJ* A.i.1, 54, 57).

Smith suggests that more sophisticated moral systems are by no means necessarily more just. For Smith, the most important moral developments occur in the context of ordinary social interaction—in whatever stage of society—rather than in complex or erudite reflections on morality. He conveys these ideas in a thumbnail history of moral teaching as he believed it emerged early in the history of every society:

> In every age and country of the world men must have attended to the characters, designs, and actions of one another, and many reputable rules and maxims for the conduct of human life, must have been laid down and approved of by common consent. As soon as writing came into fashion, wise men, or those who fancied themselves such, would naturally endeavour to increase the number of those established and respected maxims. (*WN* V.i.f.25)

Smith portrays "moral philosophy" as the attempt to connect these "maxims of common life" into a system, and he dismisses more properly formal systems as for the most part mere "sophisms," useless for the day-to-day practice of moral reasoning.[73] His own form of moral philosophy was intended to demonstrate how we actually make moral judgments: as we become self-conscious about the process by which we judge, Smith suggests, we may hope to refine our judgments. Thus, as we understand the way in which circumstances and custom structure social practices, for instance, we can acquire the appropriately critical stance toward those customs that lead us to act unjustly.[74]

Moral Philosophy and Cross-Cultural Judgments

Smith's care in passing judgment on unfamiliar practices, and his willingness to regard a wide variety of social arrangements as justifiable, follow not only from his nuanced historical theory but also from a moral theory that encourages open-mindedness toward unfamiliar values and practices. At the heart of Smith's moral theory is a notion of moral judgment as a process by which we continually revise our opinions in response to new experiences and new opportunities for comparison with the views of others.[75] Smith's moral theory recognizes that we make moral judgments in particular social and cultural contexts; but it also suggests that the broader the context in which we make our judgments, the greater possibility they have of being just. According to Smith, then, our moral judgment is likely to improve as our circle of comparison broadens, as we free ourselves from the partial, indulgent, or self-serving judgments of a narrow social group. His moral theory both regards morality as developed necessarily within the context of a particular group or society, and also warns us against allowing moral judgments to rest complacently with the inevitably partial moral views of any given group. As I discuss below, Smith also attempts a delicate balance between a very general set of universal values and an understanding of moral judgment as grounded in concrete situations. The result is an approach that accepts the possibility of cross-cultural judgments but treats unfamiliar cultural practices with interpretive generosity and without a presumptively universal moral system against which all practices are to be measured and judged.

As Smith argues in the *Theory of Moral Sentiments*, we form moral judgments by comparing our own, necessarily partial, responses to the characters, motives, and actions we witness (our own and others') with the judgments we see others forming.[76] As agents, we seek to view ourselves from the perspective of those around us, by using imagination, or "fancy," to step outside ourselves, and by attempting to bring about agreement between our own sentiments and the judgments we find being made by those who see us act. Because of our natural sympathy, such congruence is itself a source of pleasure to us.[77] Smith emphasizes the importance of remaining chastened about our own judgments as we confront different assessments by others: people are too often "partial," he argues, "with regard to the propriety of their own conduct. . . . This self-deceit, this fatal weakness of mankind, is the source of half the disorders of human life. If we saw ourselves in the light in which others see us, or in which they would see us if they knew all, a reformation would generally be unavoidable. We could not otherwise endure the sight" (*TMS* III.4.5).

We move from seeking the praise of actual spectators to asking how a well-informed and objective "impartial spectator" would judge our actions and motives. This impartial spectator emerges from within our social context but has none of the special interests that particular observers involved in the situation may have.[78] In considering the views of the impartial spectator we come to desire above all not the actual praise of those around us, but rather the confidence that our motives or actions are *worthy* of praise. In addition to a desire for the approval of our fellows, that is, nature has given us the desire to do and to be what "ought to be approved of." Our judgments of what is praiseworthy, what ought to be done, are, Smith argues, thus formed in social contexts, but they are always also partly independent of such contexts, for we may learn to ask whether as a group their judgments are biased or partial and whether what is actually praised by those around us is truly praiseworthy.[79]

We attempt to approximate the judgments of the impartial spectator's perspective by an open-minded, and open-ended, process of provisional judgments followed by revisions based on new knowledge. We develop a conception of what the impartial spectator's judgments would be by observing our own opinions and those of actual observers—members of our own society—and from these distilling a dispassionate and unbiased judgment. To rely on the judgment of the "indulgent and partial spectator" is to see our moral sentiments "corrupted" (*TMS* III.3.41). That perversion of moral judgment can result from simple *self*-indulgence, but Smith regarded the group partiality that supplies a narrow and biased *social* context for moral judgment as a greater threat to good judgment than mere egoism: "Of all the corrupters of moral sentiments, therefore, faction and fanaticism have always been by far the greatest" (III.iii.43). Because the formation of our moral judgments is, in Smith's view, a fundamentally social process, selfishness or solipsism, while it may warp our judgment temporarily, is likely to be corrected in the end by a natural desire for praise and praiseworthiness, and by a natural tendency to formulate general moral rules about the conduct of others and then apply these rules to ourselves. Smith regards faction and partiality as moral dangers precisely because in restricting the breadth of our comparisons, they halt the process by which our initial judgments might approach the just assessment of the impartial spectator.

Noting the rarity of justice not only in international affairs but also among hostile civic or religious sects within societies, Smith argues that it is difficult (though not impossible), for an individual to transcend the bounds of a strongly biased group, or a faction locked in conflict with an adversary. "In a nation distracted by faction, there are, no doubt, always a few, though commonly but a very few, who preserve their judgment untainted by the general contagion. . . . The real, revered, and impartial spectator, therefore, is, upon no occasion, at a greater distance than amidst the violence and rage of contending parties" (*TMS* III.3.43). Thus, it would seem that chauvinism and disdain for judgments or perspectives outside those of one's own group are, for Smith, far worse than simply vices in themselves: they are destructive of good moral judgment altogether. Smith's moral theory thus relies on humility and an openness to difference as a corrective for misguided moral judgments.

Smith's proposed method of constant comparison with the judgment of others, especially those outside one's particular group, lends itself to toleration of unfamiliar standards of judgment and a humility in judging different mores and institutions. It encourages skepticism regarding one's own provincial prejudices and caution in mistaking them for a universal standard. If people's judgments improve as they extend their horizon of comparison, it follows that they must take the new perspectives they encounter seriously. Smith's moral theory, I suggest, issues not in a refusal to judge or to compare customs, laws, or institutions, but rather in a posture of humility in the evaluation of unfamiliar practices. For Smith felt it possible both to judge some practices as misguided, unreasonable, or immoral, and to grant rationality and justification to a great diversity of social arrangements. He also refrained from claiming that immoral or unjust practices are correlated with a society's level of advancement.

Given that Smith believed our moral judgments are formed within particular social contexts, how did he believe it possible either to criticize practices widely approved of within a society, or to compare the practices or judgments of different societies? Scholars of Smith's moral theory have disagreed about the extent to which Smith's impartial spectator should be regarded as embedded in a particular society and to what degree Smith intended the impartial spectator's judgments to be associated with norms and values that are, in Smith's words, "natural," "arising from nature," or "as nature and reason dictate."[80] I argue that Smith believes we can know what the impartial spectator's judgments would be only by considering the judgments actual spectators form. Smith believed that an understanding of universal principles could be arrived at only through the elaboration and critique of concrete moral codes and judgments, and through careful consideration of imperfections and improvements of the rules of a great variety of societies, with attention to their circumstances.

Perhaps Smith's most strongly universalist claims about moral judgments appear at the end of the *Theory of Moral Sentiments*, where he outlines the tasks of natural jurisprudence, or "a theory of the general principles which ought to run through and be the foundation of the laws of all nations."[81] Here he describes the history of jurisprudence as the history of various societies' efforts to institute natural justice, and he held that every attempt would be marred by certain vices or injustices: "Every system of positive law may be regarded as a more or less imperfect attempt towards a system of natural jurisprudence, or towards an enumeration of the particular rules of justice" (VII.iv.36). Smith also criticizes Hobbesian voluntarism or positivism, the claim that right is what the sovereign declares it to be, for supposing "that there was no natural distinction between right and wrong, that these were mutable and changeable, and depended upon the mere arbitrary will of the civil magistrate."[82] Universalist language runs throughout the *Theory of Moral Sentiments*, in terms and phrases such as "natural property" (V.1.2), "natural sentiments of justice" (VII.4.36), and "universal disapprobation." (III.4.7)

Still, while Smith's language, especially in this discussion of natural jurisprudence, suggests he believed that in principle there are universal moral truths, valid in all times and places, these general moral truths remained for him at a high degree of abstraction. He never offered an explicit account of what moral qualities we should regard as natural, innate, or universal, and his own account of how we know what is praiseworthy is resolutely contextual. Moreover, in many instances in which Smith deploys a *language* of universality, he is apparently referring to the judgments of members of a particular society:

> The general rules which determine what actions are, and what are not, the objects of each of those sentiments, can be formed no other way than by observing what actions actually and in fact excite them. When these general rules, indeed, have been formed, when they are *universally* acknowledged and established, by the *concurring sentiments of mankind*, we frequently appeal to them as the standards of judgment. (*TMS* III.4.11)

His use of phrases such as "the common sentiments of mankind" and "natural equity" seems deliberately ambiguous, both specific to a social context and potentially universal, since what constitutes the "mankind" with whom we compare our moral judgments will, on his account, change as we broaden the scope of our communication.[83]

Natural principles serve, for Smith, primarily as a negative test for particular beliefs or actions, rather than as a system of guidance on their own. We might know when a judgment is contrary to nature, but to find out in any detail what nature approves, we must observe actual judgments made in actual societies, and these will be diverse. The only way to approach an understanding of what justice demands, then, is to examine its instantiation in particular societies and to subject the mores and practices of these societies to the kind of judgment to which, through the construct of the impartial spectator, we subject our own judgments and actions. Universal values such as equity, humanity, or justice can be given content and made meaningful only through an examination of the ways they take shape in actual social practices. Yet we can also draw on them to judge particular conventions or actions. Any tolerably complete moral system has to be built by actual societies, over time, rather than deduced from a priori principles. These actual systems will necessarily be flawed and should always be subject to critique and revision, Smith recognizes, but they are the inescapable basis of moral reasoning.

Smith's belief that moral reasoning must always take place within a social context did not result in a posture of cultural relativism and did not preclude the possibility of cross-cultural moral judgments. As all his major works show, he believed that members of different cultures can evaluate one another's beliefs and practices and can judge some superior to others—more humane, more natural, more just. The many examples of such judgments suggest several important elements of his approach to cross-cultural judgment. First, he believed that much of the diversity of morally relevant beliefs and practices observable over time and across the world reflected generally appropriate evaluations made in different situations, so that for many aspects of human life there could not be universally valid rules or standards. Second, many diverse practices that one (Europeans in particular) might be tempted to judge immoral were not in fact morally relevant. And third, he did not judge entire cultures as morally superior or inferior, and he believed, moreover, that all cultures must have generally appropriate customs or they would not long survive.

A tremendous range of customs may be shown to be reasonable or understandable given the situation of the agents. Moral judgments, Smith tells us, vary with "different situations of different ages and countries" (*TMS* V.2.7). Diverse customs and practices have developed, Smith argues, as reasonable responses to circumstances, including a society's physical environment and stage of development. It makes little sense, then, to rank virtues on any universal scale, for many virtues are appropriate to some but not all social stages.[84] Both firmness and gentleness are virtues; each is suited to certain circumstances and yet under others proves less praiseworthy, less deserving of approbation by an appropriately situated impartial spectator. "In general," Smith argued, "the style of manners which takes place in any nation, may commonly upon the whole be said to be that which is most suitable to its situation. Hardiness is the character most suitable to the circumstances of a savage; sensibility to those of one who lives in a very civilized society. Even here, therefore, we cannot complain that the morals sentiments of men are very grossly perverted" (*TMS* V.2.13). By no means will every custom or quality lauded by a society be truly praiseworthy even in context, but Smith approaches unfamiliar practices with the presumption that they are appropriate to their circumstances, and he attempts to understand why they might be valued, before criticizing some practices as infringements of such universal values as equity or humanity.

Still, Smith believed that an appropriately modest and careful observer can pass fair judgment on the customs of other places and times. Some practices in some situations might indeed violate such general standards as "equity" and "reason" or might be described as perversions of moral sentiments. He describes some immoral customs, for instance, as ossifications of once-rational (and so previously justifiable) practices. Arrangements that might be rational for a people at a particular stage of development become customary, Smith explains, and so sometimes persist long after circumstances have stopped justifying them. At that point they may be judged immoral.

Smith's discussion of infanticide in the *Theory of Moral Sentiments* illustrates his method of judgment. He seeks to understand a seemingly appalling practice in its social context while also using a notion of equity to make moral judgments across cultural and historical boundaries. Even infanticide may be excused in some societies, Smith maintains, for the "extreme indigence of a savage" makes it reasonable for such a parent to abandon a child rather than to condemn him- or herself to die with it. "That in this state of society, therefore, a parent should be allowed to judge whether he can bring up his child, ought not to surprise us so greatly." The impartial spectator, whose moral sentiments might otherwise be expected to find such a practice outrageous, can in this case enter imaginatively into the situation of the burdened parent and concur with a judgment that abandoning the child is preferable to dying with it.

The moral wrong occurs in the preservation of this practice in societies such as ancient Greece, where only "remote interest or conveniency," not necessity, motivated infanticide. The natural sentiments that otherwise would rebel against such a violation of "humanity" were suppressed by "uninterrupted custom," which led people—including philosophers, whose moral judgments should have been more considered—to accept the practice unquestioningly. The immorality of infanticide among Greeks, even "polite and civilized Athenians," stemmed, in Smith's view, partly from its being a practice abhorrent to our natural sentiments that in *that* society could not be justified by necessity, and partly from its being a custom accepted unreflectively. "When custom can give sanction to so dreadful a violation of humanity, we may well imagine that there is scarce any particular practice so gross which it cannot authorise. Such a thing, we hear men every day saying, is commonly done, and they seem to think this a sufficient apology for what, in itself, is the most unjust and unreasonable conduct" (*TMS* V.2.15). Thus, practices might come to be enshrined in a society and still be judged wrong, from either within or outside the society. Smith makes no suggestion that the natural sentiments of "savages" were similarly perverted but appears instead to assume that they could commit infanticide even while exercising sound moral judgment.

This passage exemplifies Smith's contextualization of practices that appear self-evidently immoral to his readers. Suggesting the apparent indisputability of such a judgment, he asks, "Can there be greater barbarity, for example, than to hurt an infant?" (*TMS* V.2.15). Here Smith seems to play on the term *barbarity*: he chooses a developmental word as his term of opprobrium, but in dissociating the negative moral judgment from the "savage" society, he calls into question whether societies that are savage or barbarous in the *taxonomic* sense are indeed those that behave "barbarously" in the *evaluative* sense. He then describes the sentiments behind such a judgment: the infant's "helplessness, its innocence, its amiableness, call forth the compassion, even of an enemy, and not to spare that tender age is regarded as the most furious effort of an enraged and cruel conqueror." The perspective from which this judgment is made is somewhat ambiguous. Smith's use of the passive voice blurs the question of who pities the infant or judges the conqueror cruel: is Smith articulating his readers' own sentiments, or making a universal claim about humans' natural feelings in such a situation? Although the grounds on which he determines what counted as "unjust and unreasonable conduct" are not made fully explicit, Smith offers in his own practice of moral judgment a model for approaching unfamiliar customs with both a posture of respect and a means of evaluating them. Rather than positing a list of natural or universal moral laws, condemning those who violate them, and classifying such societies as depraved or backward, Smith exercises a flexible moral imagination to consider circumstances, sentiments, and judgments as much as possible from the perspective of agents and spectators very unlike himself.[85]

Smith destabilizes widespread European condemnations of other practices found in various non-European societies. Sometimes, as with polygamy, he shows that an unfamiliar practice should not be considered unjust or unnatural, even if it might be politically inadvisable. Polygamy may be shown to have bad consequences, he argues, but it is not unjust or immoral where the law permits it. Such consequences range from immediate domestic effects, such as diminished conjugal affection, to long-term political results such as the undermining of hereditary nobilities.[86] Smith notes that other unfamiliar practices held up by Europeans as evidence of a society's cruelty, barbarity, or stupidity differ less than his readers might expect from familiar but unquestioned European fashions. The custom among some Amerindians of molding children's heads into a square shape, he writes, astonishes Europeans with its "absurd barbarity"; missionaries blame the practice for what they imagine is the "singular stupidity of those nations." But, Smith notes, they fail to recognize the custom's similarity to European ladies' use of corsets: although that fashion caused "many distortions and diseases," "custom had rendered it agreeable among some of the most civilized nations which, perhaps, the world ever beheld" (*TMS* V.1.8) While a "savage" practice might be harmful and the society better off abandoning it, Smith renders it comprehensible in much the same way that generally unquestioned European practices are, and he introduces a critical remark on the hypocrisy and xenophobia of self-assuredly "civilized" Europeans. In this instance, the broadening of one's circle of comparison in the judgment of a practice has two results: in making the strange appear familiar, it leads to a less contemptuous approach to the foreign culture while still permitting one to judge the practice as undesirable. And in defamiliarizing one's own unquestioned practice, it brings about a more critical scrutiny not only of the practice itself but also of the easy assumption that "civilization" or "refinement" is equivalent to rationality, justice, or sensible policy. Europeans, Smith proposes, are prey to the same cultural perversities as those they deem barbaric. Smith's own cross-cultural analyses, then, argued both for generosity in the evaluation of others' aesthetic and moral customs, and for heightened awareness about how such customs function in European culture, as elsewhere, to enshrine and legitimate possibly harmful practices.

In addition to urging more careful scrutiny of certain conventions, Smith resists condemning entire societies as depraved through the accumulated evidence afforded by unfamiliar customs. His position rests on two claims. First, contrary to those (from the earliest Spanish missionaries to nineteenth-century proponents of empire) who invoked strange food, clothing, or gestures as evidence of non-Europeans' fundamental inferiority, Smith recognized the moral indifference of many alien aesthetic or cultural practices.[87] Second, he insisted that the fabric of society must be clearly distinguished from isolated practices: particular blameworthy practices do not support the presumption that an entire society is depraved. A society might fall short of the demands of natural justice in particular respects, for various reasons including geographic necessity, historical accident, or custom. Still, Smith remained convinced that societies are unlikely to get morality entirely wrong. No deeply immoral society, he believed, could endure. In the case of *particular* practices, custom "is capable of establishing, as lawful and blameless, particular actions, which shock the plainest principles of right and wrong." Still no culture that was entirely misguided "with regard to the general style and character of conduct and behavior . . . could subsist a moment," Smith insists (*TMS* V.2.14–16). This claim is functionalist insofar as it rests on the idea that cultural practices preserve society. By this view, no society can be deeply unjust for long without destroying itself, collapsing under its own irrationality.[88]

The presumption that no lasting society can be utterly depraved rests on Smith's belief in the reliability of natural moral sentiments as well as in an innate human capacity to reason and reflect about them. Although sentiment and reason may be hampered by custom, and especially by religious fanaticism, both enable individuals themselves to judge moral systems. As a result, moral judgment, Smith believed, is importantly different from both aesthetic judgment and natural philosophy. Whereas aesthetic judgments are based on limitless variations of the "principles of the imagination," moral judgments "are founded on the strongest and most vigorous passions of human nature": they can be "warpt" by custom, but not "entirely perverted" (*TMS* V.2.1). Smith draws a similar contrast with regard to the development of scientific theories: false moral systems, unlike astronomical theories, cannot hold sway indefinitely.

> A system of natural philosophy may appear very plausible, and be for a long time very generally received in the world, and yet have no foundation in nature, not yet any sort of resemblance to the truth. . . . But it is otherwise with systems of moral philosophy, and an author who pretends to account for the origin of our moral sentiments, cannot deceive us so grossly, nor depart so very far from all resemblances to the truth.[89]

Natural philosophy, Smith writes, is like a distant country, about which a traveler can "impose upon our credulity the most groundless and absurd fictions." A system of moral philosophy, however, as an account of our own "desires and affections," is like a description of "the very parish which we live in" and will perish if too far from the truth. Smith is here discussing works of moral philosophy produced for a literate and therefore fairly advanced society, but his indication of what in us rebels against a false system—the moral intuitions of even "the most injudicious and unexperienced reader"—suggests a similar argument could be made about the moral systems of other societies. It is natural and universal sentiments and experience—not subtle reasoning—that make ordinary people capable of judging moral systems.

Smith's faith in the uniformity and basic rectitude of human nature led him to believe that however misguided particular practices might be, people of all societies were able and generally likely to make decent moral decisions. Such a presumption has sweeping implications for cultural criticism. It leads Smith to approach cultural variation tolerantly, to conceive diverse practices, prima facie, as reasonable responses to circumstance. It also led Smith to be particularly suspicious of those he believed had become altogether unmoored from a social context of moral judgment. Smith suggested that such disconnection occasioned extraordinary immorality precisely because the worst offenders followed the customs of no society at all. He described European slave drivers as "the refuse of the jails of Europe, . . . wretches who possess the virtues neither of the countries which they come from, nor of those which they go to, and whose levity, brutality, and baseness, so justly expose them to the contempt of the vanquished."[90] It was the very dissociation of colonial adventurers and slave traders from the enduring reasonableness and humanity of all cultures considered holistically that enabled them to act so basely and brutally.

Smith's Critique of Colonies

In his extensive treatment of colonies in the *Wealth of Nations*, Smith demonstrated that European colonial rule was both a prominent feature of Europe's emerging commercial society and largely detrimental to metropolitan, colonial settler, and conquered non-European societies alike. As he wrote in a letter of 1782, "The real futility of all distant dominions, of which the defence is necessarily most expensive, and which contribute nothing, either by revenue or military force, to the general defence of the empire, and very little even to their own particular defence, is, I think, the subject upon which the public prejudices of Europe require most to be set right."[91]

Smith's economic, moral, and political critique of colonial expansion challenged an increasingly widespread popular enthusiasm for a belligerent and expansionist colonial policy, as well as a growing conviction among Britons that their empire would prove a civilizing force in the world. Kathleen Wilson has examined the appetite for empire among eighteenth-century Britain's urban popular classes (especially in England), one stoked by opposition politicians from the 1730s as part of their campaign against the Walpole ministry. The opposition, as Wilson shows, successfully associated the interests of colonial traders with those of the nation itself.[92] Smith, in contrast, was determined not only to denounce the great monopoly companies but also to dispel the illusion that policies favored by merchants and traders benefited the nation as a whole and that colonies were essential to national wealth, power, or freedom. The opposition also managed to suggest that the expansion of British rule meant the spread of freedom both for European settlers and for barbarous subjects.[93] By the end of the Seven Years' War, imperial enthusiasts were predicting just such a triumph of British power and civilization, which they envisioned "[d]iffusing freedom and science, political order and Christian Knowledge through those extensive regions which are now sunk in superstitious barbarism" and "imparting even to the most uncultivated of our species, the happiness of *Britons*."[94] The imperialists' rhetoric, Wilson argues, "homogenized" the empire, rhetorically eliding the differences among the various British imperial territories and presuming the empire "to consist of flourishing and commercially viable colonies, populated largely by free (white) British subjects and supplemented by commercial outposts in 'exotic' climes."[95] This homogenizing move enabled supporters of mercantilist policies and imperial expansion to suggest that the empire was associated with the spread of liberty and free trade rather than with the domination of subject peoples.

In condemning the course of colonial expansion, then, Smith confronted not only a powerful interested few, but also a wide public that, over the course of several decades, had come to see its freedom, national pride, and wealth as bound up in imperial expansion. His long treatment of colonies in the *Wealth of Nations* makes clear he understood the political difficulty of persuading the British public, one increasingly committed to empire as part of its national identity, of both the folly and the cruelty of that empire. Smith was sensible of the benefits that exploration could bring to the world; in particular, he believed, it enabled an increase of trade and well-being by extending the contacts among people with potentially complementary products and needs.[96] Still, Smith argued against colonial conquest and rule as a prudent means of expanding global commerce: the expense of ruling and defending colonies, he maintained, was ruinous to both conquerors and conquered. Colonies, "a sort of splendid and showy equipage," might appeal to rulers' or adventurers' sense of glory and ambition but always cost more than they produce. "[I]f the empire can no longer support the expense of keeping up this equipage," Smith argued, "it ought certainly to lay it down" (V.iii.92). Although he often expressed doubts that European states could be convinced to relinquish their empires, Smith ended the *Wealth of Nations* with the disdainful charge that the "rulers of Great Britain have, for more than a century past, amused the people with the imagination that they possessed a great empire on the west side of the Atlantic"; he called for British leaders to awake from their "golden dream" of empire and restrict themselves to a more manageable territory. While the "shew and splendor" of colonial possession belonged to the conquering state, the resulting expansion of industry and trade that generated prosperity seemed always to belong to others.[97] Spain and Portugal might have the glory of possessing South America—but be destroyed by it: France, Holland, Flanders, and Germany enjoyed the real benefits of producing the colony's linen. Furthermore, colonies embroiled European countries in otherwise avoidable wars. Smith believed Britain's most expensive recent wars were due wholly or chiefly to colonial rivalries, beginning in 1739 with Spain and in 1755 with France.[98]

Many of Smith's strictures against colonial rule stemmed from his theory of "natural" economic development. He believed imperial ventures, with their monopoly companies and protectionist policies, interfered with the natural development of commercial economies, led to inefficient distribution of capital, and injured the general welfare of society.[99] The monopoly companies that instigated imperial exploits, and the state intervention they often required, benefited only a few investors at the expense of the broader metropolitan society—as well as the non-Europeans whose labor and land they plundered. Protectionist imperial policies damaged the interests of the metropolitan countries just as they did the prosperity of the colonies, though often far less visibly. Smith accordingly argued for free trade with Ireland in the *Wealth of Nations*, and in several letters claiming that both Ireland in particular and Britain more broadly would benefit from a lifting of "our paltry monopolies," "all these unjust and oppressive restraints," while the only losers would be a mere handful of manufacturing interests.[100]

Much of the discussion in the *Wealth of Nations* is concerned with Britain's settlement colonies in North America.[101] For the American colonies, Smith favored either complete emancipation or complete political and economic integration, both of which he believed would be politically so unpopular as to be impossible to institute peacefully. He suggested both possibilities in the *Wealth of Nations* and again in a 1778 memorandum to Alexander Wedderburn. As for complete emancipation, Smith noted the fruitlessness of demanding that a country relinquish its imperial holdings. Even if such a policy were in the country's real interest, he argued, it would be too offensive to national pride: this in spite of the fact that for the majority of citizens the empire meant nothing more than higher taxes and expensive imports. About the American colonies, he wrote,

> To propose that Great Britain should voluntarily give up all authority over her colonies, and leave them to elect their own magistrates, to enact their own laws, and to make peace and war as they might think proper, would be to propose such a measure as never was, and never will be adopted, by any nation in the world. No nation ever voluntarily gave up the dominion over any province, how troublesome soever it might be to govern it. . . . Such sacrifices, though they might frequently be agreeable to the interest, are always mortifying to the pride of every nation, and what is perhaps of still greater consequence, they are always contrary to the private interest of the governing part of it. . . . The most visionary enthusiast would scarce be capable of proposing such a measure, with any serious hopes at least of its ever being adopted. (*WN* IV.vii.c.66)

He believed the other just alternative, to extend the same principle of taxation and "fair and equal representation" in Parliament, was equally improbable because it too challenged the "private interest of many powerful individuals [and] the confirmed prejudices of great bodies of people" (V.iii.68). In spite of the unpopularity of such a view, Smith continued to argue that the solution of complete integration for "all the different provinces of the empire inhabited by people of either British or European extraction" was not only economically and politically sound, but also *just*.[102]

Such a caveat suggests Smith hesitated to make the same claim for colonies inhabited by non-European populations. Indeed, we do not find Smith's extensive discussion of the appropriate governance of the North American colonies matched by similar treatment of the best policy toward Britain's expanding colonies in Asia. His discussions of these colonies remain, instead, denunciations of existing imperial practice. Many of the vices of colonial rule over European settler colonies—such as inefficient protectionism and exorbitant military expenses—also held for Britain's growing non-European territories. These nonsettler colonies, however, were also plagued by far greater vices. He describes the ruinous logic of Europe's imperial activities in Asia and Africa, so "destructive to those which have the misfortune to fall under their government" (*WN* IV.vii.c.108). The Dutch best demonstrated the lengths to which rulers intent on their own gain will go in desolating colonial possessions, but the English in India, Smith maintained, were no better.[103] If British colonies were less devastated, this was merely because their system had not had time to take full effect.[104] Smith pointed to Bengal and other English colonies in the East Indies as contemporary examples of "sensibly decaying" societies: the different economic states of America and Bengal, Smith argued, illustrated the "difference between the genius of the British constitution which protects and governs North America, and that of the mercantile company which oppresses and domineers in the East Indies."[105] These depredations were due in large part to the "natural genius of an exclusive company," for according to Smith the dangers posed by all modern empires increase when a monopoly trading company acts as ruler of a territory, but they also stemmed from the extreme imbalance of force that enabled Europeans—with their military and economical dominance—to act with violence and injustice without suffering any ill consequences themselves.

His deeply critical treatment of the abuses of the East India Company and of the whole project of company-run states sidestepped the question of what Britain's relations with India ought to be, and indeed whether British rule of India could be justified. Perhaps Smith failed to recognize the course of expansion British rule in India had begun to take and therefore did not address larger questions about imperial relations with extensive non-European populations.[106] He supported Fox's East India Bill, the effort led by Burke, to subject the Company to strict parliamentary scrutiny (discussed in chapter 3), though like Burke he suggested that the Company was incorrigible, and that if it were allowed to remain in India it would inevitably continue to oppress and emiserate its subjects.[107] Smith wrote of the Company that "it seems impossible, by any alterations, to render those courts, in any respect, fit to govern, or even to share in the government of a great empire; because the greater part of their members must always have too little interest in the prosperity of that empire, to give any serious attention to what may promote it" (*WN* V.i.e.26). Smith did not categorically reject European rule over non-European territory, arguing, for instance, against the East India Company's exclusive territorial claims, that the "territorial acquisitions of the East India company, [are] the undoubted right of the crown, that is, of the state and people of Great Britain" (*WN* V.iii.91). Moreover, as we have seen, Smith believed a call for total emancipation of any colonies would be politically futile.

The governments established by trading companies were unnatural and iniquitous, Smith argued, for they combined two inherently contradictory interests: those of governors, whose wealth is proportionate to the wealth of their subjects (and whose true interests are therefore consonant with those of their dominions), and those of merchants, by nature transient inhabitants of any place, who thrive by defrauding producers, destroying crops to raise a commodity's price, and seizing a country's produce for quick profit. "It is a very singular government," Smith wrote, "in which every member of the administration wishes to get out of the country, and consequently to have done with the government, as soon as he can, and to whose interest, the day after he has left it and carried his whole fortune with him, it is perfectly indifferent though the whole country was swallowed up by an earthquake."[108] The East India Company merchants, like all bodies of merchants, were "plunderers of India," incapable of acting as responsible sovereigns (*WN* IV.vii.c.103). "No other sovereigns ever were, or, from the nature of things, ever could be, so perfectly indifferent about the happiness or misery of their subjects, the improvement or waste of their dominions, the glory or disgrace of their administration; as, from irresistible moral causes, the greater part of the proprietors of such a mercantile company are, and necessarily must be" (V.i.e.26). In the meantime, colonies had merely furthered the mercantilist system, to the detriment of colonies and metropolitan society alike.

Still, the destruction already suffered by the conquered peoples showed no signs of being remedied. Smith argued that all peoples' rights should be respected, but that this only happens when countries are forced to respect each other by a more equal balance of power than then existed. "To the natives . . . both of the East and West Indies," he wrote,

> these misfortunes . . . seem to have arisen rather from accident than from any thing in the nature of these events themselves. At the particular time when these discoveries were made, the superiority of force happened to be so great on the side of the Europeans, that they were enabled to commit with impunity every sort of injustice in those remote countries. Hereafter, perhaps, the natives of those countries may grow stronger, or those of Europe may grow weaker, and the inhabitants of all the quarters of the world may arrive at that equality of courage and force which, by inspiring mutual fear, can alone overawe the injustice of independent nations into some sort of respect for the rights of one another. (*WN* IV.vii.c.80)

The language of abstract rights is rare in Smith's work, and he does not specify what rights nations should be understood to have: whether rights not to be interfered with, or perhaps simply not to be robbed and destroyed. It would seem that the particular content of the rights of nations can only be worked out in practice, like systems of morality more generally, and that a considerable degree of parity of power is necessary for such rights to be fairly specified and respected.

Drawing on a theory of development that, as we have seen, emphasized the role of accident in history, Smith here suggests both the precariousness of Europe's superior force and its irrelevance from a moral point of view. Europe's strength was not the result even of any durable, not to mention innate, superiority. Whatever advances in moral refinement Europe could boast, these neither justified international preeminence, nor ensured that Europeans would treat more vulnerable others with the justice and humanity to which they were entitled. This was the case, Smith insisted, even though modern laws of war, for instance, were far "superior in moderation and humanity."[109] Smith's critique of European empires, then, was based not only on the belief that monopoly, protectionism, and imperial rule were less economically beneficial forms of international contact, but also from a thought about what equity demanded. Trade and the communication of knowledge and innovations were, Smith believed, the events most likely to bring about the equality of force necessary to ensure respect for everyone's rights.

Smith sought to explain variation in human customs and institutions and to heed his intuition that this variation could in part be ranged historically and hierarchically, with some elements described as an "improvement" over others. He respected that variation while still reserving the possibility of both moral and practical judgments of actions, laws, or practices. He succeeded in responding to the unfamiliar with sympathy, although he also preserved as a resource for judgment universal standards such as "humanity" and "justice." His efforts at impartiality led him to turn the light of criticism on his own society, and European imperialism stood out consistently as one of its vices, blunders, injustices. His consciousness that a bias in favor of the familiar or of one's own is a universal temptation that must constantly be resisted was one frequently ignored by his successors. In these respects, his theory of societal development was not only less narrow-minded and presumptuous than nineteenth-century liberal theories of progress; as we shall see in later chapters, it also led to skepticism about and even opposition to imperial conquest in ways that nineteenth-century Britain and France failed to match.

Three

Edmund Burke's Peculiar Universalism

> God forbid that, when you try the cause of Asia in the presence of Europe, there should be the least suspicion that the cause of Asia is not as good with you, because the abuse is committed by a British subject, that it should be supposed that that narrow partiality, so destructive of justice, should guide us.
>
> —Burke, "Speech on Opening of Impeachment"

The Exclusions of Empire

Adam Smith's moral philosophy enabled him, as we have seen, to view all human societies, however diverse, as rational responses to circumstances, and as deserving of respect. His complex understanding of social development led to the belief that development cannot and should not be foisted on a society from the outside, and to the idea that Europe's advanced state of development, largely the result of historical accident, was neither an indication of moral superiority nor an authorization to rule others. Despite his commitment to commercial society as largely beneficial for welfare, efficiency, and even (though less emphatically) moral refinement, Smith expressed a lively suspicion of the European traders and monopoly companies that exported this commercial society abroad.

In Burke, we find a thinker and politician in sympathy with some of the key strands of Scottish Enlightenment thought, respected by and an admirer of Adam Smith, who undertook a critical engagement with imperial politics more wholeheartedly than any other figure in eighteenth-century Britain. As I argue later in this chapter, Burke's belief that sympathy and moral imagination are essential for just international policy shared much with Smith's moral philosophy.[1] Like Smith, Burke managed to combine a commitment to universal values such as justice and humanity with a particularly sensitive appreciation for a variety of cultural forms. The pluralism for which we find resources in the writings of the Scottish Enlightenment emerges forcefully in Burke's work. Burke has often been portrayed as almost uncannily disconnected from his milieu, but I shall argue for his affinities with certain themes of the Scottish Enlightenment.

His understanding of moral judgment, for instance, shared a great deal with the strand of moral theory developed by Adam Smith and David Hume. The notions of sympathy and moral imagination enabled Burke to elaborate a critique of British imperial practice that had theoretical affinities with the thought of Smith, but that was unparalleled in its deep and sustained engagement with imperial politics. In Burke's view, the British people's failure to regard their colonized subjects, above all Indians and Irish Catholics, as appropriate subjects of sympathy encouraged the unchecked, systematic abuse of power that too often characterized British imperial rule. For an understanding of the philosophically rich and politically engaged critique of empire that was possible in eighteenth-century Britain, then, we can do no better than to turn to Burke.

Burke perceived the dangers and corruptions of empire more clearly than perhaps any of his contemporaries, and he was arguably the first political thinker to undertake a comprehensive critique of British imperial practice in the name of justice for those who suffered from its moral and political exclusions. He was the first to challenge British conduct not only in North America but also in Ireland and India, and to draw these strands together in an assault on the political morality at the root of British imperial expansion and rule. In this chapter, I draw on Burke's writings and speeches on India, Ireland, and the Caribbean island of St. Eustatius to explore his criticism of British imperial practices, and to sketch the compelling if surprising universalist commitments that underpinned it. I argue that Burke's critique of the British Empire can be read as a principled one, that its explication does not rely on details of Burke's personal or political life, and that it is not well explained as at root a conservative impulse to preserve traditional societies.

Burke developed his vision of international and imperial justice in the form of a critique of what he saw as some of the most destructive strands of political practice in the Britain of his day. These included the suspension of European moral and political norms outside Europe on the grounds that such norms were inapplicable in backward or despotic societies; and a rigid, narrow, and exclusive nationalism, one exemplified by the Protestant Anglo-Irish, but that threatened to characterize the British national self-understanding more generally. Burke's inclusive posture appears most vividly in his critique of the exclusions that Britain permitted or encouraged its colonial agents or allies—the East India Company, the Anglo-Irish, merchants and military men—to commit. Burke never claimed that imperial rule was inherently or necessarily illegitimate. Burke opposed not the imperial relation per se but rather the spirit of domination, oppression, and exclusion that often characterized British imperial conduct. He cautioned, however, that imperial rule over diverse and distant subjects was particularly vulnerable to abuse. His insistence on the moral inclusion of and political accountability to imperial subjects set extraordinarily high standards of governance, which not only the British Empire itself, but even its most high-minded defenders in the nineteenth century, persistently failed to meet.

This chapter explores Burke's arguments against the political and moral exclusion of vulnerable peoples at the mercy of British power as the empire's reach expanded: his call for the extension of an expansive, inclusive justice informed by natural law and the law of nations, by respect for unfamiliar societies, and by a particular regard for the welfare of vulnerable, especially stateless, peoples. Burke was a particularly subtle analyst of the connections between power and cultural chauvinism and of the variety of exclusions that accompany the exercise of imperial power, above all the exclusion of the ruled from the rulers' circle of moral concern, and from ordinary standards of legal justification and political accountability.

In the second section of this chapter, I argue that Burke understood the British injustices in India to be systemic, not the isolated crimes of a single man or small coterie of corrupt rulers. I suggest in the third section that Burke traced this systemic failure of British rule in India to deficiencies in the British political classes' moral and political judgment, and in an excessively constricted circle of sympathy and moral concern. In the fourth section, I argue that Burke's attack on the "geographical morality" is characteristic of his thought in that it appeals to universalism without resting securely or systematically on foundational principles, draws upon a strong conception of law while remaining attuned to the limitations of law and the importance of politics and persuasion, and invokes British tradition and self-understanding without relinquishing fury, irony, or critical distance. In the fifth section, I turn to Burke's writings on Ireland, which show that he understood a shared logic of exclusion to characterize Britain's colonial relations with its poor, Catholic neighbor as well as with the distant peoples of India. Finally, in the sixth section, I argue that Burke's critique of British imperial practices led him to argue for a revision of the British national self-understanding, for he believed that justice within the empire required that the British imagine themselves as a nation generously, inclusively, and in a manner consistent with the rights of humanity.[2] Burke, I argue, suggested that Britain must resist the parochial insularity and exclusivity that had characterized it in the past by incorporating marginal peoples such as the Irish Catholics and by conforming its actions abroad, most notably in India, to its most stringent standards of equity and respect for the rule of law.

My intention in this chapter is to draw out several connected strands of Burke's thought that are insistent, well developed, insightful, and suggestive: it is not to present a definitive reading of Burke, or to claim systematicity or perfect consistency for his thought. Important aspects of Burke's thought are not captured by this reading, and indeed run directly counter to some of his most important insights as I seek to describe them here.[3] Burke's writings, of course, evince considerable exclusions and blind spots. Some of these, like his early dismissive assumptions about the savagery of native Americans, were tempered over the course of his life. Others, most importantly his often staggering indifference to the suffering of the poor and his dismissal of any thought of including the bulk of the population in the exercise of political power, persisted through his latest works.

Any account of Burke's struggles, in imperial and international contexts, for the inclusion of colonial subjects and excluded groups within the sphere of British moral and political concern must, then, include an understanding of the limits of Burke's apprehension of injustice, as well as the limits and failings of his own political solutions. His hierarchical vision of society as a body of political inferiors and superiors in relations of subordination, and his preferred model of political action as respectful pleading by the former and conscientious stewardship from the latter, remain as unattractive and implausible as they were recognized to be by Burke's contemporary critics such as Paine and Wollstonecraft. Yet notwithstanding his hierarchical view of politics and his belief in the need for reverence for authority, Burke's writings on Ireland and India develop powerful criticisms of oligarchic politics, of the peculiar injustices of government controlled by a caste without ties of affection, interest, or identification with the governed. Burke's own refusal to regard ancien régime France in such terms, in part because of his belief in the political virtues of a landed aristocracy and in part because any injustices he recognized in the ancien régime paled for him beside the threat of revolutionary politics, should not lead us to discount the value or the depth of his criticism of rule by the unaccountable few.

Recent treatments of Burke's writings and speeches, especially on India, have done much to correct the almost exclusive emphasis in older studies on Burke's sentimentality and traditionalism.[4] In *Liberalism and Empire*, Uday Mehta identifies Burke as the sole European thinker of the eighteenth or nineteenth century who recognized the great moral and political hazards the British faced in the extraordinary plurality of the British Empire—in Burke's words, "that vast, heterogeneous, intricate Mass of interests."[5] Mehta rightly insists, contrary to a considerable literature, that Burke's analysis of empire, and his political thought more generally, did not rest on a reliance on sentiment to the exclusion of reason: "His purpose, like that of Hume, is not to abandon reason but to enlarge its ambit, to make it social and more passionate, and more informed by the uncertain vagaries that attend and form experience."[6] Although he regards Burke as in some important respects a liberal thinker, Mehta contrasts Burke's approach to empire to that of the tradition of liberal imperialism and political exclusion exemplified by Locke and Mill.[7] Mehta's account of liberal "strategies of exclusion" brilliantly analyzes the ways in which liberalism, ostensibly a universalist and "politically inclusionary" tradition, systematically excluded various groups of people, especially by positing a thick "set of social credentials"—cultural habits or psychological dispositions—deemed necessary for full political membership (46–49). Mehta has developed a subtle and inventive account of the exclusionary impulse endemic in the liberal tradition. He says little, however, about Burke's own keen and troubled perception of the practices of exclusion in British imperial politics. It is the contention of this chapter that Burke's criticism of the British Empire as it was emerging in his day was both broadly liberal—above all in its suspicion of the exercise of arbitrary and unaccountable power and its commitment to the moral equality of all human beings—and rooted in a concern to overcome the political and moral exclusions that underlay British imperial practices.

Systematic Oppression in India

Burke's interest in India began in 1767 and lasted until his death, although it was not until the late 1770s that his study of India began in earnest and he became resolute critic of the East India Company. At the beginning of his investigations into British conduct in India, the empire there still consisted primarily of fairly small coastal holdings—bases from which the East India Company could conduct trade with, and send military expeditions into, the country's interior; by his death in 1797, the British held all of Bengal and Bihar. Burke's early views on India appear to contradict his later judgments, as historians have noted, for until the late 1770s, Burke tended to defend the Company's independence against efforts by the Crown to bring the Company under greater state control (a position stemming from the hostility to monarchic power he shared with his party, the Rockingham Whigs).[8]

From 1781 to 1783, Burke served on a Select Committee on Bengal convened by the House of Commons, for which he drafted a series of searing reports on Company policies and actions. The reports served as the foundation for many of the Articles of Charge in the impeachment of Warren Hastings, governor-general of Bengal from 1773 to 1785. Burke was the chief author and defender, in 1783, of two India bills sponsored by the Fox-North coalition, which would have reorganized the Company hierarchy and made it responsible to Parliament. Burke's speech in defense of the more contentious bill (the "Speech on Fox's India Bill" of December 1, 1783) used the Company's claims that such parliamentary control was a violation of its "chartered rights" as an occasion to compare the genuine liberties protected by the Magna Carta with the Company's usurpation of governmental power and abuse of its Indian subjects. Burke's bills died with the precarious coalition; the king used the bill as an excuse to bring down the government, which was replaced by William Pitt and his administration.

After Hastings returned to England in 1785, Burke began to prepare charges against him; in April 1786 Burke's twenty-two charges were read before the House. The managers of the impeachment succeeded, to the surprise of many, in gaining the support of the House of Commons for a trial before the House of Lords. Pitt and Henry Dundas, who had been allies of Hastings at the time of the India Bill crisis, were, by 1787, supporters of the impeachment. The impeachment trial was celebrated at its opening as a battle between justice and corrupt despotism; for several weeks the London newspapers cheered the "intellectual excellence in conjunction with moral goodness" that marked Burke's character and the prosecution's case.[9] The trial was initially successful in directing the scrutiny of the British Parliament and public not only to particular questions of corruption and abuse of power under Hastings, but also to much more general questions of the morality of Britain's imperial politics and Britain's duties to less powerful non-European peoples, whether subjects of the Company or not.

Seven years of a costly trial undermined initially strong public support, and by the time of Hastings's acquittal in 1795, Burke and his fellow managers of the impeachment were seen as vengeful, irresponsible, and disloyal to the British nation. Burke himself was derided for his long-windedness and portrayed in caricatures as a drunken Jesuit (an allusion to his supposed crypto-Catholicism).[10] Burke's hostility to Hastings was, from the beginning, credited by critics to factional spirit, runaway sentiment, or Burke's naive willingness to believe biased information from a few unscrupulous sources, but such charges rest on a selective reading of the trial. P. J. Marshall's evenhanded study of the Hastings impeachment notes that while Hastings was indeed allied with Burke's political enemies beginning in 1780, and Burke's own interest in India stemmed initially from his ties to a few men with interests in India, "once his sympathies were engaged, Burke always seems to have decided his own course of action by what he genuinely believed were the best interests of the Company's Indian subjects."[11] Burke himself disputed the popular claim that his position on India was of a narrowly partisan character. In a characteristically pointed appeal to his universal moral and political obligations, and the spirit of cultural and racial exclusion that motivated his critics, he wrote to a young correspondent, "I have no party in this business, my dear Miss Palmer, but among a set of people, who have none of your lilies and roses in their faces, but who are the images of the great Pattern as well as you or I. I know what I am doing, whether the white people like it or not."[12] Despite his own insistence that his efforts at reform in India were broad and disinterested, however, just as Burke's public perceived the trial as a vindictive private crusade, recent commentators continue to insist that he "attempted to isolate colonial guilt and the rapacity of the East India Company in the person of Hastings."[13] Even Burke's admirers have judged Burke's recourse to Hastings as the focus for his critique of imperial practice to have been misguided.[14]

Far from pursuing Hastings to the exclusion of a more comprehensive critique, however, Burke's speeches throughout the trial portrayed the governor-general's actions as symptoms of much deeper, in fact systemic, corruption and abuse of power by the British in India. Burke's critique operated at three levels: he delineated the crimes of Hastings as an individual, the structural vices of the East India Company, and the failings of British rule in India generally. The last he portrayed as consequences of more widespread British moral and political deficiencies, notably Britons' restricted moral community, presumptuousness in judging other societies, and complacency about the use of their burgeoning power around the globe. While the Company was the official agent of the British government in India (thanks to a royal charter), Burke often, and indeed rightly, discussed the British rule of India as that of one *nation* over another. To be sure, he held Hastings personally responsible for taking advantage of a corrupt system. Burke believed both that moral and political responsibility could be laid at Hastings's feet—for Hastings had made full use of the opportunities for abuse inherent in the Company's government—and that the very existence of the myriad opportunities for abuse indicted the system as a whole. Indeed, the trial's ultimate failure may have been in part because it was a relentless assault on British political morality as well as a prosecution of Hastings, although Burke's more general political and social criticism was arguably better judged and more apt than his indictment of Hastings as an individual.

Although Hastings's supporters saw the impeachment trial as a product of Burke's personal hostility to the man, then, Burke consistently used the trial as an occasion to criticize the entire structure of British power in India. Burke's opening impeachment speech portrayed Hastings's crimes as just one element in a system of abuse: "an Arbitrary system must always be a corrupt one" (*WS* 6:375). Throughout the impeachment trial, and in letters of the period, Burke called attention to the *systematic* nature of the abuse of colonial power, describing British government in India in one late letter, for instance, as "Systematick iniquity and oppression."[15] Even before the trial, Burke had attempted to persuade his fellow legislators that they were in the process of establishing an "outrageous" colonial system that violated both traditional British legal standards and universal moral values, "a system which our ancestors struggled and died to exterminate, which is incongruous to the habits and peculiarities of the national character, and which we cannot admit without sacrificing at once all our prepossessions for the privileges of Britons, and the rights of humanity."[16] In contrast to colonial reformers who regarded British imperial rule as fundamentally beneficent but occasionally vitiated by the crimes of individual officials (J. S. Mill's view, as we shall see in chapter 5), Burke consistently warned that the injustices committed under Hastings were not isolated misdeeds but instead crimes nearly inextricable from the structure of British rule in India and imperial political culture.[17]

Burke tied this systematic "iniquity" most immediately to structure of the East India Company itself. The Company servants' misgovernment was due above all to their almost complete freedom from accountability either to Indians or to the British who, by providing the Company with a legal charter, bore ultimate responsibility for their actions: "They are a Republic, a Commonwealth without a people. They are a State made up wholly of magistrates. The consequence of which is there is not people to control, to watch, to balance against the power of office. There is no corrective upon it whatever."[18] While he was prepared to grant the legitimacy of the Company's charter, he expressed his disapproval of its terms, in its extravagant concessions to the Company's "claim to exclude their fellow-subjects from the commerce of half the globe . . . and to dispose . . . of the lives and fortunes of thirty millions of their fellow creatures" (WS 5:384–85). Burke's claim that the Company's "chartered rights do at least suspend the natural rights of mankind at large; and in their very frame and constitution are *liable to fall into a direct violation of them*" indicates his view that the Company's structure itself made it likely to oppress its subjects and imposed on those who had licensed such power the charge of scrutinizing its exercise with critical vigilance.[19]

Although in his speech on Fox's East India Bill he restricted himself to arguing for the Company's accountability to the British Parliament, Burke was keenly aware of the dangers posed by the peculiar political structure of a governing body legally answerable only to its superiors (the British Parliament) and not to its subjects. As he noted in preparation for a speech in 1786, "Great Empire liable to abuse of Subordinate Authority—more <especially> if it is distant—most of all if the people have no distinct priviledges secured by constitutions of their own and able to check the abuse of the subordinate Authority."[20] Burke compared the Indians' situation to that of provinces of the Roman Empire, which did have corporate status and representatives in the capital. Although Roman governors might abuse their provincial subjects—and Burke was conscious of the parallels of his trial to Cicero's prosecution of Verres, governor of Sicily—he argued that Roman provincials had access to means of redress denied to Indians.[21] The dangers of despotic power were far greater in India because Indians lacked genuine and effective means by which to appeal for redress of grievances: the British did not recognize in Indian society any corporate bodies with a legal structure and a history of legitimate authority, and it provided for no official avenues of petition or representation for Indians.

He argued further that the Company's structure and leaders stifled dissent or protest from both inside (among Company employees) and outside (from Indians). Low-level Company servants who might be in a position to protest flagrant abuses of power were co-opted by their own petty complicity in the corruption.[22] Indians, he argued, were clearly silenced by terror, as the absence of Indian petitions to British authorities attested:

> [W]hen he considered that Mr. Hastings had been for fourteen years at the head of the Government in India, and no one complaint had been sent home against him, he trembled at the enormous degree of power he had to contend with, to which alone could be ascribed the silence in question, since it was not in human nature, situated as Mr. Hastings had been, to preserve so pure, even-handed, and unimpeachable a conduct, as to afford no room for even a single accusation to be stated against him.[23]

Burke decried the execution in 1775 of the Bengali maharaja Nandakumar, who had accused Hastings of accepting bribes, not only as illegitimate in itself, but as having silenced any possibility of dissent or complaint on the part of Indians oppressed by the British.[24] "The accuser they saw hanged . . . a murder not of Nundcomar only, but of all living testimony, and even of evidence yet unborn. From that time not a complaint has been heard from the natives against their governors. All the grievances of India have now found a complete remedy."[25] Whelan holds that Burke was "running the risk of a circular argument" by claiming that both the lack of remonstrances against Hastings *and* the florid testimonials to his benevolence from grateful subjects were evidence of his oppressive governance.[26] But Burke's claim was that dissent is inevitable under an ordinarily just government. The complete absence of routine complaints and petitions from the governed—petitions that would indicate a government even minimally accessible and responsive to the interests of its subjects—indicated both the tyranny and the dishonesty of the Company's rule.[27]

For the immediate present, it was the Company, not yet the British people as a whole, that was responsible for the cruelties perpetrated in India: "The East India Company in India is not the British Nation. When the Tartars entered into China and into Hindoostan, when all the Goths and Vandals entered into Europe, when the Normans came into England, they came as a Nation. The Company in India does not exist as a Nation."[28] The British nation could still condemn, and dissociate itself from, the unauthorized actions of the Company's servants in India. "The despotic acts exercised by Mr. Hastings were done merely in his *private* character; and, if they had been moderate and just, would still be the acts of an usurped authority."[29] Hastings's trial offered the nation's representatives, both the Lords who judged and the members of Commons who impeached, the opportunity to act on the nation's natural sentiments and condemn the unnatural actions of the Company; it was a challenge to which neither House rose. It is clear, however, that Burke suspected his audience's tenuous grip on appropriate moral sentiments from the beginning. As we will see (in the fifth section), Burke appealed to Britain's reputation when it seemed that natural sentiment and charged images would be inadequate to bring his audience to see the injustice of their complacent support of the Company.

But behind the institutional failings of Company's unaccountability, as I discuss in the following section, Burke identified a deeper source of colonial injustice in the British failure to sympathize with their Indian subjects—indeed, British disdain for Indians as inferior and barbarous.

Burke's insistence on Hastings's guilt as an individual also constituted part of his effort to persuade British legislators to reform the system immediately, lest the nation as a whole become implicated in the oppression. His speeches suggest that such injustice was willful on the part of Hastings and other Company servants, but, as yet, unconscious on the part of the British nation. Part of his purpose in staging a public inquiry into the East India Company's actions in India was to make his audience aware of the extent of their own moral insularity and consequent complicity. In his speech on Fox's East India Bill (in 1783, three years before the beginning of the trial), Burke proposed that Hastings's despotic acts were private and unauthorized and that the British nation could atone for its complicity in Hastings's crimes if its representatives acted quickly to punish the wrongdoers and overhaul the system. He continued to insist in his early impeachment speech that if the nation did not punish individuals' crimes, it adopted them as its own.[30] He had little hope that the British public and its representatives were capable of such a step, however, both because of the nature of colonial rule and because of particularly British moral failings. Burke suggested that the British effort to rule India was almost bound to be unjust, even beyond the particular vices of Hastings and the

Company, and that it was the systemic injustice even more than the crimes of individuals that was nearly impossible to correct.

While Burke did not argue outright for the abolition of British rule in India, then, his speeches before and during the trial are dedicated to showing the "incorrigibility" of the Company, the tendency to abuse inherent in any attempt to govern a distant colony, and the particular evils of British rule over a people the British were content to regard as lawless and benighted.[31] Burke's treatment of the British empire in India was relentlessly and almost exclusively critical, and he offered little in the way of a positive imperial program.[32] He referred more than once to the empire in India in providential language, attributing, for instance, the "dominion of the glorious Empire" to "an incomprehensible dispensation of the Divine providence into our hands."[33] While it is true that this passage can be read (as many have read it) as suggesting that British rule in India was divinely ordained and not to be questioned, when placed in the context of Burke's persistent criticism not just of Hastings but of the whole British imperial enterprise in India, such references to the mysteriousness of the Divine plan may be read as intending to demand caution and self-doubt rather than British confidence in an imperial mission.[34] Burke insisted with reference to both America and India that if the British could not govern their imperial territories justly, they ought to release them. While Burke seemed at times to lament the loss of imperial provinces, he deplored the misconduct that gave rise to the loss as much as any blow to British power or prestige.[35] Early writings occasionally suggest use of rule to improve conditions of Indians, but this theme tends to disappear; both, it seems, because of a developing resistance on Burke's part to seeing Indians as backward, and because of Burke's growing despair that the British were capable of using their power for benevolent purposes.[36]

There is a persistent ambivalence in Burke's arguments about reform of British rule in India: he presented the myriad and almost insurmountable obstacles to reform and repeatedly argued explicitly that if British rule was not made just, beneficial to its subjects, and somehow accountable to them, then the British ought to relinquish their claims to political power in India. As he said in the speech on Fox's East India Bill, "if we are not able to contrive some method of governing India *well*, which will not of necessity become the means of governing Great Britain *ill*, a ground is laid for their eternal separation; but none for sacrificing the people of that country to our constitution" (*WS* 5:383). He went on to assure his audience that he believed that the means necessary to "preserve India from oppression" were also those that would prevent the corruption of British politics. Although he grew ever more pessimistic over the course of the 1780s that such reforms were possible, he continued to press for reforms rather than simply to call for ending British rule in India altogether.

Burke's statements that Britain was unlikely to succeed in governing India for the benefit of its subjects as it was British duty to do, and that Britain itself might be ruined in the attempt, have been variously interpreted as an assertion of the view of righteous parliamentarians that it was Britain's duty to rule and improve the country, and, more radically, as a claim that it was Britain's duty to renounce all pretensions to political power in India. Later in his East India Bill speech, Burke held in an often quoted passage that all the "circumstances" of corruption, misgovernment, and British lack of sympathy for Indians "are not, I confess, very favourable to the idea of our attempting to govern India at all. But there we are; there we are placed by the Sovereign Disposer; and we must do the best we can in our situation. The situation of man is the preceptor of his duty" (*WS* 5:404). Both supporters of the British empire and more recent critics have read this passage as establishing Burke's commitment to empire or to a colonial project.[37] Margery Sabin has recently offered a subtle and convincing reading of these lines as marking an "impasse" in Burke' argument, where Burke's "aphorism of duty . . . strains at a rhetorical level to achieve an ethical stability belied by Burke's more powerful language of indictment elsewhere."[38] Burke's language in these lines is, in the context of the speech, uncharacteristically resigned and indeed passive. The passage reminds us that Burke was not prepared to claim that British rule in India was categorically or inevitably unjust. He himself appealed to his reluctance to question existing institutions,[39] although (as Sabin notes), Burke had often remarked how new, unstable, and immature British institutions in India were. Burke's unwillingness to question the legitimacy of the Company's very existence, like his decision to "draw a veil" over the injustice and violence that had (so recently) established British power in India, marks the limits of his critique of British power in India. Within these limits his criticism is uncompromising, but this concession to the possible legitimacy of British rule in India is considerable.

Burke did not, in the end, articulate a precise political solution for India. On the one hand, he at times asserted that the sovereignty of Indian states should be shielded from encroachment or usurpation, as when he argued that he would have protected Chait Singh, the raja of Benares, from Hastings's power by ensuring that he was not "subject to our Government at all but by making him totally independent. But the moment he came into dependence upon the British Government, all the evils attached immediately upon him. . . . I declare that there is no security from this arbitrary power but by having nothing to do with the British Government" (*WS* 7:260–61). He also acknowledged, however, a place for Warren Hastings as a British governor sent to "protect" his Indian subjects. The idea of relinquishing power in India altogether was almost unthinkable in the political environment of Burke's day; Burke, like Adam Smith, surely knew that direct denunciation of empire tout court was a futile gesture. Within such constraints, he offered a thoroughgoing criticism of the British empire the implications of which, it might be argued, were lost on both his contemporaries and subsequent generations of British imperial politicians.[40]

Moral Imagination: Empire and Social Criticism

Burke's rhetorical strategy throughout the Hastings trial conveys his belief in the importance of sympathy in moral judgment. Burke believed that justice is impossible where there is a failure of moral imagination, and he fought the exclusions of imperial politics—most dramatically in the case of India but also in Ireland—by calling on his British audience to exercise moral imagination and to extend sympathy beyond their traditional circle of moral concern. Burke insisted that although Britain had developed distinctive traditions of freedom and rule of law, it could not be counted on to abide by these in its dealings with the rest of the world. While eighteenth-century proponents of British imperial expansion, as David Armitage has shown, characterized the empire as Protestant, commercial, maritime, and free (and avoided reference to precisely those elements of the empire that were not), Burke resolutely called attention to the injustices toward those who did not fit this image.[41]

Many of Burke's writings on the British Empire can be read as efforts to rouse the moral imagination and emotional indignation of his audience—his parliamentary colleagues, public opinion, even posterity—and transform the scope of their moral community and to force them to acknowledge the moral and political standing of those others.[42] Burke called attention to the particular difficulty of reforming the cruel and unjust treatment of distant, exotic people by agents of one's own country. "[I]t is an arduous thing," Burke told the House of Commons in 1783, "to plead against abuses of a power which originates from your own country, and affects those whom we are used to consider as strangers. I shall certainly endeavour to modulate myself to this temper" (*WS* 5:403). The Hastings trial was in part Burke's effort to represent Indians before the British public in a way that would render them objects of sympathy and respect: this transformation of the British perception of Indians, he believed, was essential to any lasting reform.

Sympathy was central to Burke's understanding of moral psychology and moral judgment, as it was for Hume and Smith. In his early work of moral philosophy and aesthetics, the *Philosophical Enquiry into the Origin of Our Ideas of the Sublime and Beautiful* of 1757, Burke places sympathy at the heart of moral reasoning.[43] In the *Philosophical Enquiry*,

Burke describes sympathy as the first of the social passions, the passion by which "we enter into the concerns of others" and a feeling that, by divine design, is strongest "where sympathy is most wanted, in the distresses of others."[44] Thanks to this instinctual bond to other human beings, we cannot be "indifferent spectators" of the distress of others, whether we encounter them directly, or read or hear about them (and whether the account of suffering is truth or fiction). Burke maintains that sympathy for another's suffering is not simply painful: we feel "a degree of delight . . . in the real misfortunes and pains of others," and it is this delight that compels us to attend to, even dwell on, scenes of suffering rather than shun them. At the same time, the sympathetic pain that accompanies this delight "prompts us to relieve ourselves in relieving those who suffer."[45] The connection between feeling sympathy and acting to relieve another's suffering is thus direct and immediate in Burke's moral theory: to perceive the suffering of others is—"antecedent to any reasoning"—to feel impelled to aid them.

British conduct in India in the 1770s and 1780s demonstrated to Burke that sympathy can fail, that spectators incapable of achieving an imaginative substitution of others' concerns for their own, *can* be indifferent witnesses to others' suffering. Even before Hastings's impeachment, Burke suggested that lack of sympathy in Britain was proving one of the greatest obstacles to justice in India:

> I confess, I wish that some more feeling than I have yet observed for the sufferings of our fellow-creatures and fellow-subjects in that oppressed part of the world had manifested itself in any one quarter of the kingdom, or in any one large description of men.
>
> That these oppressions exist is a fact no more denied than it is resented as it ought to be.[46]

The British public could know the facts of imperial oppression without being moved to outrage on behalf of Indians either as members of their own political community or simply as human beings. A simple recounting of British crimes in India would fail to prompt redress, Burke saw, because the British public had not learned to include Indians within its circle of moral concern.

Distance itself certainly contributed to the problem, Burke acknowledged: it was, indeed, easier to sympathize with Hastings, standing before the audience at the trial, than it was with his countless but unseen victims.[47] At first, supposing that the very unfamiliarity of Indians and their languages and cultures had enabled the British to disregard their suffering, Burke sought to render Indians intelligible as fellow human beings and potential victims of British injustice. He recognized the importance of removing technical jargon and unfamiliar names as much as possible from the reports of the select committee if Indians were to receive a fair hearing from impatient and unimaginative British politicians.[48] Similarly, in the speech on Fox's East India Bill, Burke reminded his audience,

> [W]e are in general, Sir, so little acquainted with Indian details; the instruments of oppression under which the people suffer are so hard to be understood; and even the very names of the sufferers are so uncouth and strange to our ears, that it is very difficult for our sympathy to fix upon these objects. . . . All these circumstances are not, I confess, very favourable to the idea of our attempting to govern India at all.[49]

Note the bare suggestion that Britain was unfit to govern India at all, a point Burke made in this oblique way a number of times, although he never called outright for the emancipation of India.

Burke's most elaborate effort to make the Indians intelligible and therefore sympathetic to his British audience was his comparison of the country's terrain and inhabitants with those of Germany: Indian geography was not unlike Germany's; "the Nabob of Oude might stand for the king of Prussia." Burke's extended analogy seems intended to aid his audience's imagination, to encourage their deficient sympathy. Thus he argued that his comparisons served,

> not for an exact resemblance, but as a sort of middle term, by which India might be approximated to our understandings, and if possible to our feelings; in order to awaken something of sympathy for the unfortunate natives, of which I am afraid we are not perfectly susceptible, whilst we look at this very remote object through a false and cloudy medium.[50]

If his audience could not muster sympathy for such unfamiliar people as Indians, they would have to be coaxed by drawing an imaginative link to Germans, who were easier to sympathize with only because they were more familiar.

Sara Suleri has read passages such as this as attempts by Burke to "measure India against the example of the West, so that the priority and recognized reality of European dominions become the only compass by which the geography of the colonized territory may be read"; she also maintains that Burke purposefully obfuscated Indians' situation by filling his speeches with confusing and exotic details.[51] Both suggestions, I believe, misconstrue Burke's rhetorical strategy, but they indicate the extent of the challenge he faced in his efforts both to convey an adequately textured portrait of Indian territories and societies and to remain intelligible to a fickle and ignorant public. When Burke painstakingly compared Indians to Germans, he was tailoring his imagery to the limitations of his audience, not proposing Europe as the unique or privileged source of universal standards.

But Burke came to see the British failure of sympathy as more profound than simply a misrecognition due to distance and unfamiliarity. Rather, as the Hastings trial proceeded, he began increasingly to regard Britain's moral failing as a disdain for Indians as inferior, a refusal to extend moral consideration to people outside a restricted circle, and indeed a corruption of British moral sentiments. In his closing impeachment speech, Burke's fury at what by now appeared a willful refusal on the part of the British political classes to extend their sympathy to Indians is apparent: "People that are wronged, people that are robbed, people that are despoiled have no other remedy but the sympathies of mankind, and *when these sympathies are suffered to be debauched* . . . we commit a robbery still greater" (*WS* 7:247; emphasis added). The British public, Burke seems to propose, in denying justice and sympathy to the East India Company's Indian victims, has robbed them of membership in the moral community of humanity. By this time, Burke had come to recognize that it was the elaborate and disparaging construction of Indian society as inferior to European, not simply distance or ignorance, that enabled the British political classes to countenance the Company's systematic abuse of its power in India:

> [I]f you go into a Country where you suppose mankind in a degraded, servile state, that there is no one man that can lift up his head above another, that they are a set of vile, miserable slaves, all prostrate, confounded in a common servitude, that they have no descendable lands, no inheritance, nothing that makes man proud in himself, that gives him honour and distinction, those things will take from you that kind of sympathy which naturally attaches you to men feeling like yourselves, that have hereditary dignities to support, as you peers have, who have lands of inheritance to maintain, that you will no longer have that feeling that you ought to have for the sufferings of a people whom use has habituated to such suffering.[52]

Burke recognized that pity, contempt, and certainty about one's own superiority cannot serve as the basis for sympathy, even for an adequate recognition of a victim's suffering. His speeches sought to convey not simply the extent of Indian suffering—which might produce merely condescension in his British audience—but an idea of Indians in all their humanity, which for Burke meant an understanding of their complex social conventions, hierarchies, and values.

Of course, Burke also recounted in vivid, even appalling, detail British cruelties and Indians' suffering; these narratives of oppression at first moved and eventually exasperated his audience, and they have been the focus of much of subsequent analysis of Burke's India speeches.[53] The narratives were calculated to inspire an emotional response and to undermine his audience's detachment from the crimes, which he considered a result of psychological as much as physical distance. He believed that awakening sympathy for the vulnerable on the part of his constituents and fellow legislators demanded deliberate theatrics.[54] Although he was accused of giving way to sensationalism, Burke believed his descriptions served as a means of promoting justice: "I am sensible that a cold style of describing actions, which appear to me in a very affecting light, is . . . contrary to the justice due to the people, and to all genuine human feelings about them," he announced in his speech on Fox's India Bill, anticipating the mocking response to his descriptions of horrors in India.[55] Burke noted that an East India Company employee who had been instructed to investigate disturbances against tax collectors submitted "lurid and detailed descriptions" of the torture of Indian farmers by those officials. The employee's report nicely expressed Burke's critical strategy, and Burke quoted him at the trial:

> [T]he punishments inflicted . . . for non-payment, were in many instances of such a nature that I would rather wish to draw a veil over them than shock your feelings by the detail, but . . . however disagreeable the task may be to myself, it is absolutely necessary, for the sake of justice, humanity, and the honor of government, that they should be exposed, to be prevented in future.[56]

Burke's particular emphasis on indignities to Indian nobles has tended to be read, especially alongside the *Reflections* (and following Paine's quip that Burke "pities the plumage but forgets the dying bird"), as evidence of Burke's affection for traditional hierarchies and aristocratic government and his concern for the nobility at the expense of interest in the rest of the population.[57] While Burke certainly regarded traditional hierarchies as foundations of social order and worried about their destruction, his frequent recourse to tales of the nobility had a broader rhetorical function, for he believed audiences identify more readily with the suffering of the great than with that of ordinary people. In his closing impeachment speech he justified his extended discussions of Indian nobles such as Cheit Singh: "it is wisely established in the constitution of our heart that mankind interests itself most in the fall and the fate of great personages. They are the objects of tragedy every where, which is addressed to our passions and feelings, and why? Because men of great place, men of great rank . . . cannot fall without an horrible crash upon all the others that are about them. Such Towers cannot tumble without the ruin of Cottages" (*WS* 7:340). Burke insisted that his own concern was for the many as much as the few. His emphasis on the nobility, although deliberate, was perhaps misguided in that it seems to have left many among his audience and later readers convinced of his own restricted sympathies.[58]

Later, in the *Reflections*, Burke further elaborated the place of spectacle and horror in moral judgment. Begging pardon for dwelling on the pitiful scene of the king and queen chased from Versailles on October 6, 1789, Burke wrote that our "moral opinions" rest on such scenes:

> [W]e are so made as to be affected at such spectacles with melancholy sentiments upon the unstable condition of mortal prosperity and the tremendous uncertainty of human greatness; because in those natural feelings we learn great lessons; because in events like these our passions instruct our reason. . . . We are alarmed into reflexion; our minds (as it has long since been observed) are purified by terror and pity. (*WS* 8:131–32)

One of the primary reasons for Burke's abhorrence of French revolutionaries was what he believed was their disconnection from common or "natural" moral sentiment. Mere reason, Burke maintained, destroyed what he called "the common feelings of men"—feelings that serve as a moral compass for all but the most unnatural moral "calculators." He commented that "it seems as if it were the prevalent opinion in Paris, that an unfeeling heart, and an undoubting confidence, are the sole qualifications for a perfect legislator" (*WS* 8:217). The servants of the East India Company were as guilty as the French revolutionaries of excusing crimes with elaborate reasoning; this was one of the affinities between the phenomena of "Indianism" and "Jacobinism" to whose similarities Burke often alluded.[59] Burke had pleaded with his audiences (particularly the Lords sitting in judgment of Hastings) to exercise the moral intuition of the common spectator and avoid specious and self-serving calculations. His admonition in the *Reflections*—that the "true lawgiver . . . ought to love and respect his kind, and fear himself" (*WS* 8:217)—might have been addressed to the Lords who failed, Burke suggested, to respect their "kind" in Indians, and to fear the disproportionate power wielded by the British. After Hastings was not merely acquitted but even granted a pension for his services, Burke intimated that the Lords had proven themselves no better legislators than the Jacobins.[60]

Burke's rhetorical strategy during the trial was, then, a considered product of his moral theory. He deployed deliberately shocking imagery to overcome what he feared was the insuperable indifference of the British political classes toward the injustices their countrymen perpetrated on a distant people, people the British understood ill and held in contempt. Burke saw the Hastings trial as an opportunity to bear witness to British atrocities, as much as a legal trial.[61] He failed nonetheless to prompt contrition or reform of imperial policy. Many at the time and since have attributed his failure to misguided political judgment, though Burke himself suspected his audience's insurmountable hostility to self-criticism. While his speeches were intended to transform public political judgment, he was pessimistic about how long such an alteration would take. In a private letter written after Hastings's acquittal, at a time of deep gloom for Burke, he wrote, "Above all make out the cruelty of this pretended acquittal, but in reality this barbarous and inhuman condemnation of whole Tribes and nations, and of all the abuses they contain. If ever Europe recovers its civilization that work will be useful. Remember! Remember! Remember!"[62] His arguments in the trial, then, were addressed to posterity as much as to the curious crowds in Whitehall.[63] We can read Burke's India speeches not simply as an attempt to change policy immediately, but also as the development of a theory of international and imperial justice that he hoped would serve the British in the future, when they had outgrown what he saw as their constricted moral community.

Geographical Morality and Burke's Universalism

Burke often invoked the term *geographical morality* to condemn the particular form that Britain's exclusionary politics took in India. Geographical morality, for Burke, refers to the systematic refusal to extend the moral and legal standards that the British recognized in Europe to Indians, as members of distant and alien societies. As Burke put the problem most explicitly, in the opening of the Hastings impeachment:

> [H]itherto we have moved within the narrow circle of municipal justice. I am afraid, that, from the habits acquired by moving within a circumscribed sphere, we may be induced rather to endeavor at forcing Nature into that municipal circle than to enlarge the circle of national justice to the necessities of the empire we have obtained.[64]

Although *municipal law* was a technical term for what we now tend to call domestic law, Burke's use of the word "municipal" is faintly ironic. His insistence on the failings abroad of a narrow British municipal justice undercuts the prevalent national self-image as civilized and cosmopolitan and calls into question the adequacy of Britain's moral and legal traditions to its military and economic power. He had pointed out similar failings elsewhere in the empire, in America and Ireland, though India's particular circumstances (the lack of sympathy that attended the combined differences of race, language, culture, and religion in addition to great distance) made the problem particularly acute there. With regard to America in 1774, Burke argued that Britain must ensure that its legal proceedings genuinely take into account colonists' grievances: "Justice . . . is not to be measured by geographical lines nor distances."[65] In the context of trade policy toward Ireland, he insisted on Britain's moral obligation to develop an inclusive and generous policy suited to its considerable international entanglements: "Indeed, Sir, England and Ireland may flourish together. The world is large enough for us both. Let it be our care not to make ourselves too little for it."[66]

Among the British in India, Burke argued, geographical morality took the form of a cynical exclusionary posture based on cultural and racial contempt for both the Company's subjects and independent Indian states. This rank prejudice was elaborated through theories about the nature of "oriental despotism" and the effects of climate on moral codes and social organization, all of which Burke rejected as self-serving imperialist cant. Burke characterized geographical morality as a renegade code in a world governed by universal moral and political standards: Hastings, he argued,

> has told your Lordships in his defence, that actions in Asia do not bear the same moral qualities as the same actions would bear in Europe. My Lords, we positively deny that principle. . . . These gentlemen have formed a plan of Geographical morality, by which the duties of men in public and in private situations are not to be governed by their relations to the Great Governor of the Universe, or by their relations to men, but by climates . . . parallels not of life but of latitudes. As if, when you have crossed the equinoctal line, all the virtues die. . . . This Geographical morality we do protest against. Mr. Hastings shall not screen himself under it.[67]

As such passages suggest, Burke's impeachment speeches depicted Hastings as the embodiment of this morality, but Burke made clear that it informed British policy in India more generally: "[T]hat the people of Asia have no laws, rights, or liberties, is a doctrine that is to be disseminated wickedly throughout this country" (*WS* 6:363). Burke countered the relativistic claim that different moral and legal standards in the despotic East might permit the British to suspend their own political and moral standards in two ways: he offered alternative representations of Asian societies as governed by law, stable property relations, and a recognition of certain rights; and he insisted that the British had an obligation to extend universally the fundamental standards of respect, lawfulness, and humanity that applied at home. Burke viewed his task, then, not so much as one of establishing new standards but rather as holding British behavior up to norms that were well established and fairly uncontroversial in Europe but that Europeans regularly transgressed farther afield.

Burke's speeches present Britain's practice of geographical morality in India as exclusive, and therefore unjust and oppressive, in at least two senses. First, in granting Europeans the liberty to treat members of other societies in ways they would never treat other Europeans, it straightforwardly licenses oppression, cruelty, and the use of force and fraud. Second, and more subtly, in characterizing other societies as inherently or historically lawless or barbaric, it permits the coercion and exclusion of their inhabitants even in the name of assisting them. In response, Burke argued, first, that the British had an obligation to apply their own most stringent moral norms to their dealings in India and elsewhere, and second, that Indian society could not in truth be characterized as lawless or despotic. Burke acknowledged that British laws need not be applied verbatim in India.[68] But he argued that no account of Eastern societies—as arbitrary, despotic, or corrupt—could legitimate behavior by Europeans that patently contradicted their own moral and legal standards: "I hope and trust that your Lordships will not judge by Laws and institutions, which you do not know, against those Laws and institutions which you do know, and under whose power and authority Mr Hastings went out to India" (*WS* 6:347). Although Burke would go on to give his own rendition of the content of many Asian legal systems, here he acknowledges the difficulty Europeans face in attempting to judge actions by unfamiliar standards.

Hastings's defense maintained that the British were justified in exercising arbitrary power in India because Asian rulers themselves did not abide by the rule of law. The British had no choice, Hastings claimed in his defense, but to make use of despotic local practices in order to protect their commerce and territory in India. Burke more than once quoted Hastings's claim that the "whole history of Asia is nothing more than precedents to prove the invariable exercise of arbitrary power" (*WS* 6:107, 109). Hastings's lead counsel, Edward Law, invoked what was to become a standard justification for Britain's ostensibly benevolent despotism in India when he informed the Lords that India, "up to the period when, I will say, it was blessed by the administration of the English, has been the devoted seat of everything that is detestable in the shape of misgovernment and tyranny."[69] Hastings's defenders argued that it was inappropriate, and indeed dangerous, for the British to apply European moral and legal standards in societies that had never recognized such norms. By exercising despotic rule in the name of order, they claimed, the British were not only yielding to necessity but also benefiting their Indian subjects. Burke's account of Hastings's principles was tendentious and partly misrepresented Hastings's views; as P. J. Marshall has noted, Burke drew heavily on a text that Hastings himself had not written, though he allowed it to be released under his name.[70] If Burke exaggerated in his characterization of Hastings himself, however, his determination to unsettle the notion of oriental despotism was remarkable and even prescient.

In calling on Asian practice as a justification for the Company's conduct, Hastings's defenders invoked a trope increasingly pervasive in late-eighteenth-century discourse, thanks especially to Montesquieu.[71] Indeed,

Burke named Montesquieu as a culprit in the dissemination of the false portrait of India as a society without laws, rights, or honor, proposing that "every word that Montesquieu has taken from idle and inconsiderate Travellers is absolutely false."[72] In response to the presumption of oriental despotism, Burke decoupled despotism from Asia, pointing out that despotism is a universal vice, one that cannot be said to characterize any particular society, and to which none is immune. He also repeatedly called attention to the fact that oriental despotism was a construction, imagined and deployed by Europeans out of ignorance, or more often cynical self-interest.[73] In his closing impeachment speech, Burke upbraided the "wickedness of these pretensions, that the people have no Laws or rights," citing the extensive and sophisticated commentaries of Muslim law, one of which, as he noted, had been translated into English at Hastings's own request.[74] The suggestion that these legal commentaries could have been written "by a people who have no property is so very ridiculous that one would think the very assertion was sufficient to refute it." Burke insists throughout the trial speeches that Muslim law recognizes certain individual rights, forbids rulers to impose taxes on subjects without their consent, specifies the qualities required of a rightful ruler, and designates the conditions for legitimate rebellion. According to Burke, then, the thesis of oriental despotism was both malicious and self-evidently absurd to anyone with any knowledge of Indian society.[75]

While Burke acknowledged that the British had encountered some despotic local rulers in India, he rejected the Company's assertions that the only policy open to them was to participate in the misdeeds they encountered. Hastings, he argued, had taken as his models a few exceptional tyrants, such as might be found in any society, and transformed these exceptions into his own rule.[76] In contrast to the portrait of Asian societies as benighted masses habitually at the mercy of omnipotent sovereigns who arbitrarily abrogated property and other personal rights, Burke argued that "in Asia as well as in Europe the same Law of Nations prevails, the same principles are continually resorted to . . . Asia is enlightened in that respect as well as Europe" (*WS* 6:367). In his early writing on India, Burke himself had repeated European conventional wisdom that despotic Muslims were tyrannizing the more docile and industrious Hindu population. In an essay of 1779, he argued that the British had lent their military, an "unnatural and extrinsic force," to help a local Muslim despot, the nawab of the Carnatic, to "waste, rob, and oppress a vast tract of country, once the most populous and flourishing on earth."[77] But after his close study of India in the early 1780s, Burke revised his account of Indian governance to deny that Muslim rulers and legal systems were traditionally arbitrary or despotic and that their Hindu subjects required the protection of the British.

In part Burke argued his case for the lawfulness of Indian society based on evidence drawn from legal codes that historically had informed its governance: the laws of Tamerlane, Akbar, and Genghis Khan, the Koran, the "Gentoo code," the "constitutions of Oude."[78] But behind Burke's rather general references to these Asian systems of law was his assertion that a universal law—"the law of humanity, Justice, Equity, the Law of Nature and of Nations" (*WS* 7:280)—underlies the laws of all societies. In his opening impeachment speech, Burke insisted on the agreement of all legal systems on fundamental principles of good governance and the rule of law:

> Let him run from law to law; let him fly from the Common law and the sacred institutions of the Country in which he was born; let him fly from Acts of Parliament, from which his power originated. . . . Will he fly to the Mahometan law? That condemns him. . . . Let him fly where he will; from law to law. Law thank God meets him everywhere. . . . I would as willingly have him tried upon the law of the Koran, or the Institutes of Tamerlane, as upon the Common Law or the Statute Law of this Kingdom. . . . In short, follow him where you will; let him have Eastern or Western Law; you find everywhere arbitrary power and peculation of Governors proscribed and horridly punished. (February 16, 1788, *WS* 6:365–66)

All these systems of law shared a fundamental hostility to arbitrary power on Burke's account: he could describe a sort of closing of ranks of the world's legal systems against the threat posed by Hastings, the Company, and their willful geographical morality.

Burke tended to invoke natural law and the law of nations in the same breath. He did not deduce a set of moral principles from a theory of natural law, but rather looked to its instantiation in actual societies. It is from the law of nations—from a study of the customs of societies across time and space—that he believed more specific principles could be gleaned. If the laws of all the societies of the world were examined, Burke claimed in opening the impeachment, "they would be found to breathe but one spirit, one principle, equal distributive justice between man and man, and the protection of one individual from the encroachments of the rest. The universality of this principle proved its origin."[79] A perennial problem for theories of the law of nations has been how to establish the content of such law, which risks being either too minimal to be useful or else too easily disproven by social facts, by actual disagreement about fundamental principles of justice. It might be argued that Burke's argument risks circularity, in that it posits the rule of law as a feature of all legal systems but implicitly rejects any polity not founded on the rule of law as illegitimate or even a contradiction in terms. Burke's conviction that all societies of any stability share certain general legal and moral principles stemmed from a belief similar to Smith's view, discussed in chapter 2, that no society can long survive if it is utterly corrupt in its practices and principles.

Burke's appeals to natural law, while frequent and impassioned, gave little concrete content to the concept.[80] While some readers have attempted to depict Burke as a natural law theorist in the Thomist tradition, Burke's appeals to natural law offer almost none of the detailed or systematic moral guidance of either the Catholic or the Grotian natural law tradition.[81] Burke has been criticized for this vagueness, as in Don Herzog's claim that Burke failed to redeem the "promissory note" of his appeals to natural law.[82] But Burke did not require a theory of natural law to elaborate moral principles; such a reliance on abstract theory would, indeed, have betrayed his conviction that just standards and conduct emerge in the course of social and political life, including the long and slow work of reform.[83]

Instead, Burke's conception of natural law might best be regarded not primarily as a detailed set of rules, but rather as a means of conveying the universal scope of moral duties. Burke did not doubt that British principles and customs were largely just and reasonable when applied within the customary moral and political community: he believed his audience needed no great correction there. The failures of justice and humanity he discovered in India stemmed from the easy abrogation of British standards when Britons confronted people outside their own "municipal" context: a failure created, as we have seen, in part through simple distance, but more fundamentally as a result of British disdain for unfamiliar societies.

Burke counterposed to Hastings's geographical morality "the Law of Nature and Nations," as well as similarly universal notions such as "the law of humanity, Justice, Equity."[84] He had elaborated his understanding of the law of nations in 1781, several years before the Hastings trial, in his attempt to prosecute and redress the crimes of Admiral George Rodney and the British navy against the residents of St. Eustatius, the West Indian island, which they had seized from the Dutch in March of that year. In the course of the American war, Rodney had captured this small, rocky trading post with Dutch, British, American, and Jewish residents (a number of the Jewish residents were not citizens of any country), ostensibly as punishment for its merchants' brisk trade with the Americans. Rodney claimed all public and private property for the British government. A month after Britain first learned of the island's capture, Burke moved in Parliament for "an inquiry into the seizure and confiscation of private property in the island," a motion whose sound defeat presaged the fate of his Indian efforts. In a speech of May 14, 1781, Burke denounced the British navy for seizing the private property of St. Eustatius's residents, an action he asserted was against the law of nations.[85] His speech presents one of Burke's most comprehensive descriptions of the meaning, authority, and sources of the law of nations.

In the May 14 speech, Burke considers the law of nations a source of rigorous moral and political obligations, despite its having developed piecemeal and remained unwritten. He argues, in the universalist language that would be characteristic of his Hastings impeachment speeches, "Perhaps it might be said, there was no positive law of nations, no general established laws framed, and settled by acts in which every nation had a voice. There was not indeed any law of nations established like the laws of Britain in black letter, by statute and record; but there was a law of nations as firm, as clear, as manifest, as obligatory, as indispensable."[86] Burke's suggestion here that if a more explicit international law were to be contrived, it should be by a process "in which every nation had a voice," remains undeveloped, but it accords with his generally inclusive posture, his refusal to distinguish between standards appropriate for conduct among Europeans and those less stringent norms acceptable in imperial and non-European contexts.

In the first St. Eustatius speech, Burke emphasizes the duties of reciprocity imposed on warring countries by the law of nations, and the limits that law places on justifiable means of war: "the belligerent powers are to treat one another as having mutually justice on their side, until the final issue is known. So that although the perfidiousness of the Dutch might be a just cause for going to war, it was no excuse for aggravating the horrors of it."[87] In insisting on the validity of the law of nations, Burke offers a variety of sources of moral argument without thoroughly privileging one over the others: "First, he could prove that they were established by reason, in which they had their origin and rise; next, by the convention of parties; thirdly, by the authorities of writers, who took the laws and maxims not from their own invention and ideas, but from the consent and sense of ages; and lastly, from the evidence of precedent" (2:256–57). Burke suggested, then, that the law of nations was well established in British culture according to a variety of measures—reasoned agreement, legal precedent, political tradition. But here, as in the India speeches, Burke warned his audience that Britain was in danger of defying its own moral traditions as its power extended beyond the boundaries of its moral community and beyond its capacity to reason justly. The British failure to abide by the laws of nations in the West Indies characterized the geographical morality, unfortunately typically British as well, that seemed to supersede respect for law whenever British ships crossed a line in the ocean.

Just as in his invocations of the law of nature and nations in the impeachment speeches, in his treatment of the St. Eustatius episode Burke appeals to the law of nations as much to insist on the *universal scope* of

Britain's moral obligations as to discuss its content. The episode led Burke to explore the problem, similar to India's, of the particular vulnerability of stateless peoples, or people unprotected by a state whose sovereignty the British respected. During the parliamentary debates that followed Admiral Rodney's seizure of the island, Burke focused his attention on the special problems faced by Jews whose statelessness made them Rodney's easiest and most abused victims. While Rodney's expropriation of the island's European citizens, Burke argued, certainly violated the law of nations and "that system of war" established by convention among European states, he asserted more radically and importantly that particular moral obligations accompanied the relations between a powerful state in a position of control, and a vulnerable people. The Jews of St. Eustatius were unprotected by the military force (and by the traditions of treaty and reciprocity) that, in contests among European states, ensured that civilians' claims would be enforced.[88]

The Jews' vulnerability and statelessness gave them a special claim, Burke argued, on Britain as on all powerful states. "The persecution was begun with the people, whom of all others it ought to be the care and the wish of humane nations to protect, the Jews. Having no fixed settlement in any part of the world, no kingdom nor country in which they have a government, a community, and a system of laws, they are thrown upon the benevolence of nations, and claim protection and civility from their weakness, as well as from their utility."[89] Powerful states have a particular obligation, Burke insisted, to protect vulnerable peoples without the military power to enforce their own rights claims. He held that European conventions of war are binding not only when they can be enforced by injured states: that the powerful have a duty to fulfill the unwritten laws of international reciprocity all the more scrupulously when they encounter people unable to protect themselves. He argued that the Jews' "abandoned state and their defenceless situation call most forcibly for the protection of civilized nations. If Dutchmen are injured and attacked, the Dutch have a nation, a government, and armies to redress or avenge their cause. If Britons are injured, Britons have armies and laws, the laws of nations (or at least they once had the laws of nations) to fly to for protection and justice. But the Jews have no such power, and no such friend to depend on. Humanity then must become their protector and ally. Did they find it in the British conquerors of St. Eustatius? No" (251).

After his speech of May 14, 1781, describing Britain's obligations under the law of nations, Burke made a failed second motion in December for a general inquiry into abuses. When Burke's broader efforts to redress Rodney's crimes failed, he tried instead to secure individual compensation for Jewish former residents of the island.[90] The reporter's account of that speech calls attention to Burke's moving rhetoric: "Mr Burke heightened the pathos of this affecting case, and put it home to the bosoms of the House, in a manner that could not but rouse and excite the pity and compassion of every gentleman present."[91] The arguments for the protection of vulnerable peoples in these speeches, as well as the language and imagery, prefigure much in the India writings. In both cases Burke insists on the "nationality" of the people in question: though they were not members of states whose sovereignty was recognized by European or "civilized" states, they belonged to groups with corporate identity that ought to be recognized, beyond their claims to humane treatment simply because of their humanity. Thus Burke repeatedly referred to the Jews of St. Eustatius as members of the "Hebrew nation" (just as he ascribed nationality to the peoples of India).

As in the India writings, in the St. Eustatius speech of May 14, 1781, Burke insisted that "the eyes of Europe" (later it would be the eyes of the world) were watching British conduct, and that the British reputation for fair and humane dealing and the ministers' sense of honor—if they lacked a principled commitment to justice—ought to provoke Parliament to punish and redress the actions of its agents. Most important, both India and St. Eustatius offered instances of groups of people rendered defenseless by international imbalances of power and by a British failure to respect the humanity and rights of those outside their restricted circle of moral regard. The geographical morality practiced by the British in India was part of a broader moral and political failing that characterized British actions abroad as Britain's power expanded across the globe and outpaced the society's ability to reason justly about its obligations and its place in the world.

The Politics of Exclusion in Ireland

Burke's writings on Ireland portray particularly brilliantly the pathologies of the political, legal, and social exclusion of a group of subjects simply because of their nationality or religion. While Ireland's situation was undeniably different from India's, Burke often called attention to the similar oppressions suffered by both under British rule. It has often been argued that Burke's Irish experience made him unusually sensitive to the injustices of the empire in India, but it might also be said that Burke's increasingly intense study of India sharpened his perception of the evils of exclusion in Ireland.[92] As he grappled with Indian affairs, Burke wrote three of his theoretically most sophisticated analyses of Irish exclusion: letters written in 1782 and 1792 (all, probably, with an eye to publication) about the Irish parliament's legislative responses to Catholic agitation for relief. Burke himself noted that he had written the first of these letters, to the prominent Catholic landowner Lord Kenmare, "at the time when I began the employment, which I have not yet finished, in favour of another distressed people, injured by those who have vanquished them, or stolen a dominion over them."[93] In both India and Ireland, British arrogance and insularity, their contempt for the non-British population and their refusal to integrate with them, had exacerbated the violence of the initial conquest and made the British ill-suited to rule.[94]

In Ireland, he believed the remedy must not be emancipation (as it might in India) but could only be the full inclusion of Irish Catholics in British nationality, citizenship, and society. Burke called not for the assimilation of indigenous peoples to the conquerors' own cultures, but rather for a blending of conquerors into the local population and the formation of a new, more inclusive and heterogeneous, nationality. The British nationality that incorporated the Irish Catholics by granting them religious freedom and equal civil and political rights would be a transformed Britishness. Such a transformation would be in the interest of both Irish Catholics and Britons themselves; only the Anglo-Irish who sought power independent of Britain and domination over their Catholic compatriots would suffer.

Burke regarded the history of British involvement in Ireland as a series of abuses stemming from a spirit of conquest and domination unchecked by any accountability to or connection with the dominated indigenous population. He described the dehumanization that resulted when hatred, pretended superiority, and unchecked power enabled a small faction to oppress their fellow subjects and treat them with utter contempt. Burke catalogued the evils of exclusion with great perception: both the "absolute slavery" of the proscribed group and the corruption of a "master cast" [*sic*] of rulers who could indulge their "pride, passion, petulance, peevish jealousy, or tyrannic suspicion" with impunity (*WS* 9:601). He noted that the Anglo-Irish regarded the Catholics as outlaws, as "perpetual, unalliable aliens," kept apart "as if they were not only separate nations, but separate species" (9:626, 629). Political exclusions of entire groups, Burke argued, were a violation of both universal and specifically British principles: of natural law and human rights, of reason, of political prudence, and the principles of the British constitution: "Our constitution is not made for great, general, and proscriptive exclusions; sooner or later, it will destroy them, or they will destroy the constitution" (9:601). While Burke was not, to be sure, an advocate of universal suffrage, he perceived with great clarity the peculiar dangers that arise when a group of subjects is denied all the rights of civil, political, and social membership.

Burke suggested that the total exclusion of their subjects was an injustice peculiar to the British as conquerors.[95] While he expressed suspicion of any conquest, he believed the initial violence of conquest could be overcome if the conquerors settled, mixed with the local population, and extended rights of citizenship to the conquered peoples.[96] Because of its relentless separatism, the British colonization of Ireland was oppressive even compared to the notoriously harsh Roman occupation of Gaul. While the Roman and Mughal conquerors had tended to conquer more violently, they had mitigated the outrage of their conquests by settling, intermarrying with the indigenous people, and making their conquered realms their own. Citing Tacitus, Burke wrote of Cerealis's announcement in a speech to the Gauls that henceforth the conquerors and conquered alike would enjoy equal rights: "[W]e claim no privilege, you suffer no exclusion." Burke commented, "For a much longer period than that which had sufficed to blend the Romans with the nation to which of all others they were the most adverse, the Protestants settled in Ireland, considered themselves in no other light than that of a sort of a colonial garrison, to keep the natives in subjection to the other state of Great Britain."[97] In Ireland as in India, the crimes peculiar to the British stemmed from their insularity and spirit of exclusion.

Burke's 1782 letter to Lord Kenmare detailed the failings of a reform bill that purported to ameliorate the position of Catholics in Ireland by repealing certain disabilities against Catholic priests and permitting Catholics to acquire property. In response to Lord Kenmare's request for his opinion on the bill, Burke argued that even this apparent relief bill was "grounded at once on contempt and Jealousy"; he feared that in restating systematically the Catholic proscriptions that (hitherto confusedly) had permeated Irish law, the bill would actually hinder reform (*WS* 9:566). The letter insists on the extremity and violence of the exclusion even after the supposed liberalization of the reform:

> To look at the Bill in the abstract, it is neither more nor less than a renewed act of universal, unmitigated, indispensible, exceptionless, disqualification. One would imagine, that a Bill inflicting such a multitude of incapacities, had followd on the heels of a conquest made by a very fierce Enemy under the impression of recent animosity and resentment. No man, in reading that Bill, could imagine he was reading an act of amnesty and indulgence. . . . What must we suppose the laws concerning those good subjects to have been of which this is a relaxation! (9:567)

Part of the tremendous burden borne by Irish Catholics, Burke suggested, stemmed from the intimate connections between legal and political disabilities and broader social oppression. Catholics were excluded from the legal profession and oppressed by a court system that used the pretense of Catholic conspiracies to subject them to "inhuman proceedings"; they were "exclude[d] wholly from all that is beneficial, and expose[d] to all that is mischievous, in a Trial by Jury" (9:569). Burke noted the particular oppression suffered by a group excluded from a society that was partially democratic: jury trials and elections actually exacerbated their exclusion by furnishing individual members of the Anglo-Irish population with access to the coercive power of the state. The proscription from the vote meant not only that parliamentary representatives were completely unaccountable to Catholics but also that "if they should become obnoxious to any bigotted, or any malignant people among whom they live," elected representatives had an incentive to use state power to oppress them. As Burke argued, "The taking away of a Vote is the taking away the Shield which the subject has, not only against the oppressions of power, but of that worst of all oppressions, the persecutions of private Society, and private manners" (9:570).

The culture of contempt for Catholics that the Anglo-Irish had fostered meant that even well-intentioned and apparently enlightened reformers aggravated the Catholics' exclusion in their very efforts to aid them. Burke pointed to the efforts of the Provost of Trinity College, a man of "benevolence and enlarged spirit" whose reform efforts, though "not percievd [by him] to be fresh insults," were "remedies wholly unsuited to the nature of their complaint."[98] In describing the failures of the provost's charities, Burke tellingly drew an analogy to India, to which (as he pointed out in a later letter), he was at this moment beginning to devote his energies: "It is to feed a sick Gentû with Beef Broth, and to foment his Wounds with Brandy" (*WS* 9:572–73). Burke's conclusion about the provost's efforts indicates his great sensitivity to the pitfalls of attempting to make laws on behalf of others—not simply distant or unfamiliar others, but more specifically those whom the legislators regard with contempt or an assumption of their own superiority: "To have any respect for the character and person of a popish priest there—Oh! it is an uphill work indeed! But until we come to respect what stands in a respectable light with others, we are very deficient in the Temper which qualifies us to make any Laws or regulations about them. It even disqualifies us from being charitable towards them with any Effect or Judgment." Even the most enlightened and kindhearted reformer, if his perspective and context are those of a society that regards itself as superior to those under its power, will be almost inevitably hindered by that context from judging rightly about their interests. Even those who believe themselves above the contempt for a subordinate group that characterizes his society, who believe they are acting for the best interests of the excluded, will be incapable of aiding those who are utterly excluded, judging what is best for them, or "improving" their condition from the outside.

A culture of exclusion, Burke shows, not only gives those with the spirit of domination a free hand to oppress, it not only denies legal and social channels of redress to the excluded: it also prevents many of the more enlightened among the dominating group from perceiving their own complicity in the oppression even as they believe themselves to be alleviating it. This attention to the most subtle effects of exclusion is one of the elements of Burke's sensibility that would be lost among the "civilizing" imperial liberals who regarded their own judgment about what constitutes progress and reform as unimpeachable.[99]

All three of the later analyses mentioned above (the letters to Lord Kenmare, Langrishe, and Richard Burke) emphasize the proscription of Catholics *as a group* or "description" and the unusual virulence of that form of exclusion. The hatred and contempt that drives such exclusion is irrational and impervious to argument; the excluded can do nothing to alter their status. In these letters, Burke insists the Irish Catholics are excluded as a nationality, or because of who they are, rather than because of their religious beliefs or practices. Burke described the phenomenon in the letter to Langrishe as "[t]his way of proscribing men by whole nations"; he argued that "the Catholic, as a Catholic and belonging to a description" was denied civil and political rights (*WS* 9:629). All Catholics were, for instance, at risk of arrest for riot or (worse) conspiracy against the state, no matter what their actions or characters: Burke noted that despite recent reforms he still saw evidence of "a disposition to carry the imputation of crimes from persons to descriptions, and wholly to alter the character and quality of the offences themselves" (9:603). Crime had become not an act but a national condition.

The arguments of an earlier essay suggest that Burke came only gradually to recognize the peculiar and particularly dangerous character of a proscription based on the hatred of or contempt for a group. In contrast to his later characterization of the exclusion as national or ascriptive, Burke's early and unfinished "Tracts Relating to Popery Laws" (probably written in 1765 or earlier) tends to describe the exclusions as religiously motivated and to describe the excluded as a large number of individuals: as "the many," "the great body of the people," "so many hundred thousands of human creatures" (*WS* 9:459–62). In the 1765 tracts, Burke wryly noted the failure of the disabilities to convert Catholics: "Ireland, after almost a century of persecution, is at this hour full of penalties and full of Papists" (9:464). By the time of the later letters, Burke seems to have concluded that such arguments were beside the point, since the exclusion was not based on religion after all. He continued to argue for toleration as a religious principle, but he became convinced that the oppression of Irish Catholics had little to do with religious commitment on the part of the persecutors.[100]

In his letter to Langrishe, Burke noted that proscriptions of the native Irish by their English conquerors had long predated the Reformation and any distinction between Catholic and Protestant. The twelfth-century

Anglo-Norman conquerors of Ireland had established their ascendancy through the Kilkenny Statutes of 1366, which imposed many of the same discriminatory policies that later, under the popery laws, were carried out in the guise of religious policy. "The statutes of Kilkenny shew, that the spirit of the popery laws, and some even of their actual provisions, as applied between Englishry and Irishry, had existed in that harassed country before the words Protestant and Papist were heard of in the world."[101] The religious dispute, on Burke's account, furnished a veneer of principle for simple national hatred by the Anglo-Irish and their British supporters.[102]

Three centuries after the Kilkenny Statutes, Burke argued, the same nationalist hatred infused the English Revolution in Ireland, where it had dramatically different meanings and consequences than it did in England. After the English decisively defeated the Irish in the Battle of the Boyne (1690), they enacted harsh anti-Catholic laws. As the English were claiming their own liberties at home, Burke noted, their countrymen in Ireland were depriving the local population of their property and of civil and political rights. While in England the revolution constituted a popular struggle for liberty, one rightly remembered as an emancipation from a minority of usurpers and oppressors, in Ireland the same revolution established the tyrannical power of a small faction. "I shall not think," Burke wrote, "that the *deprivation of some millions of people of all the rights of the citizens, and all the interest in the constitution, in and to which they were born*, was a thing conformable to the *declared principles* of the Revolution."[103] Although Burke's enthusiasm for the English Revolution is often noted, the letter to Langrishe and other statements on Ireland demonstrate that he was as attentive to the injustices perpetrated in the name of national fulfillment in the 1688 revolution as he was to those of 1789. He refused, then, to see the conflict between the British rulers of Ireland and their native subjects as the oppressors would have liked to paint it, as a doctrinal dispute. National prejudice and not religious fervor, he claimed, was at the root of British and Anglo-Irish persecution of the native Irish: "What was done, was not in the spirit of a contest between two religious factions; but between two adverse nations."[104] Even the form that Catholic proscriptions took demonstrated their political and national, rather than religious, character: Catholics, Burke wrote to his son, were free to attend Mass but were considered "outlaw[s] from the British constitution," whereas a genuinely religious animus would have extirpated the Mass.[105]

Burke rejected another common explanation for the Catholic proscriptions in Ireland, supported by Langrishe himself, that more recent laws were the effect of English fears of Irish Catholic strength (one proposal was called the Bill to Prevent the Further Growth of Popery). He held, to the contrary, that the cruelty and exclusion typical of Anglo-Irish nationalism resulted from the love of domination, the power and security that came from having British force behind them, and the dehumanization of the excluded group: "[E]very measure was pleasing and popular, just in proportion as it tended to harass and ruin a set of people, who were looked upon as enemies to God and man; and indeed as a race of bigotted savages who were a disgrace to human nature itself."[106] The Anglo-Irish culture of superiority and hatred had spawned a system of oppression that pervaded both law and society: the old system, only beginning to be dismantled, was

> a complete system, full of coherence and consistency; well digested and well composed in all its parts. It was a machine of wise and elaborate contrivance; and as well fitted for the oppression, impoverishment and degradation of a people, and the debasement, in them, of human nature itself, as ever proceeded from the perverted ingenuity of man. (*WS* 9:637)

Burke's insistence on the *systematic* quality of this oppression echoes his claims in the case of India that the crimes were not those of Hastings alone or of a few colonial officials, but of a legal, social, and cultural structure that permitted injustice because its victims were denied any standing in the moral community of the powerful.

Langrishe was a relatively sympathetic Irish Protestant: a man who had been one of the foremost supporters of Catholic emancipation but who nonetheless feared the full political inclusion of the Catholic population. His comment to Burke that Catholics "ought not to *be the state*" prompted Burke's insistence that the existing total exclusion was intolerable servitude; he rejected as unworthy of discussion the slippery slope suggestion that for Protestants to grant any participation to Catholics was to surrender Ireland entirely.[107]

The most recent development in the history of oppression in Ireland was, Burke apprehended, the pretended emergence of an "Irish interest" among the Anglo-Irish and an effort on their part to co-opt the native Irish Catholics into forming a new Irish, and anti-British, national identity. He counseled the native Irish against any such alliance: they must fight, instead, for Catholic emancipation and inclusion in British nationality, a struggle in which their greatest opponents would be the Anglo-Irish themselves. "Ireland therefore, as Ireland, whether it be taken civilly, constitutionally, or commercially, suffers no Grievance. The Catholicks as Catholicks do; and what can be got by joining their real complaint, to a complaint which is fictitious, but to make the whole pass for fiction and groundless pretence?"[108] It was the Catholics, not the Irish as such, who suffered, though the true reason for their oppression was not religious but national. Burke dismissed a separate Irish nationality as the dangerous goal of a selfish few:[109] "That Ireland would . . . come to make a figure amongst the nations, is an Idea which has more of the ambition of individuals in it, than of a sober regard to the happiness of an whole people. . . . Ireland *constitutionally* is independent—*Politically* she never can be so. It is a struggle against Nature."[110] Burke meant that Ireland was too small and impoverished a country to be independent and would necessarily be dominated by or united with either France or England. Because Ireland was not viable as a state, he believed, the efforts of the Anglo-Irish to bring about an Irish nationalism hostile to Britain would have to be misguided and perhaps immoral even if the Anglo-Irish leaders of this effort had not already shown themselves to be contemptuous of the Irish Catholics they now cynically courted.[111]

Burke believed it possible and desirable for the Irish to be incorporated into the British state and nationality, though he acknowledged Ireland's ambiguous political status.[112] But he insisted that the political union of Britain and Ireland required British national self-understanding to expand to encompass the Irish, most importantly Irish Catholics. In the letter to Langrishe, Burke meditated on the destructive nature and consequences of a national pride that rests on the exclusion of another group, which he believed to characterize British nationalism as it had existed so far. He aspired to cultivate a national sentiment in the British that would supplant the "party spirit" that was exemplified by the Anglo-Irish and that he believed had deep roots in British (or more strictly English) culture more generally. In Burke's view, this exclusion must be replaced by another national self-conception, one that could also be regarded as emerging from British history.

> [I]n a Country of monopoly there can be no patriotism. There may be a party spirit—but public spirit there can be none. As to a spirit of liberty, still less can it exist, or anything like it. . . . But it will be said, in that Country, some people are free—why this is the very description of despotism. Partial freedom is privilege and prerogative, and not liberty. Liberty, such as deserves the name, is an honest, equitable, diffusive, and impartial principle. It is a great and enlarged virtue, and not a sordid, selfish, and illiberal vice. It is the portion of the mass of the citizens; and not the haughty licence of some potent individual, or some predominant faction.[113]

Burke thus held that pervasive exclusions such as that of the Irish Catholics not only constituted a patent injustice to the victims but also undermined for the British themselves specifically British constitutional traditions: the rule of law, freedom, and respect for basic rights on which the British prided themselves. In Ireland, where the vast majority were long denied true property rights, "[T]he greatest and most ordinary benefits of society are conferred as privileges, and not enjoyed on the footing of common rights" (*WS* 9:459). Burke contended that the sacrifice of the interests of one part of a community for those of another is "repugnant to the essence of the Law" (9:459, 457). Indeed, an exclusive constitution could not properly be described as law at all: "[A] Constitution against the interest of the many, is rather of the nature of a grievance than a Law: that of all grievances it is the most weighty and important" (9:462).

We might suspect that the antioligarchic spirit of Burke's writings on Ireland stands in tension with his seemingly unequivocal defense of the French aristocracy and clergy in the *Reflections*. Certainly Burke's own Whig colleagues, who saw ancien régime France precisely as a despotic country in which only "some people are free," in which liberty was a "privilege and a prerogative," believed that the arguments of the *Reflections* violated many of Burke's important moral commitments.[114] Charles James Fox, for one, claimed in a 1791 debate on France to have learned from Burke that rebellions should be regarded as justified expressions of outrage at despotism.[115] While that speech destroyed their long alliance and friendship, as Burke considered the revelation of views that he had expressed in private to be an unforgivable offense, we have other, similar statements from Burke himself, again most powerfully expressed in regard to Ireland. In the letter to Langrishe he wrote: "What I have always thought of the matter is this—that the most poor, illiterate, and uninformed creatures upon earth, are judges of a practical oppression. It is a matter of feeling; and as such persons generally have felt most of it, and are not of an over-lively sensibility, they are the best judges of it" (*WS* 9:621). He warned that the "narrowing of the foundation" was not the way to build a stable structure: "The body of disfranchised men will not be perfectly satisfied to remain always in that state. If they are not satisfied, you have two millions of subjects in your bosom, full of uneasiness" (*WS* 9:630). These statements, written two years after the *Reflections*, indicate Burke's sensitivity to the suffering of the victims of Ireland's exclusionary and oligarchic politics and his awareness that such policies could understandably incite rebellion.

If Burke was hostile to suggestions that his reaction to the French Revolution was inconsistent with his earlier statements about oligarchy and oppression, we must on the other hand remain conscious that the *Reflections* provide an incomplete and limited account of his views on these matters. His many statements about the incompatibility of broad political exclusions and the rule of law might well be applied to ancien régime France. Burke himself had articulated his commitment to the oppressed in broad terms that included not simply national groups but the poor: in a speech of 1781, he said, "When, indeed, the smallest rights of the poorest people in the kingdom are in question, I would set my face against any act of pride and power countenanced by the highest that are in it; and if it should come to the last extremity, and to a contest of blood—God forbid! God forbid!—my part is taken: I would take my fate with the poor and low and feeble."[116]

Burke's arguments in the *Reflections* have caused many readers to overlook his hostility to other forms of exclusive politics, but his sustained assault on the spirit and practice of exclusion in Ireland should chasten our tendency to draw from the *Reflections* a broader political philosophy of hierarchy and exclusion. While Burke was a consistent foe of exclusion and the politics of the "few" when these were based on nation or religion, he rarely recognized wealthy ruling classes (in both France and India) as the "few," as exclusive groups ruling in their own private interest. In such cases he hewed to a theory of trusteeship, believing that a shared sense of community among rich and poor would restrain those in power. In the letter to Langrishe, Burke reflected explicitly on the differences between "national" exclusions such as that of the Irish Catholics—exclusions of "whole descriptions" of men—and political exclusions based on class. When certain classes were denied political representation, Burke argued, they might still benefit from what he called "virtual" representation, if the rulers felt sufficient affinity with them. "Virtual representation is that in which there is a communion of interests, and a sympathy in feelings and desires between those who act in the name of any description of people, and the people in whose name they act, though the trustees are not actually chosen by them."[117] The Irish Catholics, he argued, utterly excluded from social interaction with the ruling class as well as from civil and political rights, simply because of who they were, could never benefit even from such "virtual" representation. "To them it is not *an actual*, and if possible, still less a *virtual* representation. It is indeed the direct contrary. It is power unlimited, placed in the hands of *an adverse* description, *because it is an adverse description*" (*WS* 9:601). On Burke's view, the Anglo-Irish exclusion of Catholics was the product of rationally indefensible hatred.[118] He believed proscriptions based on *property*, in contrast, could be defended by reason, though it must be noted that he argued for a broad franchise for the Irish Catholic population and protested when some members of the Catholic Committee considered seeking a property qualification (of one hundred pounds) for Catholic suffrage.

A word should be said about Burke's opposition to the Quebec Act in 1774, which might seem to betray the inclusive politics that I have argued characterizes all Burke's mature imperial positions.[119] The act, sponsored by Lord North against powerful parliamentary opposition, granted religious freedom to the Catholic minority in Canada, increased the king's power over the colony, and preserved many French laws and judicial procedures (civil law was to be French, with no jury trials in civil suits, criminal law mostly English). The act was, in its religious provisions, a gesture of imperial inclusiveness that contrasted strikingly with the proscriptions against Catholics in Britain and Ireland as well as with the exclusions of French settlers and Amerindians by the American settlers. Burke opposed the act (as did all the Rockingham Whigs), on the grounds that its political clauses increased the power of the Crown and were destructive of English liberties. As an agent of New York, he expressed concern for the rights of British subjects living in disputed territory at the Quebec border: "The Crown has a power at a stroke to turn them into slavery."[120] In a June 10 speech on the subject, Burke voiced suspicion of the motives of the Quebecois "noblesse," who had petitioned for these protections, he argued, because they "wished to have the poor under their controul" (*WS* 2:473). Burke always firmly supported the provisions for religious freedom, however, and indeed he used the Quebec Act debate as an occasion to make a broader plea for Catholic emancipation. "There is but one healing, Catholic toleration in this House . . . the thirsty earth of our own country is gaping and crying for that healing shower from heaven."[121] In his support for Catholic toleration in Canada, Burke was at odds with many of the other opponents of the Quebec bill, several of whom made virulently anti-Catholic statements in the debates.[122]

Nearly twenty years later, in his letter to Langrishe, Burke invoked as a model for Ireland the 1774 emancipation of Canada's Catholics, and the 1791 Canada Act, in which Parliament established the Church of England jointly with the Catholic Church, and at the same time further ensured Catholics' political inclusion by granting political representation to Canadians without religious limitations. Burke wrote that in passing the 1791 act, Parliament "had no dread for the Protestant church . . . because we permitted the French Catholics, in the utmost latitude of the description, to be free subjects" (*WS* 9:636). Moreover, the Quebec Act had not incited popish disloyalty to Britain, as the opponents of toleration in 1774 had warned it would; on the contrary, Canadians alone among Britain's North American subjects had not revolted. The peaceful cohabitation under British rule of Catholics and Protestants in Canada was evidence that toleration was not only just but also feasible in Ireland: "They are good subjects, I have no doubt; but I will not allow that any French Canadian Catholics are better men or better citizens than the Irish of the same communion" (9:636–37).

Immediately after linking the causes of Catholic emancipation in Quebec and Ireland, he drew a broader connection to India: "I have been many years . . . employed in supporting the rights, privileges, laws and immunities of a very remote people. I have struggled through much discouragement and much opposition; much obloquy, much calumny, for a people with whom I have no tie, but the common bond of mankind" (*WS* 9:637).

His aim in all these cases, he said caustically, was to convince a small-minded Britain "that all the Pagans, all the Mussulmen, and even all the Papists (since they must form the highest stage in the climax of evil) are worthy of liberal and honourable condition." Burke himself undoubtedly saw his struggles on behalf of these various groups as elements of a concerted project of the moral and political inclusion of vulnerable subjects throughout the British Empire.

Burke as a Theorist of Nationality

Reflections on the meaning and implications of nationality form a central and somewhat overlooked element of Burke's thinking about international justice. Burke had a particularly supple perception of British nationality as constructed, evolving, and in need of revision in order to be adequate to guide Britain in the expanded sphere the nation occupied as a global power. Recent scholarship has demonstrated the centrality of Britain's empire to the formation of a British national consciousness during the eighteenth century.[123] The 1707 Act of Union initiated the movement toward a British national identity, as the Scottish and English gentry gradually intermixed and as the Scots became involved in the building of empire.[124] Burke's work should be read in light of this process, for the subject of embryonic British nationhood looms large in Burke's writings on Ireland and India. Two central concerns about British national self-understanding emerge in these writings. Burke argued for the inclusion of the Irish Catholics among Britons, and he appealed to a national self-understanding that would demand just treatment of the vulnerable, such as Indians and West Indian Jews.

Burke took his speeches on empire and international justice as occasions for imagining the British nation. As has been observed, Burke's Irishness made him sensitive to what British nationality meant for those who invoked it or acted in its name, for although he was never entirely accepted as a Briton, he was by no means simply an outsider.[125] Britain's characteristic moral and political isolation, its limited "municipal morality," was in Burke's view, as we have seen, inadequate to guide the country's actions as it became ever more entangled in relations abroad. A recurrent theme of his speeches is the thought that if Britain did not reconstruct its moral code and its self-understanding as a nation, it would continue to violate—and to allow its agents such as Hastings and Rodney to flout—the moral standards that Burke believed underlay not only the consensus in "civilized Europe" but indeed the world's legal codes generally. Britain's geographical morality required, in short, a redefinition of the national identity.

Burke did not, as a typical caricature has it, fetishize the organic national community. Rather, he was a thinker attuned to the ways in which nations are constructed and can and must be reconstructed in response to historical developments: conquests, most dramatically, in his own age. British nationalist sentiment, and the municipal morality from which it sprang, were, in Burke's view, the source of much of Britain's oppressive and unjust behavior in its imperial history. The alternative that emerges in his writings is universalism as an enlarged mentality, resting on particularist affections but attentive to the ways that such affections can slip into exclusion. The right sort of affection for one's own is in fact essential for the humanitarianism Burke sought. As the well-known passage in the *Reflections* argues, "To be attached to the subdivision, to love the little platoon we belong to in society, is the first principle (the germ, as it were) of public affections. It is the first link in the series by which we proceed toward a love to our country and to mankind" (*WS* 8:97). Burke believed that national sentiment, appropriately chastened, could underpin international justice, and so repeated appeals to a nobler and more inclusive national sentiment are a leitmotif in Burke's works on empire.

Burke combined the strong commitment to the egalitarian application of laws and standards to all peoples described above with his better-known appreciation for local tradition to form a distinctive vision of the role of national sentiment in the formation of a moral international politics. An understanding of the nation as malleable, as constructed by its members, constitutes a central part of what I have called Burke's peculiar universalism. Burke appreciated that divisions among nations served both to protect individuals and to threaten them. William Connolly has described the tension well:

> Boundaries form indispensable protections against violation and violence; but the divisions they sustain also carry cruelty and violence. Boundaries provide preconditions of identity, individual agency, and collective action; but they also close off possibilities of being that might otherwise flourish. . . . The political question is how to come to terms with the ambiguity of boundaries, how to fight against their sacrifices and violences without sacrificing their advantages altogether. The question poses endless difficulties. . . . The most tempting thing is to suppress the question itself.[126]

The problem is of course an old one, but Burke's attentiveness to the tension and his willingness to navigate it rather than to suppress the question or declare himself for or against boundaries, makes his treatment of the problem an unusually nuanced one. The construction of nationality, as Burke presented this process in his writings on India and Ireland, involves the definition of national boundaries, the naming of members, and the elaboration of a collective self-understanding; it can be pursued in a spirit of narrow self-interest or in the service of a moral politics.[127]

The word *nation* experienced a period of terminological fluidity in Burke's day.[128] It was coming to be simply another term for "state" in eighteenth-century debate (as in Bentham's new term, *international*), although it continued to be used independent of statehood and political status. The ambiguity, of course, remains in current uses of the term. Burke invoked multiple senses of uses of the term *nation*, with differing normative implications. Sometimes he made clear that he meant the term to include statehood or political status, in which case a nation could protect its members diplomatically or militarily, while remaining inclusive and essentially benevolent. At other times, as in his discussions of the national animus of the Anglo-Irish against Irish Catholics, Burke explicitly intended an exclusive locus of loyalty not contiguous with state boundaries, and destructive of peace and political unity.

Burke opposed what might be seen as an alternative form of nation building, the anticosmopolitan nationalism of Rousseau. Rousseau made the case for this kind of nationalism most explicitly in his *Considerations on the Government of Poland*, where he proposed the active construction, through the telling of national myths and the performance of nation-building rituals, a strong, and exclusive, national Polish self-understanding. "Incline the passions of the Poles in another direction" than cosmopolitanism, Rousseau wrote, "and you will give their souls a national physiognomy that will distinguish them from other peoples, that will prevent them from mixing, from feeling at ease with, from allying themselves with those peoples."[129] Burke's was a far more fluid conception of national boundaries than Rousseau's, because of what might be called his constructivist conception of the nation: nations, for Burke, exist in the evolving self-understandings of their members. They should not rely on distinctions from other nations, as Rousseau would have it, and they can and must evolve to incorporate groups previously excluded: for Britain the most important of these was the Irish.

Burke's writings on both India and Ireland suggest that he anticipated the emergence of a pernicious, and ultimately self-destructive, British nationalism, one with centuries-old roots but also immature enough in his own time to be reformed. There are suggestions throughout his work that he believed that a more capacious sense of nationality could itself be a beneficent force in Britain's external relations. His speeches on India were intended not only to elicit empathy for Indians but also to make the British public aware of their own self-understanding as Britons and to develop a national consciousness that was less insular and exclusionary, and instead tailored to promote just actions abroad. The tropes of "geographical" or "municipal" morality that run through Burke's speeches on

Hastings, and which I have argued represent the antithesis of the law of nations, also should be read in light of this project of building a less noxious nationalism.

Burke suggested that an analogous process of revising the British national self-understanding was necessary regarding India: not for the sake of including Indians within the British nation, for they were too distant and too misunderstood by Britons for any such national amalgamation to work. Rather, he sketched for his audience in the Hastings trial the contours of a new British self-understanding as an agent in the world, and he offered them the trial as an exercise in national atonement and exoneration. One of Burke's most frequent arguments for an impeachment trial for Warren Hastings, as well as for parliamentary oversight of the East India Company's conduct, was that if they failed to hold a parliamentary trial, the British as a nation would bear responsibility for the conduct of the Company (and be seen by other nations as morally culpable). The nation must choose between tacitly sharing guilt for the Company's misdeeds, and using the political system to repudiate the Company's crimes. Britain's "democratic" political system, he argued, meant that its citizens bore responsibility for the British actions abroad that they could control.[130] Burke had little hope of reforming the worst perpetrators of crimes in India (he called the East India Company "incorrigible"), but he indicated throughout his speeches that he believed the British *nation* could still atone for its past complicity, reform the government in India, and remove the criminals from their posts.

In a 1786 speech on a bill to amend Pitt's India Act of 1784, a law that Burke believed bolstered the despotic power of the governor-general, he had shown that both national self-understanding and respect for human rights lay at the heart of his argument for moral British conduct toward Indians.

> A bold and unequivocal step is taken at last to outrage this country and this House with a proposition for the establishment of a system which our ancestors struggled and died to exterminate, which is incongruous to the habits and peculiarities of the national character, and which we cannot admit without sacrificing at once all our prepossessions for the privileges of Britons, and the rights of humanity. He wished the Committee to recollect how this measure had throughout sacrificed the many for the few. (*WS* 6:71)

Burke's effort to revise British national self-understanding exemplifies his practice of social criticism: he often practiced what might be called internal or immanent critique, presenting his audience with a portrait of their own self-understanding and then demonstrating that they had failed to live up to it. Burke's trenchant sarcasm, however, also set him apart from the society he criticized, giving his speeches a tone of detachment, moral indignation, even superciliousness.[131] If this tone alienated Burke's colleagues, it also lent an aura of confidence to his own alienation. Burke was engaged not in an earnest exposition of local principles for the benefit of a straying flock but rather in a furious, ironic, combative assault on his society's complacent immorality. I emphasize Burke's critical techniques because it is at the level of rhetorical strategy that the critic must face the challenge to remain at once fiercely oppositional and still comprehensible to the audience of his society. When one's own society strays as far from what the critic believes to be just moral principles—as Britain, in Burke's view, had done—the critic's challenge is to step beyond the society's flawed and circumscribed moral arena while remaining intelligible and compelling to his audience. Burke walked the line between connected critic and ignored outsider, emphasizing the self-professed British values from which his nation had fallen away.

This chapter has attempted to recover Burke's unusual effort to articulate what a just global politics would demand of the British nation by delineating what, to paraphrase Uday Mehta, might be called Burke's strategies of inclusion.[132] Burke's writings on empire show him to have been far more attentive to the exclusions that have permeated European justifications of empire and claims about non-European societies than nineteenth-century liberals would be, and his own arguments about law and nationality countered some of the common exclusions couched in the nineteenth century in terms of progress or nationhood. Burke's belief in the fundamental value of sovereignty, in the importance of states to the well-being of individuals, and in the merit of particular cultures and traditions, were all chastened by the conviction that the boundaries of groups, national and otherwise, are mutable and ultimately somewhat arbitrary. As we will see in chapters 5 through 7, a narrower and more determinate conception of nationality would emerge in the nineteenth century, and it would serve as one basis of arguments by Tocqueville and J. S. Mill in favor of European imperial expansion and rule. First, however, we turn to the writings of Jeremy Bentham, who, for all his considerable political and philosophical differences with Burke, shared the belief that European imperial aspirations were foolhardy and unjust, premised as these aspirations were on an unwarranted confidence in the ability of Europeans to rule competently over distant peoples whose interests they could not be expected to understand or respect.

Part Two

UTILITARIANS AND THE TURN TO EMPIRE IN BRITAIN

Four

Jeremy Bentham: Legislator of the World?

Utilitarians and the British Empire

The pervasive influence of utilitarians in the nineteenth century on the justification and exercise of British imperial power in India has led many to conclude that utilitarianism was, from its inception, an imperialist theory.[1] Eric Stokes's classic work *The English Utilitarians and India* established the important role that Benthamites—from James and John Stuart Mill, to colonial administrators, to the professors at Haileybury College who trained them—played in the expansion of British rule in India throughout the nineteenth century. Stokes relates an anecdote about Lord William Bentinck, who in 1827 had just been appointed governor-general of India. As James Mill delightedly reported to Bentham, Bentinck had told him at a farewell dinner, "I am going to British India; but I shall not be Governor-General. It is you that will be Governor-General."[2] Indeed, reformers directly or indirectly influenced by Bentham, men who believed they were carrying out the Benthamite project, were powerful in Indian administration throughout the nineteenth century. Benthamites who felt they were too regularly thwarted in England, by entrenched powers and the recalcitrant body of common law, reveled in the opportunity that they believed despotic power provided for the establishment of a complete legal code (what Bentham liked to call a *pannomion*) and a rational bureaucracy.[3]

Bentham's own views on empire, however, differed significantly from those of his followers. Not only did Bentham denounce the Spanish, French, and British empires, in writings such as *Emancipate Your Colonies*! and "Rid Yourselves of Ultramaria," beginning in the 1790s and continuing into the 1820s, but he also largely resisted the judgmental stance later utilitarians took toward non-European cultures, as well as their civilizing aspirations. A study of his "emancipation" writings and his ideas about British India should serve as a corrective to a pervasive view that either utilitarianism or English liberalism, as such, was imperialist. To John Stuart Mill's claim that "[d]espotism is a legitimate mode of government in dealing with barbarians, provided the end be their improvement, and the means justified by actually effecting that end,"[4] we have Bentham's likely response: "Reform the world by example, you act generously and wisely: reform the world by force, you might as well reform the moon, and the design is fit only for lunatics."[5]

Bentham's views on conquest, expansion, and colonial rule were not entirely consistent, as is to be expected given his remarkably long career, his voluminous and often unedited output, and his diverse audiences. A wide range of related considerations also caused his views on colonialism to vary, including his fitful pacifism, his periodically expressed hopes that emigration might aid Europe's poor, and the differences between settler colonies such as Latin America and colonies such as British India that primarily involved the domination of a large indigenous population.[6] Still, the concerns that Bentham brought to bear when considering colonial rule, in particular his belief that colonial rulers and administrators could never be trusted to rule well, and his suspicion of aspirations to civilize non-Europeans, stand in sharp contrast to the technocratic and cultural confidence of Bentham's successors. Several philosophical positions in particular stand out as introduced by Bentham's followers and largely alien to his own theory: their narrow and hierarchical understanding of progress; their belief that British rule of "backward" peoples was both morally justified (even a moral duty) and good for the conquered nations; and their conviction that certain peoples were unfit for self-government. Bernard Williams remarked about utilitarianism generally that "[i]t is not surprising that one should be reminded of colonial administrators, running on a system of indirect rule."[7] While the comment seems apt enough at first glance, I shall argue that Bentham did not regard utilitarianism as legitimating the sort of dictatorial imperial rule that characterized the hopes of many of his successors: the imposition from above without concern for the opinions of the ruled or for their interests as they themselves understood them.

The curious evolution of utilitarian theory in Britain on the subject of empire can perhaps best be observed in the writings of Bentham and John Stuart Mill, the philosophically richest thinkers in the tradition; James Mill, examined in chapter 5, played a crucial intermediary role in the transformation of the utilitarian tradition. James Mill showed Bentham's influence in several articles he wrote to deny that colonies benefited the conquering country and to argue instead that colonies were foisted on European nations by sinister private interests.[8] Yet he also wrote the *History of British India*, a work, highly influential in colonial circles, that was nonetheless remarkable even for its time in its disparagement of Indians' intellectual and moral capacities. Mill concluded that Indians were incapable of participation in their government, which, he believed, should be a "simple form of arbitrary government" by Britain.[9] When recommending policies toward India, the elder Mill was driven far more by his ideas about Indians' mental and cultural deficiencies than by his doubts as a political economist about the colony's benefit to Great Britain.

John Stuart Mill, in so many arenas a great critic of his father, adopted many of James Mill's central claims about India and British government there: most important, that there was a sharp dichotomy between civilized and uncivilized nations, that Indians were barbarians incapable of self-government, and that British "despotism" was the most appropriate form of government for the country for the foreseeable future. Mill called his father "the historian who first threw the light of reason on Hindoo society" and had only praise for the *History of British India* in his *Autobiography*.[10] J. S. Mill's writings on India and empire, and his career in the East India Company, long ignored, have received considerable attention in recent years, although this scrutiny has not extended to Mill's intellectual debts to and departures from Bentham.[11]

As I have suggested, the misunderstanding of Bentham's views on colonies began with his own disciples, and they indeed bear considerable responsibility for the misrepresentation of Bentham that has become so widespread.[12] James Mill was most influential in this regard, for it was he who took the greatest interest in governing India, and who attached the utilitarian name to his narrow-minded descriptions of Indian civilization and to his own projects for the country's domination and improvement.[13] Although there is little on record of Bentham's own judgments of James Mill's imperial projects, what we have is instructive. The following sentence is most often cited as proof of Bentham's desire to improve India by transforming its legal (and thereby its social) structure: "Mill will be the living executive—I shall be the dead legislative of British India."[14] The sentence is quoted by Stokes, Donald Winch, Uday Mehta, and many others to suggest that it expresses Bentham's fond hope of civilizing backward peoples. The rest of the original passage, however, which is never cited, shows that Bentham said these words with his characteristic irony, and with the odd relish with which he contemplated his own death and afterlife: "Twenty years after I am dead, I shall be despot, sitting in my chair with Dapple in my hand, and wearing one of the coats I wear now" (Dapple was the name Bentham gave his walking stick).[15] Bentham went on to suggest that Mill was wrong to believe his own project of legislating for India was Bentham's as well, and that the intellectual and political distance between the men was far greater than Mill understood:

> His creed of politics results less from love for the many, than from hatred for the few. It is too much under the influence of selfish and dissocial affection. . . . His manner of speaking is oppressive and overbearing. He comes to me as if he wore a mask upon his face. His interests he deems to be closely connected with mine, as he has a prospect of introducing a better system of judicial procedure in British India. His book on British India abounds with bad English, which made it to me a disagreeable book. His account of the superstitions of the Hindoos made me melancholy.[16]

John Bowring, a member of the first generation of Bentham's disciples and his amanuensis and editor, quotes Bentham's view that Mill had " 'an abominable opinion' with respect to the inaptitude of women, and one 'scarcely less abominable,' that men should not hold office till they are forty years of age" (*WJB* 10:450). On these issues, as on the political capacity of non-Europeans, James Mill showed a considerably narrower mind than his mentor.

Even Bowring, who reported these differences between the men and knew at firsthand Bentham's doubts about Mill's ideas and policies, believed that Mill's views on international politics represented a fair approximation of Bentham's own.[17] Bowring, like both Mills, praised the pacific implications of utilitarianism for politics among "civilized" nations, and then abruptly cut non-Europeans out of consideration. "The civilized part of the world is coming, day by day, nearer to just principles of international intercourse," Bowring wrote in his introduction to Bentham's works. "France affording a highway for our communication with our great oriental empire, and conveying through its government telegraph the earliest news of our operations in the east, is a symptom of progress which it would have afforded Bentham the liveliest gratification to witness."[18] The complacency of Bowring's phrase "our operations in the east," however, shared nothing with Bentham's own ambivalence toward imperial rule.

If John Stuart Mill overcame his father's prejudices about women's capacities, he remained uncritical about his father's view of the people of "backward" nations, adopting and even elaborating it himself.[19] Mill himself emphasized his distance from Bentham, but Mill's account of the evolution of utilitarianism must be read with a critical eye. For Mill claimed to humanize an austere doctrine that was insensitive to humanity's higher aspirations, to temper Bentham's theory with a respect for poetry and traditions.[20] He suggested that he had taken a narrow doctrine, one incapable of understanding most of the ways that people have interpreted and responded to the human condition, and broadened it, pluralized it.[21] In some senses, as I shall suggest, precisely the opposite is the case. Unfortunately for Bentham, and for our understanding of the history of utilitarianism (and British liberalism more broadly), James and J. S. Mill's versions of the story of utilitarianism and empire have largely prevailed.

If we take seriously Bentham's many remarks on the dangers and immorality of imperial rule, we will be more skeptical than either Bentham's immediate successors or his more recent readers that Bentham would have celebrated the consolidation of the British Empire in India. We will be able to make better sense of the writings and historical events that led Elie Halévy to elide the distance between Bentham and later utilitarians and to suggest obliquely that those later utilitarians were merely continuing after his death an imperial project that Bentham had initiated:

> Bentham was the disciple of Adam Smith and up to the end of his life stood as an adversary of the colonial system: when he became a Radical, his economic objections were reinforced by political objections against a system which handed over the colonists to the mercy of functionaries sent out by the metropolis. Yet England was preserving a part of her colonial empire and founding new colonies. Were Bentham and his disciples going to demand that all the colonies should be abandoned? Colonisation is a fact before which their logic capitulated; and besides the logic of their system is double: in so far as their philosophy advocates the artificial and despotic identification of interests, might they not be tempted to consider the colonial empire as a vast field for experiments in philanthropy and reform? Bentham had always dreamed of making laws for India: now that James Mill occupied an important post in the India Company, might not his dream become a reality?[22]

This passage wrongly attributes to Bentham the notion that interests should be identified "despotically" rather than by people—any people—themselves; and it resorts to the weak claim that the utilitarians' "logic" simply "capitulated" before the tempting prospect of a captive legislative laboratory.[23] In fact, however, Bentham did not capitulate in this way, and James Mill, for his part, never shared Smith's or Bentham's moral objections to empire. With regard to colonies, there was no unitary utilitarian logic, but rather a transformation of the tradition that reflected a broader shift in European thought on empire from the late eighteenth to the early nineteenth century, away from profound doubts about colonial aspirations and toward vehement and often self-righteous support for them.

Bentham's Critique of Colonial Rule

Bentham held that justice and prudence demanded the emancipation of colonial possessions. He believed one of the greatest advantages that new countries such as the United States and, later, Greece (after its independence from the Ottoman Empire), had over the European powers was their freedom from the burden of colonial possessions.[24] The early 1790s are often cited as the period of Bentham's turn away from enlightened despotism in favor of democracy and universal suffrage.[25] These were also the years during which Bentham first expressed his opposition to colonialism. In 1789, he wrote a series of open letters to the comte de Mirabeau in an effort to influence the proceedings of France's newly assembled Estates General. One of these letters, arguing against French colonialism, was expanded and published in 1793 as the first of his pamphlets entitled *Emancipate Your Colonies!*[26] That pamphlet includes, in rapid-fire succession, most of Bentham's anticolonial arguments. He opened: "[E]*mancipate your Colonies*. Justice, consistency, policy, economy, honour, generosity, all demand it of you: all this you shall see. Conquer, you are still but running the race of vulgar ambition: Emancipate, you strike out a new path to glory. Conquer, it is by your armies: Emancipate, the conquest is your own, and made over yourselves. To give freedom at the expence of others, is but conquest in disguise: to rise superior to conquerors, the sacrifice must be your own" (*RRR* 291). Bentham revived these arguments in the early 1820s in an attempt to persuade the new liberal government in Spain to emancipate its colonies in the New World. Many of his arguments against colonial rule remained unchanged.[27]

Many of Bentham's arguments against colonies were, not surprisingly, based on calculations of interest. As he wrote in "Rid yourselves of Ultramaria," written as a sort of open letter to the Spanish people ("Spaniards!"), "Will you sacrifice—will you sit and see your rulers sacrifice—every substantial interest to the fantastic interest that has its root in national pride?"[28] He believed that empires undermined the greatest happiness of the greatest number in both metropole and colony. He argued that they were financially unsound and inefficient; that they exacted a tax on the poor of the metropole for the benefit of the wealthy; that they encouraged unnecessary growth of the state's military apparatus but left the metropole vulnerable; and that they were fueled by illusory, misguided, and dangerous conceptions of honor and glory.

Bentham's interest-based or economic arguments against colonies were certainly typical of a strong strand of late-eighteenth-century suspicion of colonial rule, a strand that included figures such as Adam Smith.[29] These claims, which often appealed to the self-interest of the metropolitan populations, are less surprising in themselves than they are for the contrast they provide to the views of his successors. Bentham believed, with Smith and others, that colonies drained national resources, bloated the military, and jeopardized the security of the metropole. He contended that colonies could not be profitable without being oppressive and that the oppression necessary to extract a profit from a distant colony was not only unjust but likely to provoke a costly and destructive "civil war."

> Suppose . . . that hitherto . . . a colony has been a source of net profit to the ruling country. Still, it is not in the nature of the case that it should long continue so to be. Over the inhabitants of the dependency in question, power cannot be exercised,—from them such profit cannot be extracted, without manifest injury done to them, without manifest oppression exercised upon them. . . . [If] the maintenance of the power of the ruling people, or rather of the rulers of the

> ruling people, is persevered in, here then is war, civil war: a war, the expense of which, increases with the distance between the country subject to the dominion, and the country which is the seat of it,—to say nothing of the misery caused by such a war.[30]

This passage weaves together some of the main strands of Bentham's critique—economic, moral, and pragmatic.[31] It includes a typical reminder to metropolitan populations that colonial rule is not in their interest but in that of a cabal of their rulers: that they, too, are victims of colonialism. Some of Bentham's other arguments, which rested on equity, glory, and the psychology of power and corruption, may come as more of a surprise, for they appear to draw little from utilitarian principles. "If the happiness of mankind is your object, and the declaration of rights your guide, you will set them free.—The sooner the better: it costs you but a word: and by that word you cover yourselves with the purest glory" (*RRR* 312–313). It is this complex assortment of arguments that is wholly missing from James Mill's critique of colonies, which adopted the Benthamite economic position and ignored the rest of Bentham's views.

Unlike James and J. S. Mill, Bentham believed that colonial rulers could not know the subject population's interests better than the people themselves and therefore could not rule them better than they could rule themselves. Bentham had long been committed to the necessity of publicity and public opinion as a way of curbing corruption and misrule.[32] While the Mills made similar arguments regarding civilized nations, both believed that barbarous countries were incapable of benefiting not only from legislative assemblies, but even from the exercise of public opinion more broadly understood. J. S. Mill argued that "the public of India afford no assistance in their own government. They are not ripe for doing so by means of representative government; they are not even in a condition to make effectual appeals to the people of this country" (*CW* 30:49); his solution was technocratic rule by East India Company civil servants. James Mill made clear that in addition to thinking Indians unable to exercise the power of public opinion, he believed them incapable even of perceiving and acting on their own interests.[33] Bentham had, that is, a respect unmatched by any of his successors for *everyone's* ability to know what was in their interest and consequently to govern themselves. Bentham's lack of interest in distinctions between civilized and barbarous peoples, which J. S. Mill criticized as a lack of historical understanding,[34] enabled him to make the same argument for all colonial peoples, whether European settlers or native inhabitants: they knew their own interests far better than any distant metropolitans, who were sure to be ignorant about their lives and uninterested in their fate, and whose colonial policy would necessarily be dictated by their own interests.

The opening pages of *Emancipate Your Colonies*! are written in a crisp, direct style reminiscent of Tom Paine's, with a series of rhetorical questions exposing the absurdities and hypocrisies of empire. "You choose your own government: why are not other people to choose theirs? Do you seriously mean to govern the world, and do you call that *liberty*?"[35] Speaking as an honorary citizen of France, Bentham invoked the principles and icons of the Revolution and demonstrated the incoherence and injustice of conquest from the republican perspective: "with fraternity in your lips, you declare war against mankind" (*RRR* 308). "One common Bastile inclosed them and you. You knock down the jailor, you let yourselves out, you keep them in, and put yourselves into his place" (4:292). Bentham emphasized the inherent problems of distance and made the case, to which he was to return in almost all his writings on colonies, that Europeans could not possibly imagine the lives, desires, and problems of subjects—whether of European descent or not—thousands of miles away. "What care you, or what can you care, about them? . . . What conception can you frame to yourselves of manners and modes of life so different from your own? When will you ever see them? . . . If they suffer, will their cries ever wound your ears? Will their wretchedness ever meet your eyes?" (4:293). Indeed, Bentham often intertwined his arguments from interest with more abstract appeals to justice, nature, and humanity. "To yield to justice is what must happen to the mightiest and proudest nations," he wrote. "Sitting where you do, call it not *courage* to drive on in the track of war and violence. There is nothing in such courage that is not compatible with the basest cowardice" (4:307).[36]

Bentham never addressed such a critical pamphlet to the British government, and this fact, along with the essay "On the Influence of Time and Place in Matters of Legislation," has led to the claim that Bentham was an enthusiastic supporter of British rule over India and was eager to see his own legislative reforms tested there.[37] Like Adam Smith, however, Bentham was surely well aware of the futility of most appeals to a country to free its colonies.[38] In the cases of France and Spain, conscious of the great respect in which he was held by republicans in both countries, he appears to have nourished hopes that he could actually persuade them to give up their colonies.[39] He wrote to each at a time when a new liberal republican regime had just come to power, and he seems to have believed that his rational and passionate arguments could help them make a clean break with their countries' colonial pasts. He knew only too well of his limited influence in Britain, having failed, disastrously and famously, to persuade the British government to institute his panopticon prison-workhouse in the 1790s. The absence of an "Emancipation" pamphlet to the British may well have been due to his sense that such a gesture would be useless. It was not a result of Bentham's enthusiasm about the benefits of

British imperial rule, about which he wrote venomously in the course of his writings on France and Spain; indeed, he criticized the entire British political system that had fostered the empire.

Thus, we find Bentham's judgments of the British Empire, both moral and practical, scattered throughout his anticolonial writings. To the French, he wrote: "By emancipating your own colonies, you may emancipate ours: by setting the example, you may open our eyes and force us to follow it"; and "By emancipating our colonies you may thus purify our parliament: you may purify our constitution.—You must not destroy it; excuse us, we are a slow people, and a little obstinate" (*RRR* 310). It should be noted that unlike James Mill (who also argued for the emancipation of Spanish America), Bentham did not, in these arguments, tend to distinguish between settler colonies and colonies populated mostly by indigenous peoples: the arguments against empire were the same for all. For instance, he wrote to the Spanish,

> "Well" (say you) "and you with all your foreign dependencies all over the world, how do you in England manage?" Manage indeed? it would require volumes upon volumes to attempt giving your any thing like an explanation—in anything like detail. In a general point of view, a few words may serve. Uncertainty, inconsistency, complication, delay, vexation and expense, all factitious and enormous—denial of justice, oppression, extortion, corruptive influence, despotism. Enquire in East, West, South: to the North not, because no dependencies have we there. Enquire in Hindostan, in the West Indies, in South Africa, in Canada, in New Holland, in Mauritius, in Saint Helena, in the Seven Islands, over which, on pretence of protection, our rulers have extended their own yet rotten sceptre.[40]

Bentham lamented Britain's insatiable acquisition of colonies since the loss of America: colonies "pursued with that eagerness and that disastrous success, of which the bitter fruits continue to be forced down our throats in such sad abundance. Witness the last-gathered of them—the Ionian isles: and that English '*protection*,' the infamy of which, without any of the profit, vies so successfully with that of the primaeval Persian tyranny."[41] In short, Bentham viewed British colonialism with the same disapproval that he did French and Spanish, even if he described his opposition to it in less detail.[42]

Bentham did call on the British government to give up its colonies and its colonial ambitions in an essay that Bowring published as "Plan for an Universal and Perpetual Peace."[43] There Bentham pursued the two classic eighteenth-century arguments against colonization: that it is unjust to the conquered and foolish from the perspective of the metropolitan population. The plan offered as its first proposition, "That it is not the interest of Great Britain to have any foreign dependencies whatsoever."[44]

As Bentham wrote in "Panopticon versus New South Wales," his essay comparing his own prison design to the Australian penal colony, "My Lord—to confess the truth, I never could bring myself to see any real advantage derived by the mother country, from anything that ever bore the name of a *Colony*."[45]

The argument he made as well to the French and Spanish, that distance alone ensures that colonies cannot be well governed, takes on particular poignancy here with his reference to the cruelties exposed by the impeachment trial in the 1780s and 1790s of Warren Hastings: "Distant mischiefs make little impression on those on whom the remedying of them depends. A single murder committed in London makes more impression than if thousands of murders and other cruelties were committed in the East Indies. The situation of Hastings, only because he was present, excited compassion in those who heard all of the cruelties committed by him with indifference" (*WJB* 2:547–48). This passage was one of several in which Bentham expressed his support for the prosecutors in the impeachment; he maintained this support well after the long trial had wearied the patience of even its most sympathetic early advocates.[46]

Even if James and John Stuart Mill questioned whether possession of colonies profited the European colonizers, both insisted that colonial rule benefited its backward subjects. Bentham never adopted such ardor for despotic colonial rule, though his views about whether Indians and others—including citizens of the United States—could benefit from British rule remain somewhat enigmatic and indeed contradictory. Several passages scattered throughout his work, that is, conflict rather starkly with his many strong claims about the damage and injustices colonial rule inflicted on the colonized. In the "Institute of Political Economy" of 1801–4, Bentham claimed that both Egypt and America would have benefited from British government because in addition to having a government of "universal and perpetual security," Britain's "moral conduct forms the natural standard in points exempt from regulation."[47] Egypt, subject to a religion "of which incurable barbarity and ignorance seem to be inseparable features," and the new American states, an "unvaried scene of sordid selfishness, of political altercation, of discomfort, of ignorance, of drunkenness," might have profited from the stability provided by new or continued British rule. Donald Winch has described the period of 1800–1804 as one in which "Bentham's Toryism seems to have reasserted itself," possibly in response to developments in France, and it is to this revived Toryism that he plausibly attributes the "patriotic sentiments that verge on jingoism" expressed in such passages.[48] Certainly they run counter to the sustained anticolonial arguments Bentham developed at some length in both earlier and later works, including his strong claims about the impossibility of governing well from a great distance and his persistent belief that colonial rule was in the hands of a small group of "sinister interests" rather than in the hands of beneficent and farsighted governors.[49]

Bentham's arguments to France and Spain concerned European settlers in the New World, so his claims in those articles cannot be assumed to apply to colonies of large indigenous populations such as India. Although the Mills, for their part, strictly distinguished settler from nonsettler colonies in all questions of self-government, Bentham, apparently quite uninterested in questions of progress or of ranking civilizations, did not make the same careful distinction but instead spoke of all "distant dependencies" in the same language.[50] Bentham's discussion of India in *Emancipate Your Colonies*! is probably the place where he expressed the greatest doubt about Indians' capacity for self-government: "[T]he power of Tippoo is no more. Would the tree of liberty grow there, if planted? Would the declaration of rights translate into Shanscrit? Would Bramin, Chetree, Bice, Sooder, and Hallachore meet on equal ground? If not, you may find some difficulty in giving them to themselves. . . . If it is determined they must have masters, you will then look out for the least bad ones that could take them."[51] He suggested that France sell its Indian possessions to the British East India Company, and he responded with sarcasm to the anticipated French accusation that he was a hireling of the Company, arguing that even if he were, the French should see that the exchange would be in their interest. In the end, though, it mattered little from France's perspective, he thought, who ruled India. "*How* you part with the poor people who are now your slaves, is after all a subordinate consideration: the essential thing is to get rid of them. . . . Whatever be their rights, they have no such right as that of forcing you to govern them to your own prejudice." We see, then, that Bentham was capable of suggesting that democratic self-government was unlikely to emerge in India in his day, although the suggestion was framed in terms of questions and through vague, impersonal phrases such as "if it be determined." The fully articulated argument that we find in James and John Stuart Mill does not appear here, nor did Bentham ever produce the sort of theory of progress they did to support that argument.[52]

In another of the few passages in which he directly addressed British rule over India, Bentham responded ambiguously to the question of whether Indians would benefit from an end to colonial rule:

> On the question—by the metropolitan country shall this or that distant dependency be kept up?—there are two *sides*—two *interests*—that require consideration: that of the metropolis herself and that of the dependency. . . . On the question whether [the dominion of British India] would be for the advantage of *Brithibernia*, much might be said on both sides. On the question as applied to the nation of British India,—in the minds of those who have read the docu-

ments, and in particular the work of the so well-informed, intelligent, and incontestably well-intentioned Bishop Heber,—scarcely can there be a doubt. By the withdrawal of the English regiments from British India, in what respect or degree would Hindoos or Mahometans profit? Answer—in much the same as did the ancient *Britons* by the withdrawal of the *Roman* legions.[53]

Did the ancient Britons, by the withdrawal of the Roman armies, gain their liberty, or were they merely reduced to barbarism? Either view was certainly possible in Bentham's day, and he himself gives no indication here about which he meant; indeed, it is possible that he intended both answers at once. Despite the decisiveness of Bentham's language, the reference to Bishop Heber does not make the passage much more straightforward. Bishop Heber, bishop of Calcutta in the 1820s and a religious and political moderate, certainly supported missionary efforts in India, and probably believed, on the whole, that British rule benefited Indians, but he by no means considered Indians barbarous or hopeless. On the contrary, he had more than usual respect among Britons of his day for Indians' intelligence and cultural achievements, and he "disagreed with the policy of excluding even upper-class Indians from participation in government."[54] When Bentham did support certain British policies in India, it was in preference to some other, far worse, British policy, rather than from a desire to perpetuate British colonial rule. Thus when he declared that he would have voted for Fox's East India Bill (the bill supported and largely drafted by Edmund Burke), Bentham outlined the appalling alternatives:

Mr. Fox's E. India Bill I regarded as eminently good with reference to the natives, as bad rather than otherwise with reference to the *permanent* interests of our own island. It was good in as far as it took the people out of the hands of by far the worst constituted species of government conceivable, and that a secret and irresponsible one: the government of a fluctuating body of merchants . . . residing at the opposite end of the world. It was bad in as far as it concentrated a large body of influence and vested it in the hands of the Ministers. I should notwithstanding at that time have voted for the bill: by hopes from it in favour of the people of Hindostan being much stronger than my fears from it in favour of the people of Great Britain. I should have voted for it in preference to Mr. Pitt's. But I should not . . . now. The goodness of Mr. Pitt's measure has been proved by experience. A happy choice of persons at the outset put things into a good frame: in that frame, having once got into it, it seems reasonable to hope they will continue."[55]

Similarly, although the support Bentham gave to James Mill's proposed reforms for India was always grudging, for instance, he preferred them to what he called "the abominable existing system" (*WJB* 10:590).

A Rereading of Bentham's Work on India

It is clear that Bentham was deeply critical of European colonial rule on both moral and practical grounds and that he was not, as his successors were, an enthusiastic supporter of the British government in India. I have argued, as well, that the passage most commonly cited as evidence for Bentham's own appetite for colonial rule ("I shall be the dead legislative of British India") is not, when read in its entirety, as straightforward as most commentators would have it. Bentham's legislative ambitions, to be sure, were notorious, and titles such as "Idea of a Proposed All-Comprehensive Body of Law, with an Accompaniment of Reasons" (1827), and "Constitutional Code; for the Use of All Nations and All Governments Professing Liberal Opinions" (1830),[56] have encouraged the idea that he believed himself capable of legislating for the world. It has been an easy step for his followers and later readers to assume that Bentham was particularly keen on legislating for India and keeping the colony under British rule in order to see his reforms through.

In addition to the "dead legislative" passage, two other pieces of writing form the rest of the evidence usually presented that Bentham supported the British Empire as a vehicle for his aspiration to legislate for the world: a short passage in a letter to Henry Dundas, president of the East India Company's Board of Control; and the "Essay on the Influence of Time and Place in Matters of Legislation," which discusses the role of culture and climate in law and society by examining what steps would be necessary to make British laws suitable for application to Bengal. Eric Stokes's *English Utilitarians and India*, the source usually cited by later commentators, claims that "Bentham had always been eager to take a hand in framing the law system of India. In 1793 he had made an offer of his services, as a sort of Indian Solon, to Dundas."[57] In the letter Stokes cites, Bentham made no such grandiose claims; nor does the letter indicate that Bentham supported the empire because he believed India needed British, or indeed utilitarian, legislators. Instead, it merely observes,

> Something in the way of legislation may be deemed wanting for Hindostan. Divested of all local prejudices, but not the less sensible of their force, and of the necessity of respecting them, I could with the same facility turn my hand to the concerns of that distant country, as to those of the parish in which I live.[58]

The passage suggests that Bentham believed that the British rulers of India (whatever he might have thought of the justice or prudence of their position) would need to legislate for their subjects and that he thought himself capable of writing appropriate legislation. For a fuller account of how Bentham thought one should go about applying laws that one had necessarily developed in one cultural and historical context to a quite different context, we must turn to the "Essay on the Influence of Time and Place in Matters of Legislation."[59]

Bentham seems to have intended the essay to form a part of the *Theory of Legislation*.[60] It opens with the presumed response of the larger work's reader to its author's seemingly limitless ambition to legislate for everywhere and all time. Bentham's apparent insensibility to cultural particulars, his arrogant confidence in his own ability to legislate for the world, is still considered one of his great failings, so this essay is of particular interest, for it directly addresses the question of how feasible it might be to legislate universally. The essay demonstrates Bentham's awareness of the problem, as well as the limits of his understanding. Characteristically, he posed the question in abstract, general terms:

> To give the question at once a universal form: What is the influence of the circumstances of place and time in matters of legislation? what are the coincidences, and what the diversities, which ought to subsist between the laws established in different countries and at different periods, supposing them in each instance the best that can be established? (*WJB* 1:171)

In order to illustrate his argument, Bentham adopted England as his "standard" and Bengal as the country to be studied in order to determine to what degree climate, custom, religion, present laws, and other factors would make it necessary to alter the "standard" legal code for its new application.

Why England and Bengal? The explicit reasons Bentham gave for his choices of theme and variation were not what we might expect from the standard portrait of the nineteenth-century British imperialist, for he did not claim to choose England because its laws were best, or Bengal because he, as a Briton, wanted to legislate for a backward India.[61] Rather, he chose England, he wrote, because he knew it best, and because he was partial, "if to any" country, then to England. He chose Bengal because it (unlike Canada, for instance) provided a strong contrast to England in climate and manners but was a country that, given British rule, could be expected to have English laws imposed on it (whereas, he wrote, it would be difficult to imagine such an event occurring in Russia).[62] For the purposes of the essay—that is, for the purposes of this clearly artificial exercise of legislative translation—Bentham "indulged" himself in a "magnificent and presumptuous dream" that his country's laws were the best possible laws.[63] About actual English laws, however, Bentham remained as critical as ever: having developed piecemeal from their origins in a "barbarous age," they were often incoherent, unnecessarily complex, badly articulated, and likely to promote corruption. "The farther we penetrate into the recesses of English law (taking utility for our guide,)"

Bentham wrote, "the better shall we be convinced that . . . for the greater part of it, it is a piece of cobweb work, spun out of fantastic conceits and verbal analogies, rather than a mass of substantial justice cast in the mould of reason."[64]

Frustration with the absurdities and corruptions of the British legal system had driven Bentham from a legal career as a very young man.[65] In Bengal, he claimed in "Time and Place," these imperfections were compounded by the inappropriateness of British laws to Bengali society, by the British failure to see the problems with their laws, and by the incapacity of metropolitan laws to deal with colonial circumstances—especially the rampant greed and corruption that despotic rule encouraged. The imposition of a foreign legal system (especially such a mediocre one) inevitably led to resentment among the conquered people; and chauvinism prevented the British rulers from acknowledging its flaws. "When a body of very imperfect laws, such as are the best of those of which the groundwork has been laid in barbarous ages, is imported in the lump from one country into another, it will be found that opposite judgments will be entertained of it by the two nations: the one will be disposed to think a great deal better of it; the other, if possible, a great deal worse of it, than it deserves" (*WJB* 1:184). The laws were nefarious not only in their direct effects, but also because they were sure to undermine any sense of trust or goodwill that managed to emerge on the part of Indians toward their British governors:

> What, then, must have been the sensations of the poor Hindoo, when forced to submit to all these wanton and ridiculous vexations? Unable to attribute to an European mind the folly adequate to the production of such a mass of nonsense and of gibberish, he must have found himself compelled to ascribe it to a less pardonable cause; to a deliberate plan for forcing him to deliver himself up, without reserve, into the hands of the European professional blood-suckers, carrying on the traffic of injustice under the cloak of law. (1:187)

The imposition of British law on India was either foolish or wicked, probably both, Bentham suggested; under the circumstances, any effort to lessen Bengal's predicament represented an improvement. The restrained and indeed pessimistic tone of the essay, however, is far from that of the crusading legislator.

In addition, Bentham made no strong claims for the applicability of his analysis in this essay to the production of actual legislation. "Time and Place" is in large part a theoretical exercise and should not be taken as evidence of Bentham's own desire to become an "Indian Solon." Early in the essay, he offered a caveat. While he could glimpse "perfection" in the endeavour of translating a body of laws, it was clear that perfection was unattainable: in this case, it would require infinite detail in the description of the perfect English laws, of the "leading principles upon which the differences between those and the laws for Bengal appear to turn," and finally, of the way in which those principles would be put into practice to create laws for Bengal.

> According to this plan, were it rigorously pursued, a complete code of laws for England, accompanied with a collection of all the laws for Bengal which would require to be different from those which are for England, would form a part only of the matter belonging to the present head. The impracticability of this plan is such, as need not be insisted upon. (*WJB* 1:172)

Bentham's more limited goal in this essay, then, would be to sketch some of the considerations a legislator would have to take into account when attempting such a task. It should be noted, then, that while Bentham's aspirations may well have lived up to his reputation for grandiosity, he was far more aware than the "Benthamites" of the East India Company that such aspirations were unfulfillable and that in actual practice a legislator would have to be infinitely more modest. The essay, to be sure, contains flights of optimism as well, as in the following passage:

> Legislators who, having freed themselves from the shackles of authority, have learnt to soar above the mists of prejudice, know as well how to make laws for one country as for another: all they need is to be possessed fully of the facts: to be informed of the local situation, the climate, the bodily constitution, the manners, the legal customs, the religion, of those with whom they have to deal. These are the data they require: possessed of these data, all places are alike. (1:180–81)

Here it is worth noting the distinction between the legislator and the governor or administrator, for Bentham appears to propose a system that, after it being established by an all knowing legislator who has risen above prejudice, would then be run by the people of India.[66] Bentham, indeed, resisted the claim that James and John Stuart Mill would make that Indians were barbarous or incapable, and indeed he criticized the easy move made by many Europeans of assuming, when they observed bad laws, that the people they were designed for must be inferior. When you encounter ridiculous or destructive laws, he observed sarcastically, "What is to be done? There is but one thing; which is, to take the blame off the shoulders of the legislator, and lay it upon the people. Say they were stupid, stubborn, prejudiced, intractable: this will put you at your ease" (1:190). Where James Mill wrote with unrelenting scorn not only about Indian legal forms but about the Indian notables and jurists who had carried out justice under the old system, Bentham believed that the English had wantonly displaced systems, practices, and agents that, even if they would benefit from reforms, were far from wholly iniquitous. "The most remarkable circumstance connected with these absurdities in English procedure is, that the judges are aware of the evils, and every now and then act upon a different system; but where the English judge acts rightly, once in a hundred times, the Cawzee and the Bramin were in the habit of acting rightly every day" (1:187).

Bentham admired the Bengali reformer Rammohun Roy and maintained a sporadic correspondence with him. In a late letter to Roy, Bentham sounds almost sanguine about British reforms and even about James Mill (*WJB* 10:590–91). What is particularly notable in this letter, however, is the restricted scope of the reforms he envisioned: reform of the judicial structure (including the inclusion of more Indians throughout the judicial ranks) and the introduction of the panopticon. Even in this, his most enthusiastic statement about what the British might do in India, Bentham made no grand claims about civilizing India but instead proposed reforms just as he did for England, Spain, France, Latin America, Greece, and Tripoli.

Bentham also developed a suggestion for jury trials in India, in his *Principles of Judicial Procedure*. This quite rare instance in his work of a specific reform for British India (and even this one is offered in passing, as an example, rather than as an actual proposal) illustrates the contrast between his understanding of education and development and those of James and John Stuart Mill.[67] Although Bentham believed that the level of education among the general Indian population was too low to enable the proper function of juries selected from the whole population, he made no claims that Indian society as such was so rude or barbarous as to prevent the possibility of juries altogether. Bentham's views about the franchise appear to follow a similar logic. His constitutional code for Greece includes a justification for the denial of voting rights to Muslims there, but this passage demonstrates that Bentham believed that a community should be denied voting rights only in the most extreme circumstances, and for the shortest possible time. It seems clear that he did not approve of the exclusion of any community from political participation on the grounds of immaturity or incapacity for self-government.

> By self-preservation—an altogether unopposable law—by that and nothing else, for neither can any thing else be requisite, are men of this class excluded from the faculty of giving any degree of efficiency to their will to the purpose in question [i.e., from voting]. The character in which they stand subjected to the exclusion is that of enemies: natural and, for a time, unhappily irreconcilable enemies. In their case so long as the danger from admission continues, so long must the exclusion be continued. So long must it be, but not a moment longer ought to be.[68]

Although his judgment that giving the vote to Muslims in Greece would threaten the existence of the state may be contested, the passage shows how high he placed the bar for the denial of suffrage to communities within a state.

In taking these positions, Bentham bore out the argument he made in the "Time" section of the essay on "Time and Place" against the common view that the best laws for "civilized" ages must be different from the best laws for "rude" ages (*WJB* 1:190–91). Importantly, in discussing these different "ages" of society, Bentham always compared particular societies with their own pasts, European with the European past and Islamic society with the age of Mohammed, rather than positing, as both Mills did, that India or Asia generally represented the "rude" age of humanity. Systematic cultural differences between rude and civilized ages might be observed, he noted; for instance, in a rude age people might on the whole be less accustomed to cooperating spontaneously with the laws. "The differences, however, that may be occasioned by these circumstances, can at the utmost be but very slight" (1:190).

Thus his jury proposal shows Bentham discussing India not as a characteristically "barbarous" society, but rather simply as one in which there was not a large pool of people educated enough to serve usefully on juries. The "general complexion of the public mind," Bentham wrote, was too uninformed to make feasible a regular supply of competent jurors from the general population. His resourceful proposal for a limited system of Indian juries was designed on the one hand as a check, in the form of publicity and public opinion, on the judges, and on the other hand as a form of civic education, both for the relatively small number of elected jurors and for the larger public as spectators. Juries would be elected for trials of particular importance: they would hear the entire trial and deliver a public verdict. Although the judge would not be bound to comply with their verdict, "in the event of non-compliance on the part of the judge—the effect of the verdict would be, that of an appeal from his decision to the tribunal of public opinion" (*WJB* 2:137). Where the population was mixed, the juries would be composed of both Muslims and Hindus; representatives of each community would be elected by members of the other to encourage impartiality and suppress corruption. Unanimity would not be required, as that would encourage bribery of poor jurors by those defendants who could afford it. The plan sought to restrain corruption on the part of the governors and to educate the public; it accommodated communal differences while at the same time attempting to use public institutions to mitigate, over time, their harmful effects. In formulating a reform plan tailored to Indian society, Bentham resisted suggesting that that society or its members were in particular need of improvement. For reasons such as these, Bentham's proposal for jury reform in India should not be confused with the "improvements" proposed by his successors, which rested precisely on claims about the peculiar backwardness or incapacity of Indians.

Although "Time and Place" indicates that Bentham was far more aware of the problems with attempting to legislate for all people than his detractors suggest, Bentham's method—his assumption that the way to go about legislating is to produce general codes and then tailor them to circumstances—remained problematic, or at the very least, easily subject to abuse. This method became particularly dangerous when, in the hands of Bentham's disciples, the general code was enforced from outside and from above, and when Bentham's followers abandoned his convictions that people knew their own interests best, that non-European notables and officials were capable of governing well, and that all people were capable of using public opinion to curb abuses by their governors. Of all Bentham's followers, James Mill offered the most thorough account of Indian society and the British Empire, and, until his son's, the most fully developed theory of social development, in his *History of British India*. The views that he expressed there influenced not only his own policymaking as an influential agent of the East India Company, but also the opinions and policies of a generation of civil servants, including such powerful figures as Governor-General Bentinck, and theorists, John Stuart Mill foremost among them. If we are to understand how Bentham's views were transformed to become the foundation of one of the most self-confident and interventionist branches of British imperial practice, then, we must turn to the thought of James Mill.

I have argued that utilitarianism as originally conceived by Bentham did not naturally lend itself to the sort of dictatorial imperial rule that characterized the hopes of many of his successors: the imposition from above without concern for the opinions of the ruled or for their interests as they themselves understood them. Bentham, for all his aspirations to see legal systems reformed around the world, never supported British imperial rule as a convenient means of imposing his schemes on powerless or incompetent subjects. Although his peculiarities make assimilation to any period or tradition seem almost absurd, Bentham is better understood as a participant in the late-eighteenth-century movement toward skepticism of imperial conquests and aspirations than he is as a protocolonialist or a "Solon" of India. Once he is understood in this light, our picture of his successors shifts as well: James Mill, who attempted an ill-advised synthesis of conjectural history and utilitarianism, takes on a new importance, for he both foreshadowed and influenced political developments that were to become prominent in the East India Company and intellectual developments among the colonialist vanguard. And, finally, John Stuart

Mill's philosophy begins to seem less a theoretical refinement of what had been an unsubtle theory out of touch with human experience, as he portrayed it. In particular his analysis of "character," which he took to be one of his key contributions to utilitarian thought, appears to sap some of the lively ecumenism from Bentham's utilitarianism and put in its place a tendentious, unsociological, and politically destructive account of social progress, of what constituted the summit of human endeavor, and of the rights and duties that accompanied such achievement.

Five

James and John Stuart Mill: The Development of Imperial Liberalism in Britain

James Mill: An Uneasy Alliance of Utilitarianism and Conjectural History

For many readers, James Mill represents the classic instance of the utilitarian imperialist. As a highly placed member of the East India Company's executive government from 1819 until shortly before his death in 1838, Mill was, as has often been observed, well situated to institute utilitarian reforms in judicial and land-use policy, among other areas.[1] Mill's *History of British India* (1817), wholly dismissive of Indian society as barbaric and the Indian population as incapable of participation in their own governance, guided not only his own views about what was desirable and possible for the British to do in India, but also those of a generation of policymakers, including his son.[2] The intolerance and crude inadequacy of James Mill's accounts of Indian society, Sanskrit, Hinduism, and indeed all aspects of Indian civilization have been well documented and need not be labored here.[3]

But the elder Mill's thought occupies a peculiar place in the history of utilitarian views on empire, a position whose oddities and potential contradictions have not fully been explored in the literature on the subject. My discussion will instead emphasize the novelties of James Mill's approach: the ways in which his mode of analysis differed significantly from those of his major sources, Bentham and the Scottish conjectural historians. James Mill stands somewhere between the theories of social development central to the Scottish Enlightenment and the theory of progress distinctive of J. S. Mill's liberalism. The elder Mill proposed a single index of civilization: all societies, he believed, could be ranged in a historical and moral hierarchy according to the degree to which they promoted utility. In making this claim, Mill drew upon both Bentham and the Scottish historians in ways that violated the subtleties and insights of both traditions.[4] The peculiarity of Mill's position lies in its unusual combination of caustic criticism of empire, primarily on classic political economy grounds, and its disdain toward non-European societies, in particular, the conviction that India should be governed by a form of British despotism entirely unaccountable to Indians themselves. Most of his writings in both veins appeared during the same period, between about 1809 and 1823.

Mill's economic critique of colonies resembled Bentham's, although he never expressed any of the moral concerns present in Bentham's work and instead focused solely on the question of whether colonies provided financial or other benefits to the metropolitan country. These views were most fully articulated in the article "Colony," published in 1823 as a supplement to the *Encyclopaedia Britannica*.[5] In that essay, Mill analyzed the potential economic benefits of colonization for the mother country, examining the various arguments in favor of monopolizing the markets or products of colonies; he concluded, as had Adam Smith and Bentham, that almost all ostensible benefits were false and that free trade would always be more profitable than colonial possessions. Colonies were "a grand source of wars"; they drained the mother country of labor and resources that would be better invested at home; mercantilist affection for colonial mines was misplaced, for most mines merely impoverished the metropolitan country.[6] Mill's explanation for colonization also followed closely those of Smith and Bentham: a few powerful investors were able to foist on European countries policies detrimental to the general interest.

> If colonies are so little calculated to yield any advantage to the countries that hold them, a very important question suggests itself. What is the reason that nations, the nations of modern Europe, at least, discover so great an affection for them? . . .
>
> It never ought to be forgotten, that, in every country, there is "a Few," and there is "a Many"; that in all countries where the government is not very good, the interest of "the Few" prevails over the interest of "the Many" and is promoted at their expense. It is according to the interest of "the Few" that colonies should be cultivated.[7]

In short, the article appears to be a fairly straightforward summary of many of the arguments from self-interest that Bentham had offered in the 1790s. Although there are occasional moments of Bentham-like sarcasm, however, we find none of the sense of outrage that pervades Bentham's writings on empire, and none of the diversity of moral and practical arguments, which, for Bentham, converged in condemnation of empire. Mill also did not address the rights or perspectives of inhabitants of the colonies, questions that Bentham *did* consider in *Emancipate Your Colonies!* and related writings.

The *History of British India* (first published in 1817) and other articles published as he wrote the *History* indicate that although Mill never believed the governance of India was in Britain's interest, and although he viewed British law and politics themselves as deeply flawed, inegalitarian, and often unjust, he considered it Britain's duty as a civilized and progressive nation to impose its rule on India. Despite his strong criticism of the East India Company in the *History*, the Company hired him two years after its publication as assistant examiner of correspondence because, on the strength of the book, they considered him one of Britain's greatest experts on India. James Mill saw his work for the Company as a labor of immense importance for the improvement of Indian society; as he wrote to David Ricardo in 1819, "Though I might procure leave of absence for the asking, there are so many despatches to answer, and the happiness and misery of so many millions are affected by what I write, that I cannot find it in my heart to abstract a day from the labours of this place till I have got towards an end of my arrears."[8]

Mill began work on the *History* in 1806 (the year of J. S. Mill's birth). In order to turn that research to immediate account at a time of straitened finances and a growing family, he also wrote a number of articles for the *Edinburgh Review*.[9] These articles, while they make many arguments that were to resurface in the *History*, engage directly in the politics of the empire in a way that the *History* does not.[10] In "Affairs of India" of 1810, for instance, Mill argued that governing India could never be in Britain's interest. He held that the East India Company had, contra the claims of its directors, always run a deficit. He argued further that British India must always be in a state of war or in preparation for war with its barbarous and untrustworthy neighbors, the Indian principalities; and that to solve the Company's problems by having the British state take over the government of India, as some of the Company's critics had proposed, would drain Britain of millions of pounds a year and introduce unbounded opportunities for corruption into the British government.[11] Whereas Bentham suggested that such arguments proved that Britain should abandon the government of its colonies, James Mill claimed instead that despite the great dangers, the British people had a duty to keep the empire, for the sake of their Indian subjects.[12]

> If we wish for the prolongation of an English government in India, which we do most sincerely, it is for the sake of the natives, not of England. India has never been anything but a burden; and any thing but a burden, we are afraid, it cannot be rendered. But this English government in India, with all its vices, is a blessing of unspeakable magnitude to the population of Hindustan. Even the utmost abuse of European power, is better, we are persuaded, than the most temperate exercise of Oriental despotism.[13]

Although Mill was often a radical critic of British society and government, when he considered Britain in comparison with "backward" societies, he shared with other nineteenth-century supporters of British rule in India considerable complacency about the superiority of British politics and culture.[14] In addition to believing that utility could be adopted straightforwardly as a standard of judgment for any society, Mill claimed, as Bentham did not, that Britain ranked highest among all nations and that its laws, even if flawed, ought to be imposed on backward nations in anticipation of improvements in Britain.

J. S. Mill was to make similar claims about Britain's civilizing duties, and indeed James Mill's argument for "a simple form of arbitrary government tempered by European honour and European intelligence" found echoes in his son's advocacy of progressive colonial despotism.[15] But whereas his son was to defend the Company as the organization best suited for the technocratic rule India required, James Mill was always less sanguine about the ability of the Company to purge peculation and corruption from its operations. He rejected greater ministerial control over Indian government (as his son would do) on the grounds that the British people knew and cared nothing for India, and that parliamentary control would only add problems of patronage to those of embezzlement. Not surprisingly given his views of Indian backwardness, he believed that the Indians were wholly incapable of sustaining the solution of local legislative assemblies that had brought self-government to Canada and the British West Indies. In light of these obstacles to good government, James Mill proposed the quite extraordinary solution of having a member of the British royal family sent out to found a hereditary emperorship of Hindustan, to govern with the help of British advisers and to encourage settlement by "Europeans of all descriptions."[16] When he became an official of the Company, Mill abandoned such a notion and contented himself with working to transform the company from a "mercantile interest" concerned with profits to a colonial administration charged with rationalizing Indian law and society.[17]

> To us it is perfectly clear, that Hindustan cannot, for any great length of time, be governed from Great Britain, but must have a government of some kind or other on the spot;—then it follows, that of all possible governments, that of Britons, resting on the foundation of a large British society, is the most full of happy prospects, not to Britain only, but to mankind at large.[18]

He added, as his son would also argue, that the British empire could be justified not only by domestic improvements but also by the pax Britannica it would create.

> The wider the circumference of the British dominion, the more extensive the reign of peace. Did it embrace the whole of the Peninsula, and were it supported with any tolerable degree of wisdom, a very considerable period of peace would probably be ensured, during which an incalculable progress might be made in happiness and civilization.[19]

James Mill saw himself at once as a utilitarian and as an heir to the philosophical history of the Scottish Enlightenment. While he was perhaps not making a self-conscious effort to marry these two very different traditions, Mill adopted a standard of utility from Bentham and an idea of progressive social development from Scottish thinkers such as Smith and Ferguson. What emerged was a problematic fusion: an index of progress in which utility is the sole standard against which any nation can be measured. As Mill wrote in the *History*, "exactly in proportion as Utility is the object of every pursuit may we regard a nation as civilized. Exactly in proportion as its ingenuity is wasted on contemptible or mischievous objects . . . [t]he nation may safely be denominated barbarous."[20] Such a conclusion did justice to neither tradition. Mill seems to have seen his project as the application of philosophical history to good government: the technique of conjectural history should be not simply a matter of theoretical reflection but a tool of utilitarian governance.[21] And yet Mill's application of "Benthamite" principles to the consolidation of imperial rule constituted a major departure from Bentham's own position on empire.

In adopting the method of conjectural history, too, Mill transformed what was, in Smith and Ferguson, a relatively nonjudgmental description of development, into a "scale of excellence or defect" (*HBI* 1:155). Mill, educated in Edinburgh, a student of Dugald Stewart and an admirer in particular of John Millar, believed himself, in writing the *History of British India*, to be undertaking a philosophical history worthy of the tradition of Scottish conjectural history.[22] And yet Mill's practice of history vitiated that tradition in two particularly important respects. First, Mill reduced the comparatively subtle developmental gradations posited by the Scottish historians into a crude dichotomy between civilization and rudeness, and he consequently assimilated all non-European societies into a single category of social "infancy." Second, he argued for a direct correspondence between a society's stage of historical development and the mental capacity of its members.[23] As to the first, Mill was conscious of his departure from the distinctions Europeans commonly made between Amerindian nomads and the highly complex Indian agricultural, commercial, and urbanized society: he explained that Europeans had become acquainted with Indians and Americans at the same time (this in itself an odd assertion) and in comparing the two had too easily leapt to the conclusion that Indians were a far more cultivated people. Mill's insistence on the similarities among "rude" nations was partly a response to what he viewed as misguided discrimination among them (and misguided admiration for India and China) on the part of his contemporaries. Mill claimed that earlier efforts were simplistic because they too easily attributed "civilization" to Asian societies. "The Hindus were compared with the savages of America; the circumstances in which they differed from that barbarous people, were the circumstances in which they corresponded with the most cultivated nations; other circumstances were overlooked; and it seems to have been little suspected that conclusions too favourable could possibly be drawn" (*HBI* 2:113). Mill seems not to have been aware that he was merely committing the reverse oversimplification. Indeed, he appears to have thought that he was offering a uniquely complex account, one that took a "joint view of all the great circumstances taken together" (2:110).

Duncan Forbes, in his influential article "James Mill and India," argues that Mill's practice of conjectural history was a straightforward adoption of the Scottish tradition of his education. He claims, for instance, that Mill was "wholly in the tradition of the philosophical history of the eighteenth century," and writes, "Mill's approach to India was unsympathetic not simply because he was a disciple of Bentham, but because he brought with him from Scotland a conception of progress which was lacking in Bentham's thought."[24] As I have suggested, this is a double mistake, for Mill altered both Bentham's thought and the conjectural histories in directions incompatible with the views of his predecessors. Forbes tells us that "[t]here is in fact an unbroken chain of intellectual causation linking Condorcet and the Scottish 'conjectural' historians with men like Bentinck who reversed the original policy of the East India Company because they were determined to impose the pattern of a 'higher' civilization on what they regarded as a semi-barbarous country." In fact, a substantial gulf separates much Scottish conjectural history and the more simplistic theories of progress that we find in both Condorcet and James Mill, and through Mill, in administrators such as Bentinck.

Knud Haakonssen deftly presents Mill's own lack of subtlety when compared to earlier Scottish thinkers. "What is it," he asks, "that makes Mill's *History* such an arid rationalist exercise when compared with, for example, the works of Smith and Millar?"[25] Haakonssen's perceptive reply to this question turns on two elements. First, Mill is inattentive to unintended consequences; second, he tends to attribute all change to the intervention of individuals and consequently lacks any "theoretical conception of social and institutional change."[26] Related to this notion of causation is Mill's assumption that human rationality improves with each new stage of development, which I discuss further below.

Smith and Ferguson, as we saw in chapter 2, were acutely aware of the contingencies involved in historical development and brought real understanding to the ways in which the development of laws and mores was closely, and reasonably, linked to material developments (such as land-use practices). For both thinkers, development from primitive to more complex stages of social organization results from both accidental outcomes and rational responses to natural constraints such as increasing population density. Smith and Ferguson each refrained from making claims about the rationality or capacity of peoples with practices and customs radically different from those of their own society, and neither credited Europeans with superiority of reason or morals on the basis of their development of commercial society. Judgment of the individual members of various societies did not form part of their philosophical project.

James Mill, in contrast, regularly referred to the customs, laws, and sacred and secular literature of non-European societies as illustrations of their members' deficient mental capacity. Because he lacked any theory of historical development, he claimed, for example, that Indian and Chinese culture were frozen in an immobility from which they could be saved only by the intervention of a heroic lawmaker or more advanced society such as Britain. While Mill may have thought of himself as explaining historical development after the manner of the Scottish conjectural historians, his treatments of the subject bear little resemblance to theirs.[27]

James Mill certainly used the language of the Scottish conjectural historians. He spoke of stages of civilization and states of society, and argued for the importance of developing an "enlarged and accurate acquaintance with the history of society."[28] Indeed, in the *History of British India*, Mill constructs his own story of the "progress of civil society" and an account of what might be called his philosophy of history.[29] Thanks to European scholarship, he tells his readers, "we can show how they lived together as members of the community, and of families; how they were arranged in society; what rites they practised, what tenets they believed, what manners they displayed; under what species of government they existed; and what character, as human beings, they possessed. This is by far the most useful and important part of history."[30] This description sounds much like the project of the Scottish conjectural histories. Indeed, Mill may not have been aware of how considerably he diverged from the methods of Smith, Ferguson, and Millar in his *practice* of history.

In an 1809 article about China, Mill allied himself with the work of Millar, and yet, characteristically, he transformed a theory of multiple stages of historical development into a dichotomous gauge of progress. Mill writes, "Since the philosophical inquiry into the condition of the weaker sex, in the different stages of society, published by Millar, it has been universally considered as an infallible criterion of barbarous society, to find the women in a state of great degradation"; he goes on to claim that the Chinese treatment of women demonstrates that China is on a par with "savages."[31] In the same article, Mill expresses his desire to develop a more carefully theorized account of the stages of civilization than has yet been produced: "It is to be lamented that philosophers have not as yet laid down any very distinct canons for ascertaining the principal stages of civilization. The ideas of the greatest part of mankind on the subject, are therefore vague in the extreme." The remainder of the passage, however, makes clear that Mill's primary concern was not the lack of nuance in descriptions of civilizational stages, but rather an excessively low threshold for the category of civilized:

> All they do is, to fix one or two of the principal nations of Europe at the highest point of civilization; and wherever, in any country, a few of the first appearances strike them as bearing a resemblance to some of the most obvious appearances in these standards of comparison, such countries are at once held to be civilized.[32]

While Mill generally spoke of the stages of civilization, as the Scottish historians did, as though there were many such stages, he did not adopt their complex gradation of four or more stages. Scottish historians could discuss degrees of complexity among various settled societies (distinguished, for example, by the sophistication of their legal codes, type of market relations, form of government and degree of penetration of society by government). Furthermore, whereas Smith and others regarded some of the diversity of human behavior to be simply variation rather than evidence of a society's stage of civilization and viewed much of human behavior as morally indifferent, Mill insistently drew on all laws and practices as accumulated "evidence" for a society's barbarism or civility.[33]

Mill instead identified societies simply as barbarous or civilized and thus assimilated all "rude" peoples into a single category of moral and political inferiority. Thus, rather than attempting to ascertain China's "stage of civilization" with any nuance, Mill simply amassed evidence to illustrate the country's backwardness.[34] "Their government is a despotism in the very simplest and rudest form," he wrote. "There is not one of the arts in China in a state which indicates a stage of civilization beyond the infancy of agricultural society."[35] Mill's categories permitted none of the fine distinctions characteristic of Scottish conjectural histories. Consequently he found the Chinese to exhibit such classic marks of barbarity as "mendacity" and to resemble, among others, Hindus, the indigenous Peruvians observed by Garcilaso de la Vega, and the "savages of New Holland."[36] He disputed every achievement commonly adduced as evidence for the sophistication of Chinese civilization: the perfection of their porcelain (he argued that their lack of refinement in glass-making, so similar to porcelain, only proved their incapacity to innovate); their exquisite gardens and architecturally advanced arches (many rude peoples were capable of these); and their printing presses ("what an abuse of terms!

Because the Chinese cut out words on blocks of wood, and sometimes, for particular purposes, stamp them on paper").

Similar instances of "barbarity" abound in the *History of British India*, in which Mill took it upon himself to discredit what he saw as the absurdly exaggerated accounts of Indian wealth and civilization by such Orientalist scholars as Sir William Jones.[37] Mill found "rudeness" everywhere in India: in their "peculiar gratification from pretensions to a remote antiquity"; the "wildness and inconsistency" of their historical accounts; the "unskillful and rude" system of governance under ancient Hindu monarchs; and their "taste for buffoonery."[38] As with China, he dismissed Indian achievements as irrelevant. Having conceded that the beauty of their weaving surpassed the ability of all other modern nations, for example, Mill remarked that this was no great achievement, as many rude nations had been known for their fine cloth. And so with printing and dyeing: "This has never been supposed to be one of the circumstances on which any certain inference with regard to civilization could be founded," and in any case the brilliant colors of their dyes were due merely to the happy accident of climate and soil (*HBI* 2:12–15).

In short, James Mill's discussions of non-European cultures followed a persistent pattern. He recognized no differentiation among these peoples, so that all non-Europeans, from the South Sea island nomads to the peoples of the Chinese empire, were essentially "rude" or "barbarous," whatever might be said about their particular means of subsistence, forms of government, or arts and practices. And he wrote as if every aspect of these cultures that might show them to be inferior to European civilization was telling, whereas anything that might suggest refinement was either trivial or misleading.[39]

Furthermore, Mill's practice of conjectural history differs from that of the most sophisticated Scottish conjectural historians in its insistence on social and cultural development as fundamentally a matter of cognitive development. Smith, as we saw in chapter 2, as well as Ferguson and Millar, held steadfastly to the idea that all peoples were equally rational—and equally capable of insight, forethought, and creativity—and that the varieties of institutions reflected rational responses to different experiences. Although these thinkers conceded that some customs or laws might cause practices to persist after they had outlived their utility, they did not regard this fact as indicating a deficiency in the mental faculties of a society's members. James Mill, in contrast, repeatedly argued that the practices of rude peoples in general, and Indians and Chinese in particular (the peoples he wrote about in greatest detail), illustrated the debility of their minds, their inability to recognize their interests, and the enslavement of their reason to whim or passion. Despite savages' pressing need, for example, to develop means of settling disputes over resources, the requisite structures emerge only after a long period of suffering, supposedly because "slow is the progress made by the human understanding, in its rude and ignorant state" (*HBI* 2:123–24).

> A civilized government, when it is strongly its interest to be at peace with you, will, you may calculate with considerable certainty, remain at peace. On a barbarous, or semicivilized government, its view of its true interests is so feeble and indistinct, and its caprices and passions are so numerous and violent, that you can never count for a day. From its hatred of all restraint, and its love of depredation, it is naturally and essentially at war with all around it. The government of India, therefore, is not to be preserved with less than a perpetual war expenditure.[40]

For Mill, barbarous reason is obscured by caprice, a flaw to be found in Indian rulers and nomadic hunters as much as in children.[41] While Mill's language in the foregoing passage might suggest that he attributed irrationality to the structures of barbarous governments, elsewhere he asserts that individual *members* of semicivilized societies suffer from inferior mental capacities:

> Sir William Jones, and others, recognized the demand for a code of Indian law; but unhappily thought of no better expedient than that of employing some of the natives themselves; as if one of the most difficult tasks to which the human mind can be applied, a work to which the highest measure of European intelligence is not more than equal, could be expected to be tolerably performed by the unenlightened and perverted intellects of a few Indian pundits. With no sanction of reason could anything better be expected than that which was in reality produced; a disorderly compilation of loose, vague, stupid, or unintelligible quotations and maxims, selected arbitrarily . . . attended with a commentary, which only adds to the mass of absurdity and darkness; a farrago, by which nothing is defined, nothing established. (*HBI* 5:426)

With no place in his theory for structural or systematic effects of laws, institutions, or circumstances on human behaviors. Mill relies on the capacity or incapacity of individuals to explain all social difference.[42]

Finally, an inability to construct rational categories is one failing to which Mill often draws attention, attributing the fault to the *minds* of individual legislators. The list of people exempt from testifying in trials in Hindu law, for example, "indicates . . . by the strange diversity of the cases which it includes, a singular want of discrimination, in the minds by which it was framed" (*HBI* 1:190). Here as elsewhere, James Mill's conviction that utilitarian theory and its own legal distinctions and categories offered the only benchmark of rationality, illustrates a limited imagination about the possible diversity of human institutions that bears little resemblance not only to the sociological sensitivity of the Scottish conjectural historians, but also to Bentham's often overlooked appreciation for the multiple solutions to the problems of organizing social life.[43]

J. S. Mill: Character and the Revision of the Benthamite Tradition

John Stuart Mill was, of course, far subtler and less doctrinaire than his father, and his views on social development and national character are much more thoroughly and carefully theorized. To a great extent, however, he shared his father's judgments of Indian society, about the usefulness of making a dichotomous distinction between civilized and barbarous peoples, and about the proper relationship between India and its British rulers. Like his father, and indeed thanks to his father, the younger Mill had a lifelong role in Indian imperial affairs.[44] J. S. Mill entered the East India Company's service in the department of correspondence at age seventeen and advanced quickly. For much of his life he was responsible for correspondence in the Political Department, which handled relations with native Indian states and thus served as a sort of diplomatic or foreign affairs department.[45] During his tenure, Mill argued forcefully for preserving the Company's rule of India and against the abolition of the Company and its replacement by direct rule by the British state, both in 1852, when the Company charter came up for renewal, and again in 1858, after the Sepoy Rebellion, when he and the Company finally lost the long-running debate. Having objected to direct governance of India by Britain, Mill refused the government's invitation to stay on as a member of the Indian government and instead took an early retirement.

J. S. Mill's views on imperial rule, like his father's, represent a departure from those of Bentham and the thinkers of the Scottish Enlightenment. The younger Mill also retreated from the relatively subtle account of historical development elaborated by the Scots, in favor of a rough dichotomy between savage and civilized, and he too combined this historical argument with utilitarian ones to justify despotic, but civilizing, imperial rule. J. S. Mill's differences from Bentham on the question of colonization went well beyond his adoption of his father's simplistic view of India, however. It was the younger Mill's effort to introduce into utilitarian thought a consideration of "character," both individual and national, and his belief in progress, which he saw as an essential element of liberty, that mark some of his greatest departures from Bentham. These theoretical differences had significant impact on the way Mill drew on utilitarian concerns when writing about empire. Although Mill is often credited with exposing the narrowness of Bentham's vision, their writings on India and colonization in fact demonstrate Bentham's greater flexibility on questions of social organization. Bentham proves more willing, for instance, to attribute value to non-British institutions and to respect non-Europeans' ability to know their own interests and participate in their own governance, a difference between these thinkers discussed at greater length below.

Mill's effort to distance his philosophy from what he saw as the coarseness of Bentham's understanding of human nature was so successful that his own critical portrayal of Benthamite utilitarianism has survived as probably the dominant characterization of Bentham's thought. Yet Mill's portrait of Bentham has done a great disservice to the ironic and passionate person one discovers so vividly emerging from Bentham's writings: a writer who, in fact, appealed to people's sense of justice, reciprocity, and glory as well as to their pleasures and pains.[46] Mill instead memorably depicted a man of great reforming ambition but stunted emotional capacity and intellectual scope. "As an analyst of human nature (the faculty in which above all it is necessary that an ethical philosopher should excel) I cannot rank Mr Bentham very high," he wrote in "Remarks on Bentham's Philosophy," published in 1833, shortly after Bentham's death and five years before the better-known "Bentham" was published.[47] The early essay is less judicious than the later, but they share a common theme: Bentham's failure to grasp the importance of human nature, and individual and national character, in morals and politics. In Bentham's work, according to Mill,

> It is not considered (at least, not habitually considered,) whether the act or habit in question, though not in itself necessarily pernicious, may not form part of a *character* essentially pernicious, or at least essentially deficient in some quality eminently conducive to the "greatest happiness." To apply such a standard as this, would indeed, often require a much deeper insight into the formation of character, and knowledge of the internal workings of human nature, than Mr. Bentham possessed. (*CW* 10:8)

In his determination to defend this point about Bentham's thought, Mill exploited the caricature of the bachelor, out of touch with common human feelings and relations. Mill asserted that Bentham's philosophy suffered from his personal unfamiliarity with the full human experience and his emotional isolation from others. "In many of the most natural and strongest feelings of human nature he had no sympathy," Mill wrote; "from many of its graver experiences he was altogether cut off; and the faculty by which one mind understands a mind different from itself, and throws itself into the feelings of that other mind, was denied him by his deficiency of Imagination."[48] Bentham's utilitarianism considered only the immediate consequences of an action, Mill argued, whereas a philosopher of ethics must also take into account an action's effects on the formation of the actor's character. Mill held that while Bentham might remain compelling as a theorist of legislation, this deficiency in his thought prevented Bentham from becoming a moral philosopher or "analyst of human nature."[49]

Mill's second essay on Bentham, five years later, expanded on such themes through a discussion of "national character," a concept that Mill unquestioningly—and problematically—treated as something essentially like individual character, the same phenomenon at a "higher generalization" (CW 10:99). Having discarded Bentham's "theory of life" as useless for the practical reasoning of real individuals, Mill went on to argue that Bentham's inability to comprehend character also strictly limited the applicability of his philosophy to questions of social organization.

> That which alone causes any material interests to exist, which alone enables any body of human beings to exist as a society, is national character: *that* it is, which causes one nation to succeed in what it attempts, another to fail; one nation to understand and aspire to elevated things, another to grovel in mean ones; which makes the greatness of one nation lasting, and dooms another to early and rapid decay. . . . A philosophy of laws and institutions, not founded on a philosophy of national character, is an absurdity. But what could Bentham's opinion be worth on national character? How could he, whose mind contained so few and so poor types of individual character, rise to that higher generalization?[50]

Mill regarded his own attention to the formation of individual and national character as perhaps the greatest advance that his own philosophy made over Bentham's.

J. S. Mill aspired to develop a science of individual and national character, which he called ethology: he described this science in outline in a chapter of the *System of Logic*.[51] While he never developed that chapter into the treatise that he hoped might launch such a field of study, we find, scattered throughout his works, observations on national character that would have contributed to the new science.[52] The thought that an understanding of the formation of both individual and national character was essential to moral and political theory underlay much of his work.

> A theory, therefore, which considers little in an action besides that action's own consequences, will generally be sufficient to serve the purposes of a philosophy of legislation. Such a philosophy will be most apt to fail in the consideration of the greater social questions—the theory of organic institutions and general forms of polity; for those (unlike the details of legislation) to be duly estimated, must be viewed as the great instruments of forming the national character; of carrying forward the members of the community toward perfection, or preserving them from degeneracy.[53]

Mill resisted racial or biological determinism, and he emphasized that national characters were mutable over time, even in unexpected directions. Still, he tended to describe national characters through a series of dichotomies—advanced-backward, active-passive, industrious-sensuous, sober-excitable—and to assign the more flattering labels predominantly to the English and Germans, and the latter to the Irish, French, southern Europeans, and "Orientals" (with characters deteriorating as one moved south and east).[54] J. S. Mill's notion of national character, despite his insistence on its importance and his otherwise sophisticated theoretical framework, was fairly thin: it had none of the connotations of complex specificity, of a unique constellation of institutions, practices, and beliefs, that we find, for instance, in Burke or Herder.[55]

For all Mill's insistence on the importance of character and the parallel between individual and national character, it would be a mistake to assume that by national character he had in mind anything analogous to the riot of eccentricity and singularity he noted in individuals. Mill's rather impoverished understanding of national character undercuts his own criticism of Bentham's narrowness. Indeed, Mill went on to argue that the "imperfections of [Bentham's] theory of human nature" prevented him not so much from appreciating human diversity as from properly ranking nations along a scale of progress.

> For, taking, as we have seen, next to no account of national character and the causes which form and maintain it, he was precluded from considering, except to a very limited extent, the laws of a country as an instrument of national culture: one of their most important aspects, and in which they must of course vary according to the degree and kind of culture already attained; as a tutor gives his pupil different lessons according to the progress already made in his education. (*CW* 10:105)

Although Mill regularly cautioned that nations and national characters must be understood as diverse, as formed by "time, place, and circumstance," he nonetheless tended at just these moments to reduce diversity among societies to variation along a single axis of progress.[56] Mill's perfectionism, his belief in self-development as a preeminent moral duty and his conviction that societies, like individuals, must continue to "improve" or else stagnate or decline, supported a view of social progress that in many of its details restated and affirmed the much less complex ideas of his father. The differences between Bentham's "Time and Place" essay and Mill's commentary on it are therefore instructive. Mill takes national differences to signify degrees of advancement in a rigid hierarchy of progress; and, like his father, he characterizes members of "backward" societies as children. Such an approach is quite alien to that of Bentham, who accepted a great number of cultural differences as simply variety and never presumed to rank nations as inferior or superior in "character," however much he castigated despotic governments.

Differences between Mill and Bentham on questions of character partly explain their difference regarding imperial rule.[57] In "Bentham," Mill expressed great faith in our capacity to determine national character and to formulate legislation on the basis of that character, whether one comprising "objectivity" (Italian) or "subjectivity" (German), a penchant for general theory (French) or an aversion to it (English). While he held that Bentham had paid more attention to differences among peoples than his readers often acknowledged, Mill believed Bentham's failure was not to have understood these differences as lying on a scale of progress, and therefore to have lost an opportunity to use legislation to draw each people closer to advanced civilization:

> It never seems to have occurred to him to regard political institutions in a higher light, as the principal means of the social education of a people. Had he done so, he would have seen that the same institutions will no more suit two nations in different stages of civilization, than the same lessons will suit children of different ages. As the degree of civilization already attained varies, so does the kind of social influence necessary for carrying the community forward to the next stage of its progress. For a tribe of North American Indians, improvement means, taming down their proud and solitary self-dependence; for a body of emancipated negroes, it means accustoming them to be self-dependent, instead of being merely obedient to orders; for our semi-barbarous ancestors it would have meant, softening them; for a race of enervated Asiatics it would mean hardening them. How can the same social organization be fitted for producing so many contrary effects?[58]

Here Mill suggested that each society had its own particular course of progress, although all shared a trajectory toward the society of independent-minded, autonomous, and progressive individuals that we encounter in *On Liberty.* Yet elsewhere, as I argue below, Mill appeared to jettison even this limited acknowledgment of societies' various paths, to identify only two sorts of societies, barbarous and civilized.

In regarding Bentham as devoid of imagination about the possibilities of human endeavor, Mill tended to criticize as want of discrimination a quality in Bentham that might better be considered liberality or tolerant agnosticism on questions he considered morally indifferent. For Bentham, nothing was at stake, morally speaking, in a great number of questions of taste or aesthetics, and he considered it particularly egregious to base legislation or public policy on judgments of taste. To this ecumenism Mill objected that

> there were certain phrases which, being expressive of what he considered to be . . . groundless liking or aversion, he could not bear to hear pronounced in his presence. Among these phrases were those of good and bad taste. He thought it an insolent piece of dogmatism in one person to praise or condemn another in a matter of taste: as if men's likings and dislikings, on things in themselves indifferent, were not full of the most important inferences as to every point of their character: as if a person's tastes did not show him to be wise or a fool, cultivated or ignorant, gentle or rough, sensitive or callous, generous or sordid, benevolent or selfish, conscientious or depraved.[59]

Bentham refused such inferences, and this difference also informed their respective attitudes toward colonial rule: in leaving people to determine their desires and interests for themselves, Bentham took a position fundamentally less judgmental and more respectful of difference than did Mill.

In "Bentham" and his twin essay on Coleridge, Mill constructed an appealing and vivid dichotomy between two seminal minds, each of which, however, had apprehended only a half-truth.[60] Mill saw his own philosophical project as a synthesis of these half-truths and was confident that such a synthesis was possible, even if he never achieved the reconciliation. He seems untroubled by any apprehensions that there might be incompatible truths, or that values or ideas might be lost in the yoking together of Bentham's critical spirit and Coleridge's reverential one.[61] Mill's confidence that he could reconcile all these truths is, in a sense, a microcosm of his certainty that whole cultures could be deliberately engineered, his insistence that the best achievements of one society could be injected, through legislation and education, into another less fortunate one, and what is more, without any sacrifice of legitimate values or worthwhile ways of life.

Nationality and Progressive Despotism

Mill regarded the ability to progress as the essential quality of human nature and thus the proper basis for social scientific study.[62] "The most important quality of the human intellect is its progressiveness, its tendency to improvement," he wrote. "That there is such a tendency in man is certain. It is this which constitutes his superiority among animated beings. . . . It is evident then that one of the grand objects of a really good education would be to promote to the utmost this spirit of progression, to inspire an ardent desire of improvement.[63] J. S. Mill adopted a notion of progress more like that of his father than he might have cared to admit. His method stripped away the complexity we find in the earlier conjectural histories and even in the rather inexorable account of progress offered by Comte, whom Mill greatly admired. What remained was a rough distinction between barbarous and civilized peoples; the claim that nationality was a quality achieved only by those societies at a certain level of development; and an insistence that more backward societies could be improved by despotic, civilizing rule. Indeed, in Mill's account they were essentially transparent to their rulers, objects of technical knowledge, like medicine, that could be distilled into textbooks and taught to a class of disinterested experts (*CW* 30:49). Progressiveness, the cardinal human quality, was also the monopoly of a select group of societies.

Just as J. S. Mill asserted a straightforward parallelism between individual and national character, he posited a similar parallel between the self-cultivation or improvement of individuals and the cultivation and progress of a nation. Furthermore, despite his view of humans as naturally progressive, he claimed some nations or peoples lack any "spring of progress" within themselves, while other more fortunate nations—notably, the ancient Greeks and their modern European successors—had been charged with the task of bringing progress to all of humanity.[64]

One of the most striking aspects of Mill's writings on empire and on non-Europeans is the quite crude distinction he constructs between civilized and savage or barbarous peoples, a dichotomy reminiscent of his father's views on the subject but even more forcefully asserted.[65] Mill elaborated this contrast in the early essay "Civilization," and it informed his remarks on non-Europeans across a range of works: in "A Few Words on Non-intervention," in his discussion of the governance of dependencies in *Considerations on Representative Government*, and in his more specific discussions of India. Mill's commentators have often regarded his dismissive views of "uncivilized" peoples as only to be expected of a period, in John Robson's words, "when ethnography was an amateur pursuit."[66] What is notable about Mill's version of this sort of civilized-savage dichotomy, however, was not that it was based on the inadequate ethnography of the day, but that he seems not to have paid much attention to the ethnography that was available. Unlike Robertson, Kant, or even Tocqueville (as we will see in the next two chapters), Mill showed himself consistently unconcerned about the accuracy of the empirical information upon which he depended for his theoretical generalizations.

Mill instead settled for classifications that enabled him to group "the native states of India" with "savage life" in which "there is little or no law," "no commerce, no manufactures, no agriculture, or next to none" (*CW* 10:123,120). He held that the "state of different communities, in point of culture and development, ranges downwards to a condition very little above the highest of the beasts."[67] He declared in *On Liberty*, "The greater part of the world has, properly speaking, no history, because the despotism of Custom is complete. This is the case over the whole

East" (*CW* 18:272). Mill's apparent determination to ignore the complexities of Indian society is especially puzzling. He may have accepted his father's view that personal acquaintance with the country was entirely unnecessary for an adequate understanding of it.[68] Although he certainly learned a great deal about India from his East India Company work and from his career as a reviewer, his more theoretical arguments present a two-dimensional portrait of India and its inhabitants. Any effort at imaginative or empathetic understanding, so striking in Burke's writings and speeches on India, is absent in Mill.

Why was Mill, who saw a sensitivity to national character as one of his greatest contributions to the utilitarian tradition, content with so undifferentiated an account of the diversity of human societies and cultures?[69] Mill seems to have had a remarkable lack of curiosity or imagination about non-European societies. In contrast to his discussions of India, his writings on Ireland, as I argue below, show striking sympathy for the Irish peasantry. Mill's disposition to ignore the complexities of non-European societies, and Indian society in particular, seems to have stemmed in part from an uncritical acceptance of his father's own judgments on these subjects.[70] This is at best a partial explanation, although it is fair to say that Mill continued throughout his life to trust his father's *History* as one of the most reliable accounts of Indian society.[71] Beyond filial respect for a work that occupied his father throughout Mill's childhood and contributed to his own education, Mill had theoretical reasons to ignore the particularity of cultures he deemed backward. As we have seen, Mill believed that all diversity in social practices and institutions could be ranged along a scale of progress, and that the challenge for political thinkers and actors was to draw backward societies toward the state of the most advanced society. For Mill, then, once a society was deemed backward, there was little more about it that one needed to know.

Mill's understanding of progress owed much to his reading of Auguste Comte; he particularly supported Comte's view that philosophical history should follow the course of progress by paying attention primarily to the society that was in the vanguard at a given moment.[72] While commenting upon Comte's view of history, Mill offered one of his own most complex accounts of social development, recognizing stages of intellectual development, the effects of the division of labor on social evolution, and the interaction between material and intellectual causes in the progress of society. Indeed, as he praised Comte's vanguardist view of progress and societal difference, Mill obliquely criticized Bentham's excessive universalism:

> M. Comte is equally free from the error of considering any practical rule or doctrine that can be laid down in politics as universal and absolute. All political truth he deems strictly relative, implying as its correlative a given state or situa-

tion of society. This conviction is now common to him with all thinkers who are on a level with the age, and comes so naturally to any intelligent reader of history, that the only wonder is how men could have been prevented from reaching it sooner.[73]

Like Hegel, whose philosophy of history followed the course of world-historical spirit as it moved from India to China to Europe, Comte was interested not so much in the dynamics of development of particular societies, but rather in the high point of human progress, which itself progressed over time. Mill wrote of Comte's "social dynamics" that it

> look[s] only at the races and nations that led the van, and regarding as the successors of a people not their actual descendants, but those who took up the thread of progress after them. His object is to characterize truly, though generally, the successive states of society through which the advanced guard of our species has passed, and the filiation of these states on one another—how each grew out of the preceding and was the parent of the following state. (CW 10:318)

In this view, historical attention shifts away entirely from development within societies, away from dynamics of development within institutions, practices, or social formations. Instead, like Hegel, Mill emphasizes social configurations as if frozen at particular moments. The progress he observes is like the passing of a baton from one vanguard society to the next: development within societies becomes a secondary consideration.

This is a philosophical and historical perspective very different from those Scottish theories of social development that study the causes leading one configuration of practices and institutions to evolve gradually into another, and that trace the emergence and elaboration of systems of property and law within a given society. The importance of this difference between the two philosophical histories is not that one is judgmental and the other not. As we saw in chapter 2, Smith offered judgments about the effectiveness or morality of various practices, though he refrained from judgments about whole societies as well as from categorizations of any society as inherently "progressive" or "stationary." The "vanguard" approach favored by Comte, Hegel, and Mill, in contrast, subordinated particular societies to a historical story completely external to them, and consequently encouraged the designation of a society as progressive and advanced (at least at a given stage in its history, until it passed on the spirit of progress to its spiritual heir), or stagnant and backward.

However much Mill spoke of the importance of understanding cultural variation, in practice he, like his father, erased details of particular societies in favor of a single and narrow set of criteria placed along a scale of progress, a practice encouraged by the Comtian "vanguardist" understanding of history. This reductionism is especially surprising in a thinker who self-consciously undertook to integrate a Coleridgian appreciation for cultural practices whose meaning or utility is not immediately apparent. According to Mill, Bentham brusquely approved or rejected propositions according to whether they fit his own narrow view of the matter, whereas with Coleridge, Mill wrote admiringly, "the very fact that any doctrine had been believed by thoughtful men, and received by whole nations or generations of mankind, was part of the problem to be solved, was one of the phenomena to be accounted for. . . . he considered the long or extensive prevalence of any opinion as a presumption that it was not altogether a fallacy."[74] *On Liberty* is a paean to human diversity and even eccentricity, and yet never without the condition that such diversity is desirable only within the limits of "civilized" society.

Mill's conception of "civilization" changed little from his early essay "Civilization" and continued to provide a backdrop in late works such as *On Liberty* and *Considerations on Representative Government*. "Civilization," published in 1836, proposes a simple developmental scale, one in which the "ingredients of civilization . . . begin together, always coexist, and accompany each other in their growth" (*CW* 18:120). In this essay Mill sets out to understand the political and moral effects of civilization in its most developed form in Britain, and in so doing develops the category of savage primarily to foreground the key characteristics of civilized society, "the diffusion of property and intelligence, and the power of cooperation" (18:124). Here, for J. S. Mill, as for James Mill, almost any institution, practice, or art will bear the mark of a society's place in the scale of civilization, high or low (and, like his father, he identifies only these two categories).

Mill's discussions of barbarism throughout his career imply that societal development is a matter of the improvement of individuals' cognitive capacity.[75] In his choice of language, if not through a full theoretical articulation, Mill's treatment of barbarism again resembles that of his father. In "A Few Words on Non-intervention" of 1859, for instance, Mill offers two reasons for the strict distinction between the legal and political standards applied to civilized nations and those reserved for the treatment of barbarians. The first argument appeals precisely to the notion of cognitive insufficiency: "[B]arbarians will not reciprocate. They cannot be depended on for observing any rules. Their minds are not capable of so great an effort."[76] The philosophical anthropology presupposed here, if indeed it warrants the term, represents a startling retreat from the subtlety of the earlier Scottish theories. As we saw in chapter 2, Smith and Ferguson insisted that mental capacities themselves did not increase in the development from nomadic to commercial society; both thinkers believed that differences in institutions and legal structures reflected different experiences and social needs, not inferior or superior capacities for abstract reasoning. Perhaps Mill's argument should not be taken quite so literally; yet the glibness of his claims in such passages, and of the distinctions upon which they rest, seem to demand an explanation.

If Mill's category of barbarian society appeared only in "Civilization," it might be thought a literary device, a rough but effective means of highlighting what was most significant about British society and assisting the case, made at the end of the essay, for a Millian reform of British universities. Mill drew an analogy between barbarians and children not merely for rhetorical or illustrative purposes, however, but as part of a larger political argument. Far from serving simply as a foil for civilization, this category of barbarism, undifferentiated as it is, emerges repeatedly in Mill's thought to justify imperial rule and a suspension of international norms. Again, Mill shares his father's view.

In *On Liberty*, most famously, Mill qualified his scheme for minimal interference in individuals' lives by the state or by other people with the proviso that it was not to apply to children or young persons, but

> only to human beings in the maturity of their faculties. . . . Those who are still in a state to require being taken care of by others, must be protected against their own actions as well as against external injury. For the same reason, we may leave out of consideration those backward states of society in which the race itself may be considered as in its nonage. The early difficulties in the way of spontaneous progress are so great, that there is seldom any choice of means for overcoming them; and a ruler full of the spirit of improvement is warranted in the use of any expedients that will attain an end, perhaps otherwise unattainable. (*CW* 18:224)

It should be emphasized that J. S. Mill justified civilizing despotism not simply on the grounds that such rule was necessary to undermine the power of existing, oppressive political structures and social hierarchies. Rather, he held that the rational capacities of *individuals* in such societies were so immature that they were incapable of being "guided to their improvement by conviction or persuasion" (18:224). Likewise, in "Non-intervention," Mill argues for two distinct standards of international behavior: reciprocity, mutual respect for sovereignty, and the law of nations should govern relations among civilized nations, while relations between civilized nations and "barbarians" cannot, properly speaking, be considered political relations.

> To characterize any conduct whatever towards a barbarous people as a violation of the law of nations, only shows that he who so speaks has never considered the subject. A violation of great principles of morality it may easily be; but barbarians have no rights as a *nation*, except a right to such treatment as may,

> at the earliest possible period, fit them for becoming one. The only moral laws for the relation between a civilized and a barbarous government, are the universal rules of morality between man and man. (*CW* 21:119)

In dismissing those who might disagree as simply thoughtless or ignorant, Mill dismisses a long history of thought and practice, which Burke fought hard to sustain, as we saw in chapter 3: one that regarded the law of nations as applicable not just among European states but also in relations with many societies Mill considered barbarous, including Persia and India.[77]

As Pratap Mehta has argued, Mill used nationality as a normative category as well as a descriptive term.[78] In the normative sense, nationality was an achievement of civilization; as in the passage above, such an achievement brought with it rights in the international sphere.[79] Mill could apply the term in a broader descriptive sense to peoples who had not attained the requisite political culture of "common sympathies" and cooperation in a common political project. But such groups did not warrant legal and political *recognition* of their nationhood, both as a matter of "right" and because such recognition was not "good" for them:

> [N]ations which are still barbarous have not got beyond the period during which it is likely to be for their benefit that they should be conquered and held in subjection by foreigners. Independence and nationality, so essential to the due growth and development of a people further advanced in improvement, are generally impediments to theirs. The sacred duties which civilized nations owe to the independence and nationality of each other, are not binding towards those to whom nationality and independence are either a certain evil, or at best a questionable good.[80]

In the same way that *On Liberty* claims despotism is legitimate for barbarians, "Non-intervention" is striking in its use of a philosophical anthropology, at best speculative, to justify the exercise of vast coercive political and military power.

Mill's stringent definition of "nationality" appears to relax somewhat by the end of his career, when he allows that some Hindu-ruled native states of India might be considered a form of "nationality," insofar as they had a long tradition of rule and cultural and historical ties between rulers and subjects. In 1866, he wrote,

> Wherever there are really native states, with a nationality, & historical traditions & feelings, which is emphatically the case (for example) with the Rajpoot states, there I would on no account take advantage of any failure of heirs to put an end to them. But all the Mahomedan (Rampore excepted which descends from Fyzoola Khan the Rohilla chief) & most of the Mahratta kingdoms are not of home growth, but created by conquest not a century ago & the military

> chiefs & office holders who carry on the government & form the ruling class are almost as much foreigners to the mass of the people as we ourselves are. . . . In these modern states created by conquest I would make the continuance of the dynasty by adoption not a right nor a general rule, but a reward to be earned by good government & as such I would grant it freely.[81]

Despite such occasional instances of tinkering with his categorizations of some Indian peoples, however, Mill never pursued the implications of these rather casual thoughts.[82]

The passage above underlines Mill's obdurate confidence, even after he had left the East India Company, in the transparency of India and Indians as objects of administration; his considerable lack of concern about the possible unintended consequences of the interventions he advocated; and his undeterred optimism that with adequate study, British administrators could root out such unanticipated effects altogether. In this sense, Mill demonstrates the characteristically "utilitarian" indifference to the intractability of actual societies to benevolent dictatorship, as Bentham, for all his ostensible lack of human experience, never did.[83] Alan Ryan has suggested that Mill's thought combined the "moral hyperactivism implicit in utilitarianism" with a confidence that " 'we'—whoever 'we' are—occupy a morally privileged position from whose height we can decide the fate of the less privileged."[84]

Mill's own conviction that he himself occupied such a position, one not only morally but aesthetically and intellectually privileged, stemmed from his theories of national character and social progress. These were ideas very much at odds with those of Bentham, who resisted making such judgments about the "condition" of whole societies. Ryan reveals the ways in which Mill's colonial interventionism stood in tension with some of his other, seemingly more pluralistic, insights.[85] *On Liberty* calls upon society to embrace and encourage the diversity of individual characters. His vision of pluralism, however, appears significantly impoverished in light of his restricted and hierarchical understanding of appropriate forms of social interaction, political institutions, and aesthetic judgments—and his dismissiveness toward ways of life he little understood.

Mill believed that the fundamental test of a government's suitability was its capacity to assist "progress" among its subjects.[86] He contended that barbarian despots were incapable of any concerted project of improvement, and civilized despots were the only hope of nations with no internal spring of progress. Mill occasionally acknowledged that, in practice, Britain had very often failed to live up to the theory of civilizing rule. He noted, for instance, that England had so far failed in its a duty to civilize Ireland, neither incorporating the Irish into the British nation nor forcing on them the "experience of lawful rule" through despotism.[87] Yet

Mill insisted that the twin problems of corruption and ignorance that plagued colonial rule could be solved by the appropriate institution: a civil service trained to its task.

Civilizing Backward Societies: India and Ireland

Mill's views on Ireland intersect in important ways with his ideas about Britain's non-European colonies and India in particular. Throughout his career Mill regarded India and Ireland as British colonies with fundamental similarities. Both were overwhelmingly agricultural societies, "less civilized" than Britain. And in both colonies the British government had supported a rapacious nobility at the expense of wretched peasant populations.[88] In his pamphlet *England and Ireland* (1868), Mill wrote that "those Englishmen who know something of India, are even now those who understand Ireland best . . . [.] Persons who know both countries, have remarked many points of resemblance between the Irish and the Hindoo character; there certainly are many between the agricultural economy of Ireland and that of India" (*CW* 6:519).

Although they shared these features, Mill believed the countries' differences were instructive: their recent histories, as Mill read them, vindicated British rule in India and impugned it in Ireland. He claimed that Ireland, since its conquest by Britain, had been oppressed and destroyed by a small class of ruling elites. India, in contrast, was for Mill the appropriate model of colonial governance for a backward society: rule by expert and disinterested administrators who had studied the country and who sought to rule for the benefit of the entire population, and who had long been relatively independent from parliamentary politics. At times Mill went so far as to suggest that Ireland would have been better governed "despotically" by a colonial administration of the Indian type.[89]

Still, for all the similarities Mill noted between the two colonies, there are significant differences in his own approaches to each of these "backward" societies. Although Mill regarded Ireland as in need of civilizing, he attributed the country's poverty and backwardness primarily to specific policies and power structures that hampered economic development and, therefore, the emergence of civilized values and behavior. He depicted Irish peasants as rational individuals struggling under conditions of inequality and misgovernment. India's backwardness, on the other hand, Mill discussed as though due to Indian civilization or "Asiatic" culture as such, and only incidentally to particular instances of misgovernment.[90] Mill believed the Indian population not "ripe for anything like a representative system."[91] His arguments for this position relied primarily on a judgment of Indian civilization as still too backward, and the Indian people as yet too bound by custom, to be capable of gaining through representative government the "progress" he believed all governments should engender.

Mill believed England had misgoverned Ireland for five hundred years and bore much of the responsibility (along with the Anglo-Irish landlords) for the country's backward state. In *England and Ireland* (1868), he wrote that "[w]e did not give the people, in lieu of their savage independence, the despotism of a more cultivated people; we left them their own barbarous rulers, but lent to those barbarians the strength of our civilisation to keep the many in subjection."[92] For Mill, the central failure of colonial governance had been Britain's support of Ireland's unrepresentative parliament. Rather than serving as means of national self-government, he claimed, it had instead increased the vastly unequal distribution of power already in place and had thus enabled Anglo-Irish landlords to immiserate yet further their Catholic peasant tenants. Mill held, moreover, that the bulk of the Irish population was not sufficiently socially advanced to benefit from representative institutions; they lacked "that reverence for law, without which no people can be any thing but, according to their physical temperament, savages or slaves."[93] At the same time, he suggests that Irish cultural backwardness was a direct consequence of the vulnerability of the poor, and that if the poor were rendered less dependent on the landlords, cultural transformation and representative government could soon follow.

In the winter of 1846–47, as the extent of the Irish famine's devastation was becoming clear, Mill wrote a series of forty-three articles in the *Morning Chronicle*. He argued passionately, and with great empathy toward the peasantry, for a permanent solution to the poverty of the Irish countryside. The articles argue exhaustively for Mill's remedy of waste land reclamation: the state should buy uncultivated lands from large landowners for the pittance they were worth in their current condition, and either give them outright to peasant cultivators or charge a moderate fixed rent in exchange for secure tenure.[94] Just as Ireland's cottier-tenant system was both the country's "grand economic evil" and its "grand moral evil," Mill was confident his solution would not only relieve Ireland's poverty but also result in the moral improvement of the peasantry.[95]

Mill's writings on Ireland are strikingly different in tone and in critical posture from those on India. Not only does Mill write compassionately of the Irish peasants; perhaps more importantly, he takes pains to explain their actions and habits as reasonable responses to the perverse incentives generated by societal institutions.[96] Mill responds with "indignation," for example, to those who attributed the peasants' idleness to the proverbial laziness of the Irish "race" (*CW* 34:890). On occasion, it is true, he acknowledged that differences between the English "Saxon race" and Irish *might* be inherent or biological, though he deemed this unlikely.[97] He further maintained that the Irish could not, "by any device of ours," be expected to develop English industriousness, in which "the work itself might almost seem to be the motive," but rather should hope to become more like their "Celtic brethren," the French and Italian peasants, who labor for love of their "little spot of land."[98]

Nonetheless, Mill resorted only rarely to the Irish national character or stage of civilization to account for Irish pathologies: his explanation of first resort is the oppressive institutional structure imposed by improvident landlords and supported by British misgovernment. The proposals of his *Morning Chronicle* series rest on the belief that if the Irish peasants were given even the smallest incentives in the form of secure tenure at reasonable rent, they would promptly begin improving the land and buildings, limiting their family size, and invigorating their "slack labor" (*CW* 24:916). Moral improvement, the articles suggest, would not require a dramatic reconstruction of mores or beliefs, religion or family relationships. Instead, if only the "mischievous and anti-social" property arrangements in Ireland could be reformed, moral improvement would inexorably follow.

Thus Mill credited the Irish with a moral dignity and rationality that he never accorded Indians. He believed, to be sure, that economic reform and moral advancement were inseparable, and that Ireland's endemic poverty could be overcome only with a transformation of social and domestic habits that would contribute to the improvement of moral character.[99] Mill wrote that "the main superiority of the remedial measures which we advocate consist in this—that they would surround the peasant with a new moral atmosphere; they would bring a set of motives to operate upon him which he has never before experienced, tending in the strongest manner to correct everything in his national character which needs correction."[100] And yet, proposals for explicit moral education of a less advanced by a more advanced people play a surprisingly small role in Mill's reform project for Ireland. For Mill believed that the proper role of the British in Ireland entailed reform of political and property structures. With economic reform, he suggested, moral changes would naturally follow without explicit "moral" intervention: what Ireland required was not a project of moral education but simply a change in the structure of economic incentives.

In many of his writings on Ireland, Mill expresses skepticism about England's ability to govern foreign populations. He criticizes the complacency and presumptuousness of the British as colonial rulers, postures to which he seems oddly blind in the writings on India. Indeed, Mill argued in 1846 and again in 1868 that British rule had not only failed to civilize Ireland but had further barbarized it.[101] Mill's critical eye toward British self-satisfaction in Ireland is largely absent from his writings on India; on the contrary, he repeatedly pointed to British government in India as the single example of wise British governance abroad (*CW* 6:216, 519).

Mill believed the British government could not be blamed for Indian misery, but on the contrary—given the country's history of poverty and inequality—had generally done the best it could. Even the most critical of Mill's references to past mistakes in Britain's government in India tend to argue that with time, research, and training British colonial administrators would continue to improve. This is the case both in his statements on behalf of the East India Company during the 1858 debates over its dissolution and in his review of Henry Maine's *Village Communities*. This 1871 essay, one of Mill's most severe commentaries on British rule in India, judges British mistakes as innocent because committed out of ignorance. "[W]e have done, and are still doing, irreparable mischief, by blindly introducing the English idea of absolute property in land into a country where it did not exist," Mill wrote, but this "injustice has been done by the English rulers of India, for the most part innocently, from sheer inability to understand institutions and customs almost identical with those which prevailed in their own country a few centuries ago."[102] Nowhere do we find such exoneration with regard to Ireland.

Mill criticized one or another policy in India as misguided, but excused those who developed and enforced them on the grounds that they were well-intentioned. While probing and critical about British missteps in Ireland, that is, Mill tended to forgive misgovernment in India as morally innocent. He remained confident that technocratic knowledge was continually improving: past errors of judgment and even the habitual and destructive British self-confidence did not suggest to Mill that British administrators should be chastened or their civilizing program restrained. Such exculpation leaves unexamined the presumptuousness with which British administrators decided to overhaul "primitive" institutions without understanding them or, more generally, the moral burden assumed by those who claim to know better than those they rule what is in those subjects' interests.

Mill shared with many of his liberal contemporaries the conviction that, with ever more knowledge and more careful methods, British mastery of India—as a subject of knowledge and a population of subjects—could be made complete.[103] As he said during his testimony on the renewal of the Company's charter in 1852,

> India is a peculiar country; the state of society and civilization, the character and habits of the people, and the private and public rights established among them, are totally different from those which are known or recognised in this country; in fact the study of India must be as much a profession in itself as law or medicine. . . . This makes it essential that the administration of India should be carried on by men who have been trained in the subordinate offices, and have studied India as it were professionally. (*CW* 30:49)

To be sure, Mill's arguments in this and similar passages during his testimony on behalf of the Company were intended to persuade the Crown and legislature that the Company, as a professional corps of colonial administrators, could better govern India than could the British parliamentary government, given the British public's ignorance about Indian affairs, or than could representative institutions in India for the foreseeable future.[104] While Mill's position as an employee of the East India Company deserves to be recalled as we read such passages, his more theoretical writings, such as the *Considerations*, make similar arguments.[105]

Throughout his involvement with colonial matters, Mill was consistently and conscientiously concerned that colonial rule be for the benefit of the governed. With regard to India, he remained confident that it generally was, both in intention and in execution. As he wrote on behalf of the East India Company, "Your Petitioners regard it as the most honourable characteristic of the government of India by England, that it has acknowledged no such distinction as that of a dominant and a subject race; but has held that its first duty was to the people of India" (*CW* 30:82). Mill's writings on India—conditioned as they are by his own sense of India as an object of administration rather than a political society—seem to be devoid of any doubt that colonial government by a corps of administrators might itself be vulnerable to systemic problems, abuses, or injustices.

Colonial Reform and the Governor Eyre Episode

Mill, then, remained confident that British colonial civil servants could rule impartially, knowledgeably, and beneficently over peoples not yet ready for self-government, their rule untainted by racial or cultural chauvinism. In settler colonies with large indigenous or subject populations, in contrast, Mill greatly mistrusted European *colonists* and their legislatures, and he was thus particularly sensitive to the possibility of abuses in such colonies as Ireland, New Zealand, and the former slave colonies. In India, too, he noted the dangers posed by European residents not employed by the Company; early in his career he warned against "that party of English in India, to protect the natives against whose rapacity and tyranny, is one of the most difficult but most bounden duties of the Indian government."[106] As we have seen, Mill's preference for colonial officials over self-interested settlers led him in the 1840s to suggest that Ireland would have fared far better under an Indian-style civil service. And yet Mill's determination to regard colonial administrations as beneficial led him to ignore the ways in which the colonial context engendered systematic oppression and misgovernment on the part of colonial officials as well as European settlers. When the Sepoy Rebellion erupted in northern India in 1857, spawned in large part by that misgovernment, Mill continued to defend the Company's rule and to deny that British policy or behavior bore responsibility for provoking the uprising.[107]

Indeed, Mill acknowledged British culpability in the Sepoy Rebellion only several years later, as he grappled with Britain's violent response to another colonial uprising, by black and mixed-race Jamaicans in October 1865. The bloody suppression of that revolt by Governor Edward John Eyre and his deputies prompted a vigorous effort on Mill's part to see their crimes punished, and the government-led atrocities seem to have tested his faith in British colonial administration. Nonetheless, Mill's response fell short of a thoroughgoing interrogation of the premises and systemic failures of British rule over populations that Mill, like most of his countrymen, considered civilizationally inferior. Instead, as I argue below, Mill chose to insist on the criminal responsibility of Governor Eyre while largely ignoring the colonial and racial context of the official violence that Eyre oversaw.

Mill's retirement from the East India Company enabled him finally to run for political office, and in July 1865 he was elected M.P. for the Liberal bastion of Westminster. During his three years in Parliament, three subjects most occupied his thoughts: British electoral reform, Irish land reform, and the crisis in Jamaica following the Morant Bay rebellion.[108] His efforts to bring Eyre to criminal trial represent his most determined criticism of the British Empire, and the episode undoubtedly deepened Mill's concern about persistent injustices of colonial rule, in particular the troubled relations between indigenous inhabitants and "overbearing and insolent" English settlers.[109]

News of the Jamaican rebellion and the extreme violence used to suppress it reached London in November 1865, several months after Mill entered Parliament. During a relatively brief and contained riot in the Jamaican town of Morant Bay, a local justice of the peace had been killed, along with several other whites. Governor Eyre responded by imposing martial law on the region for thirty days. In the course of suppressing the uprising, colonial officials executed 439 black and mixed-race Jamaicans either without trial or after summary courts-martial of foregone conclusion; they flogged 600 others (including women); and they burned at least one thousand houses.[110]

Mill reported all of this in his second speech to Parliament on the Jamaica crisis. Furthermore, an alleged leader of the rebellion, George William Gordon, the son of a white planter and a slave and a member of the Jamaican parliament, was moved on Eyre's orders from Kingston (where any trial against him would have been under civil law) to the area under martial law; he was then convicted by court-martial of high treason and hanged. Although Gordon had not been present at the riot, Eyre and others considered him one of its primary instigators because of inflammatory speeches he had made in Kingston prior to it. Eyre believed Gordon was "morally" if not legally culpable, and a court-martial a surer means to execution than civil trial. Eyre was praised by the white planters and by some in Britain for his swift suppression of the rebellion. The British government also supported Eyre, although it recognized the extreme violence of the suppression and undertook an inquiry into the events.

Mill was from the beginning a prominent member of the Jamaica Committee, which was organized in December 1865 to monitor and publicize the official inquiry into Governor Eyre's actions; this group was for the next several years at the center of efforts to see Eyre tried and punished for his role in the rebellion's suppression.[111] Mill took over the committee's chairmanship in July, 1866 when a majority of its members decided to pursue a private prosecution of Eyre; the previous chairman, Charles Buxton, resigned in the belief that a statement by the House of Commons deploring the Jamaican authorities' use of excessive force constituted a sufficient response. Mill remained chairman of the committee until it was disbanded in 1869.

Mill gave two speeches in the House of Commons demanding that the most egregious offenders among the Jamaican authorities be brought to criminal trial, and in his *Autobiography*, he described the second as "probably . . . the best of my speeches in Parliament" (*CW* 1:281). In that speech, Mill reiterated the findings of the government commission—the killings, floggings, and burnings of Jamaicans and their houses had been unjustified, reckless, "some of them positively barbarous," wanton, and cruel—and demanded a criminal trial for the perpetrators (*CW* 28:107). He apologized for speaking of such acts in the "moderate language" appropriate to parliamentary debate, and indeed Mill's evident fury is largely blanketed under sober and legalistic language.[112]

Mill's private correspondence described far more passionately his outrage at the crimes and his belief that the punishment of Eyre was, as he put it in a letter to Edwin Arnold of the *Daily Telegraph*, a matter of "transcendant importance." "Not only every principle I have," he wrote to Arnold, "but the honour and character of England for generations to come, are at stake in the condign punishment of the atrocities of which, by their own not confession, but boast, the Jamaica authorities have been guilty."[113] In later letters Mill insisted, as Burke had done, that unless the atrocities were punished, the British political establishment would share the perpetrators' guilt,[114] and he argued that if the "abominations" of Jamaica were not punished, Britain would have no moral authority to denounce massacres committed by the Russian government or French revolutionaries.[115]

Both Mill's own writings and the committee documents that went out over his name nearly always describe the crimes, and the dangers they represent, as injuries to British subjects, or fellow subjects (or sometimes "citizens"), rather than describing the victims as colonial subjects or in terms of race. His public documents and speeches all seem careful, that is, to avoid analyzing the state's suppression of the Morant Bay rebellion as a specifically colonial event. Mill's language suggests that he meant to insist on the legal equality of colonial subjects with English subjects, though to be sure he did not propose political equality of all Jamaicans with Britons, or their incorporation into the British polity, but rather a reassertion of metropolitan authority over the colony. Eyre and his defenders, for their part, insisted on the inevitability of such events in a tense and racially divided colony.[116] To emphasize the role that racial hostility played in the crimes was potentially to exonerate the perpetrators in the eyes of the British public, which sympathized with the white planter class. By not mentioning race, then, Mill avoided playing into the hands of Eyre's defenders.

Mill himself noted privately that what was important to him was primarily to uphold the broad principle of the rule of law, rather than to rectify injustices done by a small minority of white rulers to their black subjects. In a letter Mill described his second Jamaica speech as "not on this occasion standing up for negroes, or for liberty, deeply as both are interested in this subject—but for the first necessity of human society, law."[117] He reiterated the point in his *Autobiography*:

> There was much more at stake than only justice to the Negroes, imperative as was that consideration. The question was, whether the British dependencies, and eventually perhaps Great Britain itself, were to be under the government of law, or of military license; whether the lives and persons of British subjects are at the mercy of any two or three officers however raw and inexperienced or reckless and brutal, whom a panic-stricken Governor or other functionary may assume the right to constitute into a so-called Court Martial. (*CW* 1:281)

Mill was unafraid to confront the venomous racism increasingly prevalent in British society: he had done so quite forcefully in 1850, when he responded to Thomas Carlyle's "Occasional Discourse on the Negro Question."[118] Having derided freed British slaves as little more than beasts—"black Quashees" "with their beautiful muzzles up to the ears in pumpkins"—Carlyle articulated, with a rancor that few Britons (and none so well known) had dared, the racism spreading throughout British society after the abolition of slavery in the British colonies. Carlyle declared the racial superiority of the "Saxon British," ridiculed members of British philanthropic and abolitionist circles (as well as utilitarians) as "windy sentimentalists," and obliquely proposed a return to slavery.

Mill responded by denouncing as "damnable" Carlyle's doctrine "that one kind of human beings are born servants to another kind." He declared himself with that half of "all thinking persons, who have attended to the subject, [who] either doubt or positively deny" the biological inferiority of blacks (*CW* 21:92–93). Mill went on to argue against Carlyle's racism on both factual and moral grounds. As an empirical matter, he said, the "analytical examination of human nature" demonstrated that differences among human beings were largely attributable to environment and not nature, and it was not known, given the state of science, what differences might exist by nature. Mill held that the moral argument, however, was the more important: even if whites were proven to be superior to blacks, they would not have the right to "subdue them by force, or circumvent them by superior skill." These arguments, and the essay as a whole, represented important responses to Carlyle's position. Yet Mill did not question Carlyle's claim that blacks were, for the moment, intellectually and culturally inferior to whites: rather, he disputed the cause of that inferiority and its implications, claiming that it was not natural but accidental and temporary, and that it did not license tyranny but called for humanity and a project of improvement.

In the Eyre case, Mill's motives in avoiding public mention of the racial and colonial context were in part strategic: he feared he would lose the sympathy of the British public if he were to insist on the racial aspect of the crimes.[119] His insistence on the atrocity as a general one, against British subjects, rather than a particular one, against blacks or colonial subjects, reflects a principled position.[120] In his second Jamaica speech, Mill declared that "if any Government or local administrator that chooses to proclaim martial law can place us under this regimen, we have gained little by our historical struggles, and the blood that has been shed for English liberties has been shed to little purpose." He went on to suggest that all Englishmen were threatened by Eyre's actions.[121] The use of the term "we" is an inclusive gesture; it signals Mill's intention to identify with the victims and to admit all residents of Jamaica to the protection of British laws and rights. His speeches and writings on the subject can be read as an effort to alter the British public's understanding of their rights and obligations as citizens: to enlist their support for the victimized *British subjects*, rather than for the white perpetrators that racial sympathy and national sympathy might otherwise lead them to defend.

Mill's statements about the violation of law in Jamaica tread a difficult line, however. His decision not to discuss the colonial and racial distinctiveness of the Eyre episode left him incapable of articulating and confronting the peculiar injustices of colonial rule. Although martial law was wholly a colonial phenomenon in the nineteenth century, Mill discussed the abuse of martial law as simply a problem in British law, and as a threat to specifically English liberties.[122] There seems something disingenuous in his suggestion that British state power would be turned abusively against (white) Englishmen in just the way it had been on black and mixed-race Jamaicans, for it was widely known that the executions were due to racial fear, mistrust, or hatred on the part of a white population of approximately 13,000 toward a former slave population of over 350,000.[123] Moreover, Mill did not in fact believe that Jamaica (or India) was fit to be governed by unmodified British law (or to share "English liberties") but rather that both should remain under a colonial regime insulated from British politics and largely unaccountable to their inhabitants.

What should we make of Mill's apparent worry that abuses of martial law in Jamaica threatened Britons at home? There were, it is true, some claims by conservative writers that police repression would or should increase, not only to suppress Fenian activity in Ireland (a country situated uneasily between colony and metropole in the British mind), but also in response to labor unrest in England itself. In addition, the Eyre debates were going on at a particularly precarious moment in the class relations of metropolitan Britain: there had been well-publicized demonstrations by workingmen, and in 1866 several men were killed when a group of laborers confronted police officers in an effort to enter Hyde Park. Some of the most antidemocratic Tories, such as Carlyle, had even suggested that martial law might have to be called in Britain to deal with these protests (which were mostly nonviolent, however frightening to the middle classes).[124] Still, most English participants in the debate agreed that martial law was wholly inappropriate and unnecessary in England. The Jamaica Committee's own spokesman on the issue of martial law, Frederic Harrison, argued in a series of letters to the *Daily News* that Eyre's abuse of martial law was "insidious" not because it was likely to lead to the oppression of Englishmen, but because such martial law powers "are meant to maintain our vast unresting empire."[125] Martial law remained utterly improbable as a domestic policy, though British colonial rulers had frequent and violent recourse to it.

Not only was it unlikely that martial law would be declared and abused in England, then, but Mill's insistence on this supposed danger appears a digression from the real danger: that martial law would continue to be abused in the colonies. It might be said that Mill's suggestion that Eyre's actions threatened the English themselves was intended not as a particular worry about the declaration of martial law but as a more general claim that despotism practiced abroad will come home to roost; this was a favorite theme of Burke's and of other critics of conquest such as Benjamin Constant. But Mill did not articulate the worry in such terms and, it seems, could not have done so, precisely because he avoided making a critique of colonial abuse as part of an overall system or structure of power.

Mill's speech was unusual among those of the July 31 debate in avoiding mention of the racial and colonial context of the authorities' violence. Not just Eyre's defenders but also many of his critics called attention to the risk of official atrocities in a colony divided by racial hostility. Indeed nearly all the other speakers, Eyre's critics and allies, referred to the participants as "negroes" and "the white inhabitants of Jamaica" and openly discussed the racial aspect of the crisis, though of course with different purposes. Eyre's defenders, such as Baillie Cochrane, declared that the authorities had acted courageously in the face of a murderous mob intent on massacring the island's white inhabitants.[126] And Eyre's foes, such as Charles Buxton, insisted on the racial animus of the white colonial authorities.[127]

The Liberal M.P. William Edward Forster (named colonial under-secretary in 1865) spoke most directly and perceptively to the role of race in the riot and its suppression. Although Forster did not go as far as Mill in demanding a trial and punishment for Eyre, it was he rather than the more radical speakers (Mill and Buxton) who acknowledged the temptation to abuse of power inherent in colonial rule.

> Now, how was it that Governor Eyre, whom he believed to be a humane and conscientious man, sanctioned proceedings of this kind, and how was it that British officers perpetrated atrocities from which they would have shrunk had the victims been white people? The reason was that they were not free, and he did not know that he himself or any Member of the House would have been free, from the race feeling—the feeling of contempt for what was regarded as an inferior race. This, however, only made it the more incumbent upon Parliament, able as it was to sit calmly in judgment upon these things, to affirm that there ought not to be one code of morality for one colour, and another code for another. Some persons, it was true, maintained that we could not afford to deal with other races on the principle of morality; but surely ferocity was as unwise towards black men as towards white; surely justice and mercy were as much an act of duty towards one class as towards another. It was because he felt that the fault was not so much that of an individual as of a feeling to which we were all tempted in dealing with weaker races that he wished the House to protest against the proceedings in Jamaica, and to condemn that misuse of strength to which there was always a temptation.[128]

This was a strikingly forthright admission that disdain for Britain's nonwhite subjects ran so deep in British society that it would be a continual challenge to maintain anything like justice toward them. This was the case Burke had made repeatedly with regard to India.

Forster gave what was in many ways a more realistic depiction of the extent and nature of the Jamaican abuses than did Mill. By comparing them with what had occurred under recent declarations of martial law in other colonies—such as Ceylon in 1848 and Cephalonia in the Ionian Islands in 1859—Forster set Eyre's actions in the appropriate colonial context. He noted that the extent of the official violence was far greater in Jamaica than in the other colonial cases, though the insurrection that sparked it was more limited and sooner quelled. Nor did he suggest, as Mill did, that British law was identical in Britain and Jamaica, or that the abuses in Jamaica could be said to presage what might happen to "us" as well. Forster effectively made the case, then, that the actions of Eyre and his deputies were extraordinarily violent even in colonial terms.

As the passage above illustrates, Forster understood colonial rule as generally tending to the abuse of power, which in his mind therefore somewhat extenuated Eyre's own guilt. To Forster, the abuses Eyre both oversaw and permitted to occur were almost inherent in the situation rather than the result of an individual vice or crime warranting prosecution. At the same time, his attention to the specifically colonial nature of the abuse led him recommend a more sweeping reform of colonial law that would make future governors less likely to sanction similar atrocities. Mill, in contrast, limited his target to an abuse of British law by a small group of egregious offenders, and thus did not make this broader critique of colonial practice available to himself. It might be argued that Mill did not need to take up the colonial dimension of abuse in his speech because his colleagues had already addressed it at length. Still, as I have noted, his speech is strikingly different from the others even in its terminology: in the context of the other speeches, Mill's decision not to refer to the race of the participants seems a conscious one that demands explanation.

Why, then, did Mill refrain from analyzing the events in Jamaica as peculiarly colonial? He seems to have avoided following any line of inquiry that might call into question British colonial rule more broadly, or one suggesting that British power over large populations of disfranchised non-European subjects was prone to abuses that had to be understood in terms of colonial relations.[129] Indeed, perhaps Mill responded to Eyre's actions with such vehemence precisely because Governor Eyre's suppression of the Jamaican rebellion so dramatically challenged Mill's trust in the colonial bureaucracy. Unless the perpetrators of the Jamaica atrocities were brought to trial, he argued in Parliament, "we are giving up altogether the principle of government by law, and resigning ourselves to arbitrary power."[130] And yet Mill sought to reassert the rule of law through the *criminal* law, and by tightening *metropolitan* constraints on unrepresentative local legislatures, rather than aspiring to render the Jamaican government more accountable to its subjects.[131] Rather than considering the extension of suffrage to Jamaican blacks, Mill sought a solution in the imposition of reforms through the colonial authority.[132] Such a stance is all the more striking given Mill's efforts during this very period to see suffrage in Britain radically extended, as I discuss further in chapter 8.

Mill's insistence in his speeches and public writings on the importance of restoring the rule of law by punishing Eyre seems to stem from his desire to preserve the rectitude of the colonial administration, to insulate it from the corruptions of the local white ruling class. In his public speeches and Jamaica Committee documents, he concentrated solely on the criminal culpability of Eyre himself rather than on broader reforms of Jamaican administration. Mill's involvement in the Eyre controversy suggests that even at the moment in his career when he was most passionately involved in an effort to redress colonial abuses, he resisted perceiving the deeper moral and political failings of British colonial rule. This can be seen, I would argue, in Mill's determination to see that Eyre should be held personally responsible for the atrocities, as a criminal, combined with his reluctance to discuss the suppression of the Morant Bay riot as a failing of colonial governance more broadly.

It is worth noting that while Mill insisted that a colonial government directed from London was certain to be better for *Jamaica* than parliamentary self-government with black suffrage, he pointed to the Jamaican atrocities to support an argument for the enfranchisement of *American* blacks. Just two weeks after news of the rebellion had first reached London, Mill reiterated his support for American blacks' enfranchisement in a letter to an American correspondent, Rowland Hazard, writing: "What has just taken place in Jamaica might be used as a very strong argument against leaving the freedmen to be legislated for by their former masters."[133] He argued that the federal government of the United States should be free to impose laws on the newly defeated South, but he also maintained that the oppression of American blacks could be overcome only if the former slaves were granted suffrage. Still, Mill maintained that in the case of Jamaica, England should "suspend the power of local legislation altogether, until the necessary internal reforms have been effected by the mother country."

The events in Jamaica appear to have prompted Mill to reflect more closely than he had ever done on the persistent problem of European settlers' oppression of colonized populations. Although Mill never thoroughly confronted the systematic injustices or pitfalls of British colonial rule, he began in 1866 to raise what he called "the universal colonial question—what to do with the aborigines," and to suggest that the British belief in the inferiority of Britain's non-European subjects was an important source of colonial injustices.[134] Indeed it was in this period for the first time that Mill criticized the part the British had played in sparking the Sepoy Rebellion, which had occurred nearly a decade earlier and about which he had said almost nothing in his letters at the time.[135] He believed, he now wrote, that English colonists generally "think any injustice or tyranny whatever, legitimate against what they call inferior races, at least if those races do not implicitly submit to their will."[136]

We find an uncommon moment of reflection about the connections among British atrocities in a variety of colonial settings (or in the case of the American South, British sympathy with atrocities in a feudal system of racial oppression) in a letter of October 1866. Although the letter suggests that Mill had been reflecting for some time about a British (or "English") penchant for colonial injustices, this passage is in fact rare in its willingness to confront the problem:

> [M]y eyes were first opened to the moral condition of the English nation (I except in these matters the working classes) by the atrocities perpetrated in the Indian Mutiny & the feelings which supported them at home. Then came the sympathy with the lawless rebellion of the Southern Americans in defence of an institution which is the sum of all lawlessness, as Wesley said it was of all villainy—& finally came this Jamaica business the authors of which from the first day I knew of it I determined that I would do all in my power to bring to justice if there was not another man in Parlt to stand by me. You rightly judge that there is no danger of my sacrificing such a purpose to any personal advancement.[137]

This letter alludes to the colonial dimension of the Jamaica riot's suppression in a way that Mill's public statements resolutely did not. It suggests that Mill was appalled not just by Eyre's brutality, but also by the violence of British sentiments sparked by the episode, and the corruption or degraded state of feeling in Britain that permitted widespread support for colonial and racial violence more generally.[138] Similarly, in a letter of 1868, Mill expressed his fear that the Eyre episode was likely not only to generate resentment of British rule among colonial subjects but even, by its example of violence, "to brutalize our own fellow countrymen."[139]

In his letter to Henry Samuel Chapman about "what to do with the aborigines," Mill confronts in greater depth than perhaps anywhere else the contradictions of colonial governance over a settler colony with a substantial indigenous population.[140] He wrote that while he had hoped the problem would be less severe in New Zealand, "on account of the higher qualities and more civilisable character of the Maoris," experience had shown that English greed for land and contempt for non-Europeans would prove formidable obstacles to good government. In an eloquent and deeply felt statement of the English vice at the heart of the problem, Mill laments "the overbearing and insolent disregard of the rights and feelings of inferiors which is the common characteristic of John Bull when he thinks he cannot be resisted." "Knowing what the English are, when they are left alone with what they think an inferior race," Mill wrote, he could not reconcile himself to relinquishing metropolitan control altogether and giving the colonists a free hand to mistreat the Maoris, as they surely would. He believed the settlers deserved self-government in every other respect. While he felt England had a duty to protect the Maoris from the settlers, however, he worried it would be quite ineffective to grant that self-government and leave the colonial governor as in most respects "a mere ornamental frontispiece," a governor with no other mandate than the protection of the indigenous people.

Thus, in his letter to Chapman, as in his response to the Eyre crisis, Mill struggled with concerns about colonial violence toward non-European subjects as he never had in his Indian career. In neither case did Mill imagine that the reforms necessary to restrain colonial violence might involve accountability to the non-European populations, both of which he seems to have regarded as not yet capable of participating in their own governance. He rested his hope on the rectitude of a colonial administration that he believed could be relied upon to overcome the vices he now understood to be endemic among white colonists.

Conclusion

Mill, for all his radicalism with regard to domestic politics, placed considerable faith in colonial government as a well-intentioned and legitimate despotism designed for the improvement of its subjects. Both his writings on India and his role in the Eyre affair suggest that he hesitated before a full-scale inquiry into the structure of colonial rule and the repeated abuses that structure invited. He avoided such an inquiry even though he came to acknowledge, late in life, a mistrust of British political judgment on colonial matters.

The Eyre episode, for all the humanitarian courage it elicited from Mill, exposes some of the stark contradictions and blind spots intrinsic to his notion of a benevolent imperialism. It seems that by the late 1860s, Mill had begun to perceive that defects in the British (or English) character, the temptations to abuse of power inherent in the situation of colonists, and British disdain for "inferior" peoples, all made colonial injustice a persistent danger. Although profoundly suspicious of local parliaments in stratified colonies, however, Mill did little to suggest how such bodies could be reformed, or what conditions might be imposed to make them more accountable to the populations they governed.

Mill had been elected Liberal M.P. for Westminster on a platform of universal male suffrage, and he had assured his electors of his intent to fight for women's suffrage on the same terms as men's. Yet his belief in the incapacity of non-European subjects for self-rule meant that he failed to argue for—perhaps even to imagine—conditions of accountability to colonial subjects. Until backward peoples were deemed, presumably by European administrators, capable of participating in their own governance, Mill seemed content to rely on colonial administrators themselves for appropriate restraints on the exercise of power. Other than his expressions of mistrust of the local legislature, Mill said little about how progress toward collective self-government in Jamaica might take place. He resorted, as in India, to the tidier and less political solution of administration checked by criminal courts. Mill, that is, tended to regard colonial subjects as objects of administration rather than participants in a political process.

As I argued in chapter 3, Burke used the Hastings trial as a means by which to launch a broad critique of what he saw as a form of rule in which corruption and abuse of power were systemic and possibly ineradicable. Mill, in contrast, chose throughout the Eyre trial largely to avoid the question of whether colonial rule was inherently prone to abuse, and indeed in pursuing Eyre with such vehemence he exonerated the system by pinning blame on what he insisted were the *criminal* actions of a few individuals. Mill was committed to regarding British colonial rule itself as both beneficial for its subjects and innocent of the crimes of its officers. He even went so far as to claim in a discussion of Britain's high-minded international politics that Britain was "incomparably the most conscientious of all nations in our national acts."[141]

Although Mill's attack on Eyre himself displays some of the avenging passion of Burke's prosecution of Hastings, as social criticism Mill's writings on Eyre are somewhat muted. To say that Burke's thoroughgoing critique of British colonial practice was both more perceptive and more political than Mill's is not to claim that it was politically more effective: both Burke and Mill entirely failed to achieve their immediate legal and political aims. In part, of course, these campaigns may have failed simply because both men were considerably more humanitarian than the majority of their audiences. In the case of the Hastings impeachment, Burke was right to think that the British public would be more sympathetic to the British gentleman on trial before them than to his exotic and distant victims. Mill, too, knew that justice for the black and mixed-race population of Jamaica was of less pressing concern to the British public than the preservation of the colony or the security of its white ruling class. Moreover, Mill had to contend with a more jingoistic and racist British culture than Burke ever did: the language of superiority and hostility toward subject peoples was far more widespread and well-entrenched by the second half of the nineteenth century than in Burke's day.[142]

Public criticisms of Burke and Mill during these two trials show how different the nature of the opposition was that each man faced. However widely ridiculed, Burke was grudgingly admired even by his opponents for his humanitarian sympathies.[143] Mill, on the other hand, had to contend with the virulent racism even of respected public figures such as Carlyle (and more moderate racism from Ruskin). Indeed, even those of his contemporaries most sympathetic to colonial subjects thought them hopeless on their own and so remained committed to a belief in the necessity of ameliorative European rule.[144]

Evangelical religion had contributed to the moralizing self-righteousness of the British in their colonies, even among those who did not share evangelical beliefs, and Evangelicals themselves had in the decades before 1860 become increasingly disdainful of their prospective converts. The Sepoy Rebellion in India in 1857–58 had chiefly resulted not in British efforts at reform of their own government (although the Crown did replace the Company as India's direct ruler, the structure of administration remained largely the same), but rather in a hardening of British antagonism toward Indians.[145] Thomas Metcalf has argued that the reformist spirit of earlier decades was replaced by "racial animosities": "Almost without realizing it, the British threw over the whole notion of Indian regeneration and consigned the Indian people to the status of permanent racial inferiority."[146] In such a context, Mill's continued opposition to racist argument and his commitment to benevolent and improving colonial government was perhaps the most ambitious posture liberalism could muster. The Eyre trial gives some indication of the constraints on humanitarian discourse more generally in the nineteenth century.

My claim, then, is not (or not simply) that Mill neglected to see what Burke understood about the abuses inherent in colonial rule, but more broadly that liberal colonial reform itself, and liberal cosmopolitanism, had changed by the mid-nineteenth century. British superiority and the justice of British colonial rule were nearly taken for granted by the bulk of the population by the mid-nineteenth century: a sweeping critique such as Burke undertook was almost inconceivable in Mill's day.[147] This may explain why the Eyre episode, which made obvious to all in Britain the fragility of Jamaican society nearly thirty years after emancipation, did not become the occasion for a more penetrating reexamination of British colonial governance.

Part Three

LIBERALS AND THE TURN TO EMPIRE IN FRANCE

Six

The Liberal Volte-Face in France

Shifting Political Contexts: Britain, France, and Imperial Projects

In France, as in Britain, some of the most influential thinkers in the late eighteenth century—such as Diderot and Voltaire—not only criticized the violence of Europe's imperial practices but also gave voice to a lively skepticism about Europe's pretended superiority over other peoples. Indeed, the French thinkers most critical of European empire such as Diderot and some of his coauthors of the *Histoire des deux Indes* were more categorical than the British critics I have discussed in their denunciation of empire, in part perhaps because it formed part of an uncompromising assault on ancien régime politics by thinkers with no official political role or faith in the fundamental justice of their state.[1] In France as in Britain this critical posture gave way after 1830 to a nearly universal acceptance of colonial rule as a justifiable fact of global politics, and to an assumption of European superiority largely devoid of the earlier generation's respect for non-European or precommercial societies as reasonable forms of social and political organization.

During the Revolution, French political discourse was inflected with a sense of entitlement to empire that stemmed from memories of France's earlier status as a great colonial power, and from the desire to erase the history of defeat by Britain that stretched back to the loss of territory in America, Africa, and India during the Seven Years' War.[2] But despite efforts by revolutionary governments as well as Napoleon to restore the colonial empire, France lost nearly all of its overseas territories during this period: after the Congress of Vienna in 1815, the empire included the islands of Martinique and Guadeloupe in the Caribbean, Réunion, Saint-Pierre-et-Miquelon, as well as several trading posts in India and West Africa.[3] Notwithstanding the revolutionary and imperial wars' disastrous consequences for Europe and for France, Napoleon's defeat only partly discredited his expansionist politics in the eyes of subsequent political leaders. Napoleon's imperial ambitions in Europe and beyond—including his brief foray into Egypt—were remembered with great ambivalence by many Frenchmen, who sought to retain the national confidence imparted by Napoleonic military victories while distancing themselves from "Bonapartism." The Restoration government, in an effort to recapture France's prior glory as well as to prove itself an adequate replacement for Napoleon, sought without success to rebuild the empire in India, Indochina and West Africa. The Restoration's major colonial achievement, the capture of the city of Algiers from the Ottoman Empire in 1830, took place just a month before the fall of the Bourbon regime.[4] The 1820s and 1830s, then, first under the Bourbon Restoration and then under the July Monarchy, saw a rebirth of a transformed "Bonapartism" that involved a politics of foreign expansion, though such expansionist projects were met by widely expressed worries that such adventurism was disastrous for a nation still so unstable at home.

The Revolution had done much to undermine forceful moral criticism of the expansion of French power, however, for it gave birth to the idea that France was the "universal" nation, the nation that represented the future of civilization and was charged with rescuing other peoples from tyranny and ignorance.[5] Condorcet, whose ambivalence toward European empire I discuss below, adhered to a version of this idea; while he criticized European imperial rule as it had been practiced previously, he believed Europeans ought to undertake the civilization of less advanced societies through peaceful settlement in their midst. This national self-understanding underlay debates about France's place in the world throughout the nineteenth century; after midcentury, it issued in a well-developed ideology of France's *mission civilisatrice*.[6]

Because the Revolution and empire continued to overshadow their project, liberals in France during the years of the Bourbon Restoration and the July Monarchy faced practical and rhetorical challenges their counterparts in Britain and America did not. The legacy of revolution and the continuing polarization of French politics during the Restoration meant that for French liberals, the project of building a stable national community in a democratic age was both more urgent and more hazardous than it was for their British counterparts. While liberalism in postrevolutionary France developed with considerable influence from Britain, then, its character and context differed in ways with implications for the development of liberal views on empire.[7]

During their years of insecurity under Napoleon and then the increasingly reactionary politics of the Restoration regimes, liberals developed a challenging critical voice from their position in the opposition. France's domestic turmoil and frequent regime changes encouraged many during the Restoration period to believe that the French ought to avoid the costly and distracting game of imperial expansion and concentrate efforts on building a stable order at home. Benjamin Constant forcefully articulated this suspicion of empire in his assault in 1814 on the spirit of conquest, discussed below.[8] In 1828, the centrist political leader François Guizot echoed Constant in decrying the motiveless conquests he saw throughout modern Europe, writing that adventurers "leave their country, . . . abandon their proper territory, and plunge—some into Germany, others into Italy, others still into Africa—without any other motive than their personal fantasy."[9]

When the liberals came to power after the July Revolution in 1830, however, their achievements did not live up to the promise of their earlier rhetoric, for, as G. A. Kelly has written, French liberalism's "brilliance in opposition was matched by a mediocrity in power."[10] This fading of liberals' sharp critical voice was reflected too in liberal views on conquest. The biting criticism some leveled at expansionist politics before 1830 turned, after the July Revolution, to a belief among many liberals that the French nation should assume its rightful place among world powers and that this status would require colonial expansion. France's new colonial aspirations centered on Algeria, where the French acquired a hold in the city of Algiers in 1830 and quickly extended their possessions, so that by 1847 they controlled the territory of the former Ottoman Regency of Algiers.[11] Guizot, like most of his colleagues and countrymen, soon became a supporter of the French conquest of Algeria. He later recalled that although he had sometimes balked at the violent methods of General Thomas-Robert Bugeaud, the man behind much of the Algerian conquest of the 1830s and 1840s, "As to the necessity of completely subjugating the Arabs, and of extending French rule throughout the whole extent of Algeria, I agreed with the opinion of General Bugeaud."[12] Bugeaud himself, as a member of the Chamber of Deputies, had been deeply critical in the 1830s of the French presence in Algeria, despite his own military command in the colony. His position, too, had transformed by the 1840s, so that in 1845, he was advocating, in the words of his biographer, "widespread liquidation of Muslim Algerians."[13] On the left, Louis Blanc agreed with other French socialists when he argued that "to spread out, to overflow, is a duty. What France fails to get in heroic adventures she will get in popular risings. Her prosperity is a necessary guarantee against internal troubles."[14] The very term *impérialisme* began at this moment to express aspirations for a renewal of the sense of national greatness the French had enjoyed with Napoleon's conquests. Richard Koebner has argued that it was in 1840 that the French (and even the exiled German Heinrich Heine) first dissociated the term *imperialism* from Bonapartism and used the former word to signify the emperor's military glories, in isolation from his broader political program.[15]

During the 1830s and 1840s, as French power in Algeria gradually but steadily expanded, the French empire found one of its most influential political advocates in Alexis de Tocqueville. By 1837, when he first began writing about Algeria, Tocqueville was the newly celebrated author of *Democracy in America*; he would devote a considerable portion of his years as a prominent member of the Chamber of Deputies, from 1839 to 1851, to examining the French conquest of Algeria and the consolidation of rule there, and he became one of the Chamber's foremost experts on the subject.[16] Tocqueville's defense of the violent conquest and settlement of Algeria must be read in light of his own avowed belief in human equality, his self-understanding as a humanitarian and a defender of the principles of 1789, and his commitment to an equitable and honorable international politics.[17] As a thinker justly celebrated for his defense of local self-government and a kind of pluralism, Tocqueville is a particularly apt subject for a consideration of the reasons that liberalism was so slow to incorporate deep respect for cultural pluralism into its defense of pluralism more generally. I argue below and in chapter 7 that Tocqueville's anxieties about France's halting and perilous transition to democracy and his often bleak account of modern European society led him to embrace an imperial solution that, in his most perceptive moments, he knew to be specious.

Tocqueville's writings on and political involvement in French colonial expansion in the 1830s and 1840s were both significant in their own right and representative of a striking development in the liberalism of his age. His political career as a defender of the French conquest and rule of Algeria, even if this meant great violence toward indigenous Algerians, helps us understand the eclipse, during the wave of imperial expansion in the mid-nineteenth century, of the earlier suspicion of empire exemplified by thinkers from Diderot to Constant. Anti-imperial arguments still existed, but the leftist politicians who expounded them, such as Amédée Desjobert, discussed in the fourth section of this chapter, held a marginal position in the national debate. Tocqueville, who regarded himself as a liberal best placed at the center-left of France's political spectrum, was infuriated by the anti-imperialism of those leftist deputies.[18] And if Tocqueville was in many ways an idiosyncratic liberal with a more nuanced and also more equivocal view of the conquest of Algeria than most Frenchmen had, his support for such a project of colonization was widely shared among French liberals.

Condorcet: Progress and the Roots of the *Mission Civilisatrice*

A greatly influential theory of progress that articulated the revolutionary aspiration to liberate the oppressed outside France and to eradicate the backwardness beyond Europe's borders is Condorcet's *Esquisse d'un tableau historique des progrès de l'esprit humain*, written shortly before his death in 1794 and published posthumously in 1795.[19] The *Esquisse* echoes the searing criticism of Europe's violent colonial history that had characterized so much of the innovative political thought of the preceding decades, and at the same time heralds the discourse of benevolent tutelage of backward peoples that was to underpin so many liberal defenses of empire during the nineteenth century. Condorcet, maintaining that "men of all climates [are] equals and brothers by the wish of nature," denounced the subjugation and exploitation of non-Europeans as morally wrong, as violations of human rights and human equality.[20] His narrative of progress, however, generated a moral hierarchy of social stages that conceived of modern European society as morally superior to both ancient and non-European societies, and he believed that Europeans should, and in time would, peacefully civilize the rest of the world. Despite Condorcet's own indictment of Europe's conquests as among the greatest crimes of human history, then, his account of moral and intellectual progress, and his belief that Europeans were destined to undertake the tutelage of backward peoples, were to prove influential among followers such as Comte, Saint-Simon, and, indirectly, J. S. Mill.[21]

Condorcet conceived of progress as a universal process by which error is gradually eliminated as societies attain ever greater truth, both scientific and moral. He held that unlimited progress is a law of nature and that improvement occurs in all fields of human endeavor together: that all the arts and sciences advance in unison, and that technical and intellectual progress brings about moral progress, including increasing respect for human rights in domestic law and international relations. According to Condorcet's essentially linear theory of social development, one can trace humanity's advance from simplicity and moral backwardness to technical sophistication and ever greater humanity and moral and aesthetic subtlety. He was inclined to view "earlier" practices as forms of error or depravity rather than, as Adam Smith saw them, generally reasonable solutions to the changing problems of social life under different modes of subsistence.

Condorcet's rather inexorable theory of progress, and especially his view of societal development as a matter of cognitive advancement and a triumph of reason over error, left little room for respect for the practices of societies deemed to be in earlier stages of development. Although any given nation might slip before continuing its advance, or even cease to exist as a nation, Condorcet maintained, peoples could be ranged along a single continuum:

> All peoples whose history is recorded fall somewhere between our present degree of civilization and that which we still see amongst savage tribes; if we survey in a single sweep the universal history of peoples we see them sometimes making fresh progress, sometimes plunging back into ignorance, sometimes surviving somewhere between these extremes or halted at a certain point,

> sometimes disappearing from the earth under the conqueror's heel, mixing with the victors or living on in slavery, or sometimes receiving knowledge from some more enlightened people in order to transmit it in their turn to other nations, welding an uninterrupted chain between the beginning of historical time and the century in which we live, between the first peoples known to us and the present nations of Europe.[22]

Condorcet's model for societal progress was the development of individual faculties. As he wrote in his introduction to the *Esquisse*, "The progress of the human mind . . . is subject to the same general laws that can be observed in the development of the faculties of individuals, for it is the sum of that development realized in a large number of individuals joined together in society."[23] As we have seen in the thought of William Robertson and James and J. S. Mill, such analogies between societal development and the course of an individual life tended to accompany a conception of progress as a matter of individual cognitive development rather than as a series of changes in patterns of social interaction. Such analogies also tended to support a view of progress as occurring in all areas of life (scientific, political, moral, aesthetic) in lockstep together, and to encourage the notion that members of "backward" societies were like children in need of tutelage.

Condorcet regarded despots and priesthoods as the primary enemies to progress, and his anticlericalism informed the argument of every chapter of the *Esquisse*.[24] Indeed, his anticlericalism even lay behind some of his strongest criticisms of empire, for he blamed many of the moral failings of European imperialism on "the exaggerated proselytism or the intrigues of our priests."[25] Condorcet maintained that many other apparent hindrances to progress, including imperial conquest itself, had proven beneficial in unexpected ways. As Keith Baker has argued, Condorcet conceived of history as a dialectical relation between progress and its obstacles, in which the triumph over any given impediment marked a moment of advancement but also created new obstructions.[26] For all its violence, European imperial expansion contributed to progress, in Condorcet's account, in that it had furnished new truths about humanity and the world and generated the wealth that allowed Old World peoples to overthrow their tyrants or at least to lessen their oppression.[27]

Condorcet also acknowledged, however, that Europe's conquests had occasioned some of the greatest cruelty men had ever visited on their fellows, and he echoed Montesquieu's claim that conquest "always leaves an immense debt to be discharged if human nature is to be repaid."[28] The discoveries of the New World and the new trade routes to Asia and Africa, Condorcet wrote, "will have repaid humanity what they have cost it only when Europe renounces her oppressive and avaricious system of monopoly commerce."[29] European imperialism had been characterized by "our trade monopolies, our treachery, our murderous contempt for men of another colour or creed, the insolence of our usurpations." The foolish policy of chartering monopoly companies not only increased the oppression of indigenous peoples, Condorcet argued, but compromised the liberty of conquering nations as well.[30] Condorcet stressed the greed and fanatical proselytism that drove the conquerors as the primary evils of imperialism. Citing the "depopulation of the New World" as well as religious wars and massacres in Europe, Condorcet lamented that "this stage in our history"—the eighth of ten stages, running from the invention of printing to the time of Descartes—"was more than any other sullied by terrible atrocities."[31]

But although Condorcet objected to the violence of imperial conquest and in particular to the mistrust it created, he never questioned Europeans' sense of superiority itself, or their dismissal of other social and cultural arrangements. Condorcet did not doubt that Europeans could (and should) civilize non-Europeans. Indeed, although he was sure they would do so more effectively when they themselves had progressed further, he believed that even their blunders contributed to progress—just as the Crusades, although wrong, had furthered progress by bringing Arabic science to the West.

> Can we doubt that either the wisdom or the senseless discords of European nations will add to the effects of the slow but inevitable progress of their colonies, and will soon bring about the independence of the New World? And that then the European population [in the colonies], spreading rapidly over that immense territory, will either civilize or make disappear, even without conquering them, the savage nations who still inhabit vast tracts of its land?[32]

Because Condorcet saw freedom as the foundational good, the good that underlay both scientific and moral progress, he did not lament the disappearance of societies he saw as less free: thus the "peaceful removal" of Amerindian savages seemed to him a good. Europeans

> have destroyed the feelings of respect and goodwill that the superiority of our knowledge and the benefits of our commerce at first won for us. But doubtless the moment approaches when, no longer presenting ourselves as only tyrants or corrupters, we shall become for them useful instruments or generous liberators.[33]

The violence of their imperial past had made Europeans' civilizing mission more difficult; only with time and the exercise of self-restraint could they hope to win back the trust they needed to improve Asians and Africans.

Condorcet described his vision of the colonial future in his utopian chapter on the "tenth stage" of human history, the one he imagined would succeed his own corrupt and violent era. "Peoples will learn that they cannot become conquerors without losing their liberty; that permanent confederations are their only means of maintaining their independence; and that they must seek security and not power. Gradually commercial prejudices will fade away: and a false mercantile interest will lose its ghastly power to drench the earth in blood and to ruin nations under pretext of enriching them."[34] Both the improved moral sense of the Europeans and their better understanding of their own self-interest would lead them to treat conquered peoples with greater respect and enable them more effectively to civilize and liberate all non-Europeans. European "brigands" would give way to "colonies of citizens who will spread, through Africa and Asia, the principles and the example of the liberty, enlightenment, and reason of Europe." Monks who had spread nothing but "shameful superstition" would be replaced by men who would enlighten other nations about their interests and their rights. "Zeal for truth is also one of the passions," Condorcet notes, "and it will turn its efforts to distant countries, once there are no longer crass prejudices to combat and shameful errors to dissipate at home" (326–27). The "immense distance" separating African "barbarism" and savage "ignorance" from the summits of civilization in France and Anglo-America would eventually disappear, through the efforts of such benevolent and enlightened European colonists (320).

In the *Esquisse*, Condorcet identifies these European civilizers as "colonies of citizens." Although he does not discuss their political or legal relationship to the peoples among whom they are to settle and whom they are to lead to enlightenment, he imagines the process of civilization as a largely peaceful one undertaken with the acquiescence—indeed often at the behest—of the non-Europeans to be assisted. As in several passages cited above, Condorcet again notes, seemingly without qualms, that some of the most "savage" tribes are likely to "disappear" altogether.

> These vast lands are inhabited partly by large tribes who seem to require nothing, in order to civilize themselves, but to receive from us the means, who wait only to find brothers amongst the European nations to become their friends and disciples; partly by races oppressed by sacred despots or dull-witted conquerors, and who for so many centuries have cried out to be liberated; partly by tribes living in a condition of almost total savagery in a climate whose harshness repels the sweet blessings of civilization and deters those who would teach them its benefits; and finally, by conquering hordes who know no other law but force, no other profession but piracy. The progress of these two last classes of people will be slower and stormier; and perhaps it will even be that, reduced in number as they are driven back by civilized nations, they will finally disappear imperceptibly or merge into them.[35]

Notwithstanding its eloquent denunciation of Europe's history of colonial violence, Condorcet's *Esquisse* bequeathed to its nineteenth-century readers a faith in the superiority of European civilization, a disdain for non-European cultures (alongside a commitment to human biological equality), and a certainty that Europeans' enlightened morality could and soon would replace the benighted cultures of other parts of the world through a nonoppressive process of tutelage. The global future Condorcet presents in the "Tenth Epoch" suggests a civilizing enterprise that might have looked something like the imperial liberalism of the decades to come, first among British liberals and then later in France: well-meaning, self-confident, and relatively intolerant of cultural difference.

Constant and the Distrust of Empire

We find a more penetrating critique of the systematic and unavoidable injustices of European expansion in the writings of Benjamin Constant, who witnessed—as Condorcet did not—the ruin wrought by the wars of the revolutionary and Napoleonic years. Constant's 1814 essay *De l'esprit de conquête et de l'usurpation dans leurs rapports avec la civilisation européenne* is at once a forceful assault on Napoleon's militarism and a more sweeping denunciation of any policy of conquest as inappropriate to the modern era. Constant criticizes conquest by republican states as an unjust and hypocritical denial of others' right to govern themselves, but the essay focuses above all on the dangerous implications of conquest not for the conquered, but for the liberty of the conquering people themselves. Peaceful trade, Constant argues, is the more efficient way of "possessing what is desired" by members of modern societies. Constant's essay on conquest, like many of his later speeches in the Chamber of Deputies under the Bourbon Restoration, expressed a preoccupation that was to become characteristic of nineteenth-century French liberals: how to build a stable, cohesive liberal society in the wake of revolution and Napoleonic dictatorship. A number of Constant's writings and speeches from *The Spirit of Conquest*—Constant's most theoretically rich treatment of the dangers and injustices of expansionism—until the time of his death demonstrate his engagement with problems of European imperial expansion and questions of progress, civilization, and racial difference.

Constant published the *Spirit of Conquest* as two pamphlets in Hanover in January 1814, shortly after Napoleon's defeat at the battle of Leipzig and with the emperor's conquering sweep across Europe clearly in mind. Constant had supported Napoleon's coup of the Eighteenth Brumaire in 1799, and then served as a member of Napoleon's Tribunate, but after he was expelled from government in 1802, Constant lived in "semi-voluntary exile" until Napoleon's own abdication and exile to Elba in April 1814, just a few months after the publication of *The Spirit of Conquest.*[36] When Napoleon escaped from Elba in February 1815 and returned to Paris for the Hundred Days, he considered imprisoning Constant but instead appointed him as an adviser and asked him to draft "a model legislative design for a constitutional monarchy." Constant's startling willingness to serve the man he had so lately castigated for authoritarianism has been explained by Napoleon's charisma and Constant's lack of alternatives, which together may have led Constant to persuade himself that he could be instrumental in bringing about a liberal regime under Napoleon.[37]

After the second restoration of Louis XVIII, Constant served as a deputy from 1819 until 1822, when he lost his seat; he was reelected to the Chamber in 1824 and served until his death in December 1830.[38] He welcomed the July Revolution of 1830 that installed the constitutional Orleanist monarchy, though he was not offered a position in the government. During his years in the Chamber, Constant was a leading figure of the liberal opposition to the Bourbon regime and its ministries, which became increasingly reactionary, especially after Charles X took the throne in 1824. He described the slave trade as "the most atrocious crime of which a malefactor can be guilty" and was a prominent critic of the government's failure, despite France's ostensible acquiescence with the recent British ban on the trade, to prevent French merchants from trafficking in slaves.[39] Constant also attacked French colonial policy in the West Indies: he accused the government of complicity with the white colonists' racism and with their disdain for French law and the rights of freed blacks in Martinique. He also called for complete civil and political equality for free blacks.

The immediate referent of the *Spirit of Conquest* is Napoleon's expansion across Europe and his militarization of French society, but the essay addresses questions of imperial conquest and its effects on commercial society in far broader terms.[40] In words that suggest the global scope of the phenomenon he warns against, Constant speaks of the government's desire to "conquer the world," "to acquire remote countries, the possession of which will add nothing to national prosperity," and he describes the conquering soldiers as "victims, doomed to fight and die at the far ends of the earth."[41] Constant differentiates "legitimate self-defense," which he describes as an ennobling and glorious form of war, from the aimless, ignoble, and uncivilized project of unlimited expansion: "It is one thing to defend one's fatherland, another to attack people who themselves have a fatherland to defend. The spirit of conquest seeks to confuse these two ideas. Some governments, when they send their armies from one pole to the other, still talk about the defence of their hearths; one would think they call all the places to which they set fire their hearths."[42] The sarcasm of this work recalls the language of the most bitter eighteenth-century critics of empire, including Diderot, Burke, and Herder. As an articulation of a liberal pluralist's perception of the injustices and dangers of imperial expansion, the *Spirit of Conquest* stands in striking contrast to the enthusiasm for conquest that Tocqueville and many other French liberals would express just a few decades later, when they faced the possibility of a French empire in Algeria.

Constant describes modern society as characterized by free commercial activity, a sphere of local self-government, diversity within the nation, and, above all individual liberty and a commitment by individuals to their own self-interest and material well-being. In such a context, he argues, a policy of war and conquest can only be a "gross and disastrous anachronism," a violation of the interests of the vast majority of the population.[43] The influence of Scottish Enlightenment historicism in which Constant had been steeped during his education in Edinburgh is apparent in his arguments that different laws and mores are appropriate for different eras of societal development and that war and conquest, if appropriate for certain historical periods or types of society, are incompatible with modern commercial and political society.[44] In addition to violating the interests of modern citizens in peace and commerce, he argues, the project of expansion undermines modern liberty by increasing the power of the state at the expense of the individual, the military at the expense of citizens, and the central government at the expense of localities.

When a modern state cultivates the habit of conquest, he maintains, increasingly dominant military men become estranged from and contemptuous of the liberties of civilian life. To the army, "[L]aws are superfluous subtleties, the forms of social life just so many insupportable delays. . . . Unanimity seems to them as necessary as it is for troops to wear the same uniform. Opposition, for them, is disorder."[45] Despotism and conquest abroad, he argues, contradict and subvert freedom at home, for men who have been corrupted by the inordinate power of military rule will undermine domestic liberties in their turn. Such arguments echo Burke's persistent warning against the corruption of domestic politics by "nabobs" who had gained fantastic fortunes and learned habits of despotism in India. Indeed, Constant's admiring reference to Burke's speeches in the Hastings trial suggests that he may known and been influenced by Burke's arguments.[46]

Constant warns not simply against the abuse of blunt military power in the domestic arena, but more subtly against the danger that governments will manipulate public opinion and manufacture support for imprudent expansionist projects. Given the antagonism between expansionism and modern citizens' desire for peace and prosperity, Constant maintains, those who desire aggression will inevitably corrupt democratic politics, as they seek to persuade citizens—through "vain pretexts and scandalous lies"—to support enterprises patently contrary to the people's interests. Constant favored extension of the franchise, but he warned that this process could fuel French militarism and expansionism, as broader swaths of the population became politically active and susceptible to the blandishments of cynical politicians. He skillfully predicted the direction the French debate would take when he suggested that political leaders would exploit the French people's insecurity as a nation with seductive talk of national honor:

> Even whilst abandoning itself to its grandiose projects, the government would hardly dare to tell the nation: "Let us march to conquer the world!" It would reply with one voice: "We have no wish to conquer the world."
>
> Instead it would talk of national independence, of national honour, of the rounding off of frontiers, of commercial interests, of precautions dictated by foresight, and what next? The vocabulary of hypocrisy and injustice is inexhaustible. . . . It would talk of national honour, as if a nation's honour were injured because other nations retain their own.[47]

Here as throughout the *Spirit of Conquest*, Constant anticipates some of the very arguments and rhetorical appeals Tocqueville would deploy in defense of the conquest of Algeria, most notably a relative and jealous conception of national honor that regards any release of conquered territories as damaging to the nation's international reputation.

Constant insists that popular participation in policies of conquest is invariably reluctant, arguing for instance that the French people universally—if silently—opposed Napoleon's militarism.[48] Still, the *Spirit of Conquest* also betrays Constant's fear that the modern nation may come to play an active role in policies of conquest, if its government manages, through "sophism and imposture" to "disturb [the nation's] reason, pervert its judgement and overturn all its ideas."[49] Peoples, like princes, can succumb to the temptations of the "chimerical glory" of conquest, and of "an equally chimerical uniformity" that leads them to seek to obliterate national and provincial diversity, and a popular government can rule just as tyrannically as a prince over subjugated provinces.

> The conquerors of our days, whether peoples or princes, wish their empire to present an appearance of uniformity, upon which the proud eye of power may travel without meeting any unevenness that could offend or limit its view. The same code of law, the same measures, the same regulations, and if they could contrive it gradually, the same language, this is what is proclaimed to be the perfect form of social organization. Religion is an exception; perhaps because it is despised, being seen as a worn-out error that should be left to die in peace.

> But this is the only exception. And it is made up for by separating religion as far as possible from the interests of the country.[50]

Although the liberty of the conquering nation is Constant's paramount concern in this essay, a commitment to the political and cultural autonomy of the various subject peoples also underlies his critique of conquest. Just as French regions should preserve considerable cultural autonomy and local attachments in the name of political liberty, he maintains, so should other peoples be protected from conquest and from foreign efforts to impose freedom or "better" laws on them. A people's attachments to their particular laws and culture have normative weight for Constant both because such attachments can shield subjects from the despotism of a centralized state and thus serve liberty, and because they serve as a source of a nation's "sense of its own value and dignity." Laws venerated as inherited from ancestors have greater moral effect than new laws, he argues, so that a population's regard for its laws can be more valuable than the specific content of those laws. "Even if what you put in its place is of greater value, the fact that the people respected what you are taking away from it, while you impose your own improvement upon it by force, the result of your operation is simply to make it commit an act of cowardice that demeans and demoralizes it."[51] He notes that tradition does not legitimate patent injustice: no argument from tradition can legitimate slavery or other practices that have clear victims.[52] This line of argument places Constant in sympathy with thinkers such as Burke and Herder, whose estimation of custom made them wary of radical innovation (although by no means of reform itself) and critical of the presumptions of ostensibly benevolent conquerors; he was to reiterate such a view in his late essay on Charles Dunoyer, as I discuss below.[53] Constant's attention to the political role of local culture and his commitment to the preservation of such cultures differentiate his liberalism from that of Mill, who, as we have seen, believed many local cultures would have to be effaced and local loyalties broken down in the process of building national states, and who believed that nothing was lost in the amalgamation of "backward" peoples such as the Basques and Bretons into "civilized" national societies such as France.[54]

Constant singles out as particularly hypocritical and delusory the "export" of the French Revolution, when French conquests were disguised as benevolent liberations, and injustice and aggression were masked by moralistic language:

> The French revolution saw the invention of a pretext for war previously unknown, that of freeing peoples from the yoke of their governments, which were supposed to be illegitimate and tyrannical. On this pretext, death was brought among men, some of who lived quietly under institutions softened by time and

> habit while others had enjoyed for several centuries all the benefits of liberty. Forever shameful age, when an infamous government inscribed sacred words on its guilty standards, troubled peace, violated independence, destroyed the prosperity of its innocent neighbours, adding to the scandal of Europe by its lying protestations of respect for the rights of men and zeal for humanity! The worst of all conquests is the hypocritical one, says Machiavelli, as if he had foreseen our history.[55]

Constant notes that such hypocrisy corrupts both public and private morality among the conquering people, even, and perhaps especially, when the "lies of authority"—the pretexts for aggression—fail to deceive the public. For the populace, seeing hypocrisy and deception as routes to praise and greatness for their leaders, will imitate those men in their own "more subaltern" sphere and learn to lie not only out of self-interest, but also to gratify their amour propre.[56]

The *Spirit of Conquest* offers an extraordinarily subtle social-psychological analysis of imperial expansion by modern, quasi-democratic nations. It reiterates many criticisms of empire that can be found among Constant's British and French precursors of the late eighteenth century. It adds to these an innovative account of the disastrous effects such policies of expansion have on the liberty and democratic politics of the aggressor nations. While Burke and other earlier critics of the East India Company nabobs had raised similar concerns that despotism exercised abroad would come home to roost, the question of how imperial expansion would affect democratic politics within Europe was to become ever more urgent during the nineteenth century, as France and Britain extended political participation at home. One of Constant's achievements in the *Spirit of Conquest* was to perceive so early and so clearly the social dynamics, and the moral and political dangers, of expansionism by democratic states.

While the *Spirit of Conquest* is Constant's most sustained treatment of conquest and empire, we find considerations of some of the questions central to European imperial expansion in the nineteenth century—as well as a number of more specific references to non-European societies and colonial policies—in his later essays and speeches.[57] In his discussions of progress and civilization, Constant both suggested that Europe's progressive trajectory was a distinctive achievement and also criticized those who prided themselves on European cultural superiority. He also developed the argument made in passing in the *Spirit of Conquest* that progress cannot and should not be imposed from outside a society through conquest, and he denounced French colonial policy in the West Indies as racist, deeply unjust, and a shocking defiance of principles of human equality and the rule of law.

Constant retained a more sober posture toward progress and perfectibility than Condorcet's, one informed by the historicism of his Scottish education. He described himself as a "partisan" of civilization and, like Condorcet, he described progress as a shedding of oppressive and inegalitarian ideas and practices. At the same time, however, Constant also maintained that ideas and practices can have only "relative perfection," that many practices that appear to be abuses at one time or place are useful and appropriate in another, and that "civilization" entails evils as well as great improvements. Stephen Holmes has rightly emphasized Constant's ambivalence toward progress throughout his career: "Optimism and pessimism, Condorcet and Rousseau, are mixed together promiscuously from his earliest to his latest writings."[58]

Constant's most systematic statement on progress is also his most optimistic; that essay, "De la perfectibilité de l'espèce humaine," has many affinities with Condorcet's writings on the subject.[59] Here Constant maintains that perfectibility is inherent in human nature, that human societies tend to progress toward ever greater equality, and that progress entails the replacement of error and conjecture by truth, sometimes after revolutionary moments in which erroneous opinions mount a temporary resistance but are eventually annihilated.[60] Constant identifies four pivotal moments in the progress of equality in European history: the end of theocracy, the abolition of slavery, the end of feudalism, and the abolition of noble privileges in the French Revolution. Oddly, although he was a consistent opponent of slavery in the West Indies, Constant never acknowledges in the essay that Europeans continue in his day to enslave others; his claim that slavery has been definitively abolished in Europe seems at best incomplete. Indeed, "De la perfectibilité," concerned exclusively with the development of civilization in Europe, considers neither European relations with non-European societies and peoples, nor the development of civilization outside Europe. Another essay published in the same 1829 volume, "Du développement progressif des idées religieuses," posits a similar "law of progression" in Europe, but goes on to argue explicitly that some non-European societies—he names India, Egypt, and Ethiopia—are utterly immobile. Of the Ottoman Empire, whose treatment of the Greeks appalled him, Constant wrote that it was plagued by apathy in ordinary times and "a fanaticism that awakens in great crises, fierce [*farouche*] and stupid."[61]

Constant was one of the most vocal French supporters of the battle for Greek independence from the Ottoman Empire, and the subject provoked in him expressions of contempt for Ottomans as barbaric and fanatical ("une horde de barbares . . . ardente d'enthousiasme") that stand in quite striking contrast to the pluralism of the *Spirit of Conquest* and Constant's earlier writings on religion. In 1825, he wrote an impassioned essay calling for French assistance in the Greek battle for independence from the Ottoman Empire, the *Appel aux nations chrétiennes en faveur des grecs*.[62] The essay shares with the *Spirit of Conquest* a hostility to oppressive foreign rule and a defense of national independence and self-government; Constant frequently used Ottoman rule in Greece as an example of the horrors of foreign despotism. Constant describes the Ottoman Empire in the classic terms of oriental despotism, as a "fatal union between despotism and anarchy"; he dismisses it as a "stationary" country "eclipsed by the progress of civilization" (65–67). He depicts the Ottoman conflict with their Greek subjects in apocalyptic language as a battle between Occident and Orient, Christianity and Islam, civilization and barbarism.[63] Constant's interventionist position was widely shared among British and French intellectuals and, notwithstanding his wariness of military adventurism, comes as little surprise. What startles, given Constant's long-standing cultural and religious pluralism, is the fury of his language and the crudeness of his characterization of Muslim society. Constant's proposal that Napoleon "avait quelque chose d'oriental dans son génie" (67) suggests that his dichotomy between Eastern despotism and Western liberty was in part schematic, that Constant deployed the notion of oriental savagery—as Montesquieu used the concept of oriental despotism—in part to stigmatize a form of *European* rule and not simply to praise Europe at the expense of an "other."[64] At the same time, Constant seems to be invoking the widespread horror of Bonapartism in France to insist on the danger posed by the Ottoman Empire in terms familiar to his audience.

Alongside such essays vaunting the achievements of Europe and casting major non-European societies as stagnant, barbaric, or fanatical, Constant offers a more ambivalent and less triumphalist view of progress and civilization in another essay in the 1829 *Mélanges*, a critique of the writings of the liberal lawyer and political economist Charles Dunoyer.[65] In the course of responding to Dunoyer, Constant treats three themes that bear on the subjects of empire and non-European societies: the benefits and ills of "civilization," racial equality, and the oppressiveness of colonial governments. Dunoyer had reproached Constant for speaking of "excessive civilization." Constant responds that "civilization is in the destiny of the human species" and "one cannot and should not stop it." He notes that Dunoyer is right to criticize those thinkers of the last century—Rousseau, Mably, Voltaire, and Raynal—who "in their hatred for the vexatious institutions of their own civilized country [*patrie policée*]" exaggerated the virtues and pleasures of the savage state; even the ancien régime, Bastille and all, was preferable to "savage life."[66] But Constant insists that societies must also be alert to new forms of moral weakness that accompany the development of civilization, particularly the lapse of courage and the refusal to endure hardship and privation for the sake of duty (134). For all its benefits, Constant writes, civilization promotes not moral virtue, but stability and order. Here Constant sheds the somewhat complacent confidence, which the other essays seem to share with Condorcet, that moral progress will follow from the eradication of error and the achievement of technical advances, and that Europe stands at the pinnacle of all such forms of progress. He warns in particular that the consuming love of comfort spawned by civilization leads to "a kind of resignation founded on calculation," that leaves people unwilling to defend their liberty against either internal despots or external conquerors.[67] To those, like Dunoyer, who cite the history of ancient and medieval republics in Europe as evidence of European superiority over other cultures or races, Constant replies that Europe's history also affords "testimony of another kind, eighteen hundred years of arbitrary rule" from which England and France were freed only recently, while Spain and Portugal still suffer "religious and political oppression, vexation, and inquisition" (151–52). As Constant presents them, then, Europe's history and its likely future of moral cowardice and resignation offer little reason for self-congratulation, and little ground for claims to superior nature or moral knowledge in comparison with other societies.

Moreover, Constant cites the newly established Haitian republic as evidence that other peoples, including the most oppressed, have founded institutions equal to those of Europe:

> The blacks of Haiti have become very reasonable legislators, disciplined enough warriors, and statesmen as able and as polished as our diplomats. They had to overcome the double obstacle of a nature [*organisation*] considered inferior to our own, and the education of the dreadful servitude to which our infamous calculations subjected them. They have placed themselves at the level of the most perfect races, in terms not only of the necessary arts, but of social institutions, whose intricacy we find so perplexing and whose management so difficult. Their constitution is better than most constitutions of Europe. Let us leave the physiologists, then, to attend to the primitive differences that will be surmounted sooner or later by the perfectibility with which the whole race is gifted, and let us beware of arming politics with this new pretext for inequality and oppression.[68]

Constant's target in this part of the essay is scientific theories of racial inequality, which Dunoyer, a fellow liberal, had endorsed. Though Dunoyer lamented the misfortune of "inferior" races and claimed that their inferiority did not license European subjugation of them, he accepted racial difference as a scientific fact, and a politically relevant one. Constant responds that questions of biological differences among human groups might indeed be worthy of scientific study, but such discussions must be kept entirely out of politics, for the special prestige of scientific argument makes it particularly prone to abuse by self-justifying oppressors.[69] Like many other nineteenth-century liberals in Britain and France, including both Tocqueville and Mill, Constant does not rule out the possibility that racial theories may yet prove to have some scientific truth; instead, while noting their dubious empirical basis, he insists primarily on their *political* perniciousness.[70] For political purposes, Constant maintains, the biological and moral equality of all human beings must be presupposed.

Not only are peoples such as the Haitians eminently capable of founding well-ordered societies and progressing on their own, Constant proposes in this essay, but the history of conquest demonstrates that colonial government almost invariably inhibits progress and improvement among the conquered:

> The Spanish colonies had little leisure to work for their internal amelioration while the metropole was butchering their defenders. Before civilizing [*s'adoucir*] and enlightening themselves, the Greeks had to avoid the stake and prevent the kidnapping of their children, whom the pashas dragged into Egypt to be circumcised and sold, to the great satisfaction of the abettors of intolerance and the enemies of humanity. The blacks of Saint-Domingue could not advance much in their moral education under the lash of the colonists. If one day a recipe is discovered for simultaneously bringing about desirable improvement and necessary resistance, the discovery will be precious. Until then, despite the faults of the oppressed, it will be just to increase the blame due to the crimes of the oppressors.[71]

Here as elsewhere in Constant's writings of the 1820s, the Ottoman Empire's oppression of the Greeks stands out as one of his central examples of foreign despotism.[72] Although the passage is somewhat obscure, what Constant seems to suggest is that where subjects lack sufficient political power to resist domination, attempts by their rulers (particularly foreign or colonial governors) to impose progress on them will almost inevitably degenerate into oppression. Failures of colonized societies to "progress," Constant concludes, should therefore be attributed largely to oppression on the part of the rulers and not to failings of the subject populations.

Constant most directly addressed the vices and injustices of French colonial rule in his speeches to the Chamber of Deputies protesting colonial policy in Martinique. In the early 1820s, Constant had been a prominent critic of the government's failure (or unwillingness) to stop French participation in the slave trade, from which, he argued, the government profited. Although he was a far more insistent critic of the slave trade than of slavery itself in his parliamentary speeches, Constant also devoted a number of long speeches to a scathing critique of the French government's complicity in the domination of free blacks by white creoles in Martinique. The colonial administration, he noted, had "injured [*froissés*] in the most deplorable manner" "the interests of humanity."[73] Arguing that it was the Chamber's responsibility to protect the lives and safety of French citizens, including blacks in the colonies, Constant called for the extension of civil and political rights to blacks on the same terms enjoyed by white Frenchmen, that is, with a property restriction.[74]

Constant made these arguments in the course of championing the cause of a group of free blacks who had been arrested for distributing a French pamphlet that, although politically moderate and legal in France, was considered dangerous by the white colonists of Martinique.[75] As Constant recounted in a speech of July 16, 1824, the colonial government had complied with the colons' demand that it issue search warrants against "all men of color." Although nothing was found in the searches—except, Constant noted wryly, a declaration by the freemen of their loyalty to the monarchy, and a copy of a speech made in the Chamber of Deputies[76]—numerous arrests and deportation orders were issued, and many men were condemned to perpetual hard labor. Finally, a group of men sent to France for legal proceedings were prevented from landing in France by their ship's captain, who instead illegally deported them to Senegal, a "death sentence" for many of them, Constant reported. In permitting the searches, Constant argued, the colonial governor had betrayed his duty to uphold the law and had acted on behalf of that faction of white colonists who were determined "enemies of the blacks and men of color." Constant called on the Chamber to pay reparations to those who had been so abused, and to follow Britain in granting equal civil and political rights to black freemen, on grounds of both justice and prudence, "to reunite under the same laws the free population of these colonies, by interesting them all, without distinction of color or origin, in the maintenance of an equitable and impartial legislation."[77]

Like J. S. Mill later in the century, Constant believed white colonial settlers posed a great threat to basic justice for nonwhite colonial subjects; he described their treatment of blacks in Martinique as not just a "violation of the most sacred rights," but also as "insubordination [and] rebellion" against the crown and against French law. Mill, as we have seen, sought a solution to the problem of oppressive colonists in criminal proceedings against abusive governors and in shifting power from colonial legislatures to independent administrative authorities in London. Even when he himself was a legislator, Mill did not seek greater involvement by the metropolitan Parliament, since he believed that the British public to whom they were responsible was ignorant about and indifferent to colonial subjects. Constant, in contrast, turned to the Chamber of Deputies, in part, undoubtedly (and despite his appeals to the monarchy to return to the "wise and humane ordinances of Louis XIV"), because he saw little hope for more moderate policies from the increasingly reactionary Bourbon government.[78]

As for France's major colonial project of the mid-nineteenth century, the conquest of Algeria, Constant said unfortunately little. He died in December 1830, only six months after the capture of Algiers, when the new regime had not yet developed any firm intentions to colonize territory beyond that city, and he never reflected on the prospect of such a project of colonization. Immediately after the capture of the city, in the final days of Charles X's regime, Constant wrote a brief, vituperative article in the opposition newspaper *Le Temps* criticizing the government's effort to use the Algerian expedition to bolster its own failing position. In a desperate and politically misguided effort to save itself, the Polignac ministry had recently dissolved the Chamber of Deputies and called new elections, and the government clearly hoped that the conquest would spur a patriotic fervor among the electorate that might translate into votes for the unpopular ministry. In his article, Constant called on the electors to "preserve the charter [of 1814] from the repercussions [*contre-coup*] of Algiers" and not to succumb to the regime's "illusions and seductions."[79] Such attentiveness to the danger that governments will use conquest to manipulate public sentiment and suppress political opposition bears the stamp of Constant's *Spirit of Conquest*. And yet Constant also stoops to a caricature of "barbaric" Algiers and a note of patriotic pandering that recalls the essay on Greece: "Let us wish ardently for the military successes of our brave compatriots. Let us applaud the ruin of a den of pirates, if we have the courage to accomplish it, instead of respecting the quality of sovereignty in a barbarian. May the city of Algiers be flung into its port! Honor to the French soldiers. But let us demand a strict accounting of the disproportionate sacrifices" that those soldiers suffered for an affair of royal vanity.[80]

The *Spirit of Conquest* offers an arsenal of arguments that would seem to discourage France's Algerian adventure; Constant's later essay on Greece suggests a less cautious or isolationist stance, particularly in the face of a conflict between Europe and the Ottoman Empire—or even Christianity and Islam. And yet, although he was concerned, like Tocqueville, about the fate of democracy in France, Constant never turned to foreign aggression as Tocqueville would, to shore up the process of democratization at home. Like Condorcet and like Tocqueville (whose views on progress he may indeed have influenced), Constant believed in historical progress as tangible and measurable; but unlike so many later liberals of nineteenth-century France and Britain, Constant did not invoke his theory of historical progress to justify empire, and he regarded the effort to impose progress through conquest as both unjust and futile, indeed counterproductive. Constant's trenchant critique of conquest express concerns that we might expect Tocqueville to share, but that, as we shall see, we find Tocqueville silencing or avoiding in favor of what he persuaded himself were the advantages of a North African empire.

Desjobert and the Marginalization of Anti-imperialism

In the years after Constant's death and the initial capture of Algiers, as the French debated whether to undertake a full-scale conquest of the country, criticism of French expansion became ever more impotent. Tocqueville (Gustave de Beaumont later attested) thought the leftists in the Chamber wrong "on everything to do with Algeria" and voted against them every time the issue arose.[81] The leftist alternative to Tocqueville's enthusiasm for empire during the 1830s and 1840s was perhaps best articulated by his fellow deputy Amédée Desjobert (1796–1853).[82] Few in the Chamber of Deputies can have studied Algeria more carefully than Desjobert; his knowledge certainly rivaled Tocqueville's. Desjobert was a leftist deputy in the Chamber from 1833 to 1848 and after the February Revolution was elected to the Constituent Assembly.[83] Desjobert served on the committee the Chamber named in 1847 to study the colonization of Algeria, for which Tocqueville was rapporteur. As a political economist and follower of Adam Smith and Jean-Baptiste Say, Desjobert insisted on free trade as preferable to conquest and also, with perhaps naive optimism, suggested the economic failures of the "colonial regime" would soon destroy colonialism around the globe.[84]

Although Tocqueville, as he was reading documents about Algeria in preparation for his first journey there in 1841, dismissed Desjobert's works as "polemics," he had not always been so dismissive.[85] Tocqueville must have read Desjobert's first book on the subject, *La Question d'Alger: Politique, colonisation, commerce* (1837) as soon as it was published, for he praised it in his first "Letter on Algeria" of the same year, before his election to the Chamber. In *La Question d'Alger* Desjobert drew on the same kinds of sources that Tocqueville himself used: government reports and statistics, personal testimonies by French military men in Algiers, histories of North Africa and the East and West Indies (such as Raynal's *Histoire des deux Indes* and Las Casas's *History of the West Indies*, published in French translation in Lyons in 1642).[86] Desjobert's writings posed many of the same questions as Tocqueville's, although often with a far more critical edge: Are the French good colonizers? Is representative government incompatible with colonization? Does the British empire in India provide an instructive model for French efforts in North Africa? In addition to asking, as Tocqueville did, whether colonization of Algeria was prudent—economically sound, militarily feasible, beneficial for

France as a nation—Desjobert explicitly questioned whether it was moral. He concluded it was neither. Desjobert himself admired Tocqueville, at least before the latter began to advocate the conquest of Algeria.[87]

Desjobert believed that France should pursue trade with Algeria and encourage its industrialization but that colonization, with its military and administrative expenses, would prove an economic disaster.[88] He cited British India as an example of foolish and improvident policy, maintaining that Britain spent far more on India than it could ever regain. Indeed, Desjobert praised British policy in India only in contrast to what he considered the greater failure of French Algeria, where the indigenous people had been unjustly dispossessed of their farms and Europe's urban poor shipped despite their utter lack of agricultural knowledge.[89] Desjobert credited Britain's ability to keep possession of India to its prohibition on European settlement and land ownership; similarly, he praised the Ottoman regime in Algeria for its limited character and its respect for cultural difference and the property of the indigenous people.[90] He insisted that as misguided as British rule of India was, continued possession of Algeria would be even worse, for the French could not defend Algeria against European challengers except at tremendous expense and without gravely weakening France as a nation. Desjobert's economic arguments against empire recall eighteenth-century assessments by Bentham, Burke, Smith, and Diderot, among others. But his position was an unusual one in the nineteenth century not only in France but also in England, where even advocates of free trade within Europe found reasons to support imperial ventures.[91]

Domestic political concerns also motivated Desjobert's critique: echoing Constant, he maintained that representative government and individual liberties in France ultimately were irreconcilable with colonial rule. Since democratic discussion would thwart the plans of colonial administrators, he argued, the men he liked to describe as *MM. les algérophiles* would quash debate and foist their "great enterprises" on the public, enriching themselves and enhancing their own reputations at the expense not only of sound policy but of participatory democracy itself.[92] Desjobert questioned the idea, which was to become central to Tocqueville's own position, that national honor demanded preservation of the North African empire. He was more suspicious than Tocqueville was about the ways in which the notion of national honor was manipulated by those with economic interests in conquest. Thus Desjobert began his analysis of the colonial question with an astute meditation on the role of the press and public flattery in deciding political questions, particularly those of foreign policy. He feared that the powerful interests of financial speculators in imperial expansion, combined with the weakness of the public, would drive national political discourse toward aggressive displays of national pride and muscle.

> The men who exploit Africa have made up a powerful arm of public opinion: they suggested that France was unanimous on the immense advantages that the conquest and colonization of Algiers presented, and they have won over two numerous classes of men who are always easy to persuade: those, in great number, who completely adopt an opinion when it flatters their pride without injuring their interests; and those who, finding themselves ill at ease in France, saw in brilliant promises and lies the end of their misery and a future of prosperity.[93]

Desjobert suggested that the French imagination had long been seduced by the word *colony* and often succumbed to the "fatal prestige" of bad ideas. Taken in by the lies of the Spanish and of Walter Raleigh (who embellished his discoveries in order not to be the "only dupe"), the French had launched ill-fated colonial ventures in the New World and in Africa. In Desjobert's own day, similarly audacious men were attempting equally misguided conquests and "sacrificing public fortune to their particular interests."[94] The greed and ambition of men like John Law and Napoleon had led a gullible nation to support hopeless ventures whose sole results were to kill off Frenchmen and enrich the British.[95] He quoted Baron Pichon, a civil intendant in Algiers: "The authors of novels about Algiers are not our masters, and the government of France is free to reduce them to their proper worth and to repudiate them."[96] Desjobert saw in colonial ventures mostly waste and exploitation—including that of the French public.[97]

Desjobert's criticism anticipates many of the claims Tocqueville would make in support of empire. He notes that "through an adroit confusion of language," the men with interests in colonization have masked the real question—whether expansion and colonization were just and prudent—behind the frivolous and wrongheaded question of whether France could afford the reputation of degeneracy and weakness that they held would inevitably accompany a retreat. Such men had "insinuated that England had a great interest in this abandonment, and that if we had the cowardice to bring it about, England was ready to seize our conquest and to turn to her own profit all the elements of power and the commercial advantages hidden there."[98] In his "Essay on Algeria" of 1841, Tocqueville, if not unconscious of then certainly insensible to Desjobert's critique, would make precisely the argument that France must not "abandon" Algeria, as it could ill afford the appearance of decline.[99]

Tocqueville himself, in *Democracy in America*, had recognized the particular susceptibility of modern democracy to the power of the press, and he had acknowledged that the concentration of control over the press in a few hands in Paris had strengthened this influence (whereas the proliferation of press organs in America had diluted theirs).[100] Still, Tocqueville's reflections on the press and public opinion in both volumes of *Democracy* remained strikingly optimistic. People in conditions of social equality, he argued, tend to develop a stable body of opinion that, as it rests on a set of principles to which they cling quite tenaciously, is not easily shaken by the efforts of a few. Desjobert's scenario, in which a weak and divided public is easily swayed by the blandishments of a few fairly powerful men, would appear unlikely according to Tocqueville's analysis of public opinion and the press. Despite Tocqueville's wariness of individualism—his fear that tyranny always threatens a divided and apathetic public—he never adopted Desjobert's skepticism of the motives that would cause leaders and led alike to embrace schemes of such dubious benefit to the nation as, in Desjobert's view, were conquest and expansion in North Africa.

Finally, Desjobert's argument includes a strong moral element, and it is here that his disagreements with Tocqueville are most striking. He denounces the French policy of exterminating or expelling Arab nomads from their land both on humanitarian grounds and because it is a violation of their nationality.[101] "In the course of this work," he wrote, "we have deplored the sad results of administration distinguished by the hatred or at least the neglect [*oubli*] of Arab nationality."[102] He calls for full recognition of Arab nationality, and the abandonment of any plans for colonization: France should declare that it would not recognize European colonists, and that any Europeans who remained in Algeria did so at their own risk and as subjects of the indigenous government.[103] Desjobert calls on the French to extend the same political standards to Algerians that they apply in Europe, pointing out the inconsistency of criticizing conquests in Europe while committing the same injustice elsewhere: "While we raise our voices on behalf of Catholic Poland, do we want foreigners to be able to hold up against us the Muslim Poland that is struggling in Algeria?"[104] Desjobert's emphasis on the importance of recognizing Arab nationality generated a reading of the political situation in Algeria very different from Tocqueville's. Tocqueville, although fascinated and impressed by the Algerian religious, political, and military figure Abdelkader (or Abd-el-Kader or Abd al-Qadir), studied him as an adversary to be defeated. Desjobert considered Abdelkader the "representative of Arab nationality" and believed that the French had the moral duty to recognize him as the leader of the Algerian people.[105]

For Desjobert, the immorality and the imprudence of French colonial policy coincided, and he largely avoided moralizing fervor while still making clear that he considered the French policy of expulsion and colonization unjust and immoral. His rhetorical strategy was consistently to convey moral judgment through quotations of government documents or the memoirs of colonial officials: the impassioned, moralizing rhetoric of his book tends to emerge in such passages rather than in his own voice.[106] As familiar as his critical arguments might have been from the writings of the philosophes, they could not find favor in the political climate of the day, even when Desjobert's fellow republicans took power in 1848 (and declared Algeria an integral part of France, dividing it into three *départements*). Desjobert's writings stand as a reminder that the conceptual resources for a robust anti-imperialism were available to Tocqueville and his contemporaries, even as Tocqueville, with most of France's political class, embraced the total conquest of Algeria.

Tocqueville's Sociology of Democracy and the Question of European Expansion

"Il faut une science politique nouvelle à un monde tout nouveau," Tocqueville wrote in his introduction to the first volume of *Democracy in America* (1835), always alert to the originality of his times and of his own ideas.[107] He had in mind the profound political transformations in "the Christian nations of our day": developments that appeared to be leading inexorably toward democracy and social equality. His statement might just as well have applied, however, to the equally revolutionary developments in Europe's relations with the non-European world. Tocqueville himself felt these developments were little understood in Europe; they called for investigation and explanation by someone who appreciated their novelty and the profound effect on European states and cultures they were bound to have.[108] He believed the study of empire to be central to his work as a politician and an observer of politics and society. His views on the subject also present the struggles of a complex and perceptive thinker as he attempted a difficult balancing act: that of reconciling a commitment to human equality with a defense of the subordination of non-Europeans. For Tocqueville's defense of imperial expansion both stemmed from his liberalism—in the sense that it emerged directly from his concern to build a durable liberal political order in France—and also stood in tension with what we might call liberalism's center of gravity, its insistence on the moral equality of all human beings.

Tocqueville's sociological and political analysis of Europe and France was animated by concerns strikingly similar to those of Constant, particularly a suspicion of centralized state power and a worry about the tendency of the modern state to erase diversity and local attachments among its citizens.[109] The striking affinities between their diagnoses of the challenges for modern politics in commercial and democratizing societies throw their divergent analyses of empire into particular relief.[110] Both thinkers believed that the growth of commerce had driven modern individuals out of politics and into the private realm, the realm of commercial pursuits and family matters, leaving a political vacuum that the state would fill all too eagerly. Politics in modern commercial societies, both maintained, would have fundamentally to reckon with these two tendencies of political centralization and the growth of commerce, accommodating the modern character without allowing it to destroy the social fabric. Both thinkers believed that for citizens to abandon political activity altogether was not only a great danger to basic liberties but also a form of moral debasement. "It is not to happiness alone, it is to self-development that our destiny calls us," said Constant in his famous speech on ancient and modern liberty; "and political liberty is the most powerful, the most effective means of self-development that heaven has given us."[111] Constant and Tocqueville both remained ambivalent about the legacies of the Revolution, eager to preserve what they regarded as its achievements while distancing themselves from its excesses. Each suggested in his own way that the Revolution's representation of itself—and as a result the French nation's entire self-understanding—was based on delusion, and that this delusion would continue to plague and destabilize French politics. The thinkers thus shared a preoccupation with the possibilities for freedom under modern commercial and increasingly democratic conditions, and an interest in the implications of the modern conception of freedom for domestic political structures.

Both Constant and Tocqueville also recognized a threat to liberty in the modern state posed by individuals' more general retreat from common life, although this concern was to prove paramount for Tocqueville in a way that it was not for his predecessor. Constant greeted the rise of this sort of individualism, though with distinct ambivalence, also with acceptance. For Constant, the modern citizen's detachment meant that the political structure must take account of citizens' new interests and needs, that an outdated understanding of freedom must not be forced on people, and that political leaders' ambitions for the state should conform to the ambitions and ethos of the people.[112] Stephen Holmes has argued that Constant, having lived through Napoleon's rule and conquests as an adult, resisted the temptation of regarding war as noble or salutary: he "never wrote that the desire for life is 'low.' . . . Indeed, he was enough of a philosophe to agree with de Lolme's definition of glory: the ardent desire of slaughtering others in order afterwards to boast about it."[113] Modern liberty, according to Constant, is precisely the liberty of the individual beyond the public reach, and he sought to describe a political order that could accommodate the modern individual's (admittedly ignoble) desire to seek fulfillment in private rather than political affairs.

Where Constant attributed the destructive impulse toward uniformity to the spirit of conquest, a force outside society, Tocqueville located the source in modern society itself, and his diagnosis was more dire as a result.[114] Tocqueville believed commercial and private interests undermined political community and threatened liberty far more than mere force ever could. This difference between them meant that whereas Constant regarded militarism and imperial expansion as among the primary causes of the dangers facing modern society, Tocqueville allowed himself to hope they might instead be a solution.[115]

Tocqueville's apprehension of central power is too well known to need much rehearsing. This fear is the abiding preoccupation of his work on French politics, from its preliminary articulation in an 1836 essay to its fuller exposition in his last, unfinished work, *L'Ancien Régime et la révolution*.[116] Decades before he wrote *L'Ancien Régime*, then, Tocqueville had worked out its *idée fixe*: the French state had been growing ever more centralized at least from the time of Louis XIV and probably even further back, and the Revolution, far from overturning the old order as it claimed, had simply sped the process. In the book's closing chapter, "How the Revolution Came Naturally from What Preceded it," he wrote,

> The government of the old regime had already taken away from the French any possibility, or desire, of helping one another. When the Revolution happened, one would have searched most of France in vain for ten men who had the habit of acting in common in an orderly way, and taking care of their own defense themselves; only the central power was supposed to take care of it, so that the central power, fallen from the hands of the royal government into the hands of a sovereign and irresponsible assembly, and changed from good-natured to terrible, found nothing which could stop, or even briefly slow it down. The same cause which made the monarchy fall so easily, made everything possible after its fall.[117]

Excessive state power threatened liberty not through sheer might alone, Tocqueville maintained, but also because of two distinctly modern phenomena to which it contributed (and which in their turn fed the power of the state): the erasure of local loyalties in favor of national uniformity, and the increasing detachment of citizens from politics and collective action.

After spending time among his new constituents in Normandy, Tocqueville wrote to Royer-Collard of his distress about French political disengagement. "There are no meetings of any sort, no place where a large number of men can freely exchange their feelings and thoughts on any subject. It is a distressing and alarming spectacle to those who like me dread, in the future, oppression more than anarchy," he wrote. "What strikes me most as I have more opportunity to see this population is how little it is occupied with political affairs."[118] For Tocqueville, while *individualisme* and disengagement were products of the increasing equality of conditions in all "Christian nations," the France of his day was in particular danger of such oppression. Its national vulnerability stemmed from many sources: the passion for commerce and myopic self-interest that he considered endemic in contemporary Europe, the legacy of apathy generated by ancien régime absolutism, and France's extremely unstable political situation, brought about by rapid, but incomplete, political transition—the latter problems not ones faced by Britain or America.[119]

To be sure, Tocqueville saw American township politics as an appealing alternative model of modern democracy, in which central government power is counteracted by active, organized citizens. While *Democracy in America* is often read as a blueprint for Europe's future, however, it is clear from Tocqueville's writings on France that he saw little reason to believe that his country could ever take the American route. In America Tocqueville sought the model for modern democratic government, but he also paid strict attention to the ways in which America was not, and could never be, France.[120] France was too heavily burdened with the entrenched legacies of an apolitical populace and greedy central power; equally importantly, France as a nation was hobbled by a uniquely deluded historical self-understanding.

Tocqueville's treatment of American patriotism in *Democracy* I, like many moments in this work, reveals as much about his fears for the cohesion of the French nation in the postrevolutionary period as it does about America. He clearly had France in mind when he described the society in transition from a traditional monarchy to a modern republic. Such a society could no longer rely on the "instinctive patriotism" that once bound it together through ancient customs and religious faith. Nor had it yet developed the rational patriotism of Americans, where every citizen knew that his self-interest was bound up in the health of the nation and thus took "a zealous interest in the affairs of his township, his country, and the whole state as if they were his own."[121] As a society attempts to build a new sense of national community on the ruins of the old, its cohesion *as* a society, its public political life, and the rights of the citizens are all threatened:

> Sometimes there comes a time in the life of nations when old customs are changed, mores destroyed, beliefs shaken, and the prestige of memories has vanished, but when nonetheless enlightenment has remained incomplete and political rights are ill-assured or restricted. Then men see their country only by a weak and doubtful light . . . they have neither the instinctive patriotism of a monarchy nor the reflective patriotism of a republic, but have come to a halt between the two amid confusion and misery.[122]

At such times, the country is "lost to their senses," and they stop caring for a common life they can no longer perceive. As their collective enterprise becomes invisible to them, they retreat to the concrete realm of private interest. The citizens, without a clear object on which to fix their foundering public sentiments, "retire into a narrow and unenlightened selfishness." The visual quality of Tocqueville's diagnosis already presages the form one of his key solutions would take: a dazzling national glory that will focus citizens' eyes on their public life. At the end of the chapter on American patriotism, Tocqueville presented the political dilemma of his age with a starkness that may help us better to understand his desperate and misguided grasping at an imperial "solution": "In our times we must make up our minds and dare to choose between the patriotism of all and the government of the few."[123]

The dangerous inability of the French to imagine themselves as a nation stemmed not only from the inevitably transitional phase in which the society found itself in Tocqueville's day as it lurched from monarchy to democracy, but also from a peculiarly defective historical imagination. In Tocqueville's view, perhaps the Revolution's most threatening legacy was not the unsettling political changes it produced, but rather—thanks to both hypocrisy and historical misconception—instability in France's very identity as a nation.[124] The French, first in undertaking the Revolution and then in commemorating it, persistently fooled themselves about its novelty and its significance, and thus about their own national identity.[125] They believed that their national character was now defined by the Revolution and its republican principles alone, and that their historical memory need reach back only to 1789. "In 1789 the French made the greatest effort ever undertaken by any people to cut their fate, so to speak, in two, and to put an abyss between what they had been and what they wished to become," begins *L'Ancien Régime*.

> To this end they took all sorts of precautions to bring nothing from the past into their new order; they put themselves under all sorts of constraints to make themselves different from their fathers; they overlooked nothing in their effort to make themselves unrecognizable.
>
> I have always thought that they were much less successful in their unique enterprise than observers have believed, or than they themselves believed at first. (*OC* 2.1:69)

For Tocqueville, who believed that nations are constituted by historical memory, this kind of delusion was politically disastrous.[126] He feared that France, more than other European nations (and especially in contrast to Britain) lacked a solid foundation as a national community: not only had its citizens been apolitical and its government overcentralized for too many centuries, but its very identity rested on a falsehood, a "disguise." If France were to establish the sort of solid national consciousness that had propelled Britain to political strength, it would require some other basis. Tocqueville wrote the *Ancien Régime* with the explicit purpose of recovering France's true history from the self-deceptions of the Revolution. A proper understanding of French history and its pivotal moments—such as Britain had of the Glorious Revolution of 1688—and an imperial project that demanded collective effort and promised national glory: these together seemed to promise the national foundation Tocqueville sought.[127]

In addition to attempting to recover France's true history for practical purposes, Tocqueville proposed two means of resisting the individualism and anomie that plagued France and threatened the nation's political cohesion and ultimately its citizens' liberty. These might be described, in the language of the republican tradition, as the solutions of virtue and of glory. The first entailed great enterprises that require action and sacrifice by the entire nation, political projects that forced individuals out of their private spaces and into the realm of concerted action and the display of public "virtue," although such enterprises were, he thought, rare in his day. "Are you not astonished with me, Madame, upon seeing spring from a nation that appears so devoid of public virtues, an army that demonstrates itself to be so full of virtue? So much egoism here, so much self-sacrifice there," he wrote to a friend in admiration of the French soldiers fighting in the Crimean War.[128] Virtue, for Tocqueville, was intimately bound up with self-sacrifice for the benefit of the public: "The principle of the republics of antiquity was to sacrifice private interests to the general good. In that sense one could say that they were *virtuous*."[129]

Tocqueville's second solution was to promote actions that would engender in the people a sense of national greatness. Tocqueville often invoked this sort of glory as though it were merely a redescription of public virtue, appearing just as satisfied with reputation and the appearance of greatness as he would be with actual stability and prosperity for France.[130] Both strategies invited imperial exploits (and their celebration), and Tocqueville often implied that pursuit of glory through conquest would generate the political dynamics of an involved citizenry and a strong nation.[131] He never, however, described the mechanisms through which imperial expansion—which critics such as Constant and Desjobert saw as the private domain of a few generals and speculators—would involve the whole citizenry actively in collective political projects. This lacuna in his argument suggests that, in his writings on empire, Tocqueville was often guided by wishful thinking rather than by the careful sociological analysis, the scrutiny of specific causal mechanisms in politics, for which he was justly famous. We are left with the sense that Tocqueville was as satisfied by an appearance of grandeur as by real gains in political stability or even international power.[132]

In his more clear-sighted moments, however, Tocqueville recognized glory as merely a shadow of public virtue. "I have always thought," he wrote, "that the best thing our country has left is national pride, a pride which is often puerile and boastful, but which with all its absurdities and weaknesses is still the greatest sentiment that we have and the strongest tie that holds this nation together."[133] Glory, in this sense, must substitute for virtue during a nation's most vulnerable moments; self-representation must substitute for more concrete action. As he wrote to J. S. Mill in 1841, apparently expecting agreement,

> I do not have to tell you, my dear Mill, that the greatest malady that threatens a people organized as we are is the gradual softening of mores, the abasement of the mind, the mediocrity of tastes; that is where the great dangers of the future lie. One cannot let a nation that is democratically constituted like ours and in which the natural vices of the race unfortunately coincide with the natural vices of the social state, one cannot let this nation take up easily the habit of sacrificing what it believes to be its grandeur to its repose, great matters to petty ones; it is not healthy to allow such a nation to believe that its place in the world is smaller, that it is fallen from the level on which its ancestors had put it, but that it must console itself by building railroads and by making the well-being of each private individual prosper amidst peace, under whatever condition this peace is obtained. It is necessary that those who march at the head of such a nation should always keep a proud attitude, if they do not wish to allow the level of national mores to fall very low.[134]

Mill responded to Tocqueville's confidence with a scolding. He agreed reluctantly "that the feeling of orgeuil national is the only feeling of a public-spirited & elevating kind which remains & that it ought not therefore be permitted to go down." But French politicians—and Mill did not exclude Tocqueville—had offered the French public only "low and grovelling" ideas of what "constitutes national glory and national importance"; they had sacrificed good government and solid achievement for boisterous self-importance.[135] Earlier, Mill had shown himself somewhat more sympathetic in his own account of Tocqueville's sensitivity to the importance of *orgeuil national*, national pride. Mill wrote to a friend about Tocqueville's view of the rupture of French-British relations over France's designs on Egypt: the French

> were treated, he thinks, with so great a degree of slight (to say the least) by our government that for their public men not to show a feeling of blessure would have been to lower the standard of national pride which in the present state of the world he thinks almost the only elevated sentiment that remains in considerable strength. There is really a great deal in this although it does not justify & scarcely excuses the revival of the old national animosity or even the warlike demonstrations & preparations. . . . But I do think it contemptible in England

> to treat the bare suspicion of France seeking for influence in the East as something too horrible to be thought of; England meanwhile progressively embracing the whole of Asia in her own grasp.[136]

Tocqueville had written that if political leaders had not expressed their sense of injury (*blessure*), they would have "wounded and perhaps extinguished a national passion that we will need some day." Mill's grudgingly sympathetic paraphrase does not convey Tocqueville's reliance on national pride as a bulwark for what he well knew was an often precarious representative government.

As I argue below and in chapter 7, Tocqueville turned to the conquest of Algeria as a facet of his political efforts to generate in France the national pride and public virtue he believed the nation required. The ruthlessness Tocqueville often displayed toward the conquered peoples of Algeria seems to have stemmed, in part, precisely from his deep-seated fear about the vulnerability of liberty in France. Occasionally Tocqueville showed himself to be only too aware that the widespread hope that empire would save the French nation was chimerical. Many of Tocqueville's writings on France convey his anxiety that democratic community could not be engendered through the democratic process alone. This concern should be set alongside his more often discussed belief that democracy creates for itself problems that it is ill-equipped to solve—most notably an insatiable desire among citizens for equality, even at the expense of greater prosperity or of liberty itself—as one source of Tocqueville's theory of the internal self-contradictions of democracy, and as a source of Tocqueville's own apparent self-contradictions.

Expansion and Exclusion in America

Tocqueville's earliest and best-known treatment of the relations between Europeans and subject peoples occurred in the context of his voyage to America in 1831–32, especially in the long final chapter of *Democracy* I, "Some Considerations on the Present and Probable Future Condition of the Three Races That Inhabit the Territory of the United States." Tocqueville famously claims in that chapter that American expansion, like slavery, is "American without being democratic" and therefore "collaterally connected to my subject without forming a part of it."[137] His fascination with the expansionist aspect of American history, however, and his later appeals to America as a model for French Algeria, suggest that he perceived conquest, and relations with conquered peoples, to be more integral to modern politics than such a statement would imply and that he was, from the beginning, drawing political lessons about the benefits and moral compromises of colonial expansion. He described the United States as "placed in the middle of a huge continent with limitless room for the expansion of human endeavor," and his first, hopeful, reaction on seeing Algiers in 1841 was that it was a place of "feverish activity"—"Cincinnati transported onto the soil of Africa."[138]

It is on the basis of the writings on America that Tocqueville's readers have sometimes assumed that he condemned imperial expansion, for both the "three races" chapter and the subtly observant journals, essays, and letters Tocqueville wrote in America display considerable sympathy for Amerindians and little tolerance for American justifications for their expropriation and extermination.[139] In *Democracy* I, and even more in his journals and letters of 1831, Tocqueville condemns Europeans as indifferent to the rights and lives of the indigenous people: the Spanish openly, the English and Americans hypocritically and with "egoistic" disdain for the lives of Native Americans. He explicitly charges the American settlers with exterminating (*exterminer*) the indigenous peoples, dealing with them in bad faith, and refusing to recognize their rights or their status as nations. In its most outraged moments, Tocqueville's chapter on the three races offers an eloquent attack on the hypocrisy and self-righteousness of the English settlers' grasping and inexorable expansion across America.

And yet these writings indicate Tocqueville's great ambivalence about American expansion, which he saw as characteristic of, and perhaps indispensable for, the country's political and economic vitality; this ambivalence prefigures that of the Algeria writings. He presents a complex historical argument about the causes of Amerindians' suffering that enables him at once to defend and to deplore European expansion, as well as to refrain from offering any more just alternative. For he presents an account of the development of civilization that implies the inevitability of such tragedy in the encounter between civilized conquerors and a "savage" conquered population, and that implicates the Amerindians themselves in their fate. While he expresses moral revulsion at the settlers' treatment of the Amerindians, he also persuades himself that the peoples it displaced, like the slaves of the American South, cannot be assimilated into the political community. Slaves and Amerindians, representing the extremes of servitude and liberty or license, figure symmetrically in Tocqueville's landscape of democracy—or rather outside democracy, constituting its borders. Both, in Tocqueville's view, had participated in their own exclusion from democratic politics. American slaves had had the misfortune to grow accustomed to servitude and accept it; Amerindians, "savage nations" lying at the "extreme edge of freedom," could have chosen civilization but disdained to do so, and their extreme love of liberty had facilitated the corruption of their society.[140] The vices of both extremes, in Tocqueville's schema, demonstrate by negative example the qualities needed to sustain democracy. Amerindians and slaves, incapable of participating in a democratic order, are, he suggests, destined to remain excluded: expelled from the territory, killed off, degraded beneath notice, or shunted into a state of permanent enmity with American democracy.

Tocqueville maintained that by the time he arrived in America, the Amerindians were condemned to the extinction of their people. Their future was represented in the fate of the Indian Tocqueville saw lying face-down in a Buffalo street, not dead, as he had feared, but drunk.[141] They might learn some arts of civilization in the process of being conquered, but he feared their fate would be that of the Buffalo tribes he encountered as he traveled into the interior: without any of the liberty or dignity of their former condition, and corrupted by civilization without being improved by it. "From whatever angle one regards the destinies of the North American natives," he writes, "one sees nothing but irremediable ills."[142] As William Connolly has noted, Tocqueville makes use of the "slippery language of regret without moral indictment and, more significantly, of the recognition of undeserved suffering without any plan to curtail it in the future."[143] The indignant sarcasm of the "three races" chapter can be moving, but its judgment goes no further than lamentation, and Tocqueville did not offer an alternative vision of expansion. As it is too late to improve the tribes' fortunes, Tocqueville suggests, one can only express nostalgia for their uncorrupted past and lament the Anglo-Americans' failure to improve the European record in the New World, even in his own belated and apparently enlightened age. Tocqueville's account of Amerindians and slaves in this chapter is thus a highly aestheticized one, more tableau than argument. The writings of his cousin Chateaubriand, who had made a voyage quite similar to Tocqueville's forty years earlier, seem to lurk behind his own efforts to make sense of the frontier.[144] Tocqueville's writings on the Amerindians, while informed by careful observation, have a Romantic, literary inflection that would mark his early writings on Algeria but would disappear in the later writings in favor of colder political analysis and a harshly pragmatic defense of the Algerian conquest. The elegiac voice of the melancholy "three races" chapter was unavailable to the legislator and rapporteur of parliamentary commissions on colonial military appropriations. The lessons Tocqueville drew from the American experience, then, would be far more equivocal than his conclusions in *Democracy in America* might suggest. Where Tocqueville deplored the American depredations, he would advocate similar actions in Algeria. Only in the late 1840s, after two decades of violent subjection, and after the French had secured their rule in Algeria, did Tocqueville return to the voice of elegy and the prediction of tragedy characteristic of his American writing.[145]

While Tocqueville laments the "terrible afflictions" visited by the settlers on the Amerindians, his most forceful criticism is directed not at the dispossession and killing of the indigenous peoples but rather at the self-righteousness and hypocrisy that enabled the Anglo-American settlers serenely to deny even to themselves the extent of their brutality:[146]

> The conduct of the United States Americans towards the natives was inspired by the most chaste affection for legal formalities. . . . The Spaniards, by unparalleled atrocities which brand them with indelible shame, did not succeed in exterminating the Indian race and could not even prevent them from sharing their rights; the United States Americans have attained both these results with wonderful ease, quietly, legally, and philanthropically, without spilling blood and without violating a single one of the great principles of morality in the eyes of the world. It is impossible to destroy men with more respect for the laws of humanity.[147]

Tocqueville charges individual settlers and their state governments with the greatest blame, for "jealousy" and "greed" lead them to eject the native peoples from their lands even where the settlers themselves are sparsely populated. The states, he notes, "in extending what they are pleased to call the benefit of their laws over the Indians, calculate that the latter will sooner depart than submit"; their fault, again, Tocqueville suggests, lies partly in their disingenuous claims to want to civilize the Amerindians even as they seek to make their lives so intolerable that the tribes will have no alternative but to migrate.[148] The federal government, while less directly responsible for the expulsions, Tocqueville argues, acts equally in bad faith, offering guarantees about their future security farther west that it knows it will not fulfill.[149]

And yet for all his criticism of the Americans' deceit and bad faith, Tocqueville also presents a narrative of progress in which the expulsion and eventual annihilation of the indigenous people appears inevitable. Tocqueville offers a rough account of civilizational development, using language bequeathed by eighteenth-century conjectural histories, as when he argues that it is more difficult for "civilization to establish its sway" over hunting peoples than over pastoral peoples, who have a "regular system in their migrations," and that civilization can only occur when a people has settled and begins to cultivate the soil.[150] Tocqueville regards the process of civilization as a slow transformation of mores, a taming of old prejudices (such as a disdain for steady labor) and acquisition of new ones that occurs best when "barbarous peoples have raised themselves gradually by their own efforts" through "prolonged social endeavor taking place on the same spot."[151] While Tocqueville accepts that a barbarous people may "derive enlightenment from a foreign nation," he cites the Vandals and Mongols to argue that historically this has occurred when the barbarians are the conquerors: when, as a result, there is a kind of parity between the conquerors, who have power, and the conquered, who have knowledge and arts, so that each can acknowledge the other as "his equal." When the power and "intellectual superiority" are both held preponderantly by the conquerors, Tocqueville maintains, a dynamic of immiseration, dependence, and hopeless resistance results.[152]

Tocqueville describes the Amerindians' past as lives of material wretchedness and privation combined with independence, an attachment to tradition, pride, and "savage joys."[153] He suggests that the Amerindians might be able to avert their own destruction: the tribes still out of reach of the Americans, for instance, could protect themselves by uniting and becoming civilized before the arrival of the settlers, so that they could compete with them on a footing of greater equality and hope to survive as a people. Tocqueville admits that there is little likelihood of such an event; he suggests that the Amerindians themselves are partly responsible for their condition, in that there are some still strong enough to resist but who, "with the childish carelessness of the morrow characteristic of the savage man, wait for danger to reach them before bothering about it."[154] Still, Tocqueville sees the indigenous peoples' own failure to resist their destruction as itself a tragic but inexorable consequence of general causes "almost impossible for them to avoid," including ruinous economic competition from people skilled at farming and manufacture and united by customs, language, and laws. He insists that the Amerindians suffer structural disadvantages, rather than biological inferiority or even deeply rooted cultural defects; they have as much "natural genius" as Europeans, but lack the time necessary to develop the resources of civilized society.

If at times he voiced aspirations that empire served the cause of progress, Tocqueville never succumbed to the comfortable faith in civilizing colonial despotism that characterized British liberalism in his day. He observed of America, India, and Algeria that European rule, far from civilizing barbarous peoples sufficiently that they could assume governance of themselves, had instead brutalized or destroyed them.[155] The *mission civilisatrice* was to become the key tenet of French republican imperialism later in the century, especially during the scramble for Africa, but at this point French debates about empire focused less on the conqueror's civilizing duties than did British discourse.[156] J. S. Mill, as we have seen, regarded despotism by an "advanced" nation as the best and perhaps only means of generating political and civilizational advancement among "backward" peoples. Tocqueville, for all his enthusiasm for colonial expansion, better understood the costs and moral compromises of Europeans' self-delusions about beneficent conquest. Mill, likewise, withheld the status of nation from "unimproving" peoples, giving an exclusive definition of nationality as a political achievement of civilized societies and insisting that "barbarians have no rights as a *nation*, except a right to such treatment as may, at the earliest possible period, fit them for becoming one."[157] Tocqueville, in contrast, recognized the nationality, and the political character, of "half civilized" societies, and he perceived that it was precisely their character as nations—bound by ties of tradition, custom, language, historical memory, and territory—that was annihilated by European conquest.[158] The social ties that had bound Native Americans before the arrival of Europeans, he argued, had been severed by war, starvation, and misery. "Their homeland [*patrie*] has already been lost, and soon they will not have a people," he wrote; "families hardly remain, the common name is lost, and the traces of their origin vanish. Their nation has ceased to exist."[159]

Tocqueville resisted arguments that the nomadic tribes of either America or Algeria were not making adequate use of their territory, or that they lacked political organization, property rights, or even (incipient) nationhood. He rejected with scorn the argument, grounded in a Lockean theory of property, that the Amerindians had no right to their land, as they had not cultivated or improved it, that settlers who could use the land more efficiently than indigenous peoples had a right to claim and defend it.[160] As he wrote his mother in December 1831, the American settlers "have discovered . . . that, it being proved (listen to this) that a square mile could nourish ten times as many civilized men as savages, reason indicated that wherever civilized men could establish themselves, the savages would have to move away. What a beautiful thing logic is."[161]

He further criticized the Americans for invoking Indians' status as foreign nations but then refusing to acknowledge their nationality in law: "[A]lthough the Americans have often treated with them as with foreign nations, the states in which they are found have not been willing to recognize them as independent peoples, and they have undertaken to make these men, who have scarcely left the forests, submit to their magistrates, their customs, and their laws."[162] In quoting a petition from the Cherokees to the federal government, Tocqueville highlighted their own self-understanding as sovereign nations: "What crime have we committed which could deprive us of our country [*patrie*]?" The Committee on Indian Affairs responded with typical Anglo-American casuistry, Tocqueville observes: "one is astonished," he writes, "at the facility and ease with which the author . . . disposes of arguments founded on natural right and reason, which he calls abstract and theoretical principles. The more I think about it, the more I feel that the only difference between civilized and uncivilized man with regard to justice is this: the former contests the justice of rights, the latter simply violates them."[163] And yet despite his astute acknowledgment of the political self-understanding of Amerindian spokesmen and his endorsement of the justice of their claims for political recognition, Tocqueville resists making a political argument that America should respect their sovereign status and assumes instead an elegiac voice: "Such is the language of the Indians; what they say is true; what they foresee seems to me inevitable."[164]

Tocqueville could not admit the possibility that the justice embodied in American democracy produced and perhaps even required injustice, William Connolly has argued, and so he "demoralized" the violence involved in the expropriation and extermination of Amerindians, even as he recognized it as a tragedy.[165] Although Connolly does not address the writings on Algeria, these texts present even more starkly the moral abdication implicit in Tocqueville's position on national consolidation and its "necessary" exclusions. For in the case of Algeria, Tocqueville did not enjoy the luxury of the observer: his claims that Algerians must be excluded from the rights and legal protections of French settlers necessarily take the form of judgment and prescription rather than elegy or retrospection. Tocqueville relied on other strategies for avoiding a clear confrontation with the injustice, on his own terms, of his position on Algeria; he devoted himself largely to administrative details regarding French relations with the indigenous people, saving his broader and more philosophical arguments for discussions of the regime's despotism toward European emigrants to Algeria, and, most importantly, of the colony's importance to France.[166]

Tocqueville's writings on Amerindians and his thoughts on Algeria should be read in light of one another. American expansion, and thus relations with the indigenous people, proved to be far more important for Tocqueville's understanding of modern democracy than his phrase "American but not democratic" suggests. Moreover, just as many of Tocqueville's reflections on American democracy stemmed directly from his preoccupation with democracy's career in France, his interest in the American frontier took on a certain urgency that grew out of his sense that the English had succeeded where the French had failed.[167] After his visit to the northwestern fringes of settlement, where Anglo-American farmers had begun to overtake French trappers, Tocqueville concluded that the French, although of the first rank among continental nations, were, as a nation, ill-suited to colonization.[168] The French, Tocqueville believed, were at once too stolidly domestic and too unreliably adventurous. They hated to leave their homeland and the comfort of their hearths, but once they did, they became savage adventurers fit only for the wild life of the soldier or the trapper, not for the steady labor of the pioneer farmer.

Although he excoriated the Anglo-American settlers' greed and hypocrisy, Tocqueville could not resist admiring the character that had enabled them to turn the impenetrable Michigan forests to profit. His thoughts consistently returned to the American model as he attempted to discover how France could make an America of Algeria. Just as, in his words of 1841, "Africa has henceforth entered into the movement of the civilized world and will never leave it," Tocqueville first perceived in America that European liberalism and democracy were to develop alongside, and in part to be defined by, European expansion and rule over subject peoples. As his thoughts about nationhood, progress, and civilization developed, America would continue to serve as a point of reference: for the pitfalls of imperial expansion and the self-delusions of civilized society in its treatment of those it excluded, as well as for the achievements of a democratic society in the process of founding itself.

Seven

Tocqueville and the Algeria Question

Tocqueville as an Architect of French Algeria

Tocqueville followed the French colonization of Algeria, which he later described as "la plus grande affaire de ce pays," from its inception.[1] In 1833, three years after the French army captured Algiers from the Ottoman Empire, the twenty-seven-year-old Tocqueville and his cousin Louis de Kergorlay, who had participated in the conquest, seem briefly to have considered purchasing land in Algeria and becoming settlers. Tocqueville sketched a list of questions he intended to pose to the venerable orientalist Sylvestre de Sacy, including: "Is spoken Arabic a difficult language to learn? How long would a man of average abilities and devoting himself to it exclusively require to acquire enough for it to be useful in everyday life?"[2] Though he soon abandoned any plans to settle in Algeria, he continued to study Algerian history and culture, investigate the Turkish administration of Algeria, and read the Koran.

Tocqueville placed French colonialism at the center of his political agenda from the beginning of his legislative career. In 1837, during his first, failed, effort to win a seat in the Chamber of Deputies, he published two "Letters on Algeria," the first product of his study of the country.[3] He won a seat in the Chamber in 1839 (representing Valognes, near the town and estate of Tocqueville), and in 1841, after a thorough study of government reports on the colony, Tocqueville made his first trip to Algeria in the company of his brother Hippolyte and his friends Gustave de Beaumont and Claude de Corcelle.[4] This voyage, the first of Tocqueville's two visits to the country, took place just as the French began the total conquest and active colonization of Algeria. Tocqueville considered direct observation crucial for an understanding of the colonial project, and his visits left him firmly convinced that colonization of Algeria was essential to France's interests.[5]

Tocqueville's writings on Algeria share with all his other major works a fascination with new societies and an eagerness to analyze their social and political development. His enthusiasm for these projects is consistently palpable. When he studied the development of laws and mores under dramatically new circumstances, the creation of new polities out of diverse groups newly thrown together, and the mediation between existing customs and consciously developed practices, Tocqueville displayed most clearly his singular blend of sociological observation and moral purpose. The active role that government necessarily plays in colonization preoccupied Tocqueville as well: though he also grew ever more wary of the strength of the colonial administration, he was drawn to the idea of the colony as a laboratory for ideas of governance. And yet, despite his obvious delight at the possibilities presented by new societies, Tocqueville's avowed suspicion of the revolutionary spirit marks these writings as well, for he had something of the Burkean "reluctance to destroy any established system of government, upon a theory" as well as his own famous commitment to the customs and habits that grow organically from the practice of local self-government.[6]

There is a certain tragedy in the development of Tocqueville's engagement with Algeria. He began, filled with national pride and fierce determination, by imagining a French bastion in North Africa that might establish France's international reputation as a great power. He overcame his early ambivalence about the conquest with resolutions to see it through. As he wrote in an 1840 letter to Corcelle, for instance: "I think that we will never do all the great things we set out to do in Algeria, and, all things considered, we have quite a sad possession there. But, on the other hand, I remain more convinced than ever: 1st that there is no middle ground between complete abandonment and, I don't say conquest, but total domination; 2nd that this domination . . . is quite practicable."[7] Tocqueville stopped writing about Algeria more than a decade before his death, not only distracted by the 1848 revolution that he had so long foreseen, but also dismayed by many of the consequences of the French presence in North Africa. He remained, though, unwilling to reject the colonial project. As Tocqueville's explicit involvement in the Algerian question drew to a close at the end of the 1840s, he seems to have become more sensitive to the moral problems of empire, without relinquishing any of his earlier faith that a French colony could and should be maintained in Algeria. In a later letter to Corcelle, he wrote, "How can we manage to create in Africa a French population with our laws, our mores, our civilization, while still preserving vis-à-vis the indigenous people all the considerations that justice, humanity, our interest well understood, and, as you have said, our honor strictly oblige us to preserve? The question has these two sides. One cannot usefully imagine the first without seeing the second."[8]

Scholars of Tocqueville's writings on America and France have often remarked on the tension in his writings between sociological analysis and moral judgment.[9] Most of his sociological work is driven, at least in part, by a distinctly moral goal. Although *Democracy in America*, for instance, should not be read as straightforward normative democratic theory, Tocqueville studied America with the idea that democracy is more just than aristocracy and more appropriate in the modern world, and that American democracy might provide the only model that preserves the liberty, once found among aristocrats, without which democracy becomes tyranny.[10] And yet in Tocqueville's reflections on empire, his rich sociological analysis of colonial societies often appears disjoined from what might be called the "moral" reflections: both Tocqueville's defense of the conquest and rule of non-European societies, and his criticism of colonial injustices. Because Tocqueville was committed philosophically to the belief that sociological analysis is inextricable from moral prescription, his apparent willingness to separate them in his writings on empire is all the more puzzling.

Tocqueville's writings display deep and unresolved ambivalence about European empires. He expressed enthusiasm about the greatness and novelty of imperial conquest and rule (and, far less often, a belief in its goodness or justice), but also horror at its violence, and occasionally disappointment at Europeans' consistent failure to realize their *mission civilisatrice*, although he also criticized defenders of such a mission as hypocritical.[11] Tocqueville never forgot or denied the violence of imperial conquest, but his moral judgments about it vary wildly: from a sort of daring acceptance of the need for violence, which some scholars have attributed to his "aristocratic" bent, to a belief that to repeat the depredations of the Spanish and Anglo-Americans in the New World would violate the laws of humanity.[12] What is more, Tocqueville never explicitly confronted his own ambivalence, or acknowledged the contradictions his commitment to the conquest of Algeria imposed on his thought.[13]

The equivocations of a single, late, letter offer a particularly stark display of Tocqueville's ambivalence about colonial expansion. In 1857, during the rebellion in India, he wrote to Lord Hatherton, a British former M.P., that he had "never for an instant doubted your triumph, which is that of Christianity and of civilization."[14] Still, Tocqueville told Hatherton, after as careful a study as he could make without visiting India, he had concluded that England had done little more in the colony than take the place of indigenous governments and rule with the same methods, if somewhat more mildly and equitably. "I admit to you," he wrote, "that the thought still stays with me from this study that the English had not in a century done anything for the Indian populations that might have been expected from their enlightenment and their institutions. I think that more could have been expected from them."[15] He described the British "task" as "not only to dominate India, but to civilize it. These two things, indeed, are closely connected."[16] As in his Algeria writings, Tocqueville was unwilling to rule out domination and the use of violence. This letter thus displays three recurrent modes of Tocqueville's writings on empire: a vague hope that European empire will civilize the rest of the world; a doubt, based on careful study of administrative records, that European governments ever in fact succeed in improving their colonial subjects; and an acknowledgment of violence as a necessary element of colonial rule.

The ambivalence of Tocqueville's writings on empire is not, as one might suspect from a reading of *Democracy in America*, simply that of someone who understood that the multiple goods of political life do not go together neatly but rather must be limited, balanced, and compromised. Nor should we be satisfied with another explanation given for Tocqueville's belief that conquest was justified: that his French nationalism excused, in his mind, whatever injustices he believed were necessary in the pursuit of national glory or power.[17] Rather, I suggest, Tocqueville's anxieties about the difficulty of maintaining political engagement in France in an age of democratization led him to approve of the exercise of French power in Algeria and elsewhere (India, if possible) and largely to ignore the claims of those France sought to dominate.

From Assimilation to Domination: Tocqueville's Early Colonial Vision

Tocqueville's early thoughts about European relations with indigenous peoples in America clearly influenced his prescriptions in his earliest essays on Algeria, his two "Letters" of 1837. At this early stage in the foundation of a French colony in Algeria, when the broader French public was still unsure of the wisdom of attempting to expand French territory in North Africa, Tocqueville was already declaring that "with time, perseverance, ability, and justice, I have no doubt that we will be able to raise a great monument to our country's glory on the African coast."[18] The two "Letters" offer an informed and focused attack on the past seven years of French colonial policy in North Africa and present Tocqueville's vision of colonial society and the means of achieving it; these views would change considerably after he visited the country.

These articles demonstrate Tocqueville's early indebtedness to literary tropes of the Orient. The literary quality of the early writings would be replaced several years later by a more empirical tone, bolstered by his own observations and by statistics gleaned from government documents.[19] Here, however, drawing on familiar eighteenth-century images, he cast the Ottoman regime as a stagnant despotism, one that had kept the local tribes in a state of political immaturity and prevented them from pursuing forms of self-government of which they were clearly capable. He criticized the Ottoman regime as "not truly speaking a government but a continuation of conquest, a violent exploitation of the conquered by the conquerors."[20] The Turkish Janissaries occupied the country merely to levy taxes to be sent off to Turkey; they took no interest in governing the indigenous population and remained aloof from them, disdaining even their own children by Arab women (the mixed-race population known as *koulouglis*). As a result, perhaps, of his confinement of "oriental" qualities to the Turkish rulers, Tocqueville displayed in these early writings a much greater interest in local forms of social organization and much greater confidence in the existence of political structures among the indigenous Algerians, and in Algerians' capacity for political action and organization, than he would acknowledge in later works. Like so many other European observers of tribal peoples, Tocqueville, on first encountering them, was captivated by their nobility and their love of freedom.[21]

At the same time, Tocqueville proposes in these early articles that France quash the Algerians' incipient national organization in order to bring about the assimilation of natives and settlers to form a "new civilization" under French rule. He suggests that the French should work toward this assimilation through an initial stage of legal pluralism and religious toleration. If the several groups that made up Algerian society were governed by laws they could respect, he argues, laws tailored to their own social, economic, and developmental circumstances, the new government would gain the moral authority it certainly lacked at that early stage. He argues that the Algerians could become "free, respected and sedentary" through the rule of law, if the French treated them with respect and learned Algerian languages and customs; the "races" would then "intermix," "amalgamate," and "become reconciled."[22] The influence of Tocqueville's observations about America are apparent here: he had faulted the Anglo-Americans precisely for forcing the indigenous peoples too quickly to live under European laws, and for not permitting them to become "sedentary" to some extent on their own terms.[23] He was not more specific about the political arrangements he envisioned, although it does seem that at this moment at least Tocqueville imagined full assimilation of Algerians into French politics and society, and a gradual relaxation of the "exceptional" laws that must, he believed, govern any colonial society. It was not until he visited Algeria four years later and began to debate colonial policy as a member of the Chamber of Deputies that Tocqueville began to express doubts about the feasibility of assimilation and to propose dramatically different relations to the state for European colons and for the indigenous inhabitants.[24]

These early articles also express a plea for humility on the part of the French: if they went into the country believing they had everything to teach the natives, they would fail not only the conquered people but also their own interests. Tocqueville argued that the French had already displayed such counterproductive arrogance by deporting the former Ottoman rulers instead of drawing on their knowledge of the country and its inhabitants, and by destroying their records and even their roads. Instead of adopting the Ottomans' well-established scheme of property documentation and taxation, the French had instead violently imposed a less effective and more brutal system and had found themselves forced to extort money and goods "from our unhappy subjects by means far more Turkish than those the Turks ever used."[25]

Tocqueville's early vision of legal pluralism demanded ethnographic understanding on the part of the French sufficient to distinguish among the characters and needs of the different peoples of Algeria, and accordingly his early articles are devoted in large part to examining the differences between the mostly sedentary Kabyle tribes (Berbers living in the Atlas), and the more nomadic Arab population. He described the Kabyles, whom he as well as later French administrations were to favor over the Arabs,[26] as living an ideal stage of society in which freedom and equality coexisted with an admirable level of social and political organization. The Kabyles, he suggested, were the true "natural men" whom Rousseau had sought among Amerindian tribes. "If Rousseau had known the Cabyles," he wrote,

> [H]e would not have uttered such nonsense about the Caribs and other Indians of America: he would have sought his models in the Atlas; there he would have found men subject to a sort of social police and nonetheless almost as free as the isolated individual who enjoys his savage independence in the heart of the woods; men who are neither rich nor poor, neither servants nor masters; who name their own leaders, and hardly notice that they have leaders, who are content with their state and preserve it.[27]

Although Tocqueville expressed less admiration for the nomadic Arabs, he was struck by their careful documentation of collective property rights and by their well-developed religious aristocracy of marabouts. Tocqueville, who had read the Koran with an eye to its political and military implications, devoted particular attention to the marabouts' use of their religious authority as a basis for political power.[28]

Tocqueville clearly viewed the national consolidation of Algeria as an imminent possibility, and as an event delayed not by the Algerians' barbarism or political immaturity, but by the superior military power of the Ottoman Empire. He argued that the French, in their confusion and despite their heavy-handedness, had presented indigenous leaders with a chance for resurgence. Knowing nothing of the political organization developing among the local tribes, the French were unwittingly driving all the tribes into the arms of a single capable leader, the marabout Abdelkader, and thus encouraging an Arab national unity that would make it impossible to subject the Arabs to French rule.[29] Although it appeared that under Ottoman domination, the Arabs "had entirely lost the habit of governing themselves," Tocqueville believed that the Algerians' capacity for political organization had merely been weakened, rather than destroyed, by centuries of Turkish rule. He was deeply impressed by the speed with which Abdelkader—a "puny young man, who was at the time but twenty-five years old"—had emerged out of the anarchy and, within a few years of the Turkish defeat, established his national movement as the primary political and military force in western Algeria.[30] The immediate result of the French conquest was thus to open a space for political organization, of which the Arabs, and in particular their religious aristocracy, were quick to take advantage. "The most rapid and certain effect of our conquest was to give back to the marabouts the political existence they had lost," he noted. The French, Tocqueville argued, should permit this renewed self-government but control it and put it to their own use.[31] The two extremes that most worried Tocqueville were complete anarchy, and unification of the Arabs under a single leader. He argued that the French had to cultivate leaders such as Abdelkader, since they could not possibly govern the country directly (the tribes disappeared into the desert whenever the French tried to control them), but they had to encourage the rise of a number of rivals, for the national organization of Algerians under a single indigenous leader would likely destroy French hopes of dominance.

Tocqueville noted that Abdelkader had exercised considerable political wisdom in organizing the Arabs in western Algeria: the marabout emphasized his religious heritage and preserved the Arabs' customs he believed would strengthen unity and support for his leadership, while also borrowing from Turks and Europeans features of administration and military organization.[32] In his more cynical essay of 1841, Tocqueville would call Abdelkader the "Muslim Cromwell," a reference both to the marabout's manipulation of religious passions for political ends and to his political ability.[33] Despite his genuine admiration for the leader's success at national organization, however, Tocqueville studied Abdelkader primarily in order to spot his weaknesses and to learn better how to conquer and govern Algeria. Tocqueville believed that Abdelkader's political sophistication and ability justified a vigorous French response, whereas implicit in his treatment of America's westward expansion had been the notion that what made that conquest deplorable, namely the Amerindians' naïveté and lack of political organization, also made it inevitable. In the case of Abdelkader, the conquest would not be inevitable at all, but rather had to be carefully planned to overcome his political astuteness.[34]

Tocqueville's initial vision of French Algeria, then, is one of many groups living firmly under French rule, but with different laws and different degrees of autonomy until they could be assimilated to form a single population living under French laws and French governors.[35] Two of the most striking aspects of Tocqueville's early views on Algeria—his interest in Arab forms of political organization and self-governance, and his desire to see the integration of French settlers and Algerians through a policy of toleration and pluralism—would both largely disappear in his later works, after he visited Algeria, became convinced that integration was impossible, and turned increasingly to strategies of military domination.

When Tocqueville arrived in Algeria in May 1841, he set out to understand the country much as he had America and Ireland in the previous decade, beginning with impressions about the society drawn from its architecture and visual aspect, and interviewing military officials, civilian administrators, doctors, lawyers, bishops, and prominent citizens. Already we see his interest shift from Algeria's indigenous inhabitants to the new colonial society. His immediate impression, noted in his journal and early letters, was of restless activity reminiscent of the American frontier and a racial and cultural mixture even more bewildering. Tocqueville allowed himself a romanticism in his first responses to the country that would be short-lived: for the moment, it was a "[d]elicious country, Sicily with the industry of France." "Astonishing contrast," Tocqueville observed: "the Sahel the image of nature cultivated by industry and the most advanced civilization; the plain: *wilderness*."[36] Of Algiers he wrote,

> First appearance of the town: I have never seen anything like it. Prodigious mix of races and costumes, Arab, Cabyle, Moor, Negro, Mahonais, French. Each of these races, tossed together in a space much too tight to contain them, speaks its language, wears its attire, displays different mores. This whole world moves about with an activity that seems feverish. The entire lower town seems in a state of destruction and reconstruction. On all sides, one sees nothing but recent ruins, buildings going up; one hears nothing but the noise of the hammer. It is Cincinnati transported onto the soil of Africa.[37]

But it was on this first visit to Algeria that Tocqueville first recognized the real violence of colonial warfare and its likely consequences for both Frenchmen and Algerians. Of the abundant plains described above, he also wrote, "A promised land, if one didn't have to farm with gun in hand."[38] Tocqueville had already observed the brutalizing effects of colonial rule on both the indigenous people and their occupiers in America. His resolute defense of further conquest and occupation in the face of this knowledge indicates the degree of his commitment to the expansion of the French Empire.[39]

Always of delicate health, Tocqueville contracted dysentery and had to cut short his planned journey around the country; he wrote the "Essay on Algeria" while recuperating in France. Although the work remained unpublished during his lifetime, the "Essay" was Tocqueville's first extended effort to produce a colonial policy. Written with most of his parliamentary career ahead of him, the "Essay" can be read as a blueprint for a colonial society by a powerful, prominent, and increasingly respected expert on the subject. It is also the most uncompromising of Tocqueville's writings on Algeria. Although written only four years after the "Letters on Algeria," the "Essay" reveals a dramatic shift in Tocqueville's position on colonization. He had become far more concerned with the role Algeria would play in the securing of France's international reputation, and less interested in the contours of the new society for that society's own sake. Seeing Algeria for himself had caused Tocqueville to abandon his early hopes for integration of the French and Algerian populations into a single "new civilization." Only people who have never been to Africa, he now wrote, could entertain the "chimera" of a fusion of the two peoples. His scorn for the idea of a rapprochement between French and Algerians, as well as his new disdain for critics of empire who had never visited the country—such as Amédée Desjobert—give this text a haughty and even cruel edge.[40] Tocqueville's use of such terms as *ignorant*, *savage*, and *half-civilized* to describe the indigenous population became more frequent, and his military recommendations increasingly harsh.

Over the course of the next decade, the ambivalence about imperial violence that Tocqueville had demonstrated in his earlier writings about America would creep back into his thoughts on North Africa, but the "Essay" shows little evidence of such ambivalence or self-doubt. It is here that Tocqueville defends General Bugeaud's infamous *razzias* (violent raids on villages), writing, "I have often heard men in France whom I respect, but with whom I do not agree, find it wrong that we burn harvests, that we empty silos, and finally that we seize unarmed men, women, and children. These, in my view, are unfortunate necessities, but ones to which any people who want to wage war on the Arabs are obliged to submit."[41] With clear-sightedness as well as a callous indifference to the welfare of its victims, Tocqueville acknowledged, as British liberals such as Mill did not, the violence that imperial conquest required.

By 1841, Tocqueville's earlier respect for Abdelkader as an emerging "national" leader had largely disappeared: now he saw the marabout as a clever but unprincipled man who would manipulate the religious passions of his followers, and adopt Europeans strategies of warfare, to unite his countrymen and expel the French. Tocqueville now compared Abdelkader to a medieval European king who sought to consolidate his own power by crushing the feudal lords: Arab society was, he suggested, at the very stage Europe had passed through hundreds of years earlier. Rather than simply trying to crush him, the Europeans should seek to dissolve Abdelkader's power by bribing his allies and offering them real protection if they deserted. As it was, throughout the world the French had repeatedly abandoned their own indigenous allies and proven that French friendship was fatal. "Isn't it finally time," Tocqueville wrote, "to show, even if only in a tiny corner of the desert, that people can attach themselves with France without losing their fortunes or their lives?"[42] Even so, he now believed that such alliances must be temporary and that Algerians, no matter how accommodating to their French invaders, must always be treated as a separate and subject population.

After his firsthand investigation of the country, Tocqueville had concluded that military domination without colonization was a futile strategy. As the Arab population would be unrelentingly hostile to the expropriation of land necessary for widespread European settlement, the French would have to adopt uncompromising strategies for defeating the inevitable Arab resistance. In addition to halting all trade with indigenous tribes, the strategy entailed *razzias*, imprisoning unarmed civilians, including women and children, and destroying any towns the Arabs might try to establish. This position, Tocqueville believed, was the moderate one: he both rejected the summary execution of civilian prisoners advocated by many in the military, and scorned as soft and idealistic those Frenchmen who protested against *razzias* and crop-burning. "[I]n order for us to colonize to any extent, we must necessarily use not only violent measures, but visibly iniquitous ones," Tocqueville wrote. "The quarrel is no longer between governments, but between races . . . the day a European plow touches the soil."[43]

Tocqueville's interests had, as a result of his tour, shifted decisively in the direction of the European settlers and their laws and away from relations between the French and the indigenous people.[44] Having decided that colonization was the primary purpose of military domination and that relations with Algerians would consist largely of violence, Tocqueville set about devising an ideal legal and administrative structure for the European colonists. Current conditions were, he believed, intolerable. Settlers must encounter a "perfect image of their homeland" in Algeria, or they would never stay and the colony would fail. With conditions in Algeria as bad as they appeared to Tocqueville and his companions, only the settlers' "ignorance and misery" in Europe could explain their decision to emigrate there.[45] The fundamental rights of modern society—respected in even the most despotic European countries—were security of persons and property, and these were violated regularly and wantonly by the colonial authorities. Europeans could be arrested and summarily deported without any legal guarantees or appeal process, and the authorities could, and often did, seize property for "public purposes" without indemnifying the owners. Thus, he had discovered, "a man who has left Algiers to spend eight days in Toulon could find his house razed on his return." What the colonial governors failed to understand was that Europeans would leave the comforts and protections of European societies only if they had good reason to expect to get rich in Algeria: property rights were far more important to them than political participation or freedom of speech.[46] Property arrangements were a disaster at that moment, Tocqueville argued. Speculators with no intention of cultivating had snapped up all the land, boundaries were in dispute everywhere, and many plots had been sold to several buyers. Forced expropriations, disastrous in principle, were necessary here to sort out the mess and place property on a firm footing; otherwise cultivation would cease and the colony would fail.[47]

Finally, Tocqueville used the "Essay on Algeria" as an occasion to develop detailed institutional reforms: Algeria suffered from both too little centralization and too much. Responsibility for Algerian affairs was scattered among a slew of ministries in Paris and Algiers, so that nobody was accountable, and at the same time communities in Algeria were prevented from taking charge of their own affairs by scores of centralizing, bureaucratic regulations.[48] The Parisian bureaucrats must give up their aesthetically pleasing, uniform designs and allow authorities on the spot to tailor policies to local conditions: as it was, a town had to apply to the Paris ministries for funds to fix the church roof. The dangers of centralization had preoccupied Tocqueville from the time of his earliest writings on France and America. Here, for the first time, he outlined his ideas for a new society in the face of France's tendency to centralization. When he applied his historical research to institutional design in his own day, the result was a far less radical critique of centralization than his other works would suggest.

Tocqueville's two trips to Algeria gave him great insight into the vices of imperial governance, although his concern remained largely with the injustices done to French settlers, rather than to Algerians. Much of Tocqueville's sociological perception thus was devoted to the problems of the colonists: his critique of the military and civil government's treatment of the French colons is far more elaborate than his consideration of French-Arab relations. Tocqueville reserved sharp criticism for the arbitrary and high-handed treatment of the colonists by the government, especially by the civil government.[49] His criticism of the arbitrariness and unaccountability of the colonial government shared much with Burke's diagnosis of the problems of imperial governance, though it rarely extended, as Burke's had, to relations with the indigenous people. Tocqueville maintained that colonial government suffered above all from the exceptionalism with which the French had chosen to treat their colony. That Algeria was an "exceptional" society, he argued, enabled the administrators to excuse vast executive powers by decree; summary expropriation, arrest, and deportation; and seizure of property. In short, French Algeria was deprived of due process and the rule of law on the grounds that its situation was too new and uncertain to permit even the most basic freedoms that Europeans had come to expect.[50]

When defending such freedoms, Tocqueville relied for the most part not on arguments about citizens' rights to such freedoms but on the historicist argument that citizens of even the most despotic European nations had begun to recognize freedom of person and property, and that the French expected in addition freedom of the press, trial by jury, and other more sophisticated freedoms. He defended the substance of the French revolutionary rights of men and citizens without relying on the Revolution's justificatory strategy. While this approach allowed him to hold that certain rights were due to Europeans in Algeria but not to the indigenous peoples, it left him without grounds to defend the infringement of liberties that he recognized the native Algerians themselves expected.

After his second trip to Algeria in 1846, Tocqueville was appointed to draft two reports by a parliamentary commission convened for the purpose of examining military requests for additional funds for their operations in Algeria.[51] The first report, whose ostensible subject was the question whether the fast-growing military force in Algeria could be reduced, ranged far more broadly to discuss the security of French possession of the colony, relations between France and the indigenous Algerians, and what Tocqueville saw as the administration's misgovernment of French settlers. The second report considered and rejected a plan for military colonization, which had been one of General Bugeaud's pet projects and was proposed by the subsequent administration. Though more narrowly focused than the first, in its discussion of various means of settling the new country, this report allowed Tocqueville to address the question of the foundation of new societies that had occupied him from the time of his visit to America.

Tocqueville, while necessarily including a great many technical details absent from his earlier writings, thus took a broad and relatively philosophical view of his mandate as commission reporter. Although the reports are more assured and imperious in tone than Tocqueville's often troubled and ambivalent private letters, the positions he advocated in the report accord with his other statements on empire, including his arguments in the "Essay on Algeria," and it is reasonable to read the report as presenting Tocqueville's own views. The reports argued that, thanks to General Bugeaud, colonial war had become a science. Power, peace, and knowledge had been mutually reinforcing. Domination of the tribes and establishment of a tenuous peace had allowed the French to study them, for "you can study barbarous people only with arms in hand." Algerian society had become transparent—"indigenous society is no longer veiled to us"—and domination simpler.[52] The reports' many references to the importance of knowledge for domination suggest that Tocqueville and his colleagues viewed investigations in Algeria such as his own as instrumental to French rule there. Thanks to research into the

Arabs' and Kabyles' history and social institutions, the conquerors could now determine the "true and natural limits of our domination" and thus devote resources to achievable ends.

In contrast to Tocqueville's earlier writings, which actively advocated conquest in the face of official indecision and general indifference, these reports spoke of the conquest, and the settlement, of Algeria as a fait accompli. The task now was to rule securely without having to continue the dramatic troop escalations of the past decade, to develop a proper legal system for the existing European population and to promote its growth, and to govern the Arabs, now seen as a society apart, with strict justice, encouraging them to adopt certain aspects of Western civilization while keeping them in their place. Tocqueville preserved a hope that European rule over the indigenous Algerians would become regularized, sustained through custom and a recognition of French authority rather than remaining "accepted only as the work of victory and the daily product of force."

By 1847 Tocqueville had been chastened by the wanton violence of the French army and had concluded that the government in Algeria was disorderly, tyrannical, and "profoundly illiberal" (*OC* 3.1: 197). As a result of his 1846 trip to Algeria (when he managed to escape from his Potemkin-style tour and meet some of the indigenous leaders), Tocqueville came to see that the very means he had countenanced five years before had sown disaster among the native population and produced a society of settlers more violent and oppressive than the army itself.[53] Indigenous farmers had been dispossessed of their land and then hired by lazy settlers at paltry wages to do the same work they had once done as small landowners. Muslim society, although "backward and imperfect," had been far from uncivilized; the French had made it barbaric.[54] The reports show Tocqueville often unsympathetic to the indigenous people but more ambivalent about French imperial expansion than he had been in the earlier works.[55]

In his early studies of Algerian society, Tocqueville had found much support for his belief in the importance of religion to social order, and he now criticized the French administration for having made havoc not just of property rights, but more destructively of indigenous legal and religious institutions and education. The French had encountered a society that had been poor and nomadic, but also well ordered, with extensive networks of religious schools and charities; they had demolished these, leaving "Muslim society much more miserable, more disordered, more ignorant, and more barbarous than it had been before knowing us."[56] Fanaticism would always find leaders; to suppress the religious schools and charitable foundations in the name of enlightening or abolishing Islam would only be to cede power to impostors and demagogues. In the interest of stability, the

French should resurrect Algeria's once flourishing educational network, from the primary schools through Koranic legal training.[57] In sum, the French owed the Arabs good government and "exact, but rigorous, justice . . . when they act reprehensibly toward us."[58] Plans for the assimilation of Arabs, such as Tocqueville earlier had supported, and efforts to transplant "European civilization" to North Africa, were, he now believed, futile and misguided. At best the French could hope to weaken indigenous hostility to French rule and win the population's support not through ideas but by demonstrating their common interests.

Tocqueville argued that France could attempt to promote acceptance of its rule by respecting the Algerians' laws and customs and demonstrating the extent to which their interests matched French interests, although he did not elaborate much in these later reports on the mechanisms of rule that would replace violence. At the same time, Tocqueville believed that the Algerians' mobility meant that French rule must be aggressive and harsh. In order to govern, the French had not only to seize the administrative apparatus from the Ottomans but also to subjugate the population. Tocqueville had questioned his British correspondents about British means of governing the populations of India, New Zealand, and the African Cape. He learned from their method of indirect governance through indigenous notables, and advocated the same for Algeria.[59] The "art of the conqueror" required controlling the natives' disposition toward their European governors: Tocqueville believed that until the French had established some moral authority among the population, they could rule only by co-opting indigenous leaders and governing through them.[60]

The *rapports* of 1847 include Tocqueville's most complete statement of French obligations to the indigenous peoples of Algeria, and the strict limits of those obligations. Here, as he surveyed the past two decades of France's presence in Algeria, his greatest criticism of French treatment of the indigenous peoples was that the French were inconsistent, sometimes too benevolent and other times unexpectedly severe. French benevolence, in the form of free transportation to Egypt for the pilgrimage to Mecca, new mosques, and honorific titles, extended "to the point of forgetting its position as conqueror." He added, "There is neither utility in allowing, nor a duty to allow, our Muslim subjects exaggerated ideas of their own importance, nor to persuade them that we are obligated to treat them under all circumstances precisely as though they were our fellow citizens and our equals. They know that we have a dominant position in Africa; they expect to see us keep it. To abandon it today would be to astonish and confuse them, and to fill them with erroneous or dangerous notions."[61] He held that Muslims were not fellow citizens or equals; moreover, it was just to treat them as inferiors, since that was what they expected from French domination. Still, while it would be wrong to leave the best land for the Arabs, the French must be scrupulous about indemnifying indigenous property holders for the property they took.

Having dismissed the hope for an assimilation of Algerians and Frenchmen, the reports proposed a vision of a separate European society in Algeria, again drawing on Tocqueville's knowledge of the British experience. The French should professionalize colonial administration by establishing a school like the East India Company's college at Haileybury.[62] They should make property sales simple and quick to encourage settlement, as Lord Durham's famous report about Canada had instructed. As it was, the sale or rental of the smallest plot had to be approved by the minister of war: at that rate, the new society was bound to be stillborn. Centralization in Paris and an insistence on the letter of the bureaucratic law had led to a breakdown of the rule of law. Denied liberty, the colonial authorities took license, sneakily and irregularly.

Moments of caution in the reports indicate a retreat from the harshness of Tocqueville's 1841 "*Essay.*" The intervening years had been those of Bugeaud's governor-generalship in Algeria: an era of what Tocqueville had come to see as increasing military arrogance and intransigence, of growing hostility between soldiers and civilian settlers, and of the brutal *razzias* that had terrorized the Arab population without subduing them. Tocqueville, along with many in Paris, had by this point turned against Bugeaud and his tactics, and the first report indicated that new restraint with a typically accurate Tocquevillian prediction:

> If on the contrary we were to demonstrate by our behavior—without saying so, for these things are often done but never admitted—that in our eyes the old inhabitants of Algeria are merely an obstacle to be pushed aside or trampled under foot, if we surrounded their populations, not to lift them in our arms toward well-being and enlightenment but to destroy and smother them, the question between the two races would be that of life or death. Algeria would become, sooner or later, a closed field, a walled arena, where the two peoples would have to fight without mercy, and where one of the two would have to die. May God save us, gentlemen, from such a destiny!
>
> Let us not, in the middle of the nineteenth century, begin the history of the conquest of America over again.[63]

The humanity of the passage must not be exaggerated, for it was underpinned by the new confidence that Tocqueville expressed at the beginning of the first report, when he asserted that France's "domination" over Algeria had never been more secure. Still, in both reports, the last extended treatment Tocqueville would give to the question of empire, we glimpse as well his increasing disillusionment with the colonial experiment. The next few years, the last of his political career (1848–51), would be almost wholly occupied with France's domestic crisis. Tocqueville would devote his final decade, as a private citizen, to the study of French history, in his lifelong effort to craft a historical vision and a political order for France that could bear the weight of modern democracy.

The British Empire as Rival and Model

Throughout his years in the Chamber, Tocqueville studied the British Empire as both a rival and a model of successful conquest. Tocqueville's affection and admiration for England, and especially for English domestic political traditions, is well known.[64] His great interest in England's imperial experience has been less noted. From his earliest observations of the American frontier, Tocqueville had decided the British were extraordinarily adept colonizers, that they had a national aptitude for colonization that the French lacked. Later, in addition to his observations on Ireland, he pursued his investigation of the British Empire through an extended study of India, and in exchanges with his English correspondents, several of whom—most notably John Stuart Mill—were highly placed in the British colonial administration.[65] Indeed, some of Tocqueville's last reflections on European imperial expansion appear in letters to British friends in 1857–58, as Britain struggled to quash the Sepoy Rebellion in India.

Tocqueville's extensive notes on India, written in the early 1840s at the peak of his interest in Algeria, show Tocqueville seeking to benefit from the British experience given that the British had, in India, already wrestled with a number of key problems in colonization: the establishment of a judicial system, the development of education policy, the fixing of property rights. In all these areas, the influence of the British example on Tocqueville's views is marked. Although he was aware that the British empire in India was tremendously costly in economic terms, and believed the French empire in Algeria was likely to be so as well, he was convinced that the political gains were worth the expense.[66] On this economic question Tocqueville was in agreement with many of his British friends and sources, who, while they thought the empire was likely to remain an economic drain, believed it was worth continuing, often from a sense of duty.[67]

Tocqueville did, however, have important disagreements on the subject of colonization with the British liberals with whom he corresponded: these stemmed from their different justifications for empire. His British friends regarded conquest by a civilized nation of a barbarous one as a duty undertaken in service of human progress though costly for the conquering country; they disowned justifications based on the glory or political needs of the conqueror. Tocqueville, in contrast, remained suspicious of pretensions that empire was a civilizing enterprise and insisted that greatness and the political strength it would produce were sufficient justifications for conquest. Unlike J. S. Mill, for instance, who maintained that despotic rule over "barbarians" was justified only when it was calculated to improve them, but who also had great faith in British rule in India as truly improving, Tocqueville could admit that he believed the French had barbarized the Algerians rather than benefited them and still argue for expanding French rule.

Tocqueville argued for the maintenance and expansion of the French Empire primarily for two reasons: he believed that such a grand enterprise could build political solidarity and engagement among the French population, and he feared that France would lose its international position and reputation if it continued to fall behind Britain in the quest for overseas possessions.[68] As I noted in chapter 6, Tocqueville's British friends were dismayed by what they saw as his, and France's, frankly jingoistic attitude toward international politics, which justified conquest and belligerence on the grounds of national interest and even glory.

The gulf that separated Tocqueville from the British regarding foreign and colonial policy became apparent from the moment he joined the Chamber of Deputies. Tocqueville's concern about France's international position, and even more about the implications of a French "decline" for the country's internal stability, led him temporarily to abandon his lifelong Anglophilia in favor of frank animosity toward this rival in the Mediterranean. Although his views evolved during the decade away from the strident nationalism he displayed during the early 1840s, Tocqueville was consistent in his belief that French domestic stability and international reputation both required France to play a prominent role in the extension of European control over Asia and North Africa and in particular to check English dominance.

Tocqueville's first speech before the Chamber, in 1839, was a passionate engagement in what came to be called the Eastern question, in which the European powers took sides in a dispute between the Ottoman sultan and his vassal in Egypt, Mohammed (Méhémet) Ali.[69] The decade of Tocqueville's parliamentary career and his interest in Algeria thus began with a foreign policy crisis during which Tocqueville displayed a nationalist belligerence that shocked the British, who knew him as an admirer of England's culture and constitutional tradition. Contrary to Tocqueville's view that Britain and Russia had naturally opposed interests in the affair, the two countries had unexpectedly allied with the Ottoman Empire against Mohammed Ali and his French supporters.[70] Tocqueville took a resolutely anti-Britain position throughout the Eastern crisis. He criticized Adolphe Thiers (premier and minister of foreign affairs in 1840) for his conciliatory posture toward England. After Thiers told him in a private conversation that France should ally with England and agree to let the latter have Egypt as a colony, Tocqueville noted to himself that this view was "trop modeste"; as far as he was concerned France must on no account cede more political power in the Mediterranean to Britain, even if Thiers were right to think that France should not expand its own North African colonies eastward (*OC* 3.2: 269–72).

Tocqueville was convinced for most of his political career that his colleagues undervalued French colonies and their political worth for France. He devoted such energy to the question of colonization because he felt he had grasped the historic importance of conquest as few Frenchmen in his day had done. In a brief but suggestive sketch, Tocqueville described the Eastern question as central to the spirit of the age: it was characteristic of him, as indeed of much of nineteenth-century European thought, to attempt to capture the movement of history and the essence of that moment.[71] The "movement of the European race into Asia" is the "movement of the century," Tocqueville wrote (*OC* 3.2: 279). In his second major speech in the Chamber, on November 30, 1840, Tocqueville drew on these thoughts to draw a portrait of the age that suggested that if France continued to lag behind in European colonial expansion, the country would not simply decline in importance but would become a sort of anachronism:

> What is happening in Egypt and Syria is only part of an immense picture, only the beginning of an immense scene. Do you know what is happening in the Orient? An entire world is being transformed; from the banks of the Indus to the Black Sea, in all that immense space, societies are crumbling, religions are being weakened, nationalities are disappearing, all the [old] lights are going out, the old Asiatic world is vanishing, and in its place the European world is rising. Europe in our times does not attack Asia only through a corner, as did Europe in the time of the crusades: She attacks . . . from all sides, puncturing, enveloping, subduing.[72]

While it seems the English liberals with whom Tocqueville corresponded believed much the same thing, they never had to be as self-conscious as he about the idea that to be a modern nation was to colonize. As citizens of the dominant colonial and maritime power they could, for the most part, simply carry out their intentions without agonizing about their national reputation or possible decline.

Their horror at Tocqueville's belligerence, then, demonstrated not so much their high-mindedness or their morally advanced politics, as they would have it, as their political security. The surprise and dismay expressed by Tocqueville's longtime correspondent Nassau William Senior, a political economist and lawyer, at what he saw as Tocqueville's offensive nationalism, was a characteristic British response:

> The speech which you addressed to the French Chamber would have been utterly ruinous to any English statesman. What, it would have been said, to think of going to war merely to prevent our being excluded from taking part in the affairs of Syria or Egypt? or to show that we are not unable to go to war? Now you laid down to the French Chamber these . . . causes as fit causes of war. In the English House, either of Lords or Commons, we should consider such proposals as scarcely deserving a serious answer.[73]

It was precisely this view and this supercilious tone that indicated England's unassailable international position, in contrast to Tocqueville's sense that his country was falling from greatness into *décadence*.[74] As Seymour Drescher has noted, Tocqueville and his English friends soon set aside their rancor over the Eastern question and French expressions of nationalism.[75] Tocqueville had already begun to study British India, however, as both a model and something of a threat.

In the summer of 1843, Tocqueville set out to write a work on the British empire in India, an analysis that would, he hoped, "dispel the clouds that still seem to hide the foundation of the English empire in India and connect this event to the general causes that govern human affairs" (*OC* 3.1: 445). He gave up on the latter aim ("trop ambitieux," he penciled in the margin) and indeed never completed the work on India, on the grounds that the book would be flawed, given that he could not visit the colony himself.[76] Still, his reflections on India remain a source of insights about British imperialism in the mid–nineteenth century as well as of Tocqueville's own striking version of imperial liberalism.

The combination of admiration and envy Tocqueville felt for Britain made him a perceptive analyst of the contradictions of British imperial ideology. While the English criticized Tocqueville for his unbecoming nationalism, he quite astutely noted their self-serving adherence to a myth of empire as benevolent. Whereas a belief in progress and in the civilizing mission was an article of faith among the British liberals and philosophic radicals who dominated Indian policymaking after 1828, Tocqueville remained suspicious both of the rigid dichotomy between civilized and barbarous peoples employed by thinkers like the Mills and of European confidence that their rule benefited and improved their non-European subjects.

If the English conquered less violently than others, Tocqueville suggested, the particular vice of their enterprise lay in English self-righteousness and in their sense of moral superiority to their subjects. As in America, Tocqueville emphasized the English tendency to hypocrisy, or perhaps self-deception: English and Anglo-American settlers regularly pursued their own interests, always flattering themselves that they acted with humanity and benevolence. The hypocrisy that enabled the English to insist on the benevolence of their colonial rule was so engrained, he suggested, that they had come to use such language not only when addressing Indians but also among themselves. At the same time, Tocqueville described the English as continually struggling against the evidence to maintain the claim that their rule was for their subjects' benefit:

> *Duplicity and hypocrisy of English politics.* The English did nothing in India but what all the other European nations would have done in their place. In short they were perhaps more moderate in their use of their omnipotence, and less violent than many others would have been in their place. This is not what astonishes me. What I cannot get over is their perpetual attempts to prove that they act in the interest of a principle, or for the good of the natives, or even for the advantage of the sovereigns they subjugate; it is their frank indignation toward those who resist them; these are the procedures with which they almost always surround violence. They use this language not only with the natives or with European society in general, but among themselves. In the reports of the governor-general with the court of directors and even with his subordinates in India, one finds this style everywhere. (*OC* 3.1: 505)

These observations are particularly striking given how difficult it is to find any such acknowledgment among the British themselves. The commitment to empire *as a moral enterprise* was shared across a broad swath of the British political spectrum, from the philosophic radicals to Evangelicals to staunch antidemocrats such as James Fitzjames Stephen.

Although by the 1840s French political opinion was hardly less enthusiastic about non-European conquests than British opinion, the French tended in this period to be less vulnerable to the temptation to justify colonialism with such complacent certainty about the benefits to the conquered. For his own part, Tocqueville always recognized the violence of colonial conquest and refused to regard European rulers as an unmixed blessing: not only the French, whom he believed were particularly inept colonizers, but even the exemplary English in India.

> The English delivered the whole peninsula from perpetual wars, ravages, incursion of armed bands that constantly ruined it. And, in the parts directly subjected to them, they have substituted a regular and moderate government for the capricious and often violent administration of the indigenous princes. Nonetheless, the primary effects of their domination have been to augment misery, malaise, the number of crimes. (*OC* 3.1: 478–79)

Tocqueville perceived, with a clarity that few Englishmen did, the tension between two premises of the British liberal colonial enterprise of his day. The first premise was not simply that all humans are equal, but that because of this equality or identity, all human cultures are commensurable and human progress can be measured along a single scale. The second was that the English, because of their great cultural advancement, were utterly different in ideas and capacities—even as individuals—from their native subjects. These two ideas were certainly reconcilable in principle: both rested on a linear theory of cultural progress, and it was believed that however barbarous Indians were at present they would eventually be made capable of advanced civilization and self-government. In practice, however, as Tocqueville saw, the conviction of English superiority tended to produce a caste mentality among the British rulers of India that was in many ways more corrosive, and more offensive to the governed, than the caste mentality of Brahmanism.[77]

Tocqueville argued that it was precisely Christian Europe's understanding of the unity of humanity that had made Europeans such determined conquerors. "It is the idea of the common origin of the human race," he wrote in his notes on India, "of the similitude of men and the obligation that they are all to know and worship the same God, that introduced proselytism and persecution into the world."[78] British colonial rule, Tocqueville believed, was particularly strongly characterized by a sense of colonial subjects as potential equals, for whom conquest was a means to a kind of salvation, whether evangelical, or secular and civilizational. Brahmanism, in contrast, was an accommodating and tolerant religion, he noted, precisely because it was a religion of privileges; religious boundaries were racial boundaries, and Hindus could afford to tolerate different practices among those who could never be their equals.

At the same time, Tocqueville maintained that Europeans conquerors were guilty—as many more violent conquerors were not—of a presumptuousness about their own moral superiority. The Mughals, for instance, had been fiercer with "the sword, but they were not and they did not judge themselves superior in all the rest. . . . The European conqueror is comparatively gentle, moderate, intelligent, but he is and he believes himself to be so different from the conquered and so much above him that he never manages to mix" (*OC* 3.1: 494). Tocqueville argued that the English sense of superiority was particularly egregious, and in 1858 he concluded that it had done more to provoke the Sepoy Rebellion than any concrete political oppression. As he told Henry Reeve, of all colonizing peoples the English was "the most disposed to hold itself apart, and (one can say it because this defect is intimately tied to great qualities) the haughtiest of all the European peoples."[79] Despite all the English had done to improve the pay and circumstances of the Indian army, the sepoys rebelled because

> the one perceived at every instant not only that he was not the equal to but that he was not even of the same nature as the other. When one looks in depth for the true cause of the revolt of your Indian army, I am convinced that you will

> find it there. . . . I believe that the horrible events in India are not in any way an uprising against oppression. It is the revolt of barbarism against pride.[80]

Further, like J. S. Mill Tocqueville had concluded that the arrogance of European settlers, more than colonial officials, posed the greatest problems for good colonial governance:

> Now, I have always noticed that wherever one introduced, not European authorities, but a European population, in the midst of the imperfectly civilized populations of the rest of the world, the real and pretended superiority of the former over the latter has accustomed them to feeling in a way so harmful to individual interests and so mortifying to the self-respect of the indigenous people that more anger resulted from that than from any political oppression.[81]

Given that British India was never a settler colony in the way that Algeria was, Tocqueville surely perceived that the likelihood of rebellion stemming from resentment was far greater in Algeria than in India; his warnings of implacable conflict in the 1847 reports indicate as much. And yet it is clear that whatever his misgivings about the effects of settler arrogance, he believed these dangers worth the risk, and he continued to argue strenuously against those who believed military conquest could succeed without civilian settlement.[82] The question of how the European settlers should interact with the indigenous population had long preoccupied Tocqueville, and these late reflections—undoubtedly inspired as much by his experience in Algeria as by his observation from afar of British India—illustrate Tocqueville's increasing pessimism about the possibilities for peaceful coexistence between indigenous and colonial populations. As we have seen, his earliest position was that a colonial society should be a new society formed from an amalgamation of both groups, including both residential mixing and eventually intermarriage.[83] During his parliamentary career, Tocqueville hewed to the position he developed after his first visit to Algeria: settlement was intrinsic to the colonial enterprise, but the European population would necessarily remain separate from the indigenous one, living under different laws and with little hope of merging even in the distant future. Tocqueville's frustration with the arrogance of the European settlers in Algeria, however, may, by the end of his life, have led him to feel that European insolence and local resentment were bound to overrun even these policed boundaries between the European and non-European communities.

Even as he admired Britain's imperial achievements, in his analysis of that rival empire Tocqueville was able to perceive and articulate the moral and political transgressions of imperial expansion that he never brought himself to acknowledge in the case of France. Tocqueville confided to Nassau Senior in 1857 that while he "rejoiced" at Britain's success in suppressing the Sepoy Rebellion, Britain's posture of arrogance had, not without reason, infuriated not only their subjects but the rest of the world as well.

> This affair [the Sepoy Rebellion], like that of the Crimea, has made clear how little the English nation, taken as a whole, excites the sympathy of foreign peoples. Everything in this last circumstance was made to interest: the similarity of race, religion, civilization. The ruin of the English in India couldn't have profited anyone except perhaps barbarism. Despite all that, I believe I can affirm that on the whole European continent, while detesting the barbarities committed against you, no one wished for your triumph. This, no doubt, comes in good part from the evil passions of men that make them always watch with pleasure the reverses of the fortunate and the strong. But it comes also from a less dishonest cause: from the conviction held by all the peoples of the world that England never considers anything but from the perspective of her greatness; that more than any other modern nation she lacks all sympathetic feeling for anyone else; and that she never notices what happens among foreigners, what they think, feel, suffer, or do, that relative to the part that England can play in these various incidents, she thinks only of herself, even when she seems the most occupied with them. There is certainly some exaggeration in this point of view. But I could not say that the truth is absolutely absent from it.[84]

Tocqueville, who justified France's imperial expansion in Algeria, including the violent dispossession and even slaughter of its inhabitants, on the basis of arguments about the importance of the conquest for French politics and the country's self-respect and international reputation, never acknowledged that what he charged here of the British could be said of his own imperial program as well.

Slavery in the French Empire

Tocqueville was as concerned to preserve French rule in the West Indian colonies as in Algeria, and here too a paramount concern was France's rivalry with Britain for both political power and international reputation. Tocqueville regarded the abolition of slavery as indispensable to the maintenance of French power in the colonies and argued repeatedly in speeches and articles that there could no longer be a question whether to abolish slavery, but only when.[85] Britain, having banned the slave trade in 1808, had emancipated slaves in all British colonies in 1838; this fact was at the heart of Tocqueville's case for abolition. To be sure, Tocqueville's persistent calls for abolition were rooted in his moral opposition to slavery, and especially to modern race slavery, as, in Cheryl Welch's words, "unnatural in the sense that it transgressed the most basic laws of equity," as well as "unnatural in the sense that it extinguished in the hearts of slaves those spontaneous instincts that alone assured their potential humanity."[86] Tocqueville's parliamentary speeches and articles on slavery in the French West Indies indicate, in addition to this underlying moral objection, his conviction that abolition was demanded by France's honor and national identity, as well as by the nation's interests, above all its interest in preserving its colonies. Notwithstanding Tocqueville's passionate and absolute moral condemnation of slavery, his prudential concerns shaped his belief that its abolition should be accompanied by ongoing restrictions on freed slaves' movement and property rights.

Along with many other prominent liberals, Tocqueville joined the Société Française pour l'Abolition de l'Esclavage, a moderate abolitionist society, soon after its founding by the duc de Broglie in 1834.[87] "On an ideological level," Seymour Drescher has argued, Tocqueville "wrote in a friendly atmosphere of consensus" and "well-nigh universal agreement that slavery was morally evil."[88] Tocqueville also shared with much of French political society a hostility to the biological racism that was advanced, most famously, by his disciple Gobineau.[89] As Tocqueville wrote to Gobineau, his theories of racial hierarchy were "probably quite false; I know that they are certainly very pernicious."[90] As was true for Constant and Mill, as we have seen, Tocqueville did not deny altogether the possible scientific truth of racist theories; his objection to racism was primarily political. Constant had worried that racist theories would be manipulated by the powerful to oppress the vulnerable and that such theories' pretensions to scientific truth would make them all the harder to refute; Tocqueville, for his part, was concerned above all that theories of biological determinism foreclosed the possibility of human freedom, that they constituted "a very great contradiction, if not a complete abolition, of human liberty."[91] As George Frederickson has argued, Tocqueville's response to Gobineau conceded the inferiority of non-Europeans, but attributed such differences to education and culture rather than to nature.[92] Worrying as much about the moral and political damage racist theories posed for Europeans as about the effects of such theories on subject peoples, Tocqueville wrote to Gobineau, "What purpose does it serve to persuade lesser peoples, living in abject conditions of barbarism or slavery, that, such being their racial nature, they can do nothing to better themselves, to change their habits or to ameliorate their status? Don't you see that in your doctrine are inherent all the evils produced by permanent inequality: pride, violence, the scorn of one's fellow man, tyranny, and abjection in every one of their forms?" Like slavery, racism aroused in Tocqueville passionate moral outrage, but his opposition to racism, as to slavery, was accompanied by evasions and qualifications worth attending to: above all, a willingness to grant that non-European peoples were indeed "lesser peoples," and a conviction that peaceful and egalitarian coexistence among peoples, whether whites and blacks in the New World, or Europeans and Arabs in Algeria, was a nearly impossible aspiration.[93] In *Democracy in America* as well as his writings on Algeria, Tocqueville cast this latter conviction as sociological observation, but his pessimism about the prospects for an evolution of racial attitudes among whites led to political prescriptions, such as recolonization of freed slaves to Africa or restrictions on blacks' property rights, that seem to encourage rather than counteract white intransigence.

Tocqueville, self-consciously adopting the position of the moderate, between the extremes of radical abolitionism and colonial plantocracy, couched his arguments in the French abolition debates in terms calculated to appeal to an audience not easily moved by the purer moral arguments from human equality. What sustained slavery in the French colonies, Tocqueville argued, was the selfish, though self-defeating, shortsightedness of the colonists, the indifference of the French public to the fate of the colonies, and a listless resignation by that public of France's vocation as the nation of liberty and equality.[94] As we have seen, Tocqueville believed the mediocrity and pettiness of French politics under the July Monarchy, and the apathy of the French public, meant that there were few possibilities for great political action in his day. Like colonial expansion, he believed, abolition of slavery offered an outstanding opportunity for the sort of great action that had distinguished the revolutionary era and that seemed largely out of reach in his own day, but which was essential, in his view, to a vibrant democratic politics. Citing Britain's abolition of slavery, "not by the desperate effort of the slave, but by the enlightened will of the master," Tocqueville argued that "the world today offers some great spectacles that would astonish us if we were not weary and distracted."[95]

Tocqueville maintained that France had a duty to its own reputation and glory, and in particular to the legacy of the Revolution, that required abolition of slavery in the colonies.[96] France, he argued, must not leave it to Britain to be the primary representative of what he called *French* principles. In abolishing first the slave trade and then slavery itself in the Caribbean islands, Britain had appropriated France's very identity:

> We were the ones to give a determined and practical meaning to this Christian idea that all men are born equal. . . . Thanks to us, these ideas have become the symbol of the new politics. Shall we desert them now, when they are triumphant? The English are doing nothing at this moment but applying *our* principles in their colonies. They act in accordance with what we still have the right to call the *French sentiment*. Are they to be more French than ourselves?[97]

Tocqueville argued that Britain's example had also proven the political wisdom of abolition: the former slaves had exhibited an "almost fanatical attachment to the metropole," emancipation had not "given rise to a *single* insurrection," ordinary crime had not increased, and freed blacks were "rush[ing] into the schools."[98] French slave colonies could not long survive surrounded by free British colonies: French slaves would continually seek to escape, aided by smugglers motivated by both sympathy and the demand for labor in the British colonies. Tocqueville even suggested that regiments of freed slaves from the British colonies, some of which were only a few dozen miles from French islands, would storm the French colonies to free their slaves.[99]

Tocqueville's understanding of the national interest led to his support for gradual rather than immediate abolition as well as to the view that certain restrictions ought to be placed on freed blacks, including a requirement that they remain in the colony of their residence and limitations on their purchase of land. British emancipation, in Tocqueville's view, while vindicating his belief in the equality of races, had also demonstrated the dangers of a total, unregulated emancipation. Immediate emancipation had raised slaves' expectations for their political status and for material well-being; a better course would be slowly to improve slaves' living conditions and only later to emancipate them, remaining a step ahead of their expectations in order to forestall rebellion. Moreover, even emancipation "does not mean that colonial society must all at once take on exactly the same appearance as greater French society, nor that the emancipated Negro is to enjoy on the spot all the rights that our worker possesses."[100] Freed slaves in the British colonies, Tocqueville argued, had proven themselves to be interested in education and material improvement; when permitted to buy land, they had promptly bought what they could and set up small farms. This pattern, while it attested to their ability to improve themselves once freed from the yoke of servitude, also depleted the labor force and elevated wages, thereby threatening to disrupt the islands' sugar economies. Tocqueville sought to show that France could emancipate slaves without destroying colonial economies, and to this end he recommended severe measures for suppressing the wages of the freed slaves, claiming that the only remedy for the colonial economy was to prohibit freed slaves from buying land.[101]

As Drescher has observed, for Tocqueville, "extended public domination was perfectly compatible with the abolition of private slaveholding and the indefinite extension [i.e., postponement] of legal equality. Tocqueville's deep commitment to both the abolition of slavery and the extended conquest of Algeria, for example, was predicated on this distinction."[102] For Tocqueville, emancipation in the French West Indies, like the conquest of Algeria, offered France, at a time of waning public interest in politics, an opportunity to undertake a political project worthy of a great nation. Emancipation held the further attraction of fulfilling Christian moral duty and the French revolutionary legacy, as Tocqueville understood them. His support for emancipation was consequently less tinged with ambivalence than his commitment to the Algerian conquest, since he never overcame his doubts that French rule in Algeria could be justified by its benefits to its indigenous subjects.[103] And yet in both cases, Tocqueville's views of what French politics and French interests required prevailed over his commitment to abstract principles of equity or human equality.

Universal Rights, Nation Building, and Progress

Tocqueville's writings on empire have led some of his most able and sympathetic readers to believe that on this subject he simply deluded himself and contradicted his most firmly held principles.[104] Certainly it is difficult to reconcile Tocqueville's avowals of human equality and the right of nations, his sympathy for the Amerindians, and his disgust at "European tyranny" in America,[105] with his own ruthless statements in favor of European conquest of Algeria and India. In this chapter and the last, I have begun to suggest some explanations for the tensions and ambivalence that emerged over the course of Tocqueville's political and intellectual engagement with the question of empire. I now consider further how Tocqueville's thought bears on three theoretical and historical questions that have lain behind the broader argument of this book. First, how did nineteenth-century liberal thinkers, particularly those, like Tocqueville, who believed themselves to be upholding the Revolution's commitment to universal human rights, apply such universalist views in considering the obligations of powerful states toward vulnerable and colonized peoples? Second, how did the domestic political challenges of democratization and nation building in nineteenth-century Europe affect liberals' judgments about international justice and particularly relations with non-European peoples? And finally, how were notions of progress that had begun to emerge in eighteenth-century anthropology and political and economic thought transformed and deployed during Europe's second burst of imperial expansion in the mid–nineteenth century?

Although Tocqueville was emphatically no revolutionary, he defended the principles of 1789, which for him stood for a recognition of human dignity and equality, and equal civil liberty for all, and he suggested that some universal moral standards should govern states' international conduct.[106] As we saw in chapter 3, despite Burke's well-known antipathy to the language of the rights of man, and his consequent reputation as a thinker and politician who supported special privilege and opposed universal application of laws, Burke's opposition to British actions in India stemmed in large part precisely from a kind of universalism. Tocqueville accepted the language of rights far more casually than Burke did, but he was in many ways a less stringent universalist. Although Tocqueville's liberalism did not rest primarily on a belief that our moral obligations are structured by a set of natural rights, he often referred to such rights as though they were a matter of consensus and did not need to be defended. He argued, with the same tone of resignation that accompanied his discussions of the destructive individualism of American democracy, that "the idea of rights inherent in certain individuals is rapidly disappearing from men's minds; the idea of the omnipotence and sole authority of society at large is coming to fill its place."[107] He maintained, with little elaboration, that American treatment of both Indians and black slaves had repeatedly violated natural rights and natural laws. To witness slavery in America was to see "the order of nature overthrown," to hear "the cry of humanity complaining in vain against the laws."[108] Even when advocating the most brutal means of subduing indigenous Algerians, Tocqueville explicitly noted that he believed French imperial activities must be governed by a concern for rights and international law: "For myself, I think that all means of devastating the tribes must be employed," he wrote in the 1841 "Essay." "I except only those condemned by humanity and the right of nations."[109] Such moments suggest that Tocqueville did believe that natural individual rights establish moral obligations and define the scope and requirements of international justice, although his statements are not specific enough to suggest the precise limits that he believed individual or "national" rights imposed. We are left with something of a disjuncture between his explicitly normative statements on international justice and his defenses of imperial expansion in the name of France.

Tocqueville believed that generous principles of "equity," rather than strict applications of the letter of international law, should govern relations among European states. Given Tocqueville's insistence on honor and equity in France's relations with other European countries (despite his fierce rivalry with England and his occasional enthusiasm for war), it is reasonable to ask whether he merely subscribed to a double standard in international affairs, with one kind of justice for Europeans and another for "barbarous" nations. On this question, too, the record is incomplete because of Tocqueville's pragmatism, his apparent reluctance to discuss the normative questions of international politics in detail. Tocqueville's brief career as foreign minister under the Barrot government, from June to October 1849, included an episode that suggests that Tocqueville believed international law and rules of equity should have general, not merely European, application. In August 1849, Tocqueville reports in his *Souvenirs*, the Ottoman government granted protection to several of the leaders of the 1848 rebellion in Hungary, including Dembinski and Kossuth, who had fled the Hapsburg authorities across the Danube.[110] The Austrians and their Russian allies, according to Tocqueville, invoked inapplicable treaties and threatened war against Turkey, while the Ottoman sultan appealed to international law and to his own sense of humanity in refusing to hand over the rebels. Although Tocqueville comments that the sultan "was speaking like civilized people and Christians," while the European ambassadors "replied like Turks," he also endorses the principle appealed to by the sultan that "what was right on the left bank of the Danube should be so on the right too."[111] The sultan was civilized and Christian in his universal rather than selective application of principles, in his respect for international law, and in his humane treatment of supplicants; the Austrians and Russians failed not only to demonstrate a sense of equity, but even to observe basic legal principles.

Tocqueville did not provide the sort of explicit or systematic answer that J. S. Mill did to the question how European moral and legal standards of international action should be applied to nonsovereign and non-European peoples. Indeed, Tocqueville's explicit statements suggest that in theory he rejected claims that national imperatives justified the conquest and rule of other peoples. He believed, rather, that international law and the dictates of equity place demands on state conduct and that foreign policy must be guided by moral reflection, at least within Europe and arguably everywhere. Although discussions of humanity or the rights of man are rare in Tocqueville's large body of writing, when he mentioned such topics, he did so in a way that suggests he considered human equality and the rights of peoples to govern themselves as given, at least in the abstract. As he wrote in 1836 (when he had recently begun to study the Algerian enterprise in earnest),

> The Romans believed that they alone of the human race were fitted to enjoy independence; and it was much less from nature than from Rome that they thought they derived their right to be free. According to the modern, the democratic, and, we venture to say the only just notion of liberty, every man, being presumed to have received from nature the intelligence necessary for his own general guidance, is inherently entitled to be uncontrolled by his fellows in all that only concerns himself, and to regulate at his own will his own destiny.[112]

The passage is one of Tocqueville's more explicit declarations of the principle that all peoples have a right to self-rule. The argument also shows the extent to which Tocqueville was more categorical and less historicist than Constant, in that the notion of liberty that guided his judgment was not only the modern one (as Constant would have it), but the "only just" one. The definitiveness of such claims makes Tocqueville's defense of imperialism all the more perplexing: they should warn us against efforts to find a neat *theoretical* resolution to the contradictions in his thought.

Rather, we must look to the demands that the unstable and unsettling social and political situation placed on thinkers, such as Tocqueville, who sought both internal stability and an honorable international politics, in an effort to understand how a perceptive sociologist with a deeply moral understanding of politics could have produced such an implacable and shortsighted defense of empire.

Tocqueville's writings on empire have presented his readers with a seemingly irresolvable paradox. While it is clear that nationalism of some kind underlies his support for aggressive and violent imperial expansion, commentators have struggled with the relationship between his liberalism and his nationalism. Tzvetan Todorov attempts a straightforward equation of Tocqueville's liberalism and his nationalism: nationalism is simply liberalism writ large and applied to states. On this view, states, like individuals, have negative rights, but for states these are unlimited by any legal code. "Liberalism proclaims the right of the individual to do as she likes within certain limits established by the group," Todorov has written in attempting to explain Tocqueville's views; "nationalism does the same for states, but on the basis of the observation that no such limits exist."[113] While Todorov thus offers an elegant resolution to the apparent tensions between Tocqueville's liberalism and his imperialism, there is no evidence in Tocqueville's writings that he himself believed in any such parallel between the freedom of individuals and that of nations. The passages Todorov cites, in which Tocqueville claims that a state requires basic security if it is to seek peace and happiness, support national militaries, but they support nothing like the grand imperial ventures in India and Algeria that Tocqueville celebrated. Indeed, Todorov's claims based on his equation of nationalism and liberalism bear no resemblance to Tocqueville's stated views on empire; Tocqueville never justified empire on the grounds that it is within the *rights* of states as sovereign individuals to conquer other states.

To see Tocqueville's arguments in favor of conquest as claims about international right is to attribute to Tocqueville a consistency he himself never felt, and to ignore both the profound discomfort that infuses his writings on empire and the historical situation that produced this discomfort. Melvin Richter offers the more compelling view that "Tocqueville's stand on Algeria was inconsistent with the *Democracy.* When this issue forced him to choose, he placed nationalism above liberalism; the interests of 'progressive' Christian countries above the rights of those that were not."[114] And yet such a reading denies any connection between Tocqueville's liberalism and his nationalism. To dismiss the writings on empire as merely "self-delusion," as Richter does, is to overlook the ways in which Tocqueville's own understanding of his liberal politics—above all his commitment to establishing a stable liberal regime in France at a time of crisis—contributed to his nationalism. It is also to disregard the centrality of such "strategies of exclusion" (in Uday Mehta's phrase) to so much of nineteenth-century liberal thought in both Britain and France.[115]

Democratization and Nation Building

Tocqueville held that French power and reputation within Europe would rely, increasingly, on its colonial possessions; a wide range of colonial actions were justified by this patent need. Tocqueville's concern for French glory and reputation in Europe, and his desire that the nation join in collective enterprises in order to preserve its liberty, lay behind his enthusiasm for the colonization of North Africa, even if Tocqueville himself never articulated the argument quite so explicitly.[116] Tocqueville felt deeply the imperatives of nation building, and every one of his works attested to his fear that French liberty was fragile, far more vulnerable than the liberty of America or Great Britain. Tocqueville's fear that Frenchmen in his day were dangerously apolitical, preoccupied by their petty personal affairs, was exacerbated by the thought that there were no longer opportunities for glorious action. He saw large-scale empires—both glorious military conquest and prosperous settlement—as among the only arenas for grand political gestures in his day. Two pursuits that seemed to him worthy of a great nation were imperial expansion and the abolition of slavery in the French West Indies.[117] His fierce sense of rivalry with Britain, which competed with his admiration for the country's political and social institutions, encouraged his belief that national projects that earned British respect—as both empire and abolition were likely to do—would be of a particularly valuable kind.

In contrast to Constant's searing criticism of the military spirit, Tocqueville, despite some qualms, accepted the need for a dramatic increase of French troops for the sake of empire. Viewing a strong military presence in Algeria as a necessary condition of the settlement colony he sought (and often more sympathetic to the military than to the colonists, whom he often saw as greedy and self-absorbed), he devoted tremendous thought to the problem of civil-military relations in colonial society.[118] And as we have seen, Tocqueville admired what he considered the military's displays of civic virtue in an otherwise apathetic nation. Tocqueville thus refused to accept Constant's claim, and what would seem a liberal dogma, that a strong military and the culture to which it gives rise are fundamentally incompatible with democratic liberty.

After Constant's brilliant pamphlet on the spirit of conquest, French anti-imperialism retreated to the margins of French political debate. Tocqueville, in so many other senses Constant's rightful heir, repudiated the anti-imperialism of his fellow liberal and pluralist in the name of France. To build a cohesive, stable, and liberal domestic political order after the collapse of the ancien régime, revolutionary upheaval, and continuing political turmoil was Tocqueville's self-appointed task as a political thinker and actor. The notion of a proud French presence in Algeria, a vibrant and glorious new America filled with prosperous farms and engaged settler-citizens, played an important if too often overlooked part in Tocqueville's nation-building project. Although Constant himself did not live to face the real possibility of a French empire in North Africa, it seems clear that his project to place representative government on a firm footing without recourse to expansionism or appeals to French glory had thoroughly lost favor with the French public by the time of his death. The liberal politicians who succeeded him proved unable to present a compelling vision of anti-nationalist cosmopolitanism, and the liberalism of Constant's most prominent successors in France and England turned once more to the exclusions that have marked so much of its history.

Pluralism and Progress

Liberalism, particularly that of the nineteenth century, is often criticized for its antipluralism, its univocality. The idea of progress in history, which had informed aspects of eighteenth-century anthropology and politics, took on a singular importance with a broad spectrum of thinkers in the nineteenth. It lay behind the political theories of Comte, Hegel, and Marx, of the utilitarians and philosophic radicals in England, of the utopian socialists such as Fourier and Saint-Simon in France. Mill's perfectionist liberalism was theoretically central to his justification of empire, and the same can be said for nonutilitarian British liberals such as T. B. Macaulay. The tensions, if such they are, between Mill's liberalism and his views on empire can be explained in part by his well-theorized, if deeply flawed, view that societies progress in stages from barbaric to civilized and that Britain was morally justified and perhaps even duty-bound to exercise despotism in India until Indians were ready to rule themselves.

Mill, as we have seen, offered an explicit justification for his distinction between the healthy pluralism of a civilized society that he famously defended in *On Liberty*—in which dissent enhances debate, assists in the discovery of truth, strengthens the understanding of those who already believe true doctrines, and ultimately promotes self-government—and the deleterious pluralism of societies, among which are many peoples ostensibly incapable of self-improvement without the despotic tutelage of others. Mill's account of the benefits of pluralism stresses the motive force of individual strength of character, of "singularity." Although he occasionally cited the cultural diversity among European nations as a source of what he saw as their unique political liberty, Mill remained essentially persuaded that the cause of liberty could be best served by an imposition of the model of eccentricity he saw at home on "stationary" peoples.[119] Furthermore, he believed that the construction of the modern nation-state required the destruction of local identities and loyalties.[120]

Tocqueville is invoked precisely as an antidote to the blind progressivism of his times and celebrated for his appreciation of the importance of local self-governance and the flourishing of local practices and self-reliance.[121] He resisted formulating a full-blown account of historical development such as can be found in the work of other nineteenth-century theorists such as Mill and Hegel; he considered such attempts determinist, fatalist, and thus in some sense immoral.[122] The duty of the political thinker, he believed, was to make political actors aware of certain patterns of causation and to suggest the limitations on their actions, not to map the course of history or (for all his renown as a political prophet) to predict the future.

Tocqueville defended the local autonomy of *communities*, or, as he sometimes said, nations, where Mill restricted his pluralism to a defense of *individual* "eccentricity" within societies of a certain type. Tocqueville's defense of local diversity as a safeguard for political and moral autonomy was reminiscent of the pluralism of Constant:

> When towns and provinces formed so many different nations within the common country [*patrie*], each of them had a will of its own that opposed the general spirit of servitude; but now that all parts of the same empire, after having lost their immunities, their customs, their prejudices, and even their memories and their names, have grown accustomed to obey the same laws, it is no longer more difficult to oppress all of them together than to oppress one of them separately.[123]

Indeed, Tocqueville praised the toleration of local practices under the Roman Empire, although he attributed their pluralism to the emperors' inadequate information and administrative apparatus rather than to their enlightened cultural policy. The result for the ruled, in any case, was an escape from the tyranny and unchecked power that Tocqueville feared might be the consequence of modern administrative centralization.

> When the power of the Roman emperors was at its height, the different peoples of the Roman world still preserved diverse customs and mores. Although they obeyed the same monarch, most provinces had separate administrations. They were filled with powerful and active municipalities, and though the whole government of the empire was concentrated in the hands of the emperor alone, and he could, if necessary, decide everything, yet the details of social life and individual existence ordinarily escaped his control.[124]

In this model of empire, a distant state preserved peace, while the various subject peoples were left free to conduct their own affairs according to local custom. It was not the model Tocqueville advocated for Algeria, however. His early writings, as we have seen, did suggest that France's various subject populations should be governed by laws they could respect—laws based on the Koran for Algerian Arabs—but he envisioned this pluralism as a temporary solution, to suffice until the French and Arabs could be assimilated into a single people. By the time he had abandoned this assimilationist vision, Tocqueville had also largely given up the aspiration to impose laws Algerians could respect. Where Constant's pluralism issued in a caustic attack on imperial conquest, then, Tocqueville's "localism" abandoned any such deep commitment to the political autonomy of diverse peoples.

And yet precisely because Tocqueville appreciated the complexity and the political character of non-European societies as Mill never did, and because he never succumbed altogether to the illusion that Europe's civilizing mission provided a clear moral justification for despotic rule, Tocqueville's ambivalence about empire ran far deeper than Mill's. Tocqueville occasionally expressed enthusiasm for European imperialism on the grounds that it would contribute to progress among backward peoples, and he invoked the language of progress and barbarism, describing Algerian Arabs as "semi-barbarous,"[125] and noting, "It has been claimed that the peoples of India had already arrived at a very advanced state of civilization. I, for my part, am convinced of the contrary" (*OC* 3.1: 446). But he also preserved a suspicion that such arguments were disingenuous or delusionary, and that imperial domination barbarized conquered peoples far more often than it improved them. Whenever he witnessed empire firsthand, he rejected outright the notion that imperialists had been a civilizing force.[126]

Even in the early 1840s, when Tocqueville was advocating ruthless methods of conquest in Algeria and paid little attention to schemes of "improving" Algerians, he was critical of the English failure truly to make the welfare of their subjects the guiding principle of their rule in India (as well as apparently hopeful that English failures might make India vulnerable to a French takeover). Tocqueville's observation that European conquerors had consistently despoiled and even, in America, come close to exterminating native populations ultimately did not keep him from hoping that improving empire was possible, even if he never believed, with the English, that improvement of non-Europeans was the primary purpose and justification of empire. In the end, the English hypocrisy that he captured with such clarity may have been too tempting for Tocqueville himself to resist.

Finally, even when Tocqueville did appeal to the notion of European superiority as a reason to champion the European conquest of other peoples, he often did so in terms so pervaded by the language of glory and greatness that the result was something his liberal British correspondents would have repudiated. As he wrote to Henry Reeve in April 1840,

> If I were English, I would not view the expedition that is being prepared against China without anxiety. In my capacity as a beneficent but disinterested spectator, I can only rejoice in the thought of an invasion of the Celestial Empire by a European army. So at last the mobility of Europe has come to grips with Chinese immobility! It is a great event, especially if one thinks that it is only the continuation, the last in a multitude of events of the same nature all of which are pushing the European race out of its home and are successively submitting all the other races to its empire or its influence. Something more vast, more extraordinary than the establishment of the Roman Empire is growing out of our times, without anyone noticing it; it is the enslavement of four parts of the world by the fifth. Therefore, let us not slander our century and ourselves too much; the men are small, but the events are great.[127]

Tocqueville's great fear that his age was one of lassitude and mediocrity caused him to grasp at events that suggested otherwise with such enthusiasm that he used quite uncharacteristic language, including, here, the discourse of racial antagonism and enslavement.

Even when Tocqueville argued for conquest of non-Europeans in the name of European civilization, he did so with a fire and bellicosity very unlike the dispassionate language of benevolent technocracy with which nineteenth-century British liberals such as Mill justified imperial rule. This difference touches on other striking differences between Mill's and Tocqueville's approaches to empire, as we have examined them in chapters 5–7. Mill offered a logically coherent defense of the despotic rule of advanced societies over backward ones as indispensable to the advancement of peoples who were incapable of developing technologically, politically, and morally, on their own. Mill's undifferentiated theory of progress and his indifference to the diverse array of social and political structures led him to posit that "barbarian" societies utterly lacked political life or the resources to govern themselves. While Mill consciously and repeatedly used the term *despotism* to describe colonial rule, however, he remained almost blind to the facts and forms of pervasive violence and oppression that characterized it. When Mill did acknowledge the dangers of European chauvinism, he recognized only that of European settlers, remaining convinced that colonial bureaucracies could be insulated from and purged of such pernicious dispositions. Tocqueville, in contrast, never achieved Mill's confidence in the benevolence of empire, nor the theoretical rigor and parsimony of Mill's justification of empire on the grounds of a theory of progress. Tocqueville always acknowledged, as Mill did not, the persistent violence of empire and the difficulty, if not the impossibility, of harmonizing the interests of European conquerors and subject peoples. This clarity about colonial violence undoubtedly stemmed in part from Tocqueville's firsthand observations in America and Algeria, whereas Mill, for all his decades in the India office, never visited the colony and relied heavily on British sources for his information about conditions there (I have noted Mill's considerably greater empathy for Irish peasants). That Tocqueville recognized and accepted the violence of empire, despite his failure to develop a theoretically satisfying justification for it, testifies both to his greater clear-sightedness about the moral costs of the policies he recommended than Mill ever evinced, and the moral callousness with which Tocqueville was willing to legitimate imperial exploits. That neither Mill nor Tocqueville, nor almost any of their liberal contemporaries, could contemplate, except as a dim and distant prospect, the emancipation, "abandonment," or political independence of non-European colonies attests to the great distance liberal thinking had traversed from the resolute criticism of Europe's imperial expansion articulated by their late-eighteenth-century forebears.

Eight

Conclusion

THE SIXTY YEARS straddling the turn of the nineteenth century witnessed a significant shift in understandings of empire among eminent political thinkers in Britain and France. Hostility toward and skepticism about empire appeared ascendant in the closing years of the eighteenth century: Adam Smith, Burke, and Bentham were among many to denounce European colonial rule as unjust and presumptuous, as well as politically and economically disastrous even for the conquering nations. Several generations later, however, Europe's prominent liberals were determined supporters of European imperial expansion. Historical pressures and their own philosophical commitments led many thinkers in the liberal tradition, including J. S. Mill and Tocqueville, to turn away from the views of their predecessors as well as from what we might see as the best inclinations of their tradition. The emergence of support for the violent conquest and despotic rule of non-Europeans in the mid-nineteenth century, among thinkers normally celebrated not only for their respect for human equality and liberty but also for their pluralism, implicates the liberal tradition, at this moment in its history, in an inegalitarian and decidedly nonhumanitarian international politics.

In the foregoing chapters, I have suggested that two developments in European political thought were particularly important for this shift in political thinking about colonial rule: transformations in understandings of progress and societal development; and new and pressing concerns about how to establish viable liberal governments in a democratic age. Theories of progress became more triumphalist, less nuanced, and less tolerant of cultural difference, as a sense of civilizational—and more specifically national—self-confidence came to pervade political discourse in both Britain and France.[1] In France, underlying the commitment to a *mission civilisatrice* was a conviction that the nation was, thanks to its revolutionary commitment to liberty and equality, uniquely qualified to disseminate universal values.[2] Britons, similarly, were certain of their own particular fitness to spread civilization, in light of their country's gradual and secure progress toward political equality, which they contrasted with what they saw as French political failures and instability as well as the political immaturity of eastern European and, even more, non-European societies.[3]

The superiority of European politics and culture came by the mid-nineteenth century to be taken for granted, both by prominent political thinkers and in broader public discourse, in a way that, as I have argued, it was not yet assumed to be in the earlier period. Most liberals and radicals of the nineteenth century, to be sure, maintained that European superiority should be theorized as cultural, political, and economic, not biological. Their position was at once antiracist and strongly in favor of colonial rule. Their commitment to an ameliorative colonial rule premised on assumptions of human equality and biological uniformity, however, was increasingly challenged by a "scientific" racism that by the 1860s had developed an insistent and powerful voice in colonial politics.[4] The imperial liberalism of the latter half of the nineteenth century bore a somewhat equivocal relation to the new strands of racism and anthropology premised on notions of radical and perhaps ineradicable differences among human groups. As we have seen, both Mill and Tocqueville insisted that claims about *biological* differences or inequalities were unprovable and morally and politically pernicious. And yet their willingness to see the moral and political standards that governed relations within Europe suspended in dealings with other peoples bore the mark of a discourse increasingly founded on the assumptions about the inequality of different peoples.[5]

Notwithstanding the newly emphatic civilizational confidence among both French and British thinkers of the mid-nineteenth century, we also find persistent anxiety about the solidity of Europe's achievement, and in particular, concern about the dangers that democratization posed to European civilization. Tocqueville explicitly, and influentially, expressed the fear that the spread of democratic social and political culture would compromise other values, including, most importantly, the liberty he believed was characteristic of aristocracies and difficult to replicate under conditions of equality. If Tocqueville found democracy to be providential, and just, he also confronted the emergence of democratic society with trepidation, especially where, as in France, this process entailed phases of revolution and dictatorship. We saw in chapters 6 and 7 the ways in which Tocqueville responded to such anxieties by turning to the conquest of Algeria as a political experiment that might lend dynamism and confidence to a weak French public.

Mill was far more sanguine than Tocqueville about the extension of democratic participation. And yet, as I discuss further below, Mill and democratic reformers like him, committed to the principle of universal political participation, exhibited worries about the threats greater political inclusion posed to national stability and good government. In the face of forceful opposition to a wider suffrage from conservatives and many middle-class voters, British liberals and radicals had to fight to establish the political worthiness and capacity of European women and members of the working class. These thinkers repeatedly invoked colonized and other non-European peoples to define, by their exclusion, the limits of the national political community and the boundaries of democratic society. In doing so, they sought to reassure themselves as well as their antireform audiences that the extension of the political community they called for was legitimate and would remain within reasonable limits.

In what follows, I revisit, first, some of the central insights of the eighteenth-century critics of empire I have examined to suggest in broad terms what motivated and sustained their relatively tolerant, humanitarian international politics at a time of imperial consolidation and often in the face of official and public hostility or contempt. Second, I explore some of the connections between the extension of democratic participation in mid-nineteenth-century Britain and the commitment to empire on the part of Mill and his fellow British reformers, having discussed in chapters 6 and 7 the ways in which for Tocqueville, anxieties about democratization in France contributed to support for imperial expansion. I end by considering, briefly, the disquiet about colonial injustice expressed by both Tocqueville and Mill late in their careers.

Eighteenth-Century Criticism of Empire

It is important to reiterate that none of the eighteenth-century thinkers I have considered were categorically anti-imperialist. They accepted in principle that imperial rule could, if radically reformed, be made just, although they were deeply skeptical that such reforms would ever be attempted by ill-informed and corrupt imperial elites. Their critiques of empire had other limits as well: the authors considered here communicated very little with their countries' colonial subjects and had no firsthand knowledge of non-European societies. Smith, for instance, relied fairly uncritically on European ethnographic sources for his information about societies at other stages of development. Even Burke, for all his imaginative empathy and his vast knowledge of Indian affairs, knew hardly any Indians and relied almost entirely on written documents and British sources in India for his information. As I proposed in chapter 3, Burke was keenly sensitive to the hazards and injustices that attend any effort to make political judgments about a silenced and excluded people; still, the arguments he engaged in over Britain's relations with India were contributions to wholly European debates. Furthermore, these thinkers shared the belief of nearly all their European contemporaries that the commercial society of western Europe possessed some genuine advantages over other societies. Burke, despite his great respect for the antiquity and the sophistication of Indian civilization, believed that European societies represented distinctively praiseworthy political and cultural achievements. Smith, too, for all his interpretive generosity toward the practices of non-European and precommercial societies, nonetheless ranged societies along a continuum of development that ran from savage hunting societies through European commercial societies. They did not claim, as did Johann Gottfried Herder, for instance, that nations are incommensurable expressions of human creativity.[6]

Notwithstanding such limits to their cultural and political inclusiveness, the eighteenth-century thinkers considered here fused astute insights about the injustices and excesses of European colonial power with compelling models of tolerant and self-critical cross-cultural judgment.[7] Burke in particular condemned British imperial practices so comprehensively as to raise the question whether European rule over distant and very different societies could ever be just, or justifiable. Although Burke undeniably articulated a morally powerful, and philosophically rich, vision of a humane international and colonial politics, he suffered repeated failures at the political level: his pleas for Catholic emancipation in Ireland went unheeded, his bills for reparations for the Jews of St. Eustatius were voted down, his 1783 East India Bill was defeated, Warren Hastings was acquitted in 1794. Burke's contemporaries, as well as many later readers, have attributed these failures to weaknesses in Burke's own political and rhetorical strategy, above all an excessively passionate and undisciplined identification with and pity for victims. Burke's political failures, however, perhaps better illustrate the truth of his belief that the work of expanding his countrymen's straitened and stunted sympathies was a task that would require generations.

However marginalized from mainstream views Burke's resistance to the British imperial project may have left him, it is a central claim of this study that among political thinkers, Burke was not alone.[8] It is particularly worth reiterating two general elements of Burke's approach to the problems of empire and cross-cultural judgment that were shared by the critics of empire considered here, but largely abandoned by their nineteenth-century liberal successors.

First, the earlier critics' commitment to some universal moral and political norms led them to criticize the suspension—on the grounds of the alleged cultural, moral, or intellectual inferiority of many non-European peoples—of European moral and political norms outside Europe. These thinkers assumed a relentlessly skeptical posture toward Europe's increasing cultural presumptuousness: their universalism was underpinned by the belief that all societies should be presumed to be reasonable. They were prepared to make cross-cultural judgments, but they maintained a humility and lack of presumption in undertaking to judge other societies.

Second, they counseled a chastened approach to the exercise of power, particularly imperial power over distant subjects, and insisted that such power would invariably be abused unless it was made somehow accountable to those subject to it, a task they sometimes implied would be nearly impossible.

For both Burke and Smith, justice rested upon sympathy and an appropriately inclusive circle of moral concern. Smith's more fully theorized moral philosophy proposed that we make moral judgments by comparing our own initial and necessarily partial views about actions or characters with the judgments of other spectators, and thus seek the perspective of a truly impartial spectator. We will come to the best-considered and most equitable judgments when we draw on the views of as broad a group of observers as possible, he believed; for Smith, faction and the narrowness of exclusive groups were thus even more damaging to good moral judgment than mere egoism. Burke, too, as we saw in chapter 3, believed that sympathy lies at the heart of moral and political judgment. He held that in order to remedy the injustices endemic to British rule over colonial subjects, it was not enough simply to recognize that oppression took place. Such oppression must be *resented*, and this could occur only with genuine moral respect for the victims as equals—with "that kind of sympathy which naturally attaches you to men feeling like yourselves."[9] Burke further insisted that European conduct throughout the globe must be governed by certain minimal universal moral and political standards, which he enunciated through the concepts of natural law and the law of nations, and most powerfully through a critique of the "geographical morality" by which Europeans permitted themselves to believe that the moral standards they recognized among themselves were inappropriate to the conditions of backwardness or political servitude that they identified outside Europe.

These eighteenth-century critics of empire combined such universalist commitments to "humanity" and "justice" with a sensitivity to cultural particularity that led them to respect many of the values embodied in non-European societies. As we saw in chapter 2, Smith's conviction about the equal rationality of all people led him to theorize progress without thereby generating a hierarchy of moral and political worth, and without regarding societies in "earlier" stages pejoratively, as lacking the intellectual capacity or the moral judgment of more "advanced" Europeans. Burke and Smith were alike in approaching diverse cultures and political forms with the presumption that these practices and institutions resulted from reasonable judgments by mature minds responding to the particular challenges of their circumstances, and they, like Bentham, refused to regard members of non-European societies as immature or childlike in their capacity for moral and political judgment. While they regarded the particular form commercial society had taken in Europe and especially Britain as a great good and a form of progress, they did not believe that European civilization generated the moral authority to dominate other societies.

Burke shared with many of his Scottish contemporaries, especially Adam Smith, an inclination to regard societies as entities that emerge gradually from a process of constant negotiation, preservation, and reform. Although Burke did not himself produce a full-fledged account of social development, he shared Smith's sense of wonder at the complexity of societies and at the unintended consequences of human actions. Both appreciated the astonishing array of social formations and institutions that human rationality can produce and thus respected a multiplicity of values as rational and moral. Bentham, to be sure, believed most bodies of traditional law were rife with confusion, corruption, and error, and he had a faith in abstract reasoning about law and politics that would be horrifying to the Burkean sensibility. It has been my contention, however, that the utilitarian theory he developed was far more accommodating of difference, and more respectful of non-European societies, than those of his successors in the utilitarian tradition.[10] He was latitudinarian in a way that neither Mill ever managed to be; indeed, the younger Mill criticized that quality in Bentham as a lack of discrimination. Though often audaciously sure of his own reform projects, Bentham shared neither the cultural chauvinism of James and J. S. Mill, nor the younger Mill's confidence that all human values could be reconciled, without loss, into one great progressive scheme that he, as philosopher, could envision. Bentham maintained an alertness to the injustices of imperial rule, and to the capacity and right of every individual to know and declare his or her own interests, that neither James Mill, with his overpowering hatred of the few, nor J. S. Mill, with his science of individual and national character, ever achieved.

The second broad set of affinities uniting these eighteenth-century critics of empire was their insistence upon the perils of the exercise of imperial power. They recognized the violence and injustices invariably involved in the conquest and rule of distant peoples, as well as the dangers that exercising despotic rule abroad posed to liberties at home. They warned against the great fortunes, and the habits of despotism, gained in the colonies—whether by the "nabobs" who returned to England to buy seats in Parliament, or, as Constant feared, by military officers who would grow used to imposing their will over subject populations and would surely be impatient with the messy diversity and dissent of ordinary liberal politics.

They perceived the obstacles to sympathy and understanding, and therefore to good government, that are imposed by distance, cultural difference, and especially the posture, endemic in the Europe of their day, of contempt toward supposedly primitive societies. Bentham was most concerned about geographic distance, and indeed in his criticisms of European colonies he tended to refer to colonies as "distant dependencies," as though to insist on the inevitable problems caused by distance alone. He argued that officials governing on behalf of the metropole and not sharing the interests of colonial subjects, subjects including European settlers such as the South American creoles, usually govern oppressively and invariably generate resentment among their subjects: "Exercised by imported strangers, subordinate power exercises itself by acts of oppression: or at any rate, what to this purpose comes to the same thing, is thought to do so. . . . Before one grievance, with its discontent, has reached their ears, another grievance, with its discontent, has succeeded: and thus matters go on, ill-will accumulating on both sides, till patience is lost on both sides."[11]

For Burke, it was lack of cultural sympathy, more than geographic distance, that almost ensured an unjust colonial government. In India, these causes combined to render justice nearly impossible, he believed. In the case of Ireland, the proximity of the colony meant that it should be incorporated into the metropolitan nation, but he observed that cultural incomprehension and national animosity on the part of the Anglo-Irish was not only a source of persistent injustice but also an obstacle to even well-meaning reform. Even in the case of colonies populated by settlers who were widely assumed to be part of the British moral community, Burke noted the perils of injustice inherent in the imbalance of imperial power. As he wrote in the "Letter to the Sheriffs of Bristol" with regard to the American colonists, "When any community is subordinately connected with another, the great danger of the connection is the extreme pride and self-complacency of the superiour, which in all matters of controversy will probably decide in its own favour."[12] Smith had less to say than Burke or Bentham about structures of colonial governance in nonsettlement colonies, but as we saw in chapter 2, he held that the rights of nations could be adequately protected only by a rough balance of power among them. Smith observed that the predominance of European power was a matter of historical accident and expressed a hope that the distribution of power among the world's societies would become more equal so that the rights and interests of non-European peoples might not be crushed by overweening Europeans.

These thinkers insisted on the limits of our knowledge of distant or very different societies, as well as the limits of our understanding of social change and our ability to direct its course. They regarded it as essential to justice, then, that power be in some way accountable to those over whom it is exercised. Burke was no democrat, to be sure: but he believed that structures of accountability to colonial subjects were possible and indispensable if colonies were ever to be justly administered. In his closing impeachment speech Burke charged Hastings with having "disfranchized" Indians by abrogating the rule of law and making it possible for them to be fined, exiled, imprisoned, and even killed without recourse to legal protection or appeal; he had earlier deplored the absence in British India of local juries or other means of "Redress . . . against Oppressions of Power."[13] In Ireland, Burke observed even more directly the injustices and indignities that result from the unaccountable and unlimited exercise of power by one national group over another. Even well-intentioned reformers—like the high-minded Trinity College provost discussed in chapter 3, whose reform proposal only humiliated the Catholic students it was intended to assist—will be unconscious of the effects of their power when they are able to exercise it in complete social and political isolation from those subject to it.[14] If, in his desire to defend aristocratic rule, Burke refused to acknowledge that oligarchies within nations, too, almost invariably fail to serve as the "virtual representatives" of subjects to whom they are not answerable, he nonetheless articulated a potent social and political critique of the exclusion of whole peoples, or national and religious groups, from the exercise of political power. Bentham, a more enthusiastic (if not entirely consistent) democrat, held that as individuals are the best judges of their own interests, unaccountable colonial rulers will inevitably govern worse than the subjects could rule themselves, and he saw that the arrogation of exclusive power by Europeans ignorant of local conditions and driven by "sinister" interests of their own was bound to produce oppression. Even where he fell short of advocating democratic rule, as in India, Bentham insisted on greater accountability to the governed and sought ways to involve them in structures of governance: as in his proposals for juries in India to prevent abuses. In contrast, as we have seen, the rigid developmental theories characteristic of nineteenth-century liberalism, especially in Britain, enabled thinkers to regard accountability to subject peoples as inappropriate and indeed counterproductive to the task of imposing progress on those deemed unequipped to judge for themselves either their interests or the best means of attaining them.

Democracy and Liberal Anxieties in the Nineteenth Century

Tocqueville's complex sociological approach led him to develop views of the non-European societies he discussed that were far more nuanced than those of many of his contemporaries. Like Scottish theorists of conjectural history, including Smith, Tocqueville's sociology was influenced by Montesquieu.[15] Partly as a result of this influence, and in contrast to Mill, Tocqueville's writings are marked by an ambivalent view of progress, respect for a wide variety of cultural practices, and a reluctance to rely uncritically on the reports of others. Tocqueville's insightful moral psychology and his affinity for ironical modes of argument, the moderating, tolerant, and skeptical qualities he shared with the Scots, did not undermine his support for empire but did make it deeply ambivalent.[16] There are, to be sure, competing tendencies in Tocqueville himself—a staunch sense of honor, a commitment to grandeur, a conception of patriotism as essential to effective political action—that became fused with his assumptions about the preconditions of liberal democracy and that led him to turn to imperial conquest as a central element of his project to both animate and bridle French democratic politics. These competing tendencies are partly reflective of broader French politics and culture and partly due to Tocqueville's distinctive intellectual disposition, as is attested both by the fact that Tocqueville was regarded for a decade as a leading expert on French Algeria, and by the fact that the republican *mission civilisatrice* that characterized later imperial politics departed substantially from his own ambivalent vision.

I argued in chapters 6 and 7 that Tocqueville's anxieties about the political dangers of the process of democratization in France contributed substantially to his support for French colonial expansion in Algeria, despite his considerable awareness of the violence that his colonial policies required. For Tocqueville, as we have seen, colonial expansion was instrumentally valuable for French liberal democracy. The suggestion of Tocqueville's writings on Algeria is that the development of a stable and liberal democratic regime might require the exploitation of non-European societies, might legitimate suspending principles of human equality and self-determination abroad in order to secure, first, glory and, eventually, virtue and stable liberty at home in France. In choosing to pursue national glory through empire, Tocqueville condoned—and indeed advocated—the subjugation of the Algerians for the sake of French national consolidation.

Such views constituted in an important sense a moral abdication on Tocqueville's part. But they also attest to his struggle, as a liberal political thinker, with one of the key questions of nineteenth-century politics. How were European societies to make the transition from the old autocratic regimes to republics without succumbing to anarchy or state terror? Tocqueville's arguments for French imperial expansion demonstrate forcefully the degree to which a concern to place the modern democratic nation on secure footing drew French liberals of his day into an exclusionary and violent international politics that so many of their predecessors, writing under different domestic circumstances, would have seen as a betrayal of liberal humanitarianism.

For Mill and other British liberals in the Victorian period, a vision of empire was also bound up with the process of democratization in the metropole. Mill, as we have seen, repudiated Tocqueville's views about the instrumental value of imperial expansion for domestic politics. He deeply mistrusted what he considered a characteristically French tendency to resort to aggressive international politics in order to shore up national pride. Indeed, he believed the governance of the empire must be kept as insulated as possible from the democratic process in the metropole.[17] Even as a legislator, Mill retained the commitments he had formed as a colonial official. The connection between imperial politics and democratization at home, then, is less straightforward in Mill's case than in Tocqueville's, for his explicit justifications for imperial arrangements center not on claims about how colonial rule could serve Britain but rather on their ostensible benefits for backward subjects. And yet Mill and many other British liberals and radicals consistently conceived the case for extending the franchise at home in terms of a contrast with colonial subjects whose incapacity for participation in political power they deemed self-evident. Justifications for imperial rule, and for the extension of the franchise at home, were thus perhaps as closely, if differently, linked in the British liberal discourse of the 1850s and 1860s as they were in France. Having treated the connections between democratization and empire in France in chapters 6 and 7, in what follows I discuss some of the ways in which British liberals' and reformers' views, and anxieties, about democratization at home drew on and entrenched their confidence that the "backwardness" of many non-European societies justified imperial rule.

During the debates leading up to the 1867 Reform Act, liberal arguments about how widely political participation should extend were frequently articulated in light of excluded imperial subjects.[18] Historians of the Second Reform Act have called attention to the fact that the debate was conducted not in the language of political *rights* but rather in the characteristically Millian terms of the *character* of those to be included in the broadened franchise.[19] Whether they were advocating suffrage for women or workingmen, reformers contrasted the character of those they declared worthy of participation—"respectable," independent, self-restrained, industrious—with that of the subjects they deemed it necessary to continue to exclude—improvident, dependent, enslaved to passions or customs, incapable of sustained labor.[20]

The insistence on the moral rectitude of potential voters suggests the degree to which not only the opponents of franchise reform but even some of its most radical advocates remained anxious about the possible dangers of an expanded franchise for the quality of political decisions in Britain.[21] In addition to insisting on the moral character of those to be included, reformers also sought to reassure their audience and perhaps themselves that the extension of political power was to be *limited* to the worthy. This purpose was served by the enumeration of excluded groups: whether the illiterate, paupers, or criminals. Perhaps the most widespread exclusion was that of colonial subjects and non-Europeans more generally; such invocations of "backward" peoples suggested that European societies could be seen to be decisively and securely on one side of a sharp line dividing the progressive and the politically worthy from the stationary, custom-enslaved, and politically incapable.

In these debates over the extension of suffrage within Britain, then, colonial subjects were repeatedly invoked to mark the boundaries of the community of the politically worthy, but it is striking how often this invocation remained untheorized.[22] It was a commonplace of feminist writings of the period, for instance, to reject the exclusion of women from political power on the grounds of their "immaturity" and to question the analogy between women and children used to support that exclusion. It was rare, however, for writers explicitly to call attention to the similarities between the woman-child analogy and the barbarian-child analogy, or to suggest that *any* exclusion of adults on the basis of their supposed immaturity ought to be questioned. Frances Power Cobbe was one of the few to make such a suggestion, in her often witty 1868 essay in defense of property rights and legal standing for married women, "Criminals, Idiots, Women and Minors." Cobbe writes that whereas the right of the stronger might have satisfied the "conscience of Oriental or Spartan, Roman or Norman, in dealing with his wife, his Helot, his slave, or his serf,"

> we, in our day, are perplexed and well nigh overwhelmed with the difficulties presented to us. What ought the Americans to do with their Negroes? What ought we to do with our Hindoos? What ought all civilised people to do with their women? It is all very easy to go on driving down the "high *à priori*" road of equal rights for all human beings, but as it is quite clear that children and idiots cannot be entrusted with full civil and political rights, the question always resolved itself into the further one, Where shall we draw the line? When has a human being fairly passed out of the stage of pupilage and attained his majority?[23]

In explicitly rejecting equal individual rights as a basis for political inclusion, Cobbe was echoing the claims of Mill and others that voting was not a right but a matter of desert and responsibility, and it is implicitly on these grounds that she justifies women's civil and political rights. After posing the provocative question of how any line of political exclusion can be justified, however, Cobbe drops the issue of colonial subjects' political standing and returns to her theme of women's inclusion. Indeed, as her allusion to the domineering "Oriental" suggests, Cobbe herself accepted a racialized account of European freedom in which "[o]ur Teuton race, from the days of Tacitus, has borne women whose moral nature has been in more than equipoise with their passions; and who have both deserved and obtained a freedom and a respect unknown to their sisters of the south."[24] Like Mill, Cobbe asserts the unworthiness of colonial subjects with an almost sarcastic brusqueness that suggests the point is too obvious to require justification. Still, despite her own apparent refusal here to offer a justification for the exclusion of colonial subjects, Cobbe's recognition of the continuities between this exclusion and that of women is striking. She draws attention to a rhetorical and theoretical move—in which the limits of the community of the politically competent are marked—that was ubiquitous but rarely acknowledged.

Mill had long framed his arguments for the extension of the franchise within Britain in terms not of political rights but rather of character, "moral worth," and the capacity not simply for self-rule but for the exercise of power over others, something he held could never be considered a *right*. Mill had argued repeatedly that moral worth, if it could be measured, ought to serve as a criterion for political office and participation. His plural voting scheme was designed precisely to ensure that the more intellectually (and, he hoped, by extension morally) worthy citizens had greater political power than the less worthy. As early as 1835, Mill had expressed the hope that moral worth might itself become measurable, like literacy, so that it too could be used to allocate access to political participation.[25] Indeed, Mill explicitly based his case for unequal political power not simply on claims about political competence, but about people's "unequal worth as human beings," as he wrote in 1859. "It is the fact," he wrote, "that one person is *not* as good as another; and it is reversing all the rules of rational conduct, to attempt to raise a political fabric on a supposition which is at variance with fact."[26]

For all Mill's insistence that the franchise was a responsibility to be earned and not a universal right, the rhetoric of his opponents makes clear how easily Mill's position could be misrepresented, and thus how great the pressures on Mill were to reassure his audience that there were limits to the democratic community he envisioned. One critic of reform, Robert Lowe, portrayed Mill's position as a revolutionary "a priori" doctrine of universal voting rights in an 1865 parliamentary debate over lowering the property requirement for the British franchise. Lowe tried to show by a kind of reductio ad absurdum that Mill's supposed belief in "every citizen of a State having a perfect right to share in its government" was bound to lead to political rights for colonial subjects. If universal political rights exist, he argued, "[T]hey are as much the property of the Australian savage and the Hottentot of the Cape as of the educated and refined Englishman. Those who uphold this doctrine must apply it to the lowest as well as to the highest grades of civilization, claiming for it the same universal, absolute, and unbending force as an axiom of pure mathematics."[27] Lowe's argument suggests that he expected complete agreement among his audience that the idea of barbarous colonial subjects participating in their own governance was outrageous.

Lowe's rendition of Mill's position was, of course, highly misleading, for it ignored two of the central pillars of Mill's case for broader political participation. First, while Mill did, as Lowe asserted, hold that every citizen should have a "share" in government, he was at pains to show that these shares need not, and should not, be equal.[28] Mill held that suffrage was not a universal right but a privilege and a responsibility; in this regard he and Lowe were in agreement. Second, Mill had repeatedly insisted that his case for the extension of suffrage within Britain in no way implied that colonial subjects at different stages of development should be granted political power. His arguments for extended suffrage within Britain were premised on the suitability of representative government for a society of Britain's character and level of improvement. Mill agreed with Lowe that, in Lowe's words, government ought "to be carefully scanned, modified, and altered so as to be adapted to different states of society, or to the same state of society at different times."[29] That Lowe could assert that Mill's position entailed equal votes for all Britons, and votes of any kind for colonial subjects, suggests how readily Mill's arguments for electoral reform could be tarred with the imputation that they were "revolutionary" and would lead Britain irresistibly toward outcomes that even the more radical proponents of reform agreed were undesirable, even nearly unthinkable. Lowe's speech, that is, makes clear why Mill and other reformers so emphatically marked the boundaries between those they would include and those still unworthy of political power, and why they often did so with reference to Britain's "barbarous" colonial subjects.

Already in the early essay "Civilization" Mill had sought to illustrate the limits he envisioned for democratic political development by gesturing to those non-Europeans who could be said definitively to stand outside democracy. Anticipating precisely the rhetorical move opponents like Lowe would make, Mill wrote, "There is no danger of the prevalence of democracy in Syria or Timbuctoo. But he must be a poor politician who does not know, that whatever is the growing power in society will force its way into the government, by fair means or foul" (*CW* 18:127). Mill says nothing more about the particular non-European societies he invokes here: it seems he considers naming them sufficient to indicate the absurdity of any thought that the members of such societies could be political agents or might participate through their own efforts in the movement of history toward democratic equality.

Mill's efforts to define and mark the limits of the democratic community within Britain by means of such exclusions responded not only to his antidemocratic critics, but equally to his own disquiet about British democracy. We find in Mill's thought two recurrent anxieties that political and social developments within Europe might resemble retrograde colonial and other non-European societies.

First, he was concerned that excessive political power might be gained by a portion of the British population unworthy of it for reasons similar to those that explained the unfitness of Indians and other "backward" peoples. Mill characterized the English working classes in many of the same terms he used elsewhere to describe the "semi-barbarous" people of India: they were enslaved to custom and superstition, incapable of sustained effort, and hostile to progress and innovation. As he wrote of Europeans, "None are so illiberal, none so bigoted in their hostility to improvement, none so superstitiously attached to the stupidest and worst of old forms and usages, as the uneducated."[30] Such a characterization of "barbarous" peoples had, of course, led Mill to maintain that colonial governments could not be held accountable to their subject populations: that progress must be imposed from without by appropriately trained and disposed civil servants. In the case of Britain, Mill stressed that accountability to the public promoted good government even when the public was ill-educated, and that political participation itself was essential to the improvement and education of laborers in Britain.[31]

Second, Mill's worries about the intellectual and moral condition of the British working classes were exacerbated by the concern, which he shared with Tocqueville, that the development of civilization in Europe itself endangered two of the most distinctive and precious features of Britain's national character, the "spirit of liberty" and the "spirit of improvement," and threatened to produce collective mediocrity and conformity alongside greater prosperity and equality.[32] Despite all the advantages of the age, despite the many facilities for mental cultivation now available to so many, he observed a dearth of distinctive achievement and a "decay of individual energy."[33] When Mill undertook to describe this danger of cultural and intellectual stagnation more fully in *On Liberty*, he relied on the "east" to supply the model to be avoided: "The greater part of the world has, properly speaking, no history, because the despotism of Custom is complete. This is the case over the whole east" (*CW* 18:273). While Mill appealed to China's stagnation as an argument for European rule there, he simultaneously invoked it as a portent of Europe's own fate: "We have a warning example in China," he wrote; "they have become stationary—have remained so for thousands of years; and if they are ever to be further improved, it must be by foreigners."[34] He warned that "unless individuality shall be able successfully to assert itself against this yoke, Europe, notwithstanding its noble antecedents and its professed Christianity, will tend to become another China."[35]

By seeming to draw a strict boundary between civilized and barbarous societies, Mill appeared to insulate Europe from the paternalistic policies he deemed appropriate for those other societies. Even within "civilized" societies, Mill's conception of autonomy was restricted by his views about what was in the "permanent interests of man as a progressive being," as he put it in *On Liberty.* Admirers of Mill's defense of diversity and eccentricity in *On Liberty* suggest that Mill's theory of autonomy remains compelling despite his exclusion of "backward" societies from the purview of his theory of liberty. George Kateb's subtle and sympathetic interpretation of *On Liberty* approaches Mill in this manner.[36] On such a reading, one might acknowledge that Mill's empirical account of India and other non-European societies was flawed, but argue that Mill's theory of autonomy is unaffected by such empirical misjudgments about non-European peoples. I have suggested, however, that Mill's judgments about empire and non-European societies are more deeply intertwined with his views about European society and politics than such a reading would indicate, and that his judgments about such societies indicate consistent and more general commitments on Mill's part to a narrower conception of the acceptable limits of diversity and freedom.[37] The specific connections in Mill's thought between anxieties about democratization and a commitment to imperial politics can in large part be attributed to his progressivist liberalism, to his distinctive theory of the formation of character, both individual and national, and his beliefs about the development of individual autonomy and freedom. But as we have seen, the linkage between the emergence of democracy within Europe and empire abroad characterized liberal political thought more broadly, both in Britain and in France.

Late Liberal Misgivings about Imperial Injustice

The story I have told of the interconnections between liberal nation-building in nineteenth-century France and Britain and the growth of their empires suggests that the process of democratization in western Europe generated exclusions not only internal to those societies but also globally, and that liberal thinkers of this period were deeply implicated in these exclusions.[38] Figures such as Constant and Amédée Desjobert indicate a road not taken, a strand of thinking about how the nation might be made to cohere in the face of the strains of democratization without turning to the oppression or forced inclusion of others. Constant, as a thinker with one eye turned back to the eighteenth century and the other looking ahead with great prescience to the social upheaval of the nineteenth, was well placed to resist the aggression that he saw as a betrayal of liberal principles. While these thinkers' most prominent successors may have failed to maintain such humane understandings of modern nationality, and while changing political circumstances may help us to understand why this was so, my argument is in no sense intended to suggest that the developments

I have described were inescapable or a result of any "logic" inherent in liberal theory.

Both Tocqueville and Mill themselves evinced concerns late in their careers about the moral and political hazards of the empires they had advocated. The *mission civilisatrice* that came to underpin French imperial justification in the later nineteenth century was marked more by a triumphant French republicanism than by Tocqueville's own ambivalent vision.[39] Tocquevillian liberalism, with its attachment to local self-government and its nostalgia for an honorable liberty, was increasingly eclipsed by a paradoxical alliance of racism and the ideals of the universal republic. While, as we have seen, Tocqueville was partly tempted by the notion of European conquests as triumphs of progress and Christianity over barbarism, he had always preserved a consciousness of the tremendous violence these conquests involved, a wariness about the hypocritical self-righteousness of their justifications, and a more textured understanding of other peoples as political. Warning that arrogant and domineering rule over Algerians would only produce resentment, intractable conflict, and great bloodshed, in his late writings on Algeria Tocqueville occasionally returned to the language of moral outrage and foreboding that had characterized his earlier writings on the American settlers' hypocritical and brutal treatment of native Amerindians.

Such late misgivings about the perils of colonial injustice are even more striking in Mill's case, particularly given his long-standing insistence on the legitimacy of British "despotism" over less advanced peoples and given that, unlike Tocqueville, he had scarcely ever acknowledged the violence inseparable from colonial conquest and rule. Mill, to be sure, preserved his faith that the colonial model of British India was a sound one, especially in the particular form it took under the Company; he suggested that other colonies, most importantly Ireland, would be best served by a similar arrangement.[40] But as we have seen, he worried increasingly in the 1860s that British colonial settlers were ill-suited to govern, indeed almost bound to oppress, the subject peoples they invariably regarded with contempt and ignorance.

Moreover, Mill now suggested—as Burke had done in the 1780s—that British colonial settlers displayed in an exacerbated form defects that could be found in the British public more broadly. As we have seen, he came to see the English settlers' dispossession of the Maori in New Zealand not simply as an injustice to be remedied but as evidence of a deeper British failing, "the overbearing and insolent disregard of the rights and feelings of inferiors which is the common characteristic of John Bull when he thinks he cannot be resisted."[41] Similarly, although Mill had been remarkably silent about the Sepoy Rebellion of 1857 and the violent British response to it as these events were taking place, several years later he began to point to Britain's brutal suppression of the rebellion as evidence of vices disgracefully characteristic of the nation. In *On Liberty*, Mill noted the "general display of the worst parts of our national character on the occasion of the Sepoy insurrection."[42] In a letter of 1866, Mill more pointedly reiterated the claim, citing the widespread British support for the slaveholding South in the American Civil War, and for Governor Eyre of Jamaica, as further evidence of Britain's degraded moral character: "[m]y eyes were first opened to the moral condition of the English nation (I except in these matters the working classes) by the atrocities perpetrated in the Indian Mutiny & the feelings which supported them at home."[43] Mill's new reference in this late letter to *atrocities* in India suggests that it was perhaps in the wake of the brutalities committed in Jamaica by Eyre and his staff that Mill more fully began to perceive Britain's complicity in "the oppression of subject and dependent races."[44]

Mill and Tocqueville had long perceived something apt and important about the other's—and the other country's—approach to empire. Tocqueville saw moralism and high-handedness as typical of English rhetoric and as a form of hypocrisy that would only provoke less powerful nations and subject peoples into hostility toward Europeans and ultimately into calamitous rebellion. Tocqueville's sense of France's special calling as the nation of liberty to some degree assuaged his conscience regarding imperial expansion. And yet, even as he advocated the domination and colonization of Algeria, Tocqueville always preserved an awareness of the violence inherent in colonial expansion and rule that Mill allowed himself to overlook. Mill, for his part, was right to claim that the French used a language of national glory that would have been considered atavistic and dishonorable among English liberals, though he only rarely and glancingly acknowledged the extent to which Britain's unassailable international position made possible the tone of high-minded disinterestedness that more often characterized British debates.

Mill's awareness of the ways in which the exercise of arbitrary and unaccountable power not only oppressed colonized subjects but also corrupted the character of the colonizers came tragically late, and he never came to terms with the ubiquity of this danger in colonial relations, never perceiving that the problem beset colonial officials, both civil and military, as much as settlers. Moreover, both British and French public discourse had, by the latter half of the nineteenth century, so thoroughly succumbed to a conception of non-European peoples as inferior that few shared even the partial and intermittent misgivings about empire that we find in Tocqueville and Mill.[45] Nonetheless, their late doubts perhaps represent a vindication of the skepticism about European power and European superiority so powerfully articulated by Burke, Smith, Bentham, and Constant. If the political machinery of European imperial expansion was unstoppable by the latter nineteenth century, these late doubts indicate a space, however small, for dissent against its assumptions and imperatives. And yet as Smith had warned, only "equality of courage and force . . . by inspiring mutual fear, can . . . overawe the injustice of independent nations into some sort of respect for the rights of one another" (*WN* IV.vii.c.80). Ultimately, the still unfinished project of securing such respect was to emerge not out of such hesitant concerns from within Europe but from political mobilization, and determined and at times violent resistance, on the part of the colonized.

Notes

Chapter 1
Introduction

1. Diderot, *Political Writings*, 177. This passage appeared in Raynal's *Histoire des deux Indes* (1783 edition), book 8, chap. I.iv.

2. I use the term *empire* to describe the rule of one society over others, whether directly, or indirectly through institutions such as imperial trading companies; see Burke's definition of empire as "the aggregate of many states under one common head" and J. S. Mill's definition of dependencies as "territories of some size and population . . . which are subject, more or less, to acts of sovereign power on the part of the paramount country, without being equally represented (if at all) in its legislature" (Burke, "Speech on Conciliation with America," *WS* 3:132; Mill, *Considerations on Representative Government*, *CW* 19:562. The term *colony* was used in this period primarily to describe settlement territories. For treatments of the variety of political forms encompassed within the terms *empire* and *colony*, and for the evolution of the terms *empire-imperial* and *colony-colonial* in modern Europe, see Koebner, *Empire*; Canny, "The Origins of Empire"; Pagden, *Lords of All the World*; and Finley, "Colonies." David Armitage argues that the term *British Empire* came into currency in the second quarter of the eighteenth century (*Ideological Origins*, 170–71).

3. *On Liberty* (first published 1859), *CW* 18:224.

4. For analogous developments in international law, see Alexandrowicz, *Law of Nations*.

5. It would become distracting to include quotation marks each time I make use of terms such as *civilized* and *advanced*, *backward*, *savage*, and *barbarous*, which were ubiquitous in discussions of the justifiability of European rule over non-European peoples; the problematic nature of such terms should assumed throughout and is treated at length in subsequent chapters.

6. In his "Letter to a Noble Lord," Burke wrote that his services "in the affairs of India . . . are those on which I value myself the most; most for the importance; most for the labour; most for the judgment; most for constancy and perseverance in the pursuit. Others may value them most for the *intention*. In that, surely, they are not mistaken" (*WS* 9:159).

7. Eighteenth-century German critics of European empire are beyond the scope of this study. As Germany was not yet a colonial power, German thinkers of the period were not engaged actively in debates on imperial policy in the way their British and French contemporaries were. Still, Germany witnessed intellectual developments similar to those considered here, including the eclipse in the nineteenth century of a critical posture toward imperial ambitions and the development of more inexorable theories of progress and more contemptuous views of non-Europeans. On the anti-imperial arguments of Immanuel Kant and Johann Gottfried

Herder, see Muthu, *Enlightenment against Empire*. On Leopold von Ranke's division of the world's societies into those who make history (*geschichtsbildende Völker*) and those without history (*geschichtslose Völker*), see Alexandrowicz, "Empirical and Doctrinal Positivism," 286.

8. On Tocqueville's use of the term, see chapter 6 below. Bentham described his cofounders of the University College London as "an association of liberals" (letter to Simon Bolivar, August 13, 1825; see Twining, "Imagining Bentham," 10). Mill perhaps first identified himself with "liberalism" in 1831, when he described it as "for making every man his own guide & sovereign master . . . giving other men leave to persuade him if they can by evidence, but forbidding him to give way to authority" (letter to John Sterling, October 20–22, 1831, *CW* 12:84). At the end of his life, Mill identified liberalism as on "the side . . . of modern civilization and progress" ("England and Ireland," 1868, *CW* 6:523). Constant's biographer Dennis Wood has said of Constant's politics in the late 1790s, "It is perhaps not too early to speak of Constant's developing political position as liberal" (*Benjamin Constant*, 148), and Biancamaria Fontana notes that Constant used the term *libéral* to describe himself and his "political friends," though she argues that he was referring not to a political movement, but to a "vague identification with enlightened and progressive public opinion" (*Constant and Post-revolutionary Mind*, xiii).

9. See the discussions of this problem in Haakonssen, *Traditions of Liberalism*.

10. Welch, *Liberty and Utility*, 4. The caveat about monarchical government helps to show why it may make sense to include Burke among liberal thinkers, given his abiding hostility to efforts by the British Crown to expand its power, and indeed his often strong criticism of the French monarchy in the decades before the French Revolution. Also see Kahan, *Aristocratic Liberalism*, on the difficulties of characterizing nineteenth-century European liberalism; Kahan emphasizes a concern with "the dangers of two potential despotisms, from above and below" and notes that liberals of 1830–70 in Britain, France, and Germany supported eventual, but not immediate, universal suffrage (140). I discuss connections between liberal anxieties about democratization, and liberal support for empire, in chapters 6 and 8.

11. Richard Tuck's *Rights of War and Peace* addresses precisely the ways in which international politics have been central concerns in what Tuck describes as the liberal imagination from Grotius through Kant; also see Mehta, *Liberalism and Empire*; Parekh, "Superior People" and "Decolonizing Liberalism"; Keene, *Beyond the Anarchical Society*; and Leung, "Extending Liberalism."

12. Though Mehta, in his important book, focuses explicitly on nineteenth-century Britain, he often suggests the broader argument about liberalism, referring, for instance, to the liberal tradition running from Locke to Mill (see *Liberalism and Empire*, 4–8, for instance).

13. See chapter 4 for Bentham's critique of the British Empire for "denial of justice, oppression, extortion [and] despotism" (*Colonies, Commerce, and Constitutional Law*, 225).

14. As I discuss in the epilogue, both Mill and Tocqueville evinced, late in their careers, increasing disquietude about the moral and political dangers of imperial politics and warned of the persistent injustices that began to seem to them insepa-

rable from colonial relations, at least where white settler populations were involved. Also see Mantena, "Alibis of Empire."

15. Tocqueville's characteristic irony is largely silenced in his writings on Algeria, though it is at its most biting in his discussions of Americans' hypocritical treatment of Amerindians. I suggest in chapter 6 that Tocqueville had the luxury of the unresponsible observer in America; when, in the case of Algeria, he had considerable power to affect policy, he suppressed his skeptical inclinations. Also see Welch, "Colonial Violence," esp. 248–51.

16. See *Colonies, Commerce, and Constitutional Law.* Bentham had first worked out some of his anticolonial arguments in *Emancipate Your Colonies! Addressed to the National Convention of France, Ao* [Anno] *1793, shewing the uselessness and mischievousness of Distant Dependencies to an European State* (London, 1830) (*RRR*, 289–315).

17. Diderot's critique of European imperial expansion was most searing in his anonymous contributions to the Abbé Raynal's *Histoire philosophique et politique des établissements et du commerce des Européens dans les deux Indes.* Sankar Muthu argues that Diderot's "flexible moral universalism . . . allows him both to trumpet the freedom and dignity of all humans and to consider a wide array of cultural practices and institutions (of *moeurs*) in the non-European world as rational, defensible responses to local needs and concerns" (*Enlightenment against Empire*, 76); also see Benot, *Diderot*; and Duchet, *Anthropologie ethistoire.*

18. Berlin, "Thought of de Tocqueville," 204. Not even *Democracy in America* supports such a sanguine reading, however, as I discuss in chapter 6.

19. See Hart, "United States of America," for a treatment of Bentham's early hostility to American demands, mostly in anonymous contributions to works by his friend John Lind, and Bentham's later reconciliation to and indeed passionate enthusiasm for American independence.

20. John Bowring, *Memoirs of Jeremy Bentham*, *WJB* 10:63; see Hart, "The United States of America," 65.

21. As David Armitage and Anthony Pagden have shown, even when relations with Amerindians did consume imperial energies and attention, there was a widespread perception of the British Empire as the settlement of *terra nullia* or wasteland, rather than the rule of an alien population, and an insistence that the empire thus consisted of free and equal subjects. See Armitage, *Ideological Origins*; and Pagden, "Struggle for Legitimacy"; also see Pagden, *Lords of All the World*, chap. 5.

22. Imperial historiography used to date this "second" imperial period as beginning with the loss of America in 1783 and ending before the scramble for Africa of the last decades of the nineteenth century. For an account of the British Empire in this period see Bayly, *Imperial Meridian.* For the traditional view of the "swing to the east" of the late eighteenth century and the question of connections and discontinuities between the "first" and "second" British empires, see Harlow, *Founding*; for a reassessment, see Marshall, "Caribbean and India"; and Armitage, "British Conception of Empire." Armitage and Marshall see a more important turning point in 1763 with the end of the Seven Years' War, which saw the emergence of a diverse and global British Empire, though Marshall has counseled

against regarding this break, too, as very "sharp" or "purposeful" ("Britain and the World," 4).

23. Bowen, "British Conceptions."

24. Armitage, *Ideological Origins*; and Wilson, *Sense of the People*. Also see Wilson, "Citizenship, Empire, and Modernity," 174–77. Karen O'Brien has similarly described early-eighteenth-century Britain's "cosmopolitan fantasy of the empire as the bringer of a universal British peace and free trade" ("Protestantism and Poetry," 147).

25. Armitage has shown that this self-image was "originally an ideology, not an identity; that is, it was a contribution to political argument, and not a normative self-conception" (*Ideological Origins*, 172). Richard Koebner noted that "the defection of the Americans on the one hand and the union with Ireland on the other had made spectacular changes in the relative strength of the population which in a narrower or larger sense could be called 'British' ": whereas Americans, before independence, had comprised one-fifth of the "free subjects of the imperial crown," the English Canadian population was only a tenth of what the British Americans had numbered (*Empire*, 295).

26. On the mixture of pride and anxiety provoked among the British public by Britain's rapid territorial expansion thanks to successes throughout the Seven Years' War, see Wilson, *The Island Race*, chap. 1; and Bowen, "British Conceptions."

27. See Philips, *East India Company*, chap. 1; and, on parliamentary efforts to regulate the Company's activities in the 1760s to 1780s, Sutherland, *East India Company*. These culminated in the defeat of the most radical proposal, Fox's India Bill of 1783, and the passage of Pitt's India Act, which though less thoroughly reformist than Fox's bill, nonetheless inaugurated a new period of far greater state control over the affairs of the company. Burke's central role in writing and promoting Fox's bill is discussed in chapter 3 below.

28. See Mukherjee, "Jones and British Attitudes" and *Sir William Jones*.

29. Marshall, "Hastings as Scholar and Patron."

30. See Marshall and Williams, *Great Map of Mankind*, 120–23.

31. See, for example, the discussion in chapter 6 of the leftist deputy Amédée Desjobert, a contemporary of Tocqueville and a disciple of J. B. Say.

32. On increasing confidence in European superiority as non-European empires expanded through the eighteenth century, see and Philips and Wainwright, *Indian Society*; and Marshall and Williams, *Great Map of Mankind*, 301. Marshall and Williams point out that the use of exotic or of "savage" societies as critical foils for European corruption faded by the end of the century.

33. See Muthu, *Enlightenment against Empire*.

34. See Marshall, "Moral Swing," 71. As Marshall notes, the abolitionist Wilberforce voted for the impeachment of Warren Hastings, and Burke drafted a code for the reform of slavery and voted for the abolition of the slave trade. Also see Marshall's editorial introduction to Burke, *WS* 6:5, where he notes that the famous antislavery pamphlet published under the slogan "Am I not a man and a brother?" compared British injustices in India and Africa (to argue that Commons had done comparatively little to redress the latter).

35. Mulligan wrote of British depredations in India, "Then deeds were done that British arms disgrace, / And stain the annals of the human race" (*Poems Chiefly on Slavery and Oppression*, 14). With a skepticism he shared with other eighteenth-century writers (including Adam Ferguson, Kant, and Diderot) about the reliability of the information that reached Europe about "barbarous" countries, Mulligan argued in a footnote that "the state of negroes in their own country is as darkly shaded by the apologists for slavery, as their situation in the West Indies is varnished and emblazoned . . . very false estimates have been made of the disadvantages of barbarous nations. . . . Suppose an *Indian* or a *negro* were to judge us by the same mode, and only look upon the dark parts of the picture, you would deem it arrogance in him to exclaim, 'I despise, and yet I pity these Europeans!' " (83).

36. Marshall, "Moral Swing," 72.

37. For example, see Burke's source Philip Francis; Marshall, "Moral Swing," 91.

38. "Ninth Report of Select Committee," *WS* 5:252.

39. Organizations such as the Society for the Extinction of the Slave Trade and for the Civilization of Africa, active in the 1840s and 1850s (with prominent members such as Thomas Buxton and T. B. Macaulay), demonstrate the ways in which evangelist and abolitionist movements linked the humanitarian cause of abolition with a civilizing and colonialist mission.

40. See Adas, *Machines as the Measure of Man*. The tradition of admiration for China as a model of prosperity, lawfulness, bureaucratic rationality, and enlightened government was waning by the mid–eighteenth century. While Voltaire professed to admire China's enlightened and peaceful political order (following similar praise from Leibniz, Christian Wolff, and Jesuit missionaries), a portrait of China as stagnant rather than stable was gaining ground (see Marshall and Williams, *Great Map of Mankind*, chap. 5). Also see Lach, "Leibniz and China," and "Sinophilism of Christian Wolff." Voltaire's own claims were interventions in European debates rather than considered treatments of China; see Rosenthal, "Voltaire's Philosophy of History."

41. Pomeranz argues that a number of fortuitous circumstances contributed to western Europe's uniquely rapid industrialization at the end of the eighteenth century, such as the proximity of British coal mines to water transport, and the unexpectedly pervasive usefulness of the steam engine, first perfected in damp British coal mines (the Chinese had similar technology but not the conjunction of circumstances that made experimentation with it economically feasible in England). Pomeranz, *The Great Divergence*, introduction and chap. 6.

42. Washbrook, "India, 1818–1860," 397.

43. Washbrook, "India, 1818–1860," 397. Susan Bayly, *Caste, Society, and Politics* and Dirks, *Castes of Mind*, show how British efforts to understand and control Indian society contributed to (though were not solely responsible for) greater rigidity in caste structures, impermeability of caste divisions, and an extension of caste into new regions and among groups that previously had not much emphasized caste. C. A. Bayly effectively depicts the vitality and flux in Indian society not recognized by the British, as well as the unintended and often indirect

results of British rule in creating a more hierarchical and fixed social order (*Indian Society*, especially, on caste, 11–12 and 155–58).

44. Wheeler, *The Complexion of Race*, 37. Stepan notes, "By the middle of the nineteenth century, everyone [in Britain] agreed, it seemed, that in essential ways the white race was superior to non-white races" (*Idea of Race*, 4). Also see Hudson, "From 'Nation' to 'Race'." See Bowler, *The Invention of Progress*, on the misuse of Darwinian evolutionary theory in a developmentalist discourse rooted in "Victorians' wider faith in their own superiority" (13).

45. Letter to Gobineau of November 17, 1853, *OC* 9:201–2. George Frederickson has noted that Tocqueville expressed greater certainty that Gobineau's theories were pernicious than that they were false (*The Comparative Imagination*, 105).

46. In the *Principles of Political Economy*, Mill criticized the habit of "attributing the diversities of conduct and character to inherent natural differences" (*CW* 2:319). For the reference to primitive peoples, and the subsequent passage, see Mill's letter to Charles Dupont-White (April 6, 1860), *CW* 15:691 (in French; my translation).

47. See Varouxakis, "Mill on Race," 29. Varouxakis argues that after the late 1840s, Mill grew more insistent that race mattered little (*Mill on Nationality*, 47).

48. *Considerations on Representative Government* (*CW* 19:408). As Varouxakis points out, the passage combines determinist claims with the suggestion that custom is the source of such differences.

49. Also see Mehta, *Liberalism and Empire*, on the ways in which liberal universalism (notably in Locke and Mill) distinguishes "between anthropological capacities and the necessary conditions for their actualization": while the capacities are acknowledged to be universal, various peoples are politically disenfranchised as not being in a position to realize those capacities (47).

50. J. S. Mill was prepared to speak of the unequal "moral worth" of human beings, however; see the second section below.

51. Letter to Anthony Dermott, August 17, 1779. *Correspondence*, 4:121.

Chapter 2
Adam Smith on Societal Development and Colonial Rule

1. As Smith's student John Millar recalled, "[H]e followed the plan that seems to be suggested by Montesquieu; endeavouring to trace the gradual progress of jurisprudence, both public and private, from the rudest to the most refined ages." Quoted by Dugald Stewart, in his *Account of the Life and Writings of Adam Smith, L.L.D* (1793), I.19, in *EPS* 274.

2. While Smith, for instance, generally used the language of savage and barbarian in a descriptive (to mean hunting and pastoral societies) rather than evaluative sense, a far more contemptuous use of these terms was undoubtedly widespread (though by no means universal) among those directly or indirectly inspired by his analysis.

3. *WN* I.x.b.26. Also see Forbes, "Scientific Whiggism," 650.

4. Value judgments, he noted, vary with the "different situations of different ages and countries," but each flatters itself a universal standard (*TMS* V.2.7).

5. Ferguson, *History of Civil Society* 194; another was "whose king has the most absolute power": a distinction that his British readers would have been far quicker to recognize as delusion than they would great extent of territory.

6. "For, in every stage of society, the faculties, the sentiments and desires of men are so accommodated to their own state, that they become standards of excellence to themselves, they affix the idea of perfection and happiness to those attainments which resemble their own, and wherever the objects and enjoyments to which they have been accustomed are wanting, confidently pronounce a people to be barbarous and miserable. Hence the mutual contempt with which the members of communities, unequal in their degrees of improvement, regard each other." (Robertson, *History of America*, 2:50–51). For a similar comment with a more direct critique of the imperial destruction this vice engendered, see Robertson's *Historical Disquisition*, 335. Also see the essays in Brown, *Expansion of Empire*, especially Carnall, "Contemporary Images of India."

7. Dunbar, *Essays on the History of Mankind in Rude and Cultivated Ages*, Essay 5.

8. LJ A.i.27–35, LJ B.149–50. *WN* V.i.a discusses the military arrangements natural to each of the four stages. For accounts of stadial histories, see Bryson, *Man and Society*; Nisbet, *Social Change and History*; Meek, *Social Science*; Höpfl, "From Savage to Scotsman"; and Hamowy, *Scottish Enlightenment*; and for Smith's theory of history in particular, Skinner "Adam Smith"; Haakonssen, *Science of a Legislator*, chap. 7; and Bowles, "Origin of Property." As J.G.A. Pocock has written of the *Lectures on Jurisprudence*, "We read [these texts] not as incidents in the history of books, but as records of a series of pedagogical occasions" (*Barbarism and Religion*, 2:318).

9. These included John Dalrymple's *Essay towards a General History of Feudal Property in Great Britain* (1757); Henry Home, Lord Kames's *Historical Law-Tracts* (1758); Adam Ferguson's *Essay on the History of Civil Society* (1767); William Robertson's "View of the Progress of Society in Europe," the preface to his *History of the Reign of the Emperor Charles V* (1769); and Millar's *Distinction of Ranks* (1771).

10. *TMS* VII.iv.37. The promised text was to include a historical account of the "different revolutions . . . in the different ages and periods of society" undergone by the "general principles of law and government." See Haakonssen, *Science of a Legislator*, 151; and Ross, *Life of Adam Smith*, 404–6.

11. Ronald Meek has made the case that Smith was the first in Scotland to develop a four-stages theory and that his account greatly influenced the other Scottish historians. While Dalrymple (in 1757) and Kames (in 1758) *published* versions of such a theory earlier than Smith (who first used stadial arguments in print in *Wealth of Nations* in 1776), they very likely based their own accounts on lectures Smith gave at Glasgow University in 1752–53 and perhaps even earlier in Edinburgh (Meek, *Social Science*, 99–114). Meek discusses Smith's apparent worries about plagiarism and concern to establish the originality of his theory of development in "Smith, Turgot," 147–49.

Robertson, too, was said by contemporaries to be greatly influenced by Smith's lectures on jurisprudence: according to one man who heard Smith's lectures in 1750–51, "Dr Robertson had borrowed the first volume of his History of Charles V. from them as every student could testify" (Smith, *Correspondence*, 192 n. 2). The reference is to Robertson's most theoretical account of historical development, "View of the Progress of Society in Europe," the preface to *History of the Reign of the Emperor Charles V* of 1769.

For a claim that four-stages theory was in earlier and more general circulation, see Hont, "Language of Sociability." Pocock suggests that Ferguson, who was teaching in Edinburgh in the 1760s, did not derive his understanding of the four stages from Smith or Millar but from other sources (*Barbarism and Religion*, 2:330).

12. See the editors' introduction to *LJ*, which also discusses the points of contact, and the differences, between the two sets of notes, especially the order in which they treat various subjects: *LJ* A probably based on lectures delivered in 1762–63 and *LJ* B on lectures of 1763–64 (introduction, 8). A third set of notes probably based on lectures from 1751–52, 1752–53, or 1753–54 was discovered and published in 1976. These notes, comprising about nine pages of published text, were made by John Anderson, later a professor at Glasgow, probably copied from student notes taken in the lectures. These "Anderson notes" were published with commentary by Ronald Meek; references to them will be to the pages in Meek, "New Light."

13. Smith's student Dugald Stewart first used the phrase "theoretical, or conjectural history" in his 1793 life of Smith (2:49, in *EPS* 293). The term "conjectural," though it does capture something of Smith's method, was rejected by Ferguson as a mischaracterization of his effort to produce a natural history of mankind (Wood, "Natural History of Man," 113–15) as well as by Robertson (O'Brien, *Narratives of Enlightenment*, 133).

14. For examples, see Smith's discussion of property arrangements and laws of theft (*LJ* A.i.32) and of crime more generally (*LJ* A.ii.152ff.). The fundamental importance of the mode of subsistence to Smith's account was noted by Millar, who reported that Smith sought "to point out *the effects of those arts which contribute to subsistence*, and to the accumulation of property, in procuring correspondent improvements or alterations in law and government" (emphasis added; quoted in Dugald Stewart's *Life of Smith*, in *EPS* 274–75).

15. See *WN* 25 and *LJ* A.vi.46–48 and *LJ* B.220. Like other stadial histories, Smith's theory had some difficulty accounting for movement from one stage to the next.

16. See *LJ* A.vi.25ff.: even though the laboring poor of civilized societies receive a "very small share" of the wealth they are largely responsible for producing, still they are "far better provided for in all the necessaries and conveniences of life" than even a "savage prince."

17. As I discuss below, Smith used the term *natural* and its cognates frequently and with a variety of senses, despite his skepticism about the term's traditional metaphysical connotations. When he spoke of the "natural" course of development, he tended to mean what could be expected to happen in general, or thanks to the "natural inclinations of man" when they were not thwarted by "human institutions" (*WN* III.i.3, in the chapter titled "Of the Natural Progress of Opu-

lence"). In this sense the "natural" lay somewhere between the empirical and the conjectural: it could be found in the actual historical development of every society, but one often needed to see beyond the unnatural interventions of particular agents or the persistence of customs suited to earlier stages of development. As Griswold has pointed out, the notion of nature as Smith portrays it is complicated by the fact that it "seems to generate the unnatural—cabals, misplaced interventions by political utopians or misguided philosophers" (*Virtues of Enlightenment*, 328).

18. Quoted by Dugald Stewart, *Life of Adam Smith* 4:25, in *EPS* 322.

19. Skinner, in "Adam Smith," and Meek, in *Social Science*, emphasize the importance of economic factors in social change; this view has been criticized by Donald Winch and Knud Haakonssen, among others (see Winch, "Enduring Particular Result," and *Riches and Poverty*; and Haakonssen, *Science of a Legislator*).

20. Smith uses the phrase in *WN* IV.introduction. Winch argues that materialist readings of Smith mistakenly place "severe limitations on any genuine political vision of society" ("Enduring Particular Result," 258). Meek, however, does not suggest that Smith's theory was monocausal, determinist, or apolitical; he makes clear that Smith understood there to be many causes of historical change, though he argues that economic or material factors were primary (*Social Science*, 125).

21. Haakonssen, *Science of a Legislator*, 181–83.

22. Both Winch and Meek have noted that, in Winch's words, the "range of explanatory variables" increased in the more modern societies ("Enduring Particular Result," 259).

23. Compare J. S. Mill's claim that the Greeks were the only "people in the ancient world who had any spring of unborrowed progress within themselves," which attributes Greek developments to unspecified qualities in the people themselves rather than to their condition ("Review of Grote's *History of Greece*," *CW* 11:313). As I argue in chapter 5, while Mill resisted biological explanations for differing degrees of progress, he often discussed "barbarians" as distinguished from civilized peoples by their incapacity for certain kinds of abstract thought (such as the notion of reciprocity) or by their incapacity to progress without assistance from outside the society.

24. As I discuss further in chapter 6, in his *Esquisse d'un tableau historique des progrès de l'esprit humain* (Sketch for a historical picture of the progress of the human mind), whose title indicates Condorcet's view that societal development is a function of intellectual progress, he describes societal development as "the perfection of human faculties" (3). He argues that errors have "retarded or suspended the course [*marche*] of reason" (15) and that societies can be seen "sometimes making new progress, sometimes plunging back into ignorance" (11). Unlike Smith, Condorcet maintains that societal progress is the "result" of the "development of the faculties of individuals" and follows the same laws. He confidently dubs the study of these general laws of development "metaphysics" (3).

25. *WN* I.iii.7. See also the second "Fragment on the Division of Labor": "The first improvements, therefore in arts and industry are always made in those places where the conveniency of water carriage affords the most extensive market to the produce of every sort of labour" (*LJ* 585).

26. Compare Hume's claim—despite his rejection of climate theories of national difference—that "there is some reason to think, that all the nations, which

live beyond the polar circles or between the tropics, are inferior to the rest of the species, and are incapable of all the higher attainments of the human mind" ("Of National Characters," *Essays*, 207).

27. *LJ* A.iii.118–22; also see *LJ* B.140–42. In this discussion Smith is referring to a range of forms of unfree labor; here he means serfdom.

28. "[I]t was absolutely necessary both that the authority of the king and of the clergy should be great. Where ever any one of these was wanting, slavery still continues" (*LJ* A.iii.122).

29. "Anderson Notes," 32–33, in Meek, "New Light," 197 (the Anderson notes do not mention the role of the clergy).

30. Smith had greater doubts than Hume that technological progress occurs together with progress in manners, morals, economic conditions, science, and letters, see Hume's essay "Of Refinement in the Arts," in *Essays*, 268–80, especially 270–71. Forbes, too, notes that "Hume was far less skeptical about the all-round benefits of commercial civilization than Smith" ("Sceptical Whiggism," 194).

31. When there is little to buy, great landowners such as the clergy and nobility can do little with the produce of their land other than maintain dependents.

32. Burke, a careful and sympathetic reader of Smith, argued in the 1790s, "The States of the Christian World have grown up to their present magnitude in a great length of time, and by a great variety of accidents. They have been improved to what we see them with greater or less degrees of felicity and skill. Not one of them has been formed upon a regular plan or with any unity of design" (*WS* 9:287, *Second Letter on a Regicide Peace*).

33. *WN* III.i.9. In refusing to regard Europe's path of development as the standard against which other societies should be measured, Smith demonstrated a scholarly restraint often not practiced in subsequent accounts of economic progress, down to the present day. Kenneth Pomeranz argues that studies of economic development have long been marred by a tendency to measure other societies by a "European" standard, including the false assumption that those aspects of technology in which Europe excelled were inevitably the important ones and the tendency to dismiss those aspects in which eighteenth-century Europe lagged (such as agricultural technologies) as unimportant for long-term industrial growth (*The Great Divergence*, introduction and 45ff.).

34. Smith uses the phrase "unintended and unforeseen consequences of different actions" in the course of explaining why we praise and blame not only an agent's intention, as it would seem in the abstract we ought, but also the actual consequences of his or her action (*TMS* II.iii.introduction).

35. Ronald Hamowy discusses the connections among Smith's uses of the idea of unintended consequences in his moral, historical, and economic theories and notes that one should not take Smith's account of self-regulating markets to suggest that he did not "support government intervention . . . in those areas where he felt utilitarian considerations dictated such interference" (*Scottish Enlightenment*, 20).

36. Winch, "Enduring Particular Result," 265; Karen O'Brien has observed that the " 'invisible hand' in Smith's *Wealth of Nations*, for example, does not reveal to the acting individual the moral logic of its operations, and so opens out

possibilities for a profoundly ironic interpretation of man's condition" (*Narratives of Enlightenment*, 148).

37. Emma Rothschild has drawn a compelling portrait of Smith's nondogmatic approach to social analysis, arguing that Smith "lived in an imaginative universe of profound uncertainty. Like Hume, he had come to tolerate a way of life, or a way of thinking, in which almost all judgments were incomplete, provisional, propositions to be discussed, and not to be convinced of" (*Economic Sentiments*, 156).

38. In this respect Smith differs significantly from even those historians most respectful of postsavage societies outside Europe, like Robertson. For Kames's polygenetic theory, see *Sketches of the History of Man*, Sketch 12, in which he disputes Buffon's account of the peopling of America and argues that Amerindians must be of a different species than other humans (Kames's retrograde science is apparent in his rejection of Buffon and Linnaeus's systems of classification as unnatural on the following grounds: "what will a plain man think of a system of classing that denies a whale to be a fish"). Also see Wokler, "Apes and Races," 154–56; and Stocking, "Scotland as Model," 84–86.

39. See Meek, *Ignoble Savage*, 129, 138, 145, and 155, among others. A number of the thinkers Meek discusses, notably Condorcet, Kames, and Robertson (on whom Meek's study relies heavily in this regard) can more justly be said to have thought of "savages" as ignoble.

40. See, for instance: "[W]e ought always to punish with reluctance, and more from a sense of the propriety of punishing, than from any savage disposition to revenge" (*TMS* III.6.4); "the most insolent and barbarous tyranny" (II.iii.3.3); "a barbarous and faithless wife" (III.5.11). For a counterexample, though, see Smith's reference to "the most brutal and savage barbarians . . . an Attila, a Gengis, or a Tamerlane" (VI.iii.31).

41. *Savage* came to refer specifically to hunting societies, and *barbarian* to pastoral societies, but Smith is not consistent in such usage and often uses the terms interchangeably to describe early stages of society. Ferguson, for instance, distinguishes hunting from pastoral societies in these terms: "the savage, who is not yet acquainted with property" from "the barbarian, to whom it is, although not ascertained by laws, a principal object of care and desire" (*History of Civil Society*, 81). In the following pages, I use the terms, without quotation marks, in Smith's analytical (and not evaluative) sense.

42. Pocock's claim that for Smith Europe's own history began in the pastoral stage and that he therefore severed Europe's history from America ignores a number of Smith's own statements to the contrary (*LJ* A.vi.133). Smith noted, for instance (drawing on the poems of Ossian), that at the time of the Roman rule of Britain "the Scots and the Picts . . . were much in the same state as the Americans, tho they dont appear to have had the custom of roasting men alive" (*LJ* A.iv.102). Later he noted, "In a nation of savages, as our Saxon ancestors or the present North Americans, money has an immense price." See Pocock, *Barbarism and Religion*, 2:317.

43. *LJ* A.ii.97 and iv.7; also see *LJ* B.19–20.

44. On the equality of early hunting societies, see *LJ* A.iv.42–43; *WN* v.i.b.9; occasionally he referred to them as democratic, if they could be said to have government at all.

45. *TMS* V.2.7: people's "sentiments concerning the particular degree of each quality, that is either blamable or praise-worthy, vary, according to that degree which is usual in their own country, and in their own times."

46. Ferguson believed virtue required struggle and exercise and would be lost under too comfortable conditions; see his discussions of corruption and luxury, and polished nations" precarious hold on liberty in the sixth part of the *Essay* (*History of Civil Society*, 224–64).

47. The savage learns not to "give way to . . . the passions which [his] distress is apt to excite," because others around him, concerned with their own survival, cannot afford to sympathize with such passions. A "humane and polished people, who have more sensibility to the passions of others, . . . can more easily pardon some little excess" (*TMS* V.2.10).

48. *TMS* V.2.11. While Smith rarely questions the quality of the ethnographic information he draws on, he explains savage behavior as reported in terms that assume modes of moral reasoning very similar to those of the "civilized." See Berry, *Social Theory*, 91–99.

49. Roxann Wheeler has described four-stages theory as "a racial ideology" and indeed, along with natural history, as one of the "two most common paradigms for racializing people" in the eighteenth century (*The Complexion of Race*, 179), since it provided an analytic framework for explaining differences among human groups. Smith did not use the theory to reify human groups in the way Wheeler argues many four-stage theorists did.

50. Wheeler, *The Complexion of Race*, 29–33. Nancy Stepan notes the shift in the nineteenth century from "an emphasis on the fundamental physical and moral homogeneity of man" to one on mankind's "essential heterogeneity" (*Idea of Race*, 4). Lord Kames was one of the relatively few thinkers of this period to entertain the theory of polygenesis.

51. Millar, *Origin of the Distinction of Ranks*, introduction; Ferguson, *History of Civil Society*, 108. But Ferguson also distinguished between mere ignorance and incapacity: "Every question, however, on this subject ["nations on whom we bestow the appellations of barbarous or savage"] is premature, till we have first endeavoured to form some general conception of our species in its rude state, and have learned to distinguish mere ignorance from dullness, and the want of arts from the want of capacity" (80–81).

52. Pocock, *Barbarism and Religion*, 2:315.

53. Smith, "History of Astronomy," III.2, *EPS* 49. Rousseau argued in the *Second Discourse* that savages "did not even dream of vengeance, except perhaps mechanically and on the spot, like the dog that bites the stone thrown at him" *Oeuvres complètes*, 3:157.

54. Note, however, that particular word choices in the *Lectures on Jurisprudence* do not have the definitive character they might in published works.

55. *LJ* A.i.47. The much briefer treatment at *LJ* B.150 sounds more like cognitive development accounts: "Among savages property begins and ends with possession, and they seem scarce to have any idea of any thing as their own which is

not about their bodies." It is impossible to know how close the language here came to Smith's lecture, but the differences between this and the *LJ* A passage suggest that to read it as a description of savages' cognitive limitations may be misleading. It is worth noting that in the *LJ* B passage, too, Smith suggests that members of hunting societies use a spectator method to arrive at their notion of legitimate possession.

56. Among those conditions are that "the intention of the promiser [must] be expressed so clearly that no impartial spectator can be in doubt about the content of the agreement" and that "the things that are the subject of the agreement must also be considered of significant value" (*LJ* A.ii.62).

57. *LJ* B.175; also see *LJ* A.ii.56ff.; Stein, *Legal Evolution*, 39–40; and Haakonssen, *Science of a Legislator*, 112–14, who notes that this understanding of promises "brings out very clearly a basic feature of Smith's moral philosophy, namely that it is about the *relations* between persons."

58. Smith notes as well that language in its early stages (indeed until very late in the development of society) is too imprecise to engender such certainty on the part of the recipient of a promise that a breach would be actionable. Smith's point about language is not that savages cannot think abstractly, but rather that they have not yet developed the terms in which to express commitment beyond a reasonable doubt.

59. He offers as an example rituals of "stipulation" or "solemnities" such as the Armenian custom, reported by Tacitus, in which parties to an agreement suck a bit of blood from one another's thumbs; Smith suggests that even such "horrid ceremonies," rather than illustrating the "fear and terror" or superstition of the people, make sense as a means of establishing certainty and thus obligation at a time when language alone cannot do so (*LJ* A.ii.70).

60. Mill, "A Few Words on Non-intervention," *CW* 21:118.

61. Cf. Millar, for instance, who described "that noted aversion which the people [of China] discover to every sort of innovation" (*Distinction of Ranks*, 1773 ed., 139).

62. "China has been long one of the richest, that is, one of the most fertile, best cultivated, most industrious, and most populous countries in the world" (*WN* I.viii.24); "in manufacturing art and industry, China and Indostan, though inferior, seem not to be much inferior to any part of Europe" (*WN* I.xi.g.28).

63. Smith probably relied on the volume edited by the Jesuit Jean-Baptiste du Halde, *Description de l'empire de la Chine*, first translated into English in 1736. Du Halde's account was typical of Jesuit analyses of China in its emphasis on China's traditionalism and immobility (Marshall and Williams, *Great Map of Mankind*, 83–84, and 129, and *WN* 90 n. 21), and here as elsewhere Smith does not seem to question the accuracy of his sources.

64. Marshall and Williams, *Great Map of Mankind*, 135.

65. Duncan Forbes has argued that Smith singled out China and India as opulent but "politically very backward" ("Sceptical Whiggism," 199), but Smith himself does not employ such language.

66. Pomeranz, *The Great Divergence*. He notes, for instance, that one should study the history and impact of particular inventions rather than try to account

for "the Industrial Revolution" as a unitary phenomenon. Pomeranz himself does not discuss such affinities between his own argument and Smith's.

67. Smith himself doubted some of the reports of opulence and excellent public works in China and India (see *WN* V.i.d.17–18), but he notes that what is perhaps falsely reported of the extraordinary public works in those countries could not possibly be "tolerably managed" by any European state in his day either.

68. David Spadafora has argued that in contrast to the confidence expressed by eighteenth-century English thinkers in the limitlessness of progress as part of a divine plan, Scottish thinkers of the period generally were more humble about European achievements and more tentative in their hopes for the future. Only Ferguson, he notes, expressed faith in human perfectibility and limitless progress (*Idea of Progress*, 302ff.).

69. *WN* V.i.f.49–55. Winch has rightly noted that "while Smith undoubtedly drew attention to the improvements associated with commerce," he was "concerned to record losses as well as gains" ("Enduring Particular Result," 265–66). Also see Winch, *Riches and Poverty*, chap. 8.

70. Smith also discusses the disadvantages of commerce in the final paragraphs of the 1766 *Lectures on Jurisprudence*, where he singles out the neglect of education in the more commercial parts of England, the "drunkenness and riot" that result from childhoods spent in urban labor, and the fact that commerce "sinks the courage of mankind," so that the "heroic spirit is almost utterly extinguished" (*LJ* B.331–33).

71. On benefits of material comfort for moral behavior, see *TMS* V.2.9: "Before we can feel much for others, we must in some measure be at ease ourselves. . . . All savages are too much occupied with their own wants and necessities, to give much attention to those of another person." Pocock notes that while he takes it "as granted" that for Smith "the moral life of individuals depends upon the growth and progress of both civil government and commercial prosperity," Smith's narrative of progress is nonetheless "more than a whiggish teleology" (*Barbarism and Religion* 2:321).

72. The passage continues: "In other countries the unfortunate constitution of their courts of judicature hinders any regular system of jurisprudence from ever establishing itself among them, though the improved manners of the people may be such as would admit of the most accurate. In no country do the decisions of positive law coincide exactly, in every case, with the rules which the natural sense of justice would dictate. Systems of positive law, therefore, though they deserve the greatest authority, as the records of the sentiments of mankind in different ages and nations, yet can never be regarded as accurate systems of the rules of natural justice" (*TMS* VII.iv.36).

73. Smith believed that the development of general rules was absolutely essential to the moral life (see *TMS* III.4), but he was suspicious of philosophers' claims to have special knowledge of these rules.

74. The Greek practice of infanticide and the European colonial depredations in Asia (*WN* IV.vii.c.100–108), are examples of moments when actors have failed to exercise sufficient self-criticism.

75. It is important that Smith presents his moral theory as a theory of how we come to make moral judgments, and how these evolve for both individuals and

societies, rather than as a theory of what is objectively right and wrong or virtuous and vicious. Charles Griswold plausibly describes Smith, for this reason, as a "nondogmatic skeptic" and points out that Smith's approach to knowledge generally took this form: he wrote *histories* of astronomy and physics, accounts of how human beings have come to hold the views they do, rather than theories of metaphysics or ontology (*Virtues of Enlightenment*, 170).

76. This necessarily cursory discussion draws on *TMS* I.i and III.1–2. For instance: "[W]e can never form any judgment concerning [our own sentiments and motives] unless we remove ourselves, as it were, from our own natural station, and endeavour to view them as at a certain distance from us. But we can do this in no other way than by endeavouring to view them with the eyes of other people, or as other people are likely to view them" (III.1.2).

77. We feel this pleasure of congruence even when the feelings we sympathize with are unpleasant: as, for instance, when we sympathize with the "distress" and the "just and natural resentment" of the victims of "a Borgia or a Nero" (*TMS* II.i.6).

78. See Campbell, *Smith's Science of Morals*, 127: "[T]he responses of the [impartial] spectator are identified with the consensus towards which any actual group of persons can be observed to approximate in their attitudes to the behaviour of their fellows." Cf. Griswold, *Virtues of Enlightenment*, 133: the impartial spectator can "over-awe" actual spectators, "but not so far as to suppress [their] clamor entirely." While I concur with Campbell's argument that Smith's impartial spectator should not be read as a "normatively ideal observer of behavior who stands above and criticizes the moral judgments of ordinary men," Campbell, in situating the impartial spectator *entirely* within a social context, does not grant the possibility for our judgment to transcend our immediate context that Smith (problematically, perhaps) insists on.

79. *TMS* III.2.2–8; for a lucid discussion see Haakonssen, *Science of a Legislator*, 53–56.

80. Campbell has argued for a "relativist" reading of Smith; Haakonssen and Winch, who see Smith as a member of the natural law tradition, insist on a far more universalist reading, though Haakonssen especially offers a sensitive reading of the movement in Smith's theory between concrete context and universal moral values. Haakonssen argues, "If we do not find room for the natural and universal in Smith's theory of justice, his whole project for a natural jurisprudence becomes unintelligible" (*Science of a Legislator*, 148).

81. *TMS* VII.iv.37; cf *LJ* B.1. Donald Winch discusses Smith's extensive additions and revisions in 1788–89 to this section of *TMS* in *Riches and Poverty*, 166–67.

82. *TMS* VII.iii.2.2. While Smith endorses the rationalist objections to Hobbesian voluntarism he summarizes in this passage, he goes on to argue that those who believe reason tells us directly what is right or wrong have misunderstood its role. Rather, reason contributes to moral judgment first in the process of forming "vague and indeterminate" ideas of what is admirable and second through induction, by which we form general rules of conduct out of these vaguer and more immediate judgments. Smith criticizes Mandeville, too, for seeming "to take away

altogether the distinction between vice and virtue," and deems the tendency of his theory "upon that account, wholly pernicious" (VII.ii.4.6).

83. Griswold argues that notwithstanding Smith's frequent use of the term *nature*, on Smith's view, "from the standpoint of nature, or the whole, moral distinctions disappear; therefore we cannot live in accordance with nature as a whole. . . . [Smith] suggests that moral distinctions reappear when perceived in context and that moral perception requires the work of sentiment and sympathy" (*Virtues of Enlightenment*, 319). Griswold argues that Smith was attracted to the Stoic effort to "diminish our natural affection for ourselves by viewing ourselves from a detached perspective," but that he believed that in the hands of the Stoics, "natural moral sentiments become distorted when pressed philosophically."

84. We should note that Smith uses the term *humanity* in two distinct ways: sometimes it serves as a category of general morality, as when he calls infanticide "so dreadful a violation of humanity" (*TMS* V.2.15); more often, however, the term has less than universal meaning, and connotes gentleness or "sensibility" rather than an absolute moral standard (see *TMS* V.2.13).

85. Further remarks on infanticide in the *Lectures on Jurisprudence* are almost entirely descriptive rather than evaluative: he recognizes how widespread the practice has been even when prohibited by law (as under Roman law) and observes that it is common in societies that practice polygamy. He notes that Christian missionaries in China have been reconciled to the practice: making no effort to stop it, they merely pride themselves on baptizing the babies before they are killed (*LJ* A.iii.81). The hypocrisy of these priests, rather than the Roman or Chinese practice of infanticide itself, is the object of Smith's criticism in this passage.

86. A hereditary nobility is impossible when fathers have dozens of children, Smith claims, and hereditary nobilities are bulwarks against absolutism.

87. James Mill's dismissal of Indian chronology is one good example of the use of a morally indifferent practice as evidence of the entire society's immaturity and barbarism, with deep moral and political implications, as I discuss in chapter 5.

88. Smith made a similar argument about the possibility for economic progress under imperfect conditions in the *Wealth of Nations*, where he compared societies to the human body, which manages to stay healthy under a wide variety of regimens, not merely the most perfectly healthful. "If a nation could not prosper without the enjoyment of perfect liberty and perfect justice, there is not in the world a nation which could ever have prospered. In the political body, however, the wisdom of nature has fortunately made ample provision for remedying many of the bad effects of the folly and injustice of man" (IV.ix.28). People can flourish even under imperfect systems, and no system is stagnant. For a discussion of the ways in which Smith's arguments about justice resemble functional explanations, see Campbell, *Smith's Science of Morals*, 69–79.

89. *TMS* VII.ii.4.14. Smith's contemporary James Dunbar drew on this notion in his own arguments against what he saw as European cultural arrogance and the cruelty this arrogance prompted toward non-Europeans: Europeans, he wrote, imagine that they have achieved a civilization that is entirely "generous, liberal, refined, and humane; while others, from their hard fate, or their perverseness, remain in all respects illiberal, mischievous, and rude. The general supposition

with regard to the condition of human nature, is implied in that opinion of their own superiority over other nations, which Europeans are prone to entertain." And yet, "It ought to be supposed that, if other nations were as far inferior to us, as we are willing to imagine, their condition would evidently tend to decay and extermination" (*Essays on the History of Mankind*, Essay 4).

90. *TMS* V.2.9. Burke and Diderot both made similar claims about the peculiar immorality of colonial rulers. Though a compelling explanation of some extreme injustices, particularly initial acts of violence in remote regions, this argument cannot account for the establishment of cultures of exploitation such as plantation slavery in the West Indies and American South, which Smith certainly abhorred. He called domestic slavery "the vilest of all states" (*TMS* VII.ii.1.28), but he also claimed that slavery on the North American mainland was far more humane than that on the islands because the owners were poorer and less distant from their slaves than the great planters of the West Indies (*LJ* A.iii.108). As we have seen, he did believe that once slavery was established in a republic (that is, when slave-owners were self-governing), it would be extremely difficult to abolish (*LJ* A.iii.101–2).

91. Letter to John Sinclair of October 14, 1782, *Correspondence of Adam Smith*, 262 (letter 221).

92. As Wilson argues, "It was but a short step to assert that those most committed to the expansion of commerce were pursuing the good of all British citizens, whereas those more diffident about untrammeled imperial expansion were dedicated to its subversion" (*Sense of the People*, 158).

93. An engraving of 1740 (during the War of Jenkins' Ear against the Spanish) prayed that the British "lions" might be unleashed to extend British freedom around the globe: "They soon would break all Europe's threatened chain, / Tame proud Iberia, shake ye Gallic throne, / Give freedom to the World, and keep her own" (*A Skit on Britain*, London, 1740; Wilson, *Sense of the People*, 137 and 156).

94. The *Protestant Dissenting Ministers* congratulatory address to George III, *Gentleman's Magazine*, 33 (1763), is quoted by Wilson, *Sense of the People*, 204.

95. Wilson, *Sense of the People*, 155–56.

96. Smith believed that peoples who lived in moderately different regions and climates were most useful to one another: too close, and they had the same goods and deficiencies; too distant, and each could hardly imagine the needs of the other, and so they were unlikely to produce goods the other might need (see *WN* 626).

97. "The inconveniencies resulting from the possession of its colonies, every country has engrossed to itself completely. The advantages resulting from their trade it has been obliged to share with many other countries" (IV.vii.c.84).

98. Memorandum to Wedderburn, *Correspondence of Adam Smith*, 382; also see *WN* V.iii.92.

99. Because domestic agriculture and manufacture offer better returns on investment when the level of risk is considered, he argued, capital would naturally—without government intervention on behalf of mercantilist interests—be withheld from foreign trade until all the land in the country is cultivated and the country's capacity for manufactures fully tapped. See Coats, "Smith and Mercantile System," 225–30.

100. *Correspondence of Adam Smith*, letters 201 (to Henry Dundas, November 1) and 202 (to Lord Carlisle, November 8), 1779. Even more important than fair trade policy, Smith noted to Carlisle, was political reform: "as long as it continues to be divided between two hostile nations, the oppressors and the oppressed, the protestants and the Papists," both justice and industry in Ireland would suffer.

101. On Smith's critique of British colonial policy in North America, see Winch, *Classical Political Economy*; Stevens, "Colonial Disturbances"; and Ross, *Life of Adam Smith*, chap. 26.

102. *WN* V.iii.68. Smith surmised that if such a union were to take place, the imperial capital would eventually shift to America, with the population and wealth (IV.vii.c.79).

103. "By different arts of oppression [the Dutch] have reduced the population of several of the Moluccas nearly to the number which is sufficient to supply with fresh provisions and other necessaries of life their own insignificant garrisons" (*WN* IV.vii.c.101).

104. "The English company have not yet had time to establish in Bengal so perfectly destructive a system. The plan of their government, however, has had exactly the same tendency" (*WN* IV.vii.c.101).

105. *WN* I.viii.26. It is striking that the other examples Smith gives of declining societies in his day were also due to colonial conquest, though it was the metropolitan countries, Spain and Portugal, that had suffered the decline (I.xi.g.25).

106. As E. A. Benians noted in 1925 when the British Empire was still extensive, Smith "seems not to have expected or desired the foundation of empires of some permanence as a result of Western conquest" ("Project of an Empire," 33).

107. On Fox's bill, see Smith's letter to William Eden of December 15, 1783, *Correspondence of Adam Smith*, 272 (letter 233).

108. *WN* IV.vii.c.106. As I discuss in chapter 3, Burke similarly criticized the British failure to mix their fortunes with that of India.

109. *LJ* A.i.8 The context of this assertion suggests that Smith was speaking of nations—"independent states"—of more equal power, but unfortunately we have little to go on, as the lecture notes do not include the discussion of the laws of war and peace promised in this introductory overview. *WN* discusses the relation between stages of improvement and the development of the "art of war," but that discussion is a largely technical one and says nothing about the development of laws of war.

Chapter 3
Edmund Burke's Peculiar Universalism

1. For the phrase "moral imagination," see the passage on Marie Antoinette in the *Reflections*, where Burke invokes imagination, threatened by deracinated Jacobin rationalism, as fundamental to moral social life: "all the superadded ideas furnished from the wardrobe of a moral imagination, which the heart owns and the understanding ratifies as necessary to cover the defects of our naked, shivering nature" (*WS* 8:128).

2. Burke used *Britain-British* and *England-English* fairly interchangeably to describe the colonists.

3. Stephen White makes a particularly good case that no "urge to capture a true Burke" can succeed, and he proposes portraits in the "cubist tradition of painting" (*Edmund Burke*, xx–xxi). I agree with White that any portrayal of Burke as simply a crusader against injustice would be one-sided and that "Burke's thinking about injustice can have little resonance today unless it is radically dissociated from its background assumptions concerning the Great Chain of Being, which allowed him to interpret as simply inevitable many things we would find to be unjust and subject to remedy" (*Edmund Burke*, 87); but as White recognizes, aspects of Burke's own thought can assist in the effort to overcome the rigidly hierarchical strains. In his *Address to the Colonists* (1777), Burke wrote of "these fierce tribes of Savages and Cannibals, in whom the traces of human nature are effaced by ignorance and barbarity" (*WS* 3:281–82). Also see his *Speech on the Use of Indians* (1778).

4. The best recent studies include Whelan, *Edmund Burke and India*; Mehta, *Liberalism and Empire*; O'Brien, *The Great Melody*; and David Bromwich's many essays on Burke: especially *A Choice of Inheritance*, 43–78, "Context of Burke's *Reflections*," and the introduction to his selection of Burke's writings, *On Empire, Liberty and Reform*. Harold Laski, in 1947, wrote of the "liberal element in Burke's temper" and praised "the impressive ability with which Burke saw beyond his own age to a view of colonial policy the significance of which we are only just beginning to apply. . . . He saw clearly the moral vice of predatory imperialism, and he stood by his principles in the face of obloquy, indifference and neglect" (*Edmund Burke*, 7–8). On Burke's international thought, see Welsh, *Burke and International Relations* and Armitage, "Edmund Burke and Reason of State."

Sympathetic readings have often been dismissed as taking Burke's side too uncritically. Vanech's "Painful Homecoming," criticizes Regina Janes for so heavily emphasizing "Burke's humanitarianism toward India and her people . . . that Burke is sentimentalized" (175, responding to Janes, "At Home Abroad").

5. Mehta, *Liberalism and Empire*, 154, quoting Burke, Sheffield Archives, Wentworth Woodhouse Muniments 9/23. Similarly, in his *Letter to the Sheriffs of Bristol*, Burke wrote, "It was our duty . . . to conform our government to the character and circumstances of the several people who composed this mighty and strangely diversified mass" (*WS* 3:316).

6. Mehta, *Liberalism and Empire*, 42.

7. He shows that Burke, unlike members of that liberal tradition, understood India as a political community; while Burke's "conception of social order is deeply psychological" and conscious of the importance of history and place in political communities, Mehta argues, to reduce his thought to mere "traditionalism" is to misconstrue his flexible and subtle understanding of social order (176).

8. See Marshall, *Impeachment of Warren Hastings*, chap. 1, which traces the tortuous imperial politics of the 1770s and 1780s; and O'Brien, *The Great Melody*, 257ff. O'Brien circumscribes "the Indian part" of what he, following Yeats, calls "Burke's Great Melody" to 1783–94, arguing that it was during these years that Burke was speaking not on behalf of his party, but "out of deep personal conviction which he imposes on his party" (96).

9. *Morning Herald*, February 27, 1788, which also described Burke's character as "marked by . . . unbounded philanthropy to all classes and nations of men" (British Library, Burney Collection).

10. See Robinson, *Edmund Burke*, especially plate 29. Burke's response to the ridicule was to call attention to, and vindicate, his own motives in the prosecution, as when he responded to claims he was driven by private rage: "Anger indeed he had felt, but surely not a blamable anger; for who ever heard of an enquiring anger, a digesting anger, a collating anger, an examining anger, a deliberating anger, or a selecting anger? The anger he felt was an uniform, steady, publick anger, but not a private anger" (*WS* 6:104). Burke was infamous for his prolixity, as many contemporary caricatures and satirical verses attest, and the verbosity of his speeches may well have damaged his cause with both the Lords and the public. The 1774 mock elegy *Retaliation* by Oliver Goldsmith, another Irishman, teased Burke's endless oratory, but also noted the shallow insouciance of his audience: "[Burke,] too deep for his hearers, yet went on refining, / And thought of convincing, while they thought of dining" (quoted by Robinson, *Edmund Burke*, 79).

11. Marshall, *Impeachment of Warren Hastings*, 3–6. Burke's interest in and information about India initially stemmed from his connections with William Burke, Burke's friend and (probably unrelated) "cousin" of questionable integrity who went to India in 1777 to salvage his fortunes, and Philip Francis, Hastings's rival in India, the supposed author of the "Junius" letters, and a key source of information for Burke after 1781.

12. Letter to Mary Palmer of January 19, 1786, *Correspondence*, 5:252–57.

13. Nussbaum, *Torrid Zones*, 168; also see Suleri, *Rhetoric of English India*, 54.

14. Marshall, *Impeachment of Warren Hastings*, 190. Marshall concludes that "[i]t was Burke's tragedy that he could not see Hastings in perspective. . . . Almost as soon as he turned his attention to Bengal, Burke began to acquire a distorted view both of Hastings's record and of his importance."

15. Letter to French Laurence, July 28, 1796, *Correspondence*, 9:62–3.

16. "Speech on the Bill to Amend 1784 India Act," March 22, 1786, *WS* 6:70–71.

17. Suleri has argued that Burke "in the cause of [imperialism was] forced to censor his reading of the ineluctable logic of horror," that he "curtailed" his narrative of colonial horror in order to "impute its terror to some instrument of aberration. Such an instrument was Warren Hastings, who, by functioning as a repository of ill-doing, could simultaneously protect the colonial project from being indicted for the larger ill of which Hastings was a herald" (*Rhetoric of English India*, 45). It is a mistake, first, I would argue, to suggest that Burke was committed to the cause of imperialism; rather, it might be said that he was committed to the responsible exercise of British power where it existed, and he was not prepared to condemn British rule in India as such. Second, Burke's condemnation of Hastings, I hope to make clear, in no way insulated either the Company or British power (or "the colonial project") from indictment. Suleri later argues that "the Hastings trial performed a symbolic depersonification of responsibility that illustrates the eighteenth-century's growing realization that colonialism required to be judged as a system rather than as a set of misdeeds" (56); Suleri's suggestion that

the trial managers did not explicitly intend to convey such an idea appears implausible in light of Burke's repeated insistence on the systematic nature of the abuses.

18. "Speech on Opening of Impeachment," *WS* 6:285. In his discussion of the Company charter in "Fox's India Bill," Burke had argued that that charter, "to establish monopoly, and to create power" was a "trust of power" that rendered the Company accountable to Parliament, which had granted the trust; Parliament's failure to stop the Company's "oppressions" made it an "active accomplice in the abuse" (*WS* 5:384–85).

19. *WS* 5:384; emphasis added. He argued further that even the restraint that accountability to stockholders might impose on a company's officers was missing in this case, where men bought stock in the Company to acquire the influence necessary to secure posts in India for their sons, who could plunder in a few months far more than the stock itself could ever hope to produce. "The vote is not to protect the stock, but the stock is bought to acquire the vote; and the end of the vote is to cover and support, against justice, some man of power who has made an obnoxious fortune in India" (5:437). But Burke argued that while more responsible stockholders might at least rein in the worst of the individual plundering, if Company servants were accountable only to such stockholders, it would be "indeed a defective plan of policy. The interest of the people who are governed by them would not be their primary object." Burke agreed with Smith that merchants make poor governors.

20. "Rohilla War Charge," *WS* 6:94. The charge was that Hastings had wrongly hired out Company troops to fight a war against the Afghan Rohillas on behalf of the nawab of Oudh.

21. "Provinces corporate bodies," Burke remarked about the Roman Empire in his notes for his speech on the Rohilla war charge; "the several provinces and Cities could act as Corporations and by that means proceed with a degree of courage as well as with greater resources of money than any Individuals" (*WS* 6:94; also see 6:106). The threat of abuse of Roman power in the colonies was further mitigated, Burke argued, by contiguous territory and a single language (Greek). On the affinities with Cicero and the Verres trial, see Canter, "Verres and Hastings"; and Carnall, "Burke as Modern Cicero," 76–90.

22. As Burke noted in the trial, a company servant "who has taken but one penny of unlawful emolument (and all have taken many pennies of unlawful emolument) . . . dare not complain of the most abandoned extortion and cruel oppression. . . . The great criminal has the laws in his hand. He is always able to prove the small offence and crush the person entirely who has committed it" ("Opening of Impeachment," *WS* 6:290). The absence of complaints against Hastings from within the Company, which Hastings had pointed to as proof of his good governance, was, Burke held, simply evidence that he had ensured "common participation and connivance" in the evil by his British subordinates.

23. "Rohilla War Speech," *WS* 6:106.

24. Nandakumar was convicted of forgery (which, Burke noted, was not a capital crime in India) at just the time he was accusing Hastings of accepting bribes; Burke noted that "in so extraordinary a Case" the death sentence should at the very least have been suspended until it was approved by the king. Whelan summarizes the evidence for and against the charge of judicial murder, which he

finds inconclusive (*Edmund Burke and India*, 145–49); Marshall argues that it is difficult to sustain the claim that the judges were partial to Hastings in passing the death sentence (*WS* 5:183 n. 4).

25. "Fox's India Bill," *WS* 5:436; also see the "Ninth Report of Select Committee," *WS* 5:204, in which Burke argues that the establishment of a Supreme Court had not only failed to give any substantial relief "to the Natives against the Corruptions or Oppressions of British Subjects in Power," but had merely further "deter[ed] the Natives from Complaint, and consequently from means of Redress" by proving to Indians in the Nandakumar case that a complaint was liable to be punished with death. He argued that the court could not serve the purpose such courts served in England of providing "Redress . . . against Oppressions of Power" because juries were necessary to the process, and "it was presumed (perhaps a little too hastily) that [Indians] were not capable of sharing in the Functions of Jurors." Burke here declared for the committee that "the Use of Juries is neither impracticable nor dangerous in Bengal" (*WS* 5:204–5). See chapter 4 for Bentham's similar support for Indian juries.

26. Whelan, *Edmund Burke and India*, 148. For Burke's dismissal of Indian "panegyrics" upon Hastings as "either gross forgeries or most miserable aggravations of his offences," see "Opening of Impeachment," *WS* 6:370–71.

27. See the "Speech on Almas Ali Khan" of July 1784 for Burke's argument that Indians' lack of voice exacerbated the injustices done to them. "The whole drift of this crooked policy, was to keep the poor natives wholly out of sight. We might hear enough about what great and illustrious exploits were daily performing on that conspicuous theatre by Britons: But unless some dreadful catastrophe was to take place—unless some hero or heroine was to fall—unless the tragedy was to be very deep and bloody one;—we were never to hear of any native's being an actor! No. The field was altogether engrossed by Englishmen; and those who were chiefly interested in the matter actually excluded" (*WS* 5:461).

28. *WS* 6:285. Like Smith (and indeed perhaps influenced by the argument in *Wealth of Nations*), Burke insisted on the peculiar dangers of commercial empire, perpetrated by private individuals not tempered by national policy and carried out for gain by rulers whose immediate commercial interests often conflicted directly with the welfare of their subjects.

29. "Fox's India Bill," *WS* 5:415.

30. In the margin of his "Rohilla War Charge" speech, Burke noted, "[B]efore it was the disgraces of individuals. No country disgraced by bad men—but the moment the Evil is protected the guilt is general" (*WS* 6:93n); also see opening impeachment speech (6:271).

31. Burke referred to "the incorrigible condition of the Company" ("Fox's India Bill," *WS* 5:438). As Uday Mehta argues, it is anachronistic to focus on the question of "whether Burke was or was not an imperialist in an implicit or declared sense"; more important questions are what conceptions of India, civilizational development, and political relationships between and within Britain and India underlay various approaches to empire (*Liberalism and Empire*, 158).

32. P. J. Marshall has described Burke's "vision of world-wide empire based on universal justice" but questions whether Burke's aspirations for the empire "provided the basis for a program of imperial statecraft" ("Burke and Empire," 298).

33. Letter to French Laurence, July 28, 1796, *Correspondence*, 9:62. For a similar passage, see Marshall's introduction to *WS*, volume 6, quoting an unpublished manuscript in which Burke argued that the British must "leave the Country on the foundations on which it stood, and if any change was made, it should be . . . to justify to the world the mysterious ways of that astonishing dispensation of providence by which we acquired Dominion where nature had almost forbid intercourse" (6:35). Here Burke, in noting nature's near-prohibition of any relations at all, much less coercive ones, sounds the note of caution even more emphatically.

34. I disagree with Stephen White's claim that this passage indicates Burke's "unwillingness to raise broader questions about the overall legitimacy of Great Britain's domination of India" (*Edmund Burke*, 36), for Burke indeed questioned the possibility that British rule in India could ever be even minimally just and therefore justifiable.

35. As he noted in an early speech, "Some people great Lovers of uniformity—They are not satisfied with a rebellion in the West. They must have one in the East: They are not satisfied with losing one Empire—they must lose another—Lord N[orth] will weep that he has not more worlds to lose" ("Speech on Restoring Lord Pigot," May 22, 1777, *WS* 5:40).

36. "[O]ur evident duty, and our clearest interest, was to employ [European] arts and discipline, and the power that grew out of them, to meliorate the condition of the subject and the dependent, rather than to enforce the wild claims of a pretender, or to enforce the intolerable despotism even of the lawful possessors of power. All this we might have done, and in a great measure may still do, without any sort of diminution (to speak within compass) of revenue; and with an infinite increase of our reputation. But fatally, we have suffered, for a long time, a contrary course to prevail" ("Policy of Making Conquests for the Mahometans," 1779, *WS* 5:114).

37. See Suleri, *Rhetoric of English India*, 45. As Margery Sabin has noted, "nineteenth-century imperialists" similarly, but with different motives, read the passage as "Burke's paternal blessing and ethical guide for imperial power" (*Dissenters and Mavericks*, 62).

38. Sabin, *Dissenters and Mavericks*, 62.

39. He noted, famously, that despite the "plenitude of despotism, tyranny, and corruption" that the Company had exercised, he nonetheless felt, even in this case, an "insuperable reluctance in giving my hand to destroy any established institution of government, upon a theory, however plausible it may be" (*WS* 5:387).

40. The influence of Burke's views (on empire and more generally) in the decades after his death is difficult to trace, especially given his repudiation both by the Whigs with whom he had been allied for nearly his entire political career (until they rejected him as an apostate on the question of France), and by the Tories, who agreed with him on the dangers of Jacobinism but were repelled by his support for Catholic emancipation and his criticism of the British East India Company. J. J. Sack has argued that the Tories of the first three decades of the nineteenth century resisted adopting Burke as a precursor, in large part because of his commitment to the Irish and Indian causes. He cites as an example the influential

Quarterly Review, which regarded Burke's views on India as "wild and extravagant," "greatly overcharged," showing in their "appetite for sublime horrors" a certain "defectiveness of taste" (Sack, "Memory of Burke," 627, citing the *Quarterly Review* issues of March 1813 and April 1817).

41. See Armitage, *Ideological Origins*, 8.

42. Whether Burke succeeded in arousing as much indignation against himself as against Hastings during the impeachment trial, however, is open to question. As Fanny Burney wrote in her diary entry of February 16, 1788, "Were talents such as these exercised in the service of truth, unbiassed by party and prejudice, how could we sufficiently applaud their exalted possessor? But though frequently he made me tremble by his strong and horrible representations, his own violence recovered me, by stigmatizing his assertions with personal ill-will and designing illiberality" (quoted in Carnall and Nicholson, *Impeachment of Warren Hastings*, 11).

43. Burke was deeply impressed by Smith's *Theory of Moral Sentiments*, sent to him by Hume shortly after its publication in 1759; while it had affinities with his own earlier arguments, it was a systematic work of moral theory such as Burke himself had not attempted. In the *Annual Register* of that year, Burke wrote that "making approbation and disapprobation the tests of virtue and vice, and shewing that those are founded on sympathy, he raises from this simple truth, one of the most beautiful fabrics of moral theory, that has perhaps ever appeared" (cited in Smith, *Correspondence*, 1:129n). On connections between the moral philosophy of Smith, Hume and Burke, see Einaudi, "British Background."

44. Pt. 1, sec. 13 (*WS* 1:220–22). Smith was similarly to describe sympathy as the act of imagination by which "we enter as it were into [another's] body," though the link between sympathy for another's suffering and action to relieve it is somewhat more attenuated in Smith than in Burke (*TMS* I.i).

45. *WS* 1:222. Burke insists that the delight we feel in watching a tragedy in the theater results neither from the reassuring thought that it is mere fiction, nor from our own position of comfort; on the contrary, he argues, we feel similar pleasure in cases of real misfortune, and can do so even if we ourselves are in distress.

46. "Nabob of Arcot's Debts," February 28, 1785, *WS* 5:549.

47. In chapter 4 I discuss Bentham's strikingly similar reflections on the problems of redressing distant crimes.

48. "A language so foreign from all the Ideas and Habits of the far greater Part of the Members of this House, has a Tendency to disgust them with all Sorts of Enquiry concerning this Subject. They are fatigued into such a Despair of ever obtaining a competent Knowledge of the Transactions in India, that they are easily persuaded to remand them back to that Obscurity, Mystery, and Intrigue, out of which they have been forced upon public Notice, by the Calamities arising from their extreme mismanagement" (*WS* 5:197).

49. December 1, 1783, *WS* 5:403–4. As I discuss in the fifth section below, Burke rejected "virtual" representation for Irish Catholics on similar grounds: governors with no sympathy for the governed could not be trusted to rule in their interest.

50. "Fox's India Bill," *WS* 5:390.

51. Suleri argues that Burke's "discourse anticipates the nineteenth-century attempt to reconstruct Indian history on a European model," though she later contrasts the "unimaginability Burke willed on his representations of India" with the nineteenth-century confidence, exhibited by Macaulay, that with sufficient "industry" and "sensibility," the English could impose light and shape on the obscure facts of India (*Rhetoric of English India*, 29, 51).

52. *WS* 7:264 ("Speech in Reply," May 28, 1794). In a seemingly more conciliatory moment of the same speech Burke continued to suggest that remedy was still possible, though with the trial clearly about to end in acquittal, even these words appear to be a reproach rather than a real hope: "I wish to reinstate the people in their rights and priviledges. I wish to reinstate them in your sympathy" (279).

53. Suleri, for instance, reads these narratives as part of Burke's "Indian sublime" and speaks of Burke's "obsessive reading of the deranged plot of colonialism" (*Rhetoric of English India*, 36). Kramnick emphasizes Burke's descriptions of "sexual horrors" and "unrepressed sexuality" (*Rage of Edmund Burke*, 135–36). De Bruyn argues that Burke chose "the conservative gothic as the vehicle for conveying his version of events" ("Edmund Burke's Gothic Romance," 424). Others have read Burke's rhetoric as ill-judged (Musselwhite argues that Burke's and Sheridan's speeches "just look cumbersome and inept" next to Hastings's "restrained, informed, almost disdainful" language ["Trial of Warren Hastings," 90]). Also see McCann, *Cultural Politics*, 50–53.

54. Siraj Ahmad argues that "in providing an exaggerated performance of how the sentimental character responds to imperial atrocities, Burke gave the British public a model of how it should act," and that Burke thereby showed "social mimicry," not reason or "historical development," to be the basis of civil society ("Theater of civilized self," 44).

55. *WS* 5:403. He went on, "It has been said . . . that Tacitus and Machiavel, by their cold way of relating enormous crimes, have in some sort appeared not to disapprove them . . . and that they corrupt the minds of their readers, by not expressing the detestation and horror, that naturally belong to horrible and detestable proceedings." His own descriptions of Hastings's crimes would avoid this flaw, at once rhetorical and moral. Iain Hampsher-Monk has emphasized the role that rhetoric played in Burke's moral and political theory, in particular as a form of, and model for, moral reasoning. See Hampsher-Monk, "Rhetoric and Opinion."

56. Burke, quoting a report by John Paterson, *WS* 6:418; Paterson was said to be horrified by the use of his report in the trial and wrote a letter of apology to Hastings.

57. See, for instance, Kramnick's assertion that "India was a vast stage upon which Burke could parade his conservative defense of custom. . . . Hastings, on the other hand, showed no respect for . . . prescriptive or aristocratic institutions" (*Rage of Edmund Burke*, 129). See Paine, *Rights of Man*, in *Political Writings*, 64.

58. Responding to a similar criticism of the *Reflections* by Philip Francis, Burke wrote, "When and where, my dear Sir, did you find me the advocate for any tyr-

anny either ancient or modern, either at home or abroad? When did you find me totally unmoved at the distress of hundreds and thousands of my equals, and only touched with the sufferings of guilty greatness? I find this distinction neither in my sympathies, nor in my morals" (*Correspondence*, 6:171).

59. See, for instance, Burke's letter to Earl Fitzwilliam of June 21, 1794, calling these "the two great Evils of our time" (*Correspondence*, 7:553). On the ways in which Burke's portrait of Jacobinism was informed by his views of British abuses in India, see Agnani, "Enlightenment Universalism," chap. 5.

60. Letter to Lord Loughborough (who had voted for Hastings's conviction on thirteen of the sixteen charges), ca. March 17, 1796, *Correspondence*, 8:432.

61. Marshall discusses Burke's willingness to "sacrifice legal precision in order to display Hastings's crimes to the widest possible audience" (*Impeachment of Warren Hastings*, 70–71).

62. Letter to French Laurence, July 28, 1796, *Correspondence*, 9:63.

63. David Bromwich has proposed reading Burke as a social critic whose audience includes "persons who belong, as yet, to no existing group or society" ("Context of Burke's Reflections," 314).

64. *Impeachment of Warren Hastings*, "Speech in Opening, First Day," (February 15, 1788). From Burke, *Works*, 9:343. Also (with different phrasing) *WS* 6:278–79.

65. Speech against the Boston Port Bill of 1774 (the North administration's response to the Boston Tea Party), *Parliamentary History of England*, 1182–85, quoted by Stanlis, *Burke and Natural Law*, 51. For another version of the speech, see *WS* 2:405: "Every punishment is unjust that is inflicted on a party unheard. The distance of the party is no argument for not hearing."

66. In a public letter to Samuel Span, a Bristol constituent and president of the protectionist Society of Merchants Adventurers of Bristol, in which Burke urged support for his policy of free trade with Ireland and an end to the protective tariffs cherished by the Bristol merchants (*Correspondence*, 3:433). The letter gestured to the Act of Union of 1707 that had joined England and economically backward Scotland in a single political and economic entity. Far from an act of charity, Burke insisted, the union was an economic boon to English merchants, as free trade with Ireland would be as well: "Such virtue there is in liberality of sentiment, that you have grown richer even by the partnership of poverty" (434). For Burke, geographical morality was always a practical as well as a moral mistake.

67. *WS* 6:346. Denis Diderot similarly referred to the abandonment of European moral standards by colonial adventurers: "Beyond the Equator a man is neither English, Dutch, French, Spanish, nor Portuguese. He retains only those principles and prejudices of his native country which justify or excuse his conduct. He crawls when he is weak; he is violent when strong; he is in a hurry to enjoy, and capable of every crime which will lead him most quickly to his goals. . . . This is how all the Europeans, every one of them, indistinctly, have appeared in the countries of the New World. There they have assumed a common frenzy." From the *Histoire des deux Indes*, in *Political Writings*, 178. Hume thought otherwise: the "same set of manners will follow a nation, and adhere to them over the whole globe, as well as the same laws and language" ("Of National Characters," *Essays*, 205).

68. As Burke said in his speech on the Rohilla war charge, the first article of charge against Hastings to be argued before the House of Commons (April 4, 1786): "It was a tenet in politics which he ever had, and ever would hold, that all British Governors were obliged to act by law. In India to be sure it could not be expected that they could practise Magna Charta. But there they had the law of nature and nations, the great and fundamental axioms on which every form of society was built. These, in conjunction with the collected experience of ages, the wisdom of antiquity, and the practice of the purest times, formed a system which in every country was venerable and popular" (*WS* 6:109). For a discussion of Burke's understanding of the "diversified structure of subordination," see Bourke, "Liberty, Authority, and Trust."

69. E. A. Bond, ed., *Speeches of the Managers and Counsel in the Trial of Warren Hastings*, 2:533, cited at *WS* 7:276 n. 2.

70. Hastings later argued that by arbitrary power he meant no more than discretionary power: "I never considered that my will or caprice was to be the guide of my conduct" (Bond, *Speeches*, 2:494, quoted in Carnall and Nicholson, *Impeachment of Warren Hastings*, 24). P. J. Marshall argues that Hastings's principles were less distant from Burke's than Burke recognized and attributes the misconstruction partly to a poor defense (editor's introductions, *WS* 6:16 and 6:267).

71. See Venturi, "Oriental Despotism"; and Richter, "Europe and the Other." Richter argues that Montesquieu's portrait of oriental despotism developed in large part as a critique of despotic tendencies in the French monarchy and that eighteenth-century accounts of Asian societies were driven as much by European political debates as by interest in the Asian societies themselves. Burke was arguably one of the few to engage in this debate whose interest was primarily in the condition of the Asian society he described.

72. *WS* 7:264–65 ("Speech in Reply," May 28, 1794). Betraying his own considered rejection of the stereotype, Burke invoked it in the *Reflections*, writing, "To hear some men speak of the late monarchy of France, you would imagine that they were . . . describing the barbarous anarchic despotism of Turkey, where the finest countries in the most genial climates in the world are wasted by peace more than any countries have been worried by war; where arts are unknown, where manufactures languish, where science is extinguished, where agriculture decays, where the human race itself melts away and perishes under the eye of the observer" (*WS* 8:176). While Burke is paraphrasing the ancien régime's opponents here, he appears to endorse the classic account of Turkey as an oriental despotism.

73. In his "Rohilla War Speech" (June 1, 1786), Burke asked why Hastings had not "squared his conduct" by such examples as the institutes of Tamerlane, "which were replete with the soundest principles of morality and just policy": "The truth was, they were not calculated to have justified his extortions and peculations" (*WS* 6:109).

74. *WS* 7:273 ("Speech in Reply," May 28, 1794). Burke similarly emphasized that Hastings governed in India "upon arbitrary and despotic, and, *as he supposes*, Oriental principles" ("Opening of Impeachment," *WS* 6:347; emphasis added).

75. Another contemporary of Burke's who questioned the characterization was the French explorer Abraham-Hyacinte Anquetil-Duperron, whose *Législation orientale* (1778) was intended as an empirical study of the laws and property systems of Turkey, Persia, and India ("the three countries taken to be the most absolute"), which would demonstrate the error of European depictions of the east as lawless and despotic; see Whelan, "Oriental Despotism." In *Edmund Burke and India*, Whelan notes that Burke does not seem to have been familiar with Anquetil-Duperron's work (246).

76. "Speech in Reply," May 28, 1794, *WS* 7:257.

77. *WS* 5:117, 120. Burke made this case in his *Policy of Making Conquests for the Mahometans* (1779), which, far more than writings of just a few years later, characterizes Muslim rulers as rapacious (referring, for instance, to "the intolerable burden of the Mahometan yoke," *WS* 5:114) and suggesting that Indian societies did not have "settled law or constitution, either to fix allegiance, or to restrain power" (113). Later works refrain from such sweepingly pejorative characterizations of Indian societies. Also see Whelan, *Edmund Burke and India*, 231.

78. "Speech in Reply" of May 28, 1794, *WS* 7:270–76. Tamerlane "never claimed an arbitrary power . . . his principle was to govern by law; . . . to address the oppressions of his inferior governors; . . . to recognize the nobility in the respect due their rank; . . . to recognize in the people protection, and to recognize the Laws throughout" (272); Genghis Khan's compilation of laws demanded that all rulers be duly elected by a lawful assembly of the princes (270). Also see "Opening of Impeachment," *WS* 6:365–66.

79. Quoted by Stanlis, *Burke and Natural Law*, 65; from the fourth day of the opening of Hastings's impeachment.

80. But see Whelan's list of charges among those Burke presented "as crimes against natural law or justice": "treaty breaking, aggressive war, property confiscations, denial of due process to Chait Singh, abuse of wardship, and violations of filial duty (in the case of the Begams of Oudh)" (*Edmund Burke and India*, 278).

81. Peter Stanlis made the most forceful case for a natural law reading of Burke in *Burke and Natural Law*, in which he amply illustrates the frequency with which Burke appeals to natural law or the law of nations (also see his "Burke and Law of Nations"). Still, Stanlis's effort to claim a foundational position for natural law in Burke's thought is ultimately unpersuasive, for it ignores Burke's other important sources of moral and political argument, attributes all of Burke's universalistic arguments—all of his appeals to "justice," for example—to a natural law foundation, and disregards differences between the status of natural law and the (more empirical) law of nations.

82. Herzog, "Puzzling through Burke," 339. Herzog presents himself as an "opponent" of Burke.

83. As Burke put the point in the *Reflections*, "The evils latent in the most promising contrivances are provided for as they arise. . . . We compensate, we reconcile, we balance. We are enabled to unite into a consistent whole the various anomalies and contending principles that are found in the minds and affairs of men" (*WS* 8:217).

84. For a compelling account of Burke's use of the law of nature, see Whelan, *Edmund Burke and India*, 275–90; he notes that Burke appealed to natural law to respond both to Hastings's claims to rule according to despotic local customs and "above all the defense of his actions in the name of 'state necessity' or *raison d'état*" (277).

85. "Inquiry into the Seizure of Private Property in St. Eustatius," in *Speeches of the Right Honorable Edmund Burke*, 2:248. The *Annual Register* of 1781 contains Burke's second account of the affair; also see Stanlis, *Burke and Natural Law*, 90–92.

86. "Inquiry into Seizure," 2:256.

87. "Inquiry into Seizure," 2:260.

88. Burke, like Smith, recognized that the rights of nations that had suffered at European hands might be vindicated only when there was a greater equality of force.

89. "Inquiry into Seizure," 2:251.

90. See "Motion for an Inquiry into the Confiscation of the Effects Taken on the Island of St. Eustatius," December 4, 1781, *Speeches of Hon. Edmund Burke*, 2:313–25.

91. *Speeches of Hon. Edmund Burke*, 2:263.

92. For instance, on the affinities between the East India Company and the Protestant ascendancy in Ireland, see Burke's letter to Langrishe, May 26, 1795, *Correspondence*, 8:254.

93. *WS* 9:635. The letter to Lord Kenmare, written in 1782, was published in Dublin in 1783 and again in 1791; the letters to Richard Burke and Sir Hercules Langrishe were both written 1792; the latter was published in Dublin in February 1792 (see *WS* 9:594 and 640). Langrishe, an old friend of Burke's who sat in the Irish Parliament, was one of the members of the Protestant ruling class most sympathetic to Catholic demands.

In a parliamentary speech of 1785, Burke said that "they must be ignorant or inhuman, who said, that Ireland in her present circumstances so feelingly called on Great Britain as the undone millions of India" ("Speech on Debate on Address," January 25, 1785, *WS* 9:585). Also see Janes, "High Flying," on the relation between India and Ireland in Burke's thought.

94. See Mahoney, *Edmund Burke and Ireland*; Fuchs, *Edmund Burke, Ireland, and the Fashioning of Self*, and O'Brien, *The Great Melody*, for accounts of Burke's views on Ireland. James Conniff defends Burke's political judgment on Ireland against some of Mahoney's charges of irrationality and strategic error in "Edmund Burke's Reflections on the Coming Revolution in Ireland"; see Conniff's *Useful Cobbler*, chap. 10, for an account of Burke as an "impatient reformer on Irish questions" (265). I regret that the important book by Luke Gibbons, *Edmund Burke and Ireland*, appeared too late for me to be able to take account of its findings and arguments.

95. In the letter to Langrishe, for instance: "[N]o nation in the world has ever been known to exclude so great a body of men (not born slaves) from the civil state, and all the benefits of its constitution" (*WS* 9:628).

96. For Burke's suspicion of conquest see, for instance, his statement that the 1688 revolution in Ireland was "to say the truth, not a revolution, but a conquest,

which is not to say a great deal in its favour" (letter to Langrishe, *WS* 9:614), or his description in the early "Essay towards an Abridgement of the English History" of "the unhappy, but sometimes necessary task of subduing a rude and free people" (*WS* 1:368).

97. Letter to Langrishe, *WS* 9:615. See also Burke's 1783 comparison between the British and the Mughals in India: "[T]he Asiatic conquerors soon abated of their ferocity, because they made the conquered country their own" ; and "Every other conqueror of every other description has left some monument, either of state or beneficence, behind him. Were we to be driven out of India this day, nothing would remain, to tell that it had been possessed during the inglorious period of our dominion, by anything better than the ourang-outang or the tiger." "Fox's India Bill" (WS 5:401–2). A decade later, in closing the Hastings impeachment, Burke further demoted Hastings in the bestial ranks: "We never said he was a tiger and a lion. We said he was a Weasel and a Rat" ("Speech in Reply," May 28, 1794, *WS* 7:277).

98. *WS* 9:615. The provost, John Hely-Hutchinson, had intended to create sizarships (scholarships that included some work duties) for Catholics at Trinity College; Burke noted that as long as Catholics were denied access to the entire university, the "charities" Hely-Hutchinson had in mind not only were inadequate but, because the positions were "servile," might indeed exacerbate the Catholics' subjection.

99. Burke's resistance to the popular Whig vision of history as moving in progressive stages from parochial barbarity to enlightened, commercial cosmopolitanism is a hallmark of his writings on both France and the empire. For a discussion of the many strands of Whiggism, and of Burke's misgivings about them, see J.G.A. Pocock, *Virtue, Commerce, and History*, 215ff.

100. "Toleration being a part of moral and political prudence, ought to be tender and large"; it ought, if only out of prudence, to permit "not only very ill-grounded doctrines, but even many things that are positively vices" for the sake of good of the commonwealth (*WS* 9:605).

101. *WS* 9:615. Similarly, he wrote to Richard Burke of the religious arguments made by the Anglo Irish, "I speak here of their pretexts, and not of the true spirit of the transaction, in which religious bigotry I apprehend has little share" (*WS* 9:646).

102. In the "Tracts Relating to Popery Laws," Burke had also remarked on the similarity of pre-Reformation oppressions to more recent ones, but once again he noted this fact with an ironic comment on English religious inconsistency, rather than concluding explicitly that religion was not at the root of the proscriptions: under King Richard II (reigned 1377–99) the English "compelled the people to submit, by the forfeiture of all their civil rights, to the Pope's authority, in its most extravagant and unbounded sense. . . . No country, I believe, since the world began, suffered so much on account of Religion; or has been so variously harassed both for Popery and for Protestantism" (*WS* 9:471).

103. Letter to Langrishe, *WS* 9:614. He went on, "In England it was the struggle of the great body of the people for the establishment of their liberties against the efforts of a very small faction, who would have oppressed them. In Ireland it was the establishment of the power of the smaller number, at the expence of the

civil liberties and properties of the far greater part; and at the expence of the political liberties of the whole. It was, to say the truth, not a revolution, but a conquest, which is not to say a great deal in its favor."

104. Letter to Langrishe, *WS* 9:615. The Protestant celebrations of the Battle of the Boyne (July 1, 1690)—a battle that might be seen as the culmination of the Irish phase of the Revolution of 1688—in Northern Ireland today continue to be among the most aggressive displays of Protestant power in the north, provoking violence and unrest every July.

105. Letter to Richard Burke, *WS* 9:652.

106. Letter to Langrishe, *WS* 9:616. The oppressive penal laws, he wrote, "were manifestly the effects of national hatred and scorn towards a conquered people; whom the victors delighted to trample upon, and were not at all afraid to provoke." In the "Tracts Relating to Popery Law," Burke had argued that penal laws bore a close resemblance to the revocation of the Edict of Nantes, which, he noted, had been effected when Louis XIV was at the height of his authority at home and power abroad (*WS* 9:459).

107. *WS* 9:598. Burke did note in a letter to Richard Burke that only a "strange man, a strange Christian, and a strange Englishman" could prefer the current "enslaved, beggard, insulted, degraded" Ireland to a flourishing Catholic Ireland even if not a single Protestant remained (*Correspondence*, 7:118, March 23, 1792).

108. *Correspondence*, 8:247. Burke's argument recalls the position of Scottish Catholics in the twentieth century, who have been among the strongest supporters of union with Britain on the grounds that union tempers the oppressive tendency of local Protestants. I am grateful to Richard Tuck for pointing out the analogy.

109. The selfish few were those of "Francis Street": a meeting of Dublin Catholics at which "strongly radical and anti-English speeches were delivered" (*WS* 9:668 n. 1).

110. In a letter of May 1795, *Correspondence*, 8:246–47. A close union with England was Ireland's best hope, Burke continued; Ireland should avoid allying with France, a power "either despotick, as formerly, or anarchical as at present." That Burke referred here to ancien régime France as despotic is worth noting, as he made no similar claim in the *Reflections* and is often believed to have rejected the thought altogether.

111. Burke's hostility to the formation of a separate Irish nation-state (and national identity) should be distinguished from the view that backward nationalities should be assimilated into more advanced as J. S. Mill, for instance, advocated, as we shall see in chapter 6.

112. He insisted on Ireland's status as a separate kingdom, but he also described England as the seat of their common empire: "Ireland was not a *sub*-ordinate, but a *co*-ordinate state; it was as free and independent of this country, as any foreign power, connected only by the band of one common king" (*WS* 9:586). "He hoped Ireland would ever look up to this country as this seat of empire" (590).

113. *WS* 9:641–42; from the letter to Richard Burke of 1792. Reform was necessary for both moral and pragmatic reasons. "This way of proscribing men by whole nations, as it were, from all the benefits of the constitution to which

they were born, I never can believe to be politic or expedient, much less necessary for the existence of any state or church in the world" (9:612). See Bowen, *Protestant Crusade in Ireland*, for a discussion of the increasingly vigorous Protestant evangelical crusade that followed rural unrest in Ireland.

114. A less sympathetic Anglo-Irish observer claimed that Burke had supported the American revolutionaries and opposed the French because the former were allied with then-Catholic France, while the latter had attacked Christianity and especially Catholicism: "Hence *illae lachrymae of that gentlemen, and hence his recantation of republicanism*" (*Irish Parliamentary Register*, 15:352–53; quoted by R. B. McDowell in the "Introduction to Part II, *WS* 9:420 n. 6).

115. "Having been taught by his right hon. friend," Fox said, "that no revolt of a nation was caused without provocation, he could not help feeling a joy ever since the constitution of France became founded on the rights of man, on which the British constitution itself was founded. . . . From his right hon. friend he had learned that the revolt of a whole people could never be countenanced and encouraged, but must have been provoked" (O'Brien, *The Great Melody*, 423; from Fox speech, May 6, 1791). Also see Kramnick, "Left and Edmund Burke," 190–94.

116. Quoted by Bromwich in *Empire, Liberty, and Reform*, 5.

117. *WS* 9:629. Burke argued that virtual representation could be superior to actual representation when such affinity could be counted on, since it corrects the possible waywardness of the people's choice. He did not elaborate the claim that virtual representation "must have a substratum in the actual"; he seems to have meant that if there is a sense of community among a nation's people, good government can be secured even through restricted representation. James Conniff has argued that Burke saw his theory of trusteeship fail when the House of Lords refused to convict Hastings and proved themselves incapable of serving as "surrogates for the Indian people," but as we have seen, Burke had long doubted that British legislators could serve such a function (Conniff, "Burke and India," 292).

118. "For my own part, I do not know in what manner to shape such arguments, so as to obtain admission for them into a rational understanding. Every thing of this kind is to be reduced, at last, to threats of power" (*WS* 9:626).

119. Linda Colley, for instance, concludes from Burke's opposition to the Quebec Act that "Burke was profoundly opposed to the North Administration's efforts to broaden Britain's power base in North America by extending limited concessions to groups other than its white, Protestant colonists" ("A Magazine of Wisdom," 5).

120. *Proceedings and Debates*, June 6, 1774, 5:78; see Lawson, *Imperial Challenge*, 141.

121. *Proceedings and Debates*, June 7, 1774, 5:131; see Lawson, *Imperial Challenge*, 142.

122. Lawson notes that the opponents of the Quebec Act were a diverse group who could come to no agreement regarding its various provisions; while Burke and Fox supported the religious toleration clauses, zealous Protestants like Isaac Barré and other M.P.s furiously rejected the bill as "popish from beginning to end." Such distinctions were lost in misreporting by the newspapers, from which, Lawson, writes, "it is hard not to believe that Burke and Fox were the most ardent

Protestant bigots, which could not have been further from the truth" (Lawson, *The Imperial Challenge*, 138–43).

123. See Colley, *Britons*; Wilson, *Sense of the People*; and Langford, *Polite and Commercial People.*

124. For the connection between the Act of Union and the "British" character of the empire, see Robertson, "Empire and Union." It has been argued that Hastings especially, though English, channeled Company patronage disproportionately toward Scottish aspirants and that Scots were "closely connected to every charge" in the impeachment (Riddly, "Warren Hastings," 33). Colley further claims that a central goal in the Hastings trial was to expose and punish Scottish participation in the imperial project (*Britons*, 128–30).

125. Conor Cruise O'Brien has developed this theme in *The Great Melody*; also see Vanech, "Painful Homecoming," for a brief but nuanced treatment.

126. Connolly, *The Ethos of Pluralization*, 163.

127. As her subtitle, *Forging the Nation*, suggests, Colley asserts just such a process of the construction of British nationality from the Act of Union through Queen Victoria's coronation.

128. See Hont, "Permanent Crisis"; and Cobban, *Nation State*, 30–31.

129. Rousseau, *Oeuvres complètes*, 3:960.

130. Despite its limited suffrage (which he supported), Burke considered England democratic, as he shows in his comments about England's obligations to its democratic inheritance, in his speech on the bill to amend the 1784 India Act, on March 22, 1786, *WS* 6:69: "To what had democracy, in all ages and all countries, owed most of its triumphs, but to the openness, the publicity, and the strength of its operation."

131. Michael Walzer has described what he calls the "connected" social critic in *Interpretation and Social Criticism.* Such a critic is "a serious, not a comic, figure because his principles are ones we share" (48). David Bromwich charges "culturalists" such as Walzer with "trying to shed a habit of irony," although irony "seems to be the natural condition of the social critic" ("Culturalism," 89).

132. Uday Mehta coined the apt phrase "liberal strategies of exclusion" in his article of that title.

Chapter 4
Jeremy Bentham: Legislator of the World?

1. Scholars that have portrayed utilitarianism as an inherently imperialist doctrine and attributed to Bentham the views on empire expressed by his self-declared disciples include Halévy, *Growth of Philosophic Radicalism*; Stokes, *English Utilitarians and India*; Iyer, *Utilitarianism and All That*; and Mehta, *Liberalism and Empire*. For a recent corrective to this argument, see Allison Dube, "Tree of Utility." William Thomas has written that "[James] Mill is very much Bentham's pupil in much of what he says about Indian government," but he demonstrates as well the elder Mill's departures from Bentham, and some of the other sources of influence on Mill's interpretation of India, especially "puritanism" and Christian missionary testimony (Thomas, *The Philosophic Radicals*, 101 and 96–119).

2. Stokes, *English Utilitarians and India*, 51; from *WJB* 10:577.

3. The influence of utilitarian reformers in the transformation of Victorian England has been much debated: while scholarship of the 1950s and 1960s tended to downplay utilitarian influence, more recent scholarship suggests that utilitarian ideas affected reform both directly, through Bentham's followers in administration, and indirectly, through reformers who were quite unaware of the Benthamite origins of the reforms they sought; see Conway, "Nineteenth-Century Revolution."

4. Mill, *On Liberty* (1859), *CW* 18:224.

5. *WJB* 4:416. The moon was Bentham's usual analogy for distant dependencies. In a passage typical of Bentham's quirky and biting wit on the subject of colonies, he wrote of the Spanish imperialists: "Spain is *one*! such will be their *arithmetic*. It has its *Peninsular* part and its *Ultramarian* part! such will be their *geography*. As well might it be said—Spain and the Moon are *one*! it has its *earthly* part: it has its *lunar* part. Such, it is but too true, is the language of your *Constitutional Code*. But, a body of human law, how well soever arranged in other respects, does not suffice for converting *impossibilities* into *facts*" " Rid Yourselves of Ultramaria," in *Colonies, Commerce, and Consitutional Law* (52).

6. Stephen Conway has discussed Bentham's ambivalent pacifism in "Bentham on Peace and War" and "The Nineteenth-Century British Peace Movement." Some of Bentham's economic objections to settler colonies were overcome at the very end of his life, when he was persuaded by the arguments of Edward Gibbon Wakefield for "systematic colonization" of Australia: see Semmel, "Philosophic Radicals and Colonialism," 518–19. But Semmel, by discussing the "Benthamite Radicals" as a group, too readily assimilates Bentham's views and doubts about colonialism to the more consistently enthusiastic views of his followers. It is also important to note the great extent to which Bentham left the writing of his later works to his disciples; see Robson, "Mill and Bentham," 257.

7. In Smart and Williams, *Utilitarianism*, 138.

8. These anti-imperialist arguments are presented most thoroughly in "Colony," written in the late 1810s as a supplement to the fifth edition of the *Encyclopaedia Britannica* (1823).

9. "A simple form of arbitrary government, tempered by European honour and European intelligence, is the only form which is now fit for Hindustan" (Mill, "Affairs of India," 156). Even Alexander Bain, whose biography of James Mill is on the whole deaf to criticism of Mill and often verges on hagiography, wrote of the *History*, "The analysis of the Hindoo institutions is methodical and exhaustive, and is accompanied with a severe criticism of their merits and their rank in the scale of development. . . . Being written while the public was prepossessed by an excessive admiration for Hindoo institutions and literature, due to Sir W. Jones and others, the review was too disparaging—the bow bent too far in the opposite direction" (*James Mill*, 176–77).

10. "The Positive Philosophy of Auguste Comte" (1865), *CW* 10:320; also see Mill's *Autobiography*, *CW* 1:27–29.

11. Stokes's *English Utilitarians* was one of the few works to deal in any depth with the question of Mill's views on empire until the 1990s. Some of the best

recent works include Zastoupil, *Mill and India*; Moir, Peers, and Zastoupil, *Mill's Encounter with India*; Mehta, *Liberalism and Empire*; and Lloyd, "Mill and East India Company." While some of Mill's most important texts on India were published in 1990 in *CW* 30, Mill's many dispatches for the East India Company, housed in the British Library's Oriental and India Office Collection, are unlikely to be published; see Robson, "Civilization and Culture," 369 n. 27. Only Fred Rosen's brief but suggestive article "Eric Stokes, British Utilitarianism, and India" begins to address these connections.

12. One exception is Eileen Sullivan, who draws a contrast between J. S. Mill's justification of empire and "a liberal tradition which was primarily anti-imperialist," including Smith, Bentham, and James Mill ("Liberalism and Imperialism," 599). Although Sullivan notes that James Mill argued for "arbitrary government" by Britain over India, she concludes rather abruptly that he, like Bentham, was fundamentally an anti-imperialist.

13. Halévy's *Growth of Philosophic Radicalism*, which itself heavily influenced Stokes's reading of the utilitarian tradition, is also partly to blame for conflating Bentham's thought with that of James Mill. Fred Rosen has discussed this problem, claiming that "Halévy uses their association to suggest that they created a sect isolated from both the Whig tradition and from other more libertarian, radical movements. This conflation of the two fails to appreciate the fact that Bentham, if not Mill, addressed a wide and varied audience on a number of different levels . . . [and] tends to minimize the creative side of Bentham's thought[,] which is not as strong in Mill" ("Elie Halévy," 923).

14. We should note that it was the notoriously unreliable Bowring who attributed these words to Bentham (*WJB* 10:450; Stokes and others cite the wrong page). The sentence is repeated or paraphrased in almost every treatment of the subject. Even Sullivan, in a nuanced account that is almost alone in drawing attention to the contrast between Bentham's views on empire and those of J. S. Mill, claims that Bentham "was primarily interested in reforming the Indian legal system though he left most of the specific discussion to James Mill. Bentham came to believe that through James Mill he would be the dead legislator of India" ("Liberalism and Imperialism," 604).

15. The image Bentham describes here strikingly resembles the Auto-Icon, Bentham's preserved body that still sits at the University College London, as well as the instructions Bentham gave in an addendum to his will for the construction of the Auto-Icon. I am grateful to Richard Tuck for making the connection with the Auto-Icon and to Fred Rosen for confirming Dapple's identity.

16. *WJB* 10:450. The last sentence is suggestive, though Bentham unfortunately says no more on the subject. Some of Bentham's other treatments of the beliefs of Indians of various religions suggest a more respectful attitude than Mill's, as I discuss below. It should, perhaps, be noted that John Stuart Mill was so outraged by Bowring's inclusion of these remarks in his "Memoirs of Bentham" that he wrote a long letter to the *Edinburgh Review*, which had quoted these words in a review of the "Memoirs." Mill called the passage "idle word[s spoken] . . . under some passing impression or momentary irritation" (*CW* 1:536). It is also worth noting the similarity of Bentham's judgment of James Mill to an observation Burke made in the *Reflections* on the unsuitability of dogmatic critics for

political reform: "It is undoubtedly true, though it may seem paradoxical; but in general, those who are habitually employed in finding and displaying faults are unqualified for the work of reformation, because their minds are not only unfurnished with patterns of the fair and good, but by habit they come to take no delight in the contemplation of those things. By hunting vices too much, they come to love men too little" (*WS* 8.218).

17. In his "Introduction to the Study of Bentham's Works," Bowring wrote, "From observations here and there scattered through [Bentham's] works, his opinions on the subject might be gathered; but it was almost solely in the great article by Mr Mill on the 'Law of Nations' in the Encyclopaedia Britannica, that the public could find a distinct account of the utilitarian theory of International law" (*WJB* 1:75).

18. *WJB* 1:75. J. S. Mill, as I argue below, similarly drew an almost impermeable boundary between the civilized and the uncivilized worlds, though he theorized the distinction more carefully than Bowring did.

19. In the *Essay on Government*, James Mill wrote that women justly may be denied suffrage, as "the interest of almost all of [them] is involved either in that of their fathers or in that of their husbands"; J. S. Mill later wrote that this paragraph was "the worst. . .he ever wrote." See James Mill, *Political Writings*, xxii and 27.

20. On Bentham's narrowness, it is worth calling attention to the popular misconception about Bentham's supposed philistinism, initiated by J. S. Mill's remark that Bentham found "pushpin and poetry" equally valuable. As Ross Harrison has explained, Bentham was discussing political and legal structures rather than personal ethics. Bentham's point was that if the people of a state value something, their pleasure in it should be taken into account by the governing authorities. Harrison notes that while this latter point is still a matter of debate, "it is nothing like as contentious as the suggestion that it is an appropriate system of personal values" (*Bentham*, 5). Bentham did not mean, or believe, that intellectual or artistic cultivation is nonsensical or pointless.

21. Anderson, "Mill on Bentham," adopts Mill's assessment of Bentham's limitations. Uday Mehta echoes Mill's view that Bentham's utilitarianism was more "mechanical and authoritarian" than Mill's own (*Liberalism and Empire*, 101); while this may be a fair description of their respective theories about European government and society, it misrepresents, I think, their views about non-Europeans.

22. Halévy, *Growth of Philosophic Radicalism*, 510. After quoting the "dead legislative" passage, Halévy writes, "Twenty-eight years after his death the Indian penal code came into force; it had been drawn up by Macaulay under the influence of Bentham's and James Mill's ideas, so that Bentham, who had failed to give a legal code to England, did actually become the posthumous legislator of the vastest of her possessions."

23. Fred Rosen has argued compellingly that Bentham was a more committed democrat than either Mill ("Elie Halévy," *Bentham and Representative Democracy*, and *Bentham, Byron, and Greece*); also see Crimmins, "Bentham's Political Radicalism Reexamined," asserting that Bentham's "democratic convictions" long preceded his encounter with James Mill (262). For an influential statement

of the contrary view, see Douglas Long, who argues that Bentham regarded liberty as merely instrumental to security and that "attempts by recent commentators [such as Mary Mack] to show that Bentham was fundamentally a 'democrat' or a 'liberal' seem to miss the point" (*Bentham on Liberty*, 206–8).

24. In a letter addressed to Greek legislators, Bentham wrote, "You stand clear from the temptation afforded by distant dependencies: you stand exempt from the danger of splitting upon that rock. . . . In this respect, you have the advantage over Spain, Portugal, England, France, and the Netherlands" (*Securities against Misrule*, 195).

25. See, for instance, Mack, *Jeremy Bentham*, 412–13; and Harrison, *Bentham*, 8–9.

26. In *RRR* 289–315. On the letters to Mirabeau, see Mack, *Jeremy Bentham*, 417–19.

27. Donald Winch has argued that Bentham's anticolonialism was simply an "early," largely superseded, phase of his career. Winch (*Classical Political Economy*), following the general lines of Stokes's argument, regards Bentham's thought as an integral episode in a tradition of "classical liberal imperialism" stretching from the eighteenth century through J. S. Mill. While Winch rightly characterizes the "story" of Bentham's views on colonization as one of "recurring ambivalence," he uses a selection of passages to argue that Bentham tended to support both settler colonies and rule over territories such as India. His conclusion that such a tradition encompassed thinkers with such diverse views on empire as Adam Smith, Bentham, and the Mills leads to mischaracterizations, particularly of Smith and Bentham. In a more recent article Winch insists on Bentham's "dream of being 'the dead legislative hand of British India,' " and he continues to regard the "imperialism . . . of Bentham and his colonial reforming followers" as a continuous movement ("Colonies and Empire," 153–54).

28. Bentham, *Colonies, Commerce, and Constitutional Law*, 92. "Rid Yourselves of Ultramaria," Bentham's "most sustained piece" on the emancipation of Spanish America, remained in manuscript, although Bentham published a number of other essays on Spanish affairs in the 1820s, after the restoration of the liberal constitution and the reinstatement of the Cortes. Bentham did most of the writing of "Rid Yourselves" in 1821. See Schofield's introduction, xv and xliv.

29. Sullivan discusses similarities between Smith's and Bentham's arguments in "Liberalism and Imperialism," 600–603.

30. In "Constitutional Code," book 1, chap. 6 ("Financial Law"), *WJB* 9:33.

31. Douglas Long holds, without elaboration, that Bentham supported the emancipation of colonies only on economic grounds (*Bentham on Liberty*, 209).

32. See Rosen, "Elie Halévy," 928, who argues that Bentham's "emphasis on publicity and public opinion predated his democratic theory but nonetheless played an important role in it."

33. With "a barbarous, or semicivilized government, its view of its true interests is so feeble and indistinct," James Mill wrote, that it acted mostly from ungoverned passion and was completely unreliable. He thought the same was true for the individual members of such societies ("Affairs of India," 147).

34. J. S. Mill often criticized Bentham as an unhistorical thinker: see *CW* 10:325, where he refers to "philosophers who, like Bentham, theorize on politics

without any historical basis at all"; and his (incorrect) argument in "Bentham" that Bentham believed the same legislation was appropriate for every society: "He places before himself man in society without a government, and, considering what sort of government it would be advisable to construct, finds that the most expedient would be a representative democracy. Whatever may be the value of this conclusion, the mode in which it is arrived at appears to me to be fallacious; for it assumes that mankind are alike in all times and all places, that they have the same wants and are exposed to the same evils, and that if the same institutions do not suit them, it is only because in the more backward stages of improvement they have not wisdom to see what institutions are most for their good" (443).

35. *RRR* 292. The writings on empire are some of Bentham's rhetorically most powerful works; neither James nor John Stuart Mill (undoubtedly a far greater writer than his dry, didactic father) could match Bentham's sardonic humor, which appears in abundance in works such as *Emancipate Your Colonies*! Bentham himself did not think well of James Mill's style, claiming that the *History of British India* "abounds with bad English, making it to me a disagreeable book"; toward the end of his life, he wrote to Rammohun Roy that Mill's *History* contained some useful practical information, "though as to style, I wish I could, with truth and sincerity, pronounce it equal to yours" (*WJB* 10:590).

36. The security, political, and economic interests of the metropole all militated against empire. Bentham envisioned the National Assembly responding to his arguments, "*Oh, but they are a great part of our power.*" He responded, "Say rather, *the whole of your weakness*. In your own natural body you are impregnable; in those unnatural excresences you are vulnerable" (*WJB* 4:414).

37. In 1838, after Bentham's death, his 1793 essay to France was published in London by an anonymous supporter, who titled it "Canada. Emancipate Your Colonies!" and attached a preface, signed "Philo-Bentham," applying his arguments to the British Empire.

38. For Smith's argument, see page 54, above.

39. William Hazlitt quipped that Bentham's influence increased in proportion to the distance from his house in Westminster (*Spirit of the Age*, 3–4).

40. From "Emancipation Spanish. From Philo-Hispanus to the People of Spain," in *Colonies, Commerce, and Constitutional Law*, 153.

41. "Rid Yourselves of Ultramaria," in *Colonies, Commerce, and Constitutional Law*, 137.

42. Lea Campos Boralevi argues that Bentham held different views about existing colonies, which he saw as a complex problem involving the oppression of colonial inhabitants, and about the prospect of future colonization, which he regarded as primarily an economic problem and favored as a way to release excess of capital or labor to the benefit of the colonizing nation (*Bentham and the Oppressed*, 127). While Boralevi is right to point to Bentham's sporadic enthusiasm for colonization as a release of labor and capital, she fails to note the many reasons he offers against new plans of colonization, as in the passage just quoted.

43. This piece was Essay 4 of his *Principles of International Law* (in *WJB* 2:535–60), and it demonstrates how wrong Bowring was to suggest that James

Mill's writings on international law offered a fair approximation of Bentham's own views (see *WJB* 1:75). Recent editors and other scholars have pointed out difficulties with the text as it appears in the Bowring edition: see Hoogensen, "Bentham's International Manuscripts." Hoogensen argues that the "Plan" was a "compilation of at least three essays" found among Bentham's manuscripts—"Pacification and Emancipation," "Colonies and Navy," and "Cabinet No Secresy"—which were "dismembered, reconfigured, and arbitrarily 'sewn' together" (3–4).

44. *WJB* 2:546. "The following, then, are the final measures which ought to be pursued:—1. Give up all the colonies. 2. Found no new colonies" (2:548).

45. *WJB* 4:206. Boralevi emphasizes that his general opposition to colonial rule stemmed far more from its negative consequences for the colonizing country than from a concern about the oppression of the colonized. While Boralevi's treatment of this topic is one of the most sensitive in the literature, she nonetheless assimilates his view of Indians to those of the Mills and Bentham's other followers in the colonial administration. While his writings include scattered doubts about the readiness of Indians for democracy, Bentham's posture of respect for such colonized non-Europeans, such as his insistence on Indian participation in juries, and his failure or refusal to develop a theory of progress justifying colonization, mark him as crucially different from his followers.

46. See chapter 3 on Edmund Burke's leading role in the Hastings impeachment trial. Bentham's point about the difficulty people have in mustering sympathy for distant sufferers is strikingly Burkean.

47. Bentham, *Economic Writings*, 3: 356–7.

48. Winch, *Classical Political Economy*, 34.

49. In "Rid Yourselves of Ultramaria," Bentham identified twenty-nine classes of people with sinister interests in colonial dominion (*Commerce, Colonies, and Constitutional Law*, 38–39).

50. See James Mill's "Colony," for instance, where he distinguishes colonies "in which the Idea of People is the predominating Idea" (4) (settler colonies) and those in which the idea of territory predominates, as in India, whose inhabitants can be ignored, for the purposes of determining the colony's benefits to the metropole (7).

51. *Emancipate Your Colonies*! *WJB* 4:417. Bice referred to Vaishya (a trading caste), Sooder to Sudra (an agricultural caste); see *WS* 7:266.

52. A puzzling postscript was attached to this essay in 1829; it reads, "As a citizen of Great Britain and Ireland, he is thereby confirmed in the same opinions, and accordingly in the same wishes. But, as a citizen of the British Empire, including the sixty millions already under its government in British India, and the forty millions likely to be under its government in the vicinity of British India . . . his opinions and consequent wishes are the reverse" (*WJB* 4:418).

53. "Official aptitude maximized—expense minimized" (*WJB* 5:268–69). By Brithibernia, a typical neologism, Bentham simply meant the British and Irish understood together as a nation.

54. See Laird, introduction to *Bishop Heber*, 32.

55. 1790; quoted by Mack, *Jeremy Bentham*, 396–97, citing University College Collection, Box 126, p. 7.

56. The term "legislator of the world," or "legislador del mundo," was bestowed on Bentham by the Guatemalan politician, José del Valle, who asked for Bentham's help in creating a civil code for Guatemala. See Bentham, *Legislator of the World* (xi and xxxiv); Dinwiddy, *Bentham*, 17; and Williford, *Jeremy Bentham on Spanish America*. On Bentham's numerous codification projects for countries around the world, see Schofield, "Jeremy Bentham: Legislator of the World."

57. Stokes, *English Utilitarians and India*, 51. Leslie Stephen had earlier claimed likewise that "Bentham was as ready to legislate for Hindoostan as well as for his own parish" (*The English Utilitarians*, 300).

58. Bentham to Henry Dundas, May 20, 1793, *Correspondence of Jeremy Bentham*, 4:430. Dundas was president of the Board of Control, the chief governing body in the East India Company, at this time (editor's note).

59. Uday Mehta writes that Bentham, like other British liberals, wrote "copious[ly]" on the British empire in India (*Liberalism and Empire*, 4); this essay, however, is a rare example (perhaps the only one) of an extended discussion of India by Bentham. Occasional examples from Indian law come up in the course of Bentham's work, and many of these are discussed here.

60. First published, along with the rest of the *Theory of Legislation*, in *Traités de Législation civile et pénale*, edited by Etienne Dumont (1802), the essay appears in *WJB* 1:169–94.

61. Whereas later, less theoretically minded utilitarians often simply assumed the excellence of British laws and legal structure, Bentham himself was generally careful to distinguish the ideal legal codes that he composed from scratch and what he knew to be the very imperfect British system, marred as it was by its uncritical dependence on custom and precedence.

62. "I take England, then, for a standard; and referring everything to this standard, I inquire, What are the deviations which it would be requisite to make from this standard, in giving to another country such a tincture as any other country may receive without prejudice, from English laws? I take my own country for the standard, partly because to that country, if to any, I owe a preference; but chiefly because it is that, with the circumstances of which I have the best opportunity to be informed" (*WJB* 1:171).

63. *WJB* 1:171. Allison Dube notes that this line introduces the "satirical dimension" of the entire essay ("Tree of Utility," 35). Dube argues convincingly that the essay demonstrates that it is a mistake to identify Bentham, as Stokes and his followers have done, as one of the utilitarian "crusading men of system," given Bentham's "humility," his understanding of the great limits on what a legislator can hope to achieve. I disagree, however, with Dube's claim that "most of what has passed for utilitarian thought on India . . . is not utilitarian at all, though parts of it may be awarded the consolation title of liberal" (40–41), for their understandings of utility as the highest goal of public policy, and in particular their (rather different) efforts to marry utility with theories of progress, deeply informed the imperial policies of both James and John Stuart Mill, as I argue in the next chapter.

64. *WJB* 1:186. Bentham condemned English laws as much for the absurdities apparent in their refined form as for those left over from a barbarous age. After describing the labyrinthine process involved in an English lawsuit, he concluded, "And who would think it? This mass of absurdity is the work of modern refinement, not of ancient barbarism. . . . Why, then, were these simple and pure forms abandoned? why were they not re-established, when new tribunals were instituted in another country, instead of transferring this system of possible equity and certain misery to Bengal?" (1:188).

65. Lafleur, "Bentham and the *Principles*," vii.

66. His successors, in contrast, saw a much more prominent role for such "impartial" governors—notably John Stuart Mill in his depiction of the perfectly trained and knowledgeable technocrats who would govern India and whose ranks would only very slowly be opened to Indians themselves. Bentham was much less confident than John Stuart or even James Mill that Company civil servants could indeed preserve impartiality and resist corruption or the pursuit of their own private interests.

67. "Jury-Trial," in *Principles of Judicial Procedure*, *WJB* 2:137–38. For the contrast with James Mill, see Mill's *Encyclopaedia Britannica* article on education, in *Political Writings*, 139–94.

68. Bentham, *Securities against Misrule*, 263.

Chapter 5
James and John Stuart Mill: The Development of Imperial Liberalism in Britain

1. Stokes, *English Utilitarians and India*, 48. James Mill entered the company as assistant examiner of correspondence and in 1830 was promoted to the position of chief examiner, a post John Stuart Mill took up in 1856.

2. The question of how J. S. Mill's judgments about India might have been affected by his father's is taken up in the final sections of this chapter.

3. See, for thorough accounts, Majeed, *Ungoverned Imaginings*; Makdisi, *Romantic Imperialism*; and Thomas, *The Philosophic Radicals*, 98–119, which astutely points out the "puritanism" of Mill's interpretation of India, as well as his reliance on missionary sources for "detailed accounts the grosser customs of a people he had placed so low in his scale of civilization" (108). Uday Mehta has aptly noted that "Mill's views regarding India, its past and its present" were "pathetically foolish in their lack of nuance" (*Liberalism and Empire*, 90). J. H. Burns offers a concise and often searing critique of James Mill's method and judgments; he concludes that "the almost blood-curdling arrogance of Mill's cultural chauvinism" is unredeemed by either felicity of language or "any clearly articulated method" ("The Light of Reason," 18).

4. Jane Rendall has identified a generation of "Scottish orientalists" between Robertson and Mill who shared the commitment to "philosophical history" characteristic of the Scottish Enlightenment and, for the most part, had lived in India; she argues that they "shared a common European assumption of superiority, but not Mill's dogmatic rejection of all that constituted Indian culture," and many sought to refute Mill's account of India. These figures included William Erskine,

Mountstuart Elphinstone, and Vans Kennedy; many were students of Dugald Stewart (Rendall, "Scottish Orientalism," 44 and passim).

5. Mill also used the article to attack penal colonies, which, he argued, following Bentham's lead in "Panopticon versus New South Wales," were incapable of performing either of the sole functions punishment should serve: to reform the criminal, and to deter others by making his punishment sufficiently unpleasant.

6. "Colony," 32.

7. "Colony," 31.

8. Mill to Ricardo, August 14, 1819, Ricardo, *Works*, 8:51; see Mazlish, *James and John Stuart Mill*, 125.

9. For descriptions of Mill's articles year by year and his correspondence with Jeffrey, the *Review*'s editor, in which Mill pleaded with Jeffrey to accept his articles, see Bain, *James Mill*, 97–127.

10. The *History* stops abruptly at 1805, noting that "with regard to subsequent events, the official papers, and other sources of information, are not sufficiently at command" (*HBI* 6:480).

11. Mill, "Affairs of India," especially 147–53.

12. "Explore the history of the British dominion in India from first to last. Whoever was the governor;—whatever was the system of government;—at no time do find that the territory had any thing to spare for England;—at all times do you find it draining away the wealth of England;—at all times launching further and further into a boundless ocean of debt" (Mill, "Affairs of India," 147). He went on to note that, given his bleak portrait of the consequences of empire for Britain, his readers would surely ask "whether, having shown, that neither the East India Company, nor a British ministry, can ever govern India but with infinite loss to this country, we mean to propose that the connexion should be dissolved, and the people abandoned to themselves? We answer, no. We have already very strongly declared our opinion against the abandoning of the people to themselves [see *Edinburgh Review* 15:372]; and whatever may be our sense of the difficulties into which we have brought ourselves, by the improvident assumption of such a dominion, we earnestly hope, for the sake of the natives, that it will not be found necessary to leave them to their own direction" (154). Also see Mill's "Review of Malcolm."

13. "Review of *Voyage aux Indes Orientales*," 371.

14. Javed Majeed's reading of the *History of British India* as a critique as much of Britain as of India seems for this reason to be overstated (*Ungoverned Imaginings*, 133, 174, and 200).

15. Mill, "Affairs of India," 155.

16. Mill, "Affairs of India," 155–56.

17. James Mill worried, as had Smith and Bentham, about the incompatibility of the roles of merchant and governor: "The mercantile interest could not see, in the light of an official, the very stagnant condition of the native population in India" (Bain, *James Mill*, 348).

18. Mill, "Affairs of India," 135.

19. "Review of *Voyage aux Indes Orientales*," 372. For a parallel argument by J. S. Mill, see *Considerations on Representative Government*, chap. 18, where

he argued that even if settler colonies such as Canada and Australia should, in justice, be separated from Britain, continued British rule could be justified by its peaceful consequences for international relations and the added "moral influence" in the world such extensive possessions gained for Britain, "the Power which, of all in existence, best understands liberty" (*CW* 19:565).

20. *HBI*, 2:105. Javed Majeed has aptly noted that Mill's tone of definitiveness—his "pseudo-deductive style of argument which stresses the certainty of conclusions derived from unassailable premisses" owed as much to Mill's puritanical spirit as to his utilitarianism (*Ungoverned Imaginings*, 186–87).

21. "To ascertain the true state of the Hindus in the scale of civilization, is not only an object of curiosity in the history of human nature; but to the people of Great Britain, charged as they are with the government of that great portion of the human species, it is an object of the highest practical importance" (*HBI* 2:107)

22. J. S. Mill called his father "the last survivor of this great school" of Scottish moral philosophy; see Ball, introduction to Mill, *Political Writings*, xiv; also see Mehta, *Liberalism and Empire*, 93.

23. As we saw in chapter 2, some earlier Scottish thinkers such as Robertson also regarded societal development as to some extent a consequence of improved mental capacities.

24. Forbes, "James Mill and India," 23–24. He also writes, "Mill, rationalist as he was, was also a firm believer in progress, and in his historical thinking followed Condorcet, and the Scottish 'conjectural' historians, for whom the 'progress of society' was an absolute presupposition" (24). Forbes's article, although "the pioneering study" (Haakonssen, "Mill and Scottish Moral Philosophy," 629 n. 4) of James Mill's effort to marry utilitarianism with Scottish philosophical history, mischaracterizes the conjectural histories and therefore their relation to Mill's own thought. Mazlish, similarly, argues that "Mill was fairly typical of the Enlightenment attitude toward history, especially of the Scottish Enlightenment" and that "[c]onjectural history gave to James Mill a flexibility, lacking in Bentham, that was to stretch Utilitarianism almost to the breaking point" (*James and John Stuart Mill*, 118–20). Also see Thomas, *The Philosophic Radicals*, 98ff. Haakonssen's article marks a great improvement over prior treatments of the subject.

25. Haakonssen, "Mill and Scottish Moral Philosophy," 631.

26. Haakonssen, "Mill and Scottish Moral Philosophy," 631. Haakonssen identifies unintended consequences and the "heterogeneity of ends" as a single "element."

27. As Haakonssen argues, "[A]ll hopes of pluralism ["of the sort which we find in Smith and Millar"] are ruled out by Mill's actual explanatory practice" ("Mill and Scottish Moral Philosophy," 632).

28. *Edinburgh Review* 15 (July 1809): 377. See *HBI* 2:110 for another claim that Mill sought to "describe the characteristics of the different stages of social progress" with a complexity that had not yet been achieved.

29. *HBI* 1:119–22. At 2:123, he claimed that the transition from the tribal state to the "regulated and artificial system of a monarchy and laws is not sudden; it is the result of a gradual preparation and improvement." Despite such evidence that Mill was aware of subtle and continuous social development, he continued

to make use of such undifferentiated categories as the "rude and ignorant state" (2:124).

30. *HBI* 1:119. He noted that such broad accounts of social practice were all that was possible: the uselessness of Indian historical records meant that "we cannot describe the lives of their kings, or the circumstances and results of a train of battles."

31. "Review of de Guignes" (July 1809), 428. See also the *History*, where Mill writes, "Among rude people, the women are generally degraded; among civilized people they are exalted" (*HBI* 1:309; the footnote reads, "This important subject is amply and philosophically illustrated by Professor Millar"); and goes on to assimilate Hindu practices to those of "the African and other savage tribes" and to "barbarous nations, as in Pegu, in Siberia, among the Tartars, among the negroes on the coast of Guinea, among the Arabs, and even among the Chinese" (309–10).

32. Mill, "Review of de Guignes," 413. Mill went on to say that Europeans are deceived by distance; while the nearby Turks were usually regarded as barbarians, the Hindus and Chinese were seen as civilized, despite their inferiority to the Turks "in every particular which can be regarded as a mark, or as a result of civilization."

33. Thus, for example in his discussion of Indian laws in the *History*, Mill examined laws only for evidence of their rudeness. For one of many such instances, see *HBI* 1:173–74, where Mill claims that the Hindu law of family joint interest in property was the only type of law available to a people "in a state of society too near the simplicity and rudeness of the most ancient times, to have stretched their ideas of property" to the point of regarding an individual as having complete discretion in the disposition of his property.

34. This is the case despite his declaration of the need to "attain . . . accurate notions respecting the state of civilization among the Chinese" ("Review of Guignes," 412).

35. "Review of de Guignes," 414 and 424. Despite his own lack of interest in matters of literary or artistic taste, Mill also wrote of the Chinese, "Their want of taste, in the shapes and ornaments of their vessels, is now proverbial" (425).

36. "Review of de Guignes," 426. Mill remarked that the Chinese were incapable of innovation—their only skill lay in imitation; as for their mendacity, he said the same of Indians (regarding their "proneness to perjury"; see *HBI* 5:433).

37. See his comments on Jones throughout the *History*, especially 2:30–85. Also see Majeed, *Ungoverned Imaginings*, especially chap. 5; Majeed's title echoes Mill's claim that Jones had displayed a "susceptible imagination" in his admiration for "Eastern wonders" (in the "Review of *Voyage aux Indes Orientales*," 369; see Majeed, *Ungoverned Imaginings*, 163), as well as Mill's assertion that Indian historical and mythological accounts were the products of a "wild and ungoverned imagination" (*HBI*, 1:115).

38. *HBI* 1:107, 115, 144, 335. Mill's editor H. H. Wilson, an admirer of Jones, protests in a footnote that "competent authorities opine differently" (I.144); other footnotes dispute many of Mill's other instances of Indian "rudeness." On the multiple layers of debate running through the text (Mill against Jones and Wilson against Mill), see Majeed, *Ungoverned Imaginings*, 190–92. As Majeed points

out, for all his criticism of Mill's disparaging portrait of Indian civilization, Wilson shared Mill's view that British rule of India was a moral responsibility.

39. Mill did claim, once, that Indians were civilized: in an 1812 *Edinburgh Review* article, he wrote, "An immense empire, acquired by the agents of a company of merchants—sixty millions of brave and civilized men subjected to the dominion of twenty thousand—and at the same time made braver and more civilized—and happier and more secure in their happiness, in consequence of their subjugation. These are some of the wonders that strike us at first sight, when we turn our eyes to our possessions in the East" ("Review of Malcolm," 38). This statement diverges so radically from everything else Mill wrote, including the *History of British India*, which was published several years later, that it remains quite a puzzle.

40. "Affairs of India," 147–48. This passage recalls the claim, fairly common in the seventeenth and eighteenth centuries, that savages were incapable of looking to the future: perhaps the best known instance was Rousseau's claim in the *Discourse on Inequality* that savages' complete lack of foresight would cause them to sell their beds in the morning and come crying for them in the evening (*Oeuvres Complètes*, 3:144). Mill, however, applied it to Indians, which even the cruder disparagers of savages did not do.

41. He not only describes Indian *society* as being in a state of infancy, but also compares Indians themselves to children: "Among children, and among rude people, little accustomed to take their decisions upon full and mature consideration, nothing is more common than to repent of their bargains, and wish to revoke them" (*HBI* 1:161).

42. Even when he is not arguing explicitly to this effect, locutions characteristic of such a view appear: "No idea of any system of rule, different from the will of a single person, appears to have entered the minds of them, or their legislators" (*HBI* 1:141). Other such examples abound: Mill describes the "the suspicious tempers and narrow views of a rude period" (1:145) and "the ignorant and depraved people, of whose depravity we have so many proofs" (5:449). "Though no arrangement would appear more natural, and more likely to strike even an uncultivated mind, than the division of laws into civil and penal, we find them mixed and blended together in the code of the Hindus" (1:157). In the same passage, Mill acknowledges that the Roman distinction of persons and things, still dominant in England, is rude and confusing; he goes on, "It will be seen, however, that even this imperfect attempt at a rational division was far above the Hindus" (1:157). "The Hindus have, through all the ages, remained in a state of society too near the simplicity and rudeness of the most ancient times, to have stretched their ideas of property so far" (1:173). Other examples can be found at 1:192–93, 232, 2:147.

43. With characteristic definitiveness, and with the suggestion (echoed by J. S. Mill) that Indians were objects to be sorted and administered, rather than human subjects, Mill announced his intention of "extracting and ordering the dispersed and confused materials of India, once and for all" (*HBI* 1:15; quoted by Majeed, *Ungoverned Imaginings*, 122).

44. For detailed considerations of Mill's career and opinions regarding India, see especially Zastoupil, *Mill and India*; Moir, introduction to *CW* vol. 30, and the essays in Moir, Peers, and Zastoupil, *J.S. Mill's Encounter with India.*

45. As Mill explained in 1852; see Lloyd, "Mill and East India Company," 53). Moore provides the most thorough account of this aspect of Mill's Company work in "Mill and Royal India."

46. The common view that only the early Bentham was a skillful stylist has remained, despite periodic efforts to combat it, such as M. P. Mack's *A Bentham Reader*, with which the editor sought to dislodge the idea "that later Bentham is eccentrically jargonical and unreadable" (359).

47. *CW* 10:12. "Remarks on Bentham's Philosophy" was first published in Edward Lytton Bulwer, *England and the English*, 2 vols. (London: Bentley, 1833), 2:321–44 (in *CW* 10:163–70). Mill's discussion of Bentham in the *Autobiography* is considerably more generous than either of the early essays; there Mill claimed that while he still agreed with his earlier judgments, he worried that they had helped to discredit Bentham's philosophy before it had "done its work" and therefore that these articles had hindered rather than contributed to "improvement" (*CW* 1:227). He probably began writing the *Autobiography* in the early 1850s; it was first published in 1873, shortly after his death (*CW* 1:xxii ff. and 3). "Bentham" was first published in the *London and Westminster Review*, August 1838.

48. "Bentham," *CW* 10:91.

49. "It is fortunate for the world that Bentham's task lay rather in the direction of jurisprudential than of properly ethical inquiry" (*CW* 10:98).

50. *CW* 10:99. "The true teacher of the fitting social arrangements for England, France, or America is the one who can point out how the English, French, or American character can be improved, and how it has been made what it is."

51. Book 6, chap. 5: "Of Ethology, or the Science of the Formation of Character" (*CW* 8:860–74). Here Mill calls ethology "the science which corresponds to the art of education; in the widest sense of the term, including the formation of national or collective character as well as individual" (869).

52. On Mill's science of character, see Carlisle, *Writing of Character*; Collini, "Idea of Character"; Collini, Winch, and Burrow, *Noble Science of Politics*, 150ff.; Robson, "Civilization and Culture"; Varouxakis, "National Character" and *Mill on Nationality* and Feuer, "Mill as Sociologist." Terence Ball argues that Mill went much farther toward the elaboration of such a theory than is commonly recognized and regards the *Autobiography* and *The Subjection of Women* as two of Mill's "case studies" in the formation, deformation, and reformation of character ("The Formation of Character," 27).

53. *CW* 10:9. This science of ethology, Mill argued, may be called an exact science, "for its truths are not, like the empirical laws which depend on them, approximate generalizations, but real laws," though he granted that these laws were "hypothetical," that they affirmed tendencies and not particular facts (*CW* 8:870).

54. For a thoughtful analysis of this point, and Mill's ambiguities on the subject of race, see Varouxakis, "Mill on Race" and *Mill on Nationality*, chap. 3. Also see Mill's letter to Gustave d'Eichthal encouraging further study of racial difference: "You are very usefully employed in throwing light on these dark subjects—

the whole subject of the races of man, their characteristics & the laws of their fusion is more important that it was ever considered till of late & it is now quite *a l'ordre du jour* & labour bestowed upon it is therefore not lost even for immediate practical ends" (December 25, 1840, *CW* 13:456).

55. Feuer cites James Mill's *History of British India* "as a model [for J. S. Mill] of what a science of ethology could do" and presents the elder Mill's methods and judgments quite uncritically. He concludes rather too optimistically that J. S. Mill "is the only sociologist of the nineteenth century whose pages are not discoloured with the acid of bias" ("Mill as Sociologist," 110).

56. See *Autobiography*, *CW* 1:77, where, after claiming that he had "ceased to consider representative democracy as an absolute principle, and regarded it as a question of time, place, and circumstance," Mill went on to say that he now sought to understand "what great improvement in life and culture stands next in order for the people concerned, as the condition of their further progress."

57. It should be noted, however, that some of Bentham's writings on empire show that he was more interested in the effects of policy on the character of a nation's inhabitants than Mill admitted. As we have seen, for instance, Bentham argued that imperial rule was contrary to the interests of the ruling country not simply for economic or military reasons, but because it was corrupting.

58. "Remarks on Bentham's Philosophy," *CW* 10:16; for a rewording of the same argument, see "Bentham," *CW* 10:105.

59. "Bentham," *CW* 10:113.

60. In the imperious tone characteristic of these essays, Mill wrote, "Do we then consider Bentham's political speculations useless? Far from it. We consider them only one-sided" (*CW* 10:109); Mill applied the phrase "half-truth" to Bentham's thought in "Remarks on Bentham's Philosophy," *CW* 10:18.

61. See Mehta, "Liberalism, Nation, and Empire," 3–4, for a subtle articulation of this idea.

62. On Mill's views about progress, see Gibbins, "Mill, Liberalism, and Progress"; Burns, "The Light of Reason"; Kurer, *John Stuart Mill*; and Habibi, *Ethic of Human Growth*.

63. "The Universities," *CW* 26:349. Mill discussed the place of a theory of progress in the social sciences in the *System of Logic*, where he wrote, "The progressiveness of the human race is the foundation on which a method of philosophizing in the social science has been of late years erected, far superior to either of the two modes which had previous been prevalent, the chemical or experimental, and the geometrical modes" (book 6, "On the Logic of the Moral Sciences," chap. 10, "Of the Inverse Deductive, or Historical Method," *CW* 8:914).

64. He argued that the classical age "decided for an indefinite period the question, whether the human race was to be stationary or progressive." This was the case because "history points to no other people in the ancient world who had any spring of unborrowed progress within themselves" ("Review of Grote's *History of Greece*," *CW* 11:313). Also see Kurfirst, "J. S. Mill and Oriental Despotism."

65. Bhikhu Parekh has argued that Mill's naive account of Eastern cultures served essentially as a foil for Mill's notion of Europe (see "Liberalism and Colonialism," and "Decolonizing Liberalism," 89–90).

66. Robson, "Civilization and Culture," 352. Lloyd is similarly indulgent toward Mill's "belief that India was not able to govern itself," writing that although Mill's attitude "may have been a pessimistic" one, "[t]here was a good deal of evidence" to support it ("Mill and the East India Company," 71).

67. *Considerations on Representative Government*, chap. 2, *CW* 19:394.

68. James Mill had written, "Whatever is worth seeing or hearing in India, can be expressed in writing. As soon as every thing of importance is expressed in writing, a man who is duly qualified may obtain more knowledge of India in one year in his closet in England, than he could obtain during the course of the longest life, by the use of his eyes and ears in India" (*HBI* 1:xxiii). Also see "Review of *Voyage aux Indes Orientales*," 366–69.

69. Cf. Robson, "Civilization and Culture," who argues that Mill thought it necessary to understand each society's history and specific culture. Mill may have thought this is what he believed, but he did little to learn about the specificities of any non-European culture, or to adjust his theoretical framework to what he did know of them (360).

70. A number of scholars have noted the peculiar opening of J. S. Mill's autobiography, in which his mother is absent but the *History* looms large, as indeed it did throughout Mill's childhood: "I was born in London on the 20th of May, 1806, and was the eldest son of James Mill, author of the *History of British India*" (*CW* 1:5); see Mazlish, *James and John Stuart Mill*, 3; and Peers, "Imperial Epitaph," 201.

71. J. S. Mill began reading and editing the work at a young age and described it in his *Autobiography* as a "book which contributed largely to my education," crediting his intellectual development in part to "the number of new ideas which I received from this remarkable book, and the impulse and stimulus as well as guidance given to my thoughts by its criticisms and disquisitions on society and civilisation" (*CW* 1:28–29).

72. Mill, in his essay on Comte, wrote that although Comte's thought was not well known beyond a small circle of devotees, his ideas "have manifested themselves on the surface of the philosophy of the age" (*CW* 10:263). While Mill was to repudiate what he saw as Comte's authoritarianism, the understanding of history that he developed under the influence of Comte's writings remained remarkably consistent throughout his career. On Mill's borrowings, and differences, from Comte, see Mueller, *Mill and French Thought*, chap. 4; Robson, *The Improvement of Mankind*, 80–94; and Burns, "The Light of Reason," 7–9. For some of Mill's criticisms of Comte, see *The Correspondence of J. S. Mill and Auguste Comte*, especially letters 40 and 42, on the need for a better developed science of character; and letter 82 (of January 12, 1846), in which Mill states that their agreements on method have not produced agreements on more substantive questions about social systems.

73. *CW* 10:323. He also contrasted Comte to "philosophers who, like Bentham, theorize on politics without any historical basis at all" (325). Collini, Winch, and Burrow note that Mill later "matured beyond the need to distance himself from the a-historical simplicities of Bentham" (*Noble Science of Politics*, 134–35).

74. "Coleridge" (1840), *CW* 10:120.

75. For instance, he wrote in 1858, "All respect and fear of England as a nation will be materially weakened in the East; for, that there may be a firm action notwithstanding divided councils, or that a government can be really formidable which allows itself to be bearded and its acts railed at to its face, is a truth which it requires a much higher civilization than that of Orientals to understand or credit" ("The Moral of the India Debate," *CW* 30:198).

76. *CW* 21:118. In "Civilization," Mill argued similarly that the answers to the "great questions in government . . . vary indefinitely, according to the degree and kind of civilization and cultivation already attained by a people, and their peculiar aptitudes for receiving more" (*CW* 10:106).

77. C. H. Alexandrowicz has argued that with the turn of the nineteenth century the European practice of regarding the law of nations as applicable outside Europe was replaced with a positivist understanding of that law that saw it as stemming from and applicable to European states alone (*Law of Nations*, chap. 1). The resemblance of the quoted passage to James Mill's words on the subject is striking: In his *Encyclopaedia Britannica* article "Law of Nations," the elder Mill had written, "It is only then in countries, the rulers of which are drawn from the mass of the people, in other words, in democratical countries, that the sanction of the laws of nations can be expected to operate with any considerable effect" (9).

78. Mehta, "Liberalism, Nation, and Empire," 7 and passim.

79. Mill's argument for what might be called internal colonization followed a similar logic; he held that "[n]obody can suppose that it is not more beneficial to a Breton, or a Basque of French Navarre, to be brought into the current of a highly civilized and cultivated people—to be a member of the French nationality . . . than to sulk on his own rocks, the half-savage relic of past times, revolving in his own mental orbit" (*Considerations*, *CW* 19:549).

80. "Non-intervention," *CW* 21:118–19. "The criticisms, therefore, which are so often made upon the conduct of the French in Algeria, or of the English in India, proceed, it would seem, mostly on a wrong principle" (119).

81. Letter to John Morley of September 26, 1866, *CW* 16:1202–3. Moir notes, of Mill's position on the policy of lapse (British assumption of sovereignty by prohibiting adoption), "Indeed, the implied picture of Mill himself weighing the destinies of assorted Indian dynasties from his office in London has a certain cartoon quality about it" (introduction to *CW* 30:liv).

82. Moreover, as Moore rightly points out, given what Mill says in "Non-intervention" the recommendation to respect nationality in this case appears to reflect concerns about expedience and not right ("Mill and Royal India," 106).

83. Mill himself criticized the "fantasy" of the good despot in chapter 3 of *Considerations on Representative Government*, asking, "What sort of human beings can be formed under such a regimen," in which they have no "potential voice in their own destiny [?]" (*CW* 19:400).

84. Ryan, "Mill in Liberal Landscape," 532.

85. Ryan observes the limits to the diversity Mill was willing to tolerate: "There was little room in Mill's mind for the thought that what he saw as the superstitious, indolent, and intermittently violent life of the Indian subcontinent was to be enjoyed as one more variant on the theme of a diverse and contradictory human nature" ("Mill in Liberal Landscape," 531).

86. "Repeal of the Union," April 25, 1834, *CW* 6:217. As he wrote in *Considerations on Representative Government*, civilized rulers of barbarous nations should "[train] the people in what is specifically wanting to render them capable of a higher civilisation." He went on, "We need not expect to see that ideal realised; but unless some approach to it is, the rulers are guilty of a dereliction of the highest moral trust which can devolve upon a nation" (*CW* 19:416; also see 396).

87. *CW* 6:216. "We are bound not to renounce the government of Ireland, but to govern her well"; if Ireland were not civilized enough to be fully incorporated, like Scotland, then it should, like India, be "governed despotically . . . by English functionaries, under responsibility to the English parliament."

88. On Ireland, see "Repeal of the Union," April 25, 1834, *CW* 6:216 and on India, "Memorandum of Improvements" (1858), *CW* 30:94.

89. In "Repeal of the Union," which condemned proposals to repeal the union between Ireland and England (6:216).

90. "The question is, in what manner Great Britain can best provide for the government . . . of 150 millions of Asiatics, who cannot be trusted to govern themselves" ("A President in Council the Best Government for India," *CW* 30:201).

91. "The East India Company's Charter" *CW* 30:51.

92. *CW* 6:216. Mill had argued in the *Morning Chronicle*, "The English nation owes a tremendous debt to the Irish people for centuries of misgovernment, perpetrated mostly for no English interest or purpose, but for the sole interest of that colony of English descent who have got the lands of Ireland into their possession. . . . If ever compensation was due from one people to another, this is the case for it" (*CW* 24:903).

93. *CW* 6:217 (1834). This fairly early article insists much more on Ireland's civilizational backwardness than Mill's later writings would.

94. As E. D. Steele has argued, Mill's proposals for Irish land reform in both the *Morning Chronicle* and the *Principles of Political Economy* (in editions from 1848 to 1865) were "much less radical . . . than is often supposed" ("Mill and Irish Question," 419). Mill was arguing not for a widespread redistribution of cultivated lands but for the more limited distribution of waste (unimproved) lands. Still, as Mill himself noted in his *Autobiography*, his proposals contravened popular British opinion on Ireland.

95. "The Condition of Ireland" (3), *CW* 24:889 (*Morning Chronicle*, October 10, 1846).

96. He cited, for instance, the perverse structure of the cottier-tenant system, under which subsistence farmers, forced to bid against one another to occupy land, drove rents above what any of them could actually pay. (*Morning Chronicle*, October 10, 1846, *CW* 24:889–92).

97. The English "dogged tenacity of work," he wrote, "depends on peculiar circumstances of character, whether inherent in the race, or, as is far more probable, produced by peculiarities of historical development" (*CW* 24:916).

98. *CW* 24:916. He also suggested that the Irish should not emigrate in large numbers, as they were an "excitable" race (though here by the term *race* he did not mean to argue that this characteristic was biological or inherent). He went on, "[I]t is not well to select as missionaries of civilization a people who, in so great a degree, yet remain to be civilized" (915).

99. Zastoupil argues that if Mill's economic proposals were moderate (as Steele argued), his project for Ireland's moral regeneration was far more radical ("Moral Government," 711).

100. *Morning Chronicle*, November 19, 1846, *CW* 24:955.

101. "We have an opportunity of making the compensation, in the most admirable form for the permanent advantage of the receivers; in a form as well suited to educate them into better habits and higher civilization, as our past conduct was calculated to barbarise and anarchise, if the expression may be permitted, even a civilised people" (*Morning Chronicle*, October 17, 1846, *CW* 24:903).

102. (*CW* 30:222) His "Memorandum of Improvements in Indian Administration" (*CW* 30:93–160) offers a similar analysis of past mistakes. Given that Mill wrote this piece in 1858 in his official capacity as a representative of the East India Company arguing for the continuation of its rule in India, it is perhaps not surprising that he interpreted "progress" in the British administration of India in a highly favorable light.

103. In this aspiration Mill followed his father's hope that in the *History of British India* he would be "extracting and ordering the dispersed and confused materials of India, once and for all" (*HBI*, 1:xvi).

104. "[T]he public of India afford no assistance in their own government. They are not ripe for doing so by means of representative government; they are not even in a condition to make effectual appeals to the people of this country; they cannot even make their circumstances and interests and grievances known and intelligible to people so different and so unacquainted with India as the people, and even the Parliament of this country" (*CW* 30:49).

105. Chapter 18 of *Considerations* makes many of the same arguments about the superiority of colonial governance by an "intermediary body" insulated from metropolitan politics and "chiefly composed of persons who have acquired professional knowledge" (*CW* 19:573–74). Since the work was published in 1861 after the Company was disbanded, Mill takes a tone of reproach rather than persuasion here (see especially the final paragraph of foreboding).

106. "Penal Code for India" (1838), *CW* 30:30. Also see "Minute on the Black Act" (1836), *CW* 30:15. Also see *Considerations*, where he cites the English in India, the French in "Algiers," the Americans in the countries already conquered from Mexico, and the Spanish in America, arguing: "In all these cases, the government to which these private adventurers are subject, is better than they, and does the most it can to protect the natives against them" (*CW* 19:571).

107. On Mill's initial misjudgment of the severity of the rebellion, and his relatively minor role in the Company's response to it, see Zastoupil, *Mill and India*, 159–68. As Zastoupil shows, two dispatches written under Mill's authority (one by Mill himself) argued that the Company "had not threatened Indian religions or in any way misled its subjects" (161). The Board of Control, disagreeing, held missionaries, and the authorities who supported them, as well as the British policy of annexation, largely responsible for provoking the revolt.

108. See *CW* 16:1131, where Mill notes in a letter of January 1, 1866, that in addition to parliamentary reform in England, Jamaica would be one of the "great topics of the year"; news of the trial and execution of George William Gordon, a

mixed-race member of the Jamaican House of Assembly, reached London only weeks before this letter was written (see 16:1117 n. 2).

109. While Mill claimed he felt an obligation as a member of Parliament to develop a position on this last problem, he confessed to being baffled by it. See his letter to Henry Samuel Chapman, January 7, 1866, *CW* 16:1136.

110. See the accounts in Semmel, *The Governor Eyre Controversy*; Dutton, *The Hero as Murderer*; Kinzer, Robson, and Robson, *Moralist*, 184–217; Knox, "British Government"; and Hall, *White, Male*, 257–95, and *Civilizing Subjects*.

111. I have found no evidence that Mill considered the affinities between his own efforts against Eyre and Burke's leadership of the Hastings impeachment trial; this seems a striking omission. David Bromwich's suggestion that Burke never seemed to Mill "part of his usable past," in part because of James Mill and Harriet Taylor's detestation of Burke, seems a plausible explanation (private correspondence).

112. Burke erred in the opposite direction and chose not to restrain his rhetoric; he suffered for it in the press, which began by finding him eloquent but later criticized his extravagance. See page 75 above.

113. Letter of January 31, 1866, *CW* 32:160–61.

114. "This is not like a contest for some political improvement, in which the only question is whether it shall be obtained a little sooner or a little later. Ours is, morally, a protest against a series of atrocious crimes, & politically an assertion of the authority of the criminal law over public delinquents. This protest & vindication must be made now or never: & to relinquish the effort while a single unexhausted chance remains would be, in my estimation, to make ourselves to some extent participants in the crime" (letter to Lindsey Middleton Aspland, February 23, 1868, *CW* 16:1364–65).

115. Letter to William Fraser Rae, December 14, 1865, *CW* 16:1126.

116. In his speech of July 24, 1866, as he was leaving Jamaica, Eyre said that "excesses must always take place under martial law, especially when black troops, who are often wholly beyond the control of their officers, are employed" (quoted in Dutton, *The Hero as Murderer*, 321).

117. Letter to David Urquhart, October 4, 1866, *CW* 16:1205.

118. Carlyle's essay was published anonymously in *Fraser's Magazine for Town and Country*, vol. 40, February 1849; Mill's response appeared in vol. 41, January 1850, and appears in *CW* 21:86–95. The essay was reprinted in America as "West India Emancipation" in the *Commercial Review of the South and West*, June 1850, o.s., n.s. 2.4:527–38 (the edition cited here). In an 1853 reprint of the essay Carlyle changed the title from "negro" to "nigger" (see Hall, *Civilizing Subjects*, 349ff.).

119. "It was clear that to bring English functionaries to the bar of a criminal court for abuses of power committed against negroes and mulattoes, was not a popular proceeding with the English middle classes" (*Autobiography*, *CW* 1:282). In a letter of 1868 Mill claimed that he hoped to provoke public outrage against "public delinquents" even if he lost the legal case (to Lindsey Aspland, February 23, *CW* 16:1364–65).

120. I am grateful to David Bromwich for deepening my understanding of this point.

121. "[W]e want to know who are to be our masters: her Majesty's judges and a jury of our countrymen, administering the laws of England, or three naval and military officers, two of them boys, administering . . . no law at all" (*CW* 28:110, 113).

122. Since 1805, martial law had been declared twice each in Barbados, Jamaica, Ceylon, and the Cape of Good Hope and once in Canada, Cephalonia, Demerara, and St. Vincent (in 1862, in force for two years) (Dutton, *The Hero as Murderer*, 309).

123. On racism in Jamaica and England in this period, see Hall, *Civilizing Subjects* (Hall gives the population figures on page 23). The *Times* of London, a conservative but not unrepresentative paper, had written, several years before the rebellion, "Negroes, coolies and planters; what is the position of each, and what are the rights of each? Floods of pathetic eloquence and long years of Parliamentary struggling have taught us to imagine that the world was made for Sambo, and that the sole use of sugar is to sweeten Sambo's existence. The negro is, no doubt, a very amusing and a very amiable fellow, and we ought to wish him well; but he is also a lazy animal, without any foresight, and therefore requiring to be led and compelled" (January 6, 1860, quoted by Hall, *Civilizing Subjects*, 216).

124. See Semmel, *The Governor Eyre Controversy*, 106–8; Semmel also quotes a letter from Matthew Arnold (to his mother) arguing that the British government should suppress workers' riots—indeed should "put down *all* rioting with a strong hand" (134).

125. See Semmel, *The Governor Eyre Controversy*, 130.

126. Cochrane argued that "there were 500,000 of blacks in Jamaica and only 15,000 whites, and what would have been the position of Governor Eyre if he had not used the most energetic measures, and if there had been a general massacre of the whites? . . . nothing but the energy of the Governor saved the white population from extermination" (*Hansard's Parliamentary Debates*, 184, cols. 1813–14). Historians have concluded that such "extermination" was not intended by the rioters, nor likely.

127. Buxton quoted some of the correspondence that passed between the military officers during the spate of executions, including one letter from the deputy adjutant general to Colonel Hobbs: "Dear Colonel,—I send you an order to push on at once to Stony Gut, but I trust you are there already. Hole is doing splendid service with his men all about Manchioneal, and shooting every black man who cannot account for himself (sixty on line of march.) Nelson at Port Antonio hanging like fun by court martial. I hope you will not send any black prisoners. Do punish the blackguards well" (*Hansard's Parliamentary Debates*, vol. 184, col. 1776).

128. *Hansard's Parliamentary Debates*, vol. 184, cols. 1812–13.

129. It should be noted that impeachment, which might have encouraged a broader critique of Eyre's role as a colonial official, was not available to Mill as a means of bringing Eyre to justice: the process (already unusual by Burke's day) had not been employed in Britain since the impeachment of Lord Melville in 1806.

130. Speech of July 31, 1866, *CW* 28:112.

131. George Frederickson has noted Mill's "skepticism as to whether a colonial environment could be conducive to liberty and civilization without the sustained intervention of the metropolitan authorities" (*The Comparative Imagination*, 110).

132. Earlier, Mill had written to Rowland Hazard of post–Civil War America that "[e]mancipation is not enough, without making the free negroes electors and landholders" (June 7, 1865, *CW* 16:1066).

133. Letter to Rowland G. Hazard, November 15, 1865, *CW* 16:1117.

134. Letter to Henry Samuel Chapman, January 7, 1866, *CW* 16:1135–36.

135. Mill's letters and other texts written during the British suppression of the Sepoy Rebellion of 1857–58 do not betray such worries. A rare reference to the rebellion occurs during a letter to Harriet Mill of September 16, 1857: "The Indian news seems to me more bad than good, but not, I think, of any bad omen" (*CW* 25:537). The rebellion had begun the preceding May.

136. Letter to Henry Samuel Chapman, January 7, 1866, *CW* 16:1135–36.

137. Letter to David Urquhart, October 4, 1866, *CW* 16:1205–6. Mill's interesting exemption of the working classes reflects his activities on behalf of workingmen during this period and his understanding of the hostility toward them as a class among precisely those who were defending Eyre, most notably Thomas Carlyle. See Semmel, *The Governor Eyre Controversy*, on the connections between suppression of working-class agitation and support for Eyre.

138. I am grateful to David Bromwich for suggesting this line of thought.

139. Letter to William Sims Pratten of June 9, 1868, published in the *Times*, June 15, 1868, *CW* 16:1411.

140. Letter to Henry Samuel Chapman, January 7, 1866, *CW* 16:1135–36. Chapman had lived for years in New Zealand as supreme court judge.

141. "A Few Words on Non-intervention," *CW* 21:115.

142. See Stepan, *Idea of Race*; and Hall, *Civilizing Subjects*, chaps. 6–7. Hall argues that antiracist sentiment among the Protestant abolitionists of the 1830s was replaced in the 1850s by "an increasing turn to the language of race to explain and justify the inequalities and persistent differences between peoples" (338).

143. See, for instance, a satirical verse account of the Hastings trial, which accuses Burke of madness, malice, desire for a royal sinecure, and other vices, but also acknowledges, not unsympathetically, " 'Tis the cause of Mankind, led by Edmund the Brave, / His object is Man, from Man's baseness to save." (Broome, *Letters from Simpkin the Second*).

144. The abolitionist William Morgan, who was sent to Jamaica by the British and Foreign Anti-Slavery Society after the riot to follow the inquiry of the suppression and to study the condition of the victims, was, for all his horror at the situation, committed to European government as the only possible solution. Although, he wrote, the Jamaican blacks "are far from being the savage and brutalised people which their enemies represent them to be," still "they have not reached that high culture and civilisation which shows itself in an extensive demand for superior articles of dress, and furniture, and food"; only "intelligent Englishmen" could remedy their situation. See Hall, *Civilizing Subjects*, 415–16.

145. See Metcalf, *The Aftermath of Revolt*, chap. 8. Metcalf argues that one reform was a new reluctance to pursue Dalhousie's aggressive acquisition of states ruled by Indian princes (the "Native States").

146. Metcalf, *The Aftermath of Revolt*, 303–4.

147. In "The Rise of Anti-imperialism in England" and "The Climax of Anti-imperialism in England," R. L. Schuyler argued that there was a peak of anti-imperialist argument in England in the 1850s and 1860s before a return to almost universal support for empire in the 1880s. Notably, however, he found that even the most "anti-imperialist" writers of the period, such as Goldwin Smith, were arguing for the emancipation not of India, which they agreed required British rule, but of settler colonies like Canada and Australia. See especially "Climax," 539–40.

Chapter 6
The Liberal Volte-Face in France

1. The British thinkers we have considered, especially Smith and Burke but even Bentham, were far more committed to their existing social and political order and sought to bring Britain's imperial and international conduct into line with what they saw as the country's basically just political practice. On Diderot, see Benot, *Diderot*; Duchet, *Anthropologie et histoire*; and Muthu, *Enlightenment against Empire*, chaps. 2–3.

2. On French revolutionary colonial policy, see Saintoyant, *La colonisation française pendant la révolution* and *La colonisation française pendant la période napoléonienne*; Matthewson, "Jefferson and Haiti"; and Sloane, "Napoleon's Plans." On the pervasive, if often unspoken, commitment to the idea of honor in postrevolutionary France, and on the ways in which the idea of national honor became even more important after military defeat, see Reddy, *The Invisible Code*, chap. 1 and (on the importance of national honor after France's defeat by Prussia in 1870), 237.

3. See Benot, *La Révolution et la fin des colonies*.

4. Andrew and Kanya-Forstner, "Centre and Periphery," 9–10; and Quinn, *The French Overseas Empire*, 92–101 and 107–9.

5. I am indebted to Cheryl Welch for her thoughts about how to conceive these developments.

6. Woolf, "French Civilization and Ethnicity." In chapter 7, I discuss Tocqueville's belief that France's revolutionary legacy charged the nation with the task of preserving its place at the forefront of progress by, for instance, abolishing slavery. Tocqueville, as we will see, was far more ambivalent than later French liberals about whether civilizing colonized societies was possible. On the *mission civilisatrice* in the later nineteenth century, particularly in West Africa, see Conklin, *A Mission to Civilize*.

7. On the contours of liberalism in early-nineteenth-century France, see Kelly, *The Humane Comedy*; Welch, *Liberty and Utility* and *De Tocqueville*, chap. 1;

Fontana, *Constant and Post-revolutionary Mind*; and Mélonio, *Tocqueville and the French*. Constant and Germaine de Staël shared an "Anglophilic constitutionalism" (see Kelly, 18) with some of the more centrist Doctrinaires, and, later, Tocqueville.

8. Constant was, of course, not French—"even by the loose cosmopolitan standards of the eighteenth century," as G. A. Kelly has noted—but Swiss (from the *pays de Vaud*). He felt himself to be French and devoted much of his career to French politics both in government and as a publicist, but his status in French politics and society was always ambiguous. See Kelly, *The Humane Comedy*, 8–12.

9. Guizot, *Histoire de la civilisation d'Europe* (1828), 18.

10. Kelly, *The Humane Comedy*, 2. Hazareesingh describes some of the tensions in mid-nineteenth-century French liberal thought: tensions between a desire to promote political and economic change and to preserve social order; between a desire to extend political participation and to govern paternalistically; and between respect for local autonomy and a concern to preserve national unity (*From Subject to Citizen*, 165–69).

11. In 1848 the Constitution of the Second Republic declared Algeria an "integral part of France"; see Ageron, *Modern Algeria*, 28–30. On the 1830 conquest of Algiers in the last days of Charles X's reign, France's military and civil colonial policy under the July Monarchy during the first two decades of conquest of the rest of Algeria; and the long resistance and eventual defeat and capture of the Algerian leader Abdelkader, see Hamdani, *La vérité sur l'expédition*; Schefer, *L'Algérie et l'évolution*; Ageron, *Modern Algeria*; Ruedy, *Modern Algeria*, chap. 3; Julien, *L'Algérie contemporaine*, 1:1–269; Bouche, *Histoire de la colonisation française*; Stora, *L'Algérie coloniale*; Rey-Goldzuiguer, "La France coloniale"; Danziger, *Abd al-Qadir*; Collingham, *July Monarchy*, 240–57; Frémeaux, *Les Bureaux arabes*; Lorcin, *Imperial Identities*, 17–52. Early reports by French officials and many of the treaties between the French and Abdelkader can be found in Emerit, *L'Algérie à l'époque d'Abd-el-Kader*; translations of the treaties are in Danziger, *Abd al-Qadir.*

12. Guizot, *Memoirs*, 116–17.

13. Sullivan, *Thomas-Robert Bugeaud*, 55–67. Also see Bugeaud, *De la colonisation de l'Algérie* (1847), and Germain, *La politique indigène de Bugeaud.*

14. Blanc, *Histoire de dix ans*, quoted by Soltau, *French Political Thought*, 98. The Saint-Simonians were the socialists most committed to the colonization of Algeria; see Emerit, *Les Saint-Simoniens en Algérie*; perhaps the most influential statement of Saint-Simonian colonial aims was *La Colonisation de l'Algérie* (1843) by Saint-Simon's disciple Prosper Enfantin.

15. Koebner and Schmidt, *Imperialism*, 2–3, quoting a legitimist newspaper, *La Quotidienne*: "The Bonapartist party is no more. The imperialist party remains powerful . . . the imperialist party is the military party of the Empire . . . the party of the sword, the party of honor."

16. In chapter 7, I discuss Tocqueville's interest in the British conquest of India, whose revolutionary nature and implications he believed none of his contemporaries perceived; also see his notes on India in *OC* 3:1 443–553.

17. For Tocqueville's claim that he sought, as foreign minister, to develop a "liberal" foreign policy that lived up to the "principles of our Revolution: liberty, equality, and clemency," see his *Recollections*, 240 n. 6.

18. Tocqueville insisted on his own liberalism. In June 1842, he told his electorate: "I am a liberal and nothing more. I was one before 1830; I am still one" ("A MM. les électeurs de l'arrondissement de Valognes," quoted by Drescher, *Tocqueville and England*, 11). Also see his letter to Royer-Collard insisting that the "*liberal but not revolutionary* party [is] the only one that would suit me" (September 27, 1841, *OC* 11:108). Also see Tocqueville, *Recollections*, 91. For Tocqueville's efforts to secure a seat on the center left in the Chamber of Deputies, see Jardin, *Tocqueville*, 298.

19. The *Esquisse* was written in haste over eight months, when Condorcet was in hiding during the Terror in the rue Servandoni. On the circumstances of the drafting of the essay, see Baker, *Condorcet*, 342 and 350–52, and Badinter and Badinter, *Condorcet*, 589–621.

20. *Esquisse*, 191. In translating passages from the *Esquisse* I have consulted June Barraclough's translation, *Sketch for a Historical Picture of the Progress of the Human Mind*. Condorcet stated his belief in human equality eloquently in his dedication, to slaves, of his *Réflexions sur l'esclavage des nègres* of 1781: "Although I am not of the same color as you, I have always regarded you as my brothers. Nature has formed you to have the same mind [*esprit*], the same reason, the same virtues as whites. I am only speaking here of Europeans; as for those in the colonies, I wouldn't do you the injury to compare them with you; I know how often your loyalty, your probity, your courage have made your masters blush. If you were to seek a man in the American islands, you would not find him among the white people [*gens de chair blanche*]" (*Oevures complètes*, 7:63).

21. On the influence of the *Esquisse* on Comte's and Saint-Simon's views of progress, as well as the important and often unrecognized differences between Condorcet's approach to social science and that of nineteenth-century positivist sociology, see Baker, *Condorcet*, 371–82.

22. Condorcet, *Esquisse*, 11.

23. Condorcet, *Esquisse*, 3.

24. Condorcet noted elsewhere that the vicious influence of priests is universal: "[W]ithout restricting ourselves to examples near us, which strike everyone [*frappent tous les yeux*], but which one cannot cite without wounding weak minds and timid souls, it is enough to observe that the absurd superstitions of India and Egypt did not sully primitive religion; that, like all religions of the great agricultural and sedentary peoples, it began with a pure deism mixed with some metaphysical ideas, taken from a coarse [*grossière*] philosophy and expressive in the allegorical style of these early times, and that only the ambition of the priests, who had become the teachers [*précepteurs*] of these nations, converted these beliefs into a vile heap of absurd superstitions, calculated for the interest of the priests" (*Sur l'instruction publique*, 1791–92, *Oeuvres complètes*, 7:289).

25. Condorcet, *Esquisse*, 324. He argued that priests' power was particularly dangerous as it made use of the instruments of progress themselves—language and writing—to spread error among the people and strengthen their own exclusive grip on power.

26. Baker, *Condorcet*; also see Baker's introduction to his edition of Condorcet's *Selected Writings*.

27. "It is only in this [eighth] epoch that man has been able to know the globe he inhabits, to study in all countries the human race as modified by the long influence of natural causes or social institutions" (*Esquisse*, 190).

28. Montesquieu, *Spirit of the Laws*, bk 10, chap. 4, p. 142.

29. Condorcet, *Esquisse*, 191.

30. Describing monopoly companies as "these counting-houses of brigands," Condorcet wrote, "European nations will finally learn that exclusive companies are simply a tax on them, to give their governments a new instrument of tyranny" (*Esquisse*, 326).

31. Condorcet, *Esquisse* 208. In reference to the extirpation of Amerindians, Condorcet had also written, "The unfortunate creatures who lived in these new lands were treated as through they were not human beings because they were not Christians. . . . The bones of five million men covered those unfortunate lands where the Portuguese and the Spaniards brought their greed, their superstitions, and their wrath. They will lie there to the end of time as a mute witness against the doctrine of the political utility of religion; a doctrine which even to this day finds its apologists among us" (190). We should note that the brunt of Condorcet's own wrath falls on Christianity rather than on any other aspect of European society that might drive imperial ruthlessness.

32. *Esquisse*, 324; emphasis added. Note that the independence of New World colonies marked, for Condorcet, the beginning of the real work of civilizing backward peoples.

33. *Esquisse*, 324–25.

34. *Esquisse*, 361.

35. *Esquisse*, 327–28.

36. See Biancamaria Fontana, introduction to *Political Writings*, 10–13; textual research has shown that Constant drew considerable material for this work from unpublished drafts written a decade earlier, soon after his 1802 expulsion from the Tribunate.

37. See Fontana, introduction, 12, and Wood, *Benjamin Constant*, 214.

38. From 1819 to 1822 Constant represented a constituency from the Department of Sarthe; from 1824 to 1830, he served two different constituencies, first in Paris and then in the Lower Rhine. See Holmes, *Making of Modern Liberalism*, 22; Wood, *Benjamin Constant*, 228–55; and, for a detailed account of Constant's parliamentary career, Bastid, *Constant et sa doctrine*, 305–476.

39. See the speeches collected in the *Discours de M. Benjamin Constant* (quotation at 1.549): On the slave trade, June 27, 1821, April 5, 1822, and July 31, 1822; on colonial administration in Martinique, July 16, 1824, January 8, 1825, and June 3, 1826. Although he made clear his opposition to slavery, Constant did not emphasize its abolition as a political demand in his speeches in the Chamber. His arguments in the speeches against the slave trade, and for the civil rights of blacks in the colonies, suggest that he sought to tailor his demands to what was politically possible under the regime, as I discuss further below.

40. Noting the work's theoretical tone, Fontana cites Germaine de Staël's comment: "[A]re you quite sure that this style à la Montesquieu is really suited to the

circumstances and to the times?" (letter of January 23, 1814, in Fontana, *Constant and Post-revolutionary Mind*, 13).

41. Constant, *Oeuvres*, 1007; *Political Writings*, 67.

42. Constant, *Oeuvres*, 1010; *Political Writings*, 69.

43. Constant, *Oeuvres*, 995; *Political Writings*, 55.

44. On the influence of Scottish theories of development on Constant, see Fontana, *Constant and Post-revolutionary Mind*, chap. 3. Constant notes that whereas war was once a test of courage, strength, and skill, technological developments mean that it has become simply dangerous, and that whereas war was once the price of security and independence, commerce and the interdependence of states have replaced war as the foundation of security. War has thus, he argues, "lost its charm as well as its utility" (*Oeuvres*, 995; *Political Writings*, 55).

45. Constant, *Oeuvres*, 1001; *Political Writings*, 61. Constant notes the spread of "military justice" throughout Europe following the Napoleonic conquests as an example of the deterioration of freedom in the face of military habits.

46. "Mr Hastings was not punished: but that oppressor of India appeared on his knees in front of the House of Lords while the voices of Fox, of Sheridan, of Burke, avenging a humanity long trampled under foot, awoke in the soul of the English people emotions of generosity and feelings of justice, and forced mercenary motives to disguise their greed and their violence" (Constant, *Principles of Politics*, chap. 9, in *Political Writings*, 240).

47. *Oeuvres*, 1004; *Political Writings*, 64. He also noted, in defense of the French people, that their failure to condemn Napoleon's conquests "is in fact simply the effect of the terror [they] experienced" rather than genuine enthusiasm for his exploits (*Oeuvres*, 985; *Political Writings*, 45).

48. *Oeuvres*, 1010; *Political Writings*, 70.

49. *Oeuvres*, 1003–4; *Political Writings*, 64.

50. *Oeuvres*, 1014; *Political Writings*, 73.

51. *Oeuvres*, 1015–16; *Political Writings*, 74–75.

52. He defends this position not with a well-theorized argument about how one might identify universally objectionable injustices, but with a quip: "Those who appeal to habit in order to excuse injustice remind me of that French cook who was reproached for making eels suffer when she skinned them. 'They are used to it,' she said, 'I have been doing it for thirty years!' " (Constant, *Oeuvres*, 1016n; *Political Writings*, 75 n. 1).

53. Like Burke (as well as Smith, as we have seen), Constant asserted the basic agreement of all societies on fundamental moral and political principles: "The happiness of societies and the security of individuals rest upon certain positive and immutable principles. These principles are true in all climates and latitudes. They can never vary, whatever the extent of the country, its mores, its beliefs, its usages. It is incontestable in a hamlet of twenty huts, as in a nation of thirty million, that no one must be arrested arbitrarily; [or] punished without being tried according to pre-established laws and following prescribed procedures" (*Principes des politiques* quoting his own *Réflexions sur les constitutions*, 1814, *Oeuvres*, 1099).

54. Constant maintains that "this obsession with uniformity" ultimately destroys the distinctive national character and "original colours" not only of the subjugated peoples but also of the conquerors (*Political Writings*, 78).

55. *Political Writings*, 65 n. 2.

56. *Oeuvres*, 1006; *Political Writings*, 66.

57. The *Spirit of Conquest*, as I have noted, is written in highly general terms, without specific references to any conquered nations, and so it is difficult to say whether Constant had in mind primarily the European countries subjugated by revolutionary and Napoleonic France, or whether he meant to include non-European conquests and colonies such as Egypt and the French Antilles.

58. Holmes, *Making of Modern Liberalism*, 187; Holmes also notes the contrast between Constant's and Condorcet's approaches: "Unlike either Condorcet or Condorcet's conservative critics, Constant embraced 'the modern' cooly, without jubilance or hesitation" (184).

59. The essay was first published in *Mélanges de littérature et de politique* in 1829, though it was probably drafted in 1805 or at the latest 1810; see Lamberti, "De Constant à Tocqueville," 20. Also see the related manuscript, "Du moment actuel & et de la destinée de l'Espèce humaine, ou histoire abrégée de l'égalité," in *Écrits littéraires (1800–1813)*. Lamberti suggests that although Tocqueville never mentions Constant in his published works or his correspondence, he may well have read at least this volume of Constant's, which appeared when Tocqueville was twenty-four and reading widely in political thought; the volume's many reflections on the human progression toward ever greater equality have affinities with Tocqueville's own views. Lamberti rightly notes that Constant "appears as a disciple of Condorcet" in the essay, but he fails to register the ambivalence, well treated by Holmes, that pervades most of Constant's thoughts on the subject.

60. Constant opens the essay with the claim that human beings require a belief in progress in order to make sense of the social order and their place in it: only the "system . . . of the perfectibility of the human species," he writes, is "suited to give a goal to our labors, to motivate our researches, to sustain us in our incertitudes, to raise us up from our discouragements" (*Mélanges*, 387).

61. *Mélanges*, 100, 115, 105. Of India, Ethiopia, and Egypt, Constant writes: "The progressive faculty is struck with immobility; everything discovered is prohibited to it; all innovation is sacrilege. The use of that precious art that records thought and transmits it across distances is prohibited as an impiety. . . . With the Greeks, in contrast, freed from the sacerdotal yoke, at least from the heroic times, everything is progressive" (105).

62. Paris, 1825. The essay was written for a "Greek committee" formed by the Société de la Morale Chrétienne (with profits to go to "the Greeks"). It is reprinted in *Benjamin Constant, Publiciste*, 59–68. Constant had been raising the plight of the Greeks in the Chamber for several years before his 1825 "Appel." See, for instance, his speech of March 13, 1822; *Discours*, 2:117, and, later, his longer speech of May 29, 1826. Boris Anelli describes Constant's essay, along with Chateaubriand's 1825 *Note sur la Grèce*, as "la plus haute expression du philhellénisme français" ("La guerre pour l'indépendance," 197). On British liberal arguments for intervention in Greece, see Rosen, *Bentham, Byron, and Greece*; and Schwartzberg, "Lion and Phoenix."

63. Alongside the crusading language are more calculating arguments from commercial advantage: Constant notes that "generous and Christian conduct will open up a rich and prosperous career to French commerce" and that if France leaves heroic action to Britain, it will also relinquish such commercial benefits (*Benjamin Constant: Publiciste*, 64).

64. On Montesquieu's use of such a rhetorical strategy, see Richter, "Europe and the Other."

65. "De M. Dunoyer et quelques-uns de ses ouvrages." Dunoyer (1786–1862) had published *De l'industrie et de la morale dans leurs rapports avec la liberté*, the main text Constant discusses, in 1825. On Dunoyer, see Hart, "Radical Liberalism."

66. Constant adds, that "our philosophers borrowed from the banks of the Orinoco examples intended to make the inhabitants of the banks of the Seine blush" (*Mélanges*, 155–56).

67. *Mélanges*, 135. Constant employs a somewhat tendentious definition of civilization that emphasizes material well-being rather than manners or politesse: "Little does it matter to us that the word *civilization* comes from the word *civitas*; what is certain, is that its meaning has changed along the way. Civilization is no longer, in the thought of its partisans as well as its enemies, uniquely that which makes men more suited to society, but that which procures for members of society a greater sum of pleasures [*jouissances*]. Thus, it must be examined whether this sum of pleasures, becoming each day more precious to conserve, makes us more timid, less disposed to risk that which could make us lose them" (138).

68. Constant, *Mélanges*, 149–50.

69. "Power is too disposed to represent its own excesses, its capricious and willful excesses, as a necessary result of the laws of nature. It is too easy to leap from the recognized inferiority of one race and the superiority of another, to the servitude of the first; and that which philosophy considers just the demonstration of a speculative truth, the colonists have repeated for three hundred years in order to maintain the most illegitimate oppression and the most execrable ferocity" (*Mélanges*, 149).

70. Dismissing faddish theories of racial physiology, Constant notes wryly, "This system [of racial difference] is not necessary for reassuring us as to the possibility of our subjection: for if we possessed no better guarantees, our security would be ill founded. If we do not have the flattened skull of the Kalmuks, our foreheads bend no less easily before power" (151).

71. *Mélanges*, 135. The final sentences read: "Si l'on découvre un jour une recette pour faire marcher de front le perfectionnement désirable et la résistance nécessaire, la découverte sera précieuse. Jusqu'alors, malgré les défauts des opprimés, il sera juste de faire plus large la part du blâme dû aux crimes des oppresseurs."

72. Later in the essay, Constant cites the resistance against Ottoman rule of the nomadic, mountain-dwelling Klephtes of Greece to argue that barbarous peoples resist oppression more effectively than the civilized do (*Mélanges*, 138).

73. *Discours*, 2:291.

74. Constant argued that the Chamber must not approve the government's allocation of funds to Martinique as long as the colonial government violated the

rights of blacks. "Sur les déportés de la Martinique," July 16, 1824, *Discours*, 2:289–300; also see 2:301–5 and 490–98.

75. Constant described the pamphlet as containing "only very moderate representations against the pretensions of those who would deprive men of color the rights that our kings had accorded them, rights sanctioned by several centuries, and which have never been threatened except under the successors of Louis XIII and Louis the XIV, by corrupted or mistaken ministers" (*Discours*, 2:291–92).

76. The speech found by the authorities was by M. Lainé de Villevêque; at this point in his narrative, Constant is interrupted by cries, perhaps ironic, of "Oui, oui! Un discours incendiaire!" (*Discours*, 2:294).

77. Speech of June 3, 1826, *Discours*, 2:495.

78. The death of Louis XVIII in September 1824 and his replacement by Charles X further increased the power of the right-wing *ultras*. In January 1825, Constant gave a second long speech on the Martinique *déportés*, in which he made the following appeal: "Can we, in a Chamber of Deputies, in a French Chamber, regard as unimportant that which concerns the security and the life of the citizens?" (*Discours*, 2:302).

79. "Alger et les élections," *Le Temps*, June 20, 1830; *Positions de combat*, 190–92. Constant insisted that the episode was "an affair of honor" between the dey of Algiers and Charles X. Also see Wood, *Benjamin Constant*, 246–48 on Constant's political activities in these final months. The Charter of 1814 was the frame of government during the Bourbon Restoration, effective through 1830.

80. "Alger et les élections," *Positions de combat*, 191–92.

81. In a conversation with Nassau Senior after Tocqueville's death (*OC* 6.2:514).

82. In addition to the writings of Desjobert discussed below, for excerpts from anticolonialist speeches in the Chamber of Deputies by Desjobert, Xavier de Sade, Dupin, and Duvergier de Hauranne, between 1830 and 1841, see Merle, *L'Anticolonialisme européen*, 283–90.

83. Robert, *Dictionnaire des parlementaires français*, "Desjobert."

84. "The idea of colonizing Algiers could have been born from nothing but the most complete ignorance of the simplest notions of political economy, and by oblivion of the colonial events that have occurred across the globe. . . . [T]he colonial regime cannot be introduced into Africa at the moment that it is collapsing everywhere, to the unanimous acclamation of colonies and metropoles" (Desjobert, *L'Algérie en 1846*, 8).

85. Despite Tocqueville's characterization, Desjobert's tone is sober and straightforward rather than polemical.

86. See Desjobert, *La Question d'Alger*, 2–6, 50, 70ff. On some other common sources on Algeria for Frenchmen of the 1830s, see Lorcin, *Imperial Identities*, 102–8.

87. Denouncing those who sought to repeat in Algeria the crimes of America's Europeans conquerors, Dejobert quoted Tocqueville—"one of our most enlightened theorists [*publicistes*]"—on the ruin of the Native Americans, whose "implacable prejudices . . . uncontrolled passions, and still more, perhaps, their savage virtues, consigned them to inevitable destruction" (Desjobert, *La Question d'Alger*, 62).

88. "Africa is the ruin of our finances, the incessant cause of our annual deficit" (Desjobert, *L'Algérie en 1846*, 25).

89. On France's ill-fated efforts to install the urban poor in Algeria as homesteaders, see Heffernan, "Parisian Poor."

90. The Ottomans in Algeria "did not, as we did, proclaim colonization, that is, they did not threaten the natives with dispossession of the land they cultivated; and, to put such an unfortunate idea into execution, they did not bring from Asia Minor farmers who did not know how to farm at home; they did not bring from Smyrna or Constantinople townsmen who had never seen a field; they did not conjure up a swarm of speculators, who, in the midst of the terror inspired by their power, would have bought the natives' country, en masse and without understanding [*connaître*] it, with that laudable intention of selling it back bit by bit at a premium, always under the influence of their protection" (Desjobert, *La Question d'Alger*, 89). As we shall see in the next chapter, Tocqueville, too, eventually came to criticize the dispossession of indigenous farmers and the wild speculation in property occasioned by the conquest.

91. As we saw in chapter 5, James Mill was one such thinker, believing empire economically prejudicial to the colonizing country but worthwhile for the sake of the backward Indians. Also see Semmel, *Free Trade Imperialism*; and Stokes, *English Utilitarians and India*, 38–40 and 323, who quotes such pamphlets as *The Happy Era of One Hundred Millions of the Human Race, or the Merchant, Manufacturer, and Englishman's Recognised Right to an Unlimited Trade with India* (1813). Such pamphlets supported Britain's rule of India but argued that it should be limited, in Stokes's words, "to the efficient provision of law and order."

92. Desjobert, *L'Algérie en 1846*, 105.

93. Desjobert, *La Question d'Alger*, 1.

94. Desjobert, *La Question d'Alger*, 3. In his account of the sixteenth-century obsession with Eldorado, Desjobert may be drawing on Smith's *Wealth of Nations* (see *WN* IV.vii.a.19).

95. Founder of the Compagnie d'Occident (later the Compagnie des Indes), Law had been forced to flee France in 1720 after his project to develop French territories along the Mississippi River led to frenzied speculation and eventually financial collapse.

96. Desjobert, *La Question d'Alger*, 6.

97. Desjobert did seriously consider the economic and military merits and feasibility of colonization, providing a thorough account of French military expeditions from 1830 to 1836; he made clear that he wrote this history in opposition to the account provided in the *Moniteur algérien*, the official colonial journal, which he considered a settlers' rag (see *La Question d'Alger*, 14–15).

98. Desjobert, *La Question d'Alger*, 8.

99. "I do not think France can think seriously of leaving Algeria. In the eyes of the world, such an abandonment would be the clear indication of our decline [*décadence*]" (*OC* 3.i 213; *Empire and Slavery*, 59–60). Desjobert did argue that national pride would be wounded by complete abandonment of relations with Algeria, and that it would be honorable and advantageous for France to continue to influence the civilization of North Africa, and just for France to hold on to several maritime posts.

100. *Democracy* I, pt. 2, chap. 3. Tocqueville developed these thoughts further in the chapter called "Why Great Revolutions Will Become More Rare," in which he argued that it was precisely equality of conditions that led to steady public opinion and hence a stable political structure. In the second volume he would claim, "As conditions grow more equal, and men individually become less strong, they increasingly let themselves glide with the current of the crowd and find it hard to maintain alone an opinion abandoned by the rest" (*Democracy* II, *OC* 1.2:120–21; Lawrence, 520). I cite the Lawrence translation of *Democracy in America* throughout, with some modifications to the translations.

101. Desjobert insists that the French face the truth of their crimes: "The only logical thing to do in seizing the country in order to plant a European population there, was the destruction of the indigenous population. Whatever color one gives to this fact, with whatever veil one covers it, it is still extermination" (*L'Algérie en 1846*, 21).

102. Desjobert, *La Question d'Alger*, 307.

103. Desjobert, *La Question d'Alger*, 306ff. The advantages for France in his system would be, he claimed, continued suppression of piracy; peaceful possession of two or three coastal points that could be useful during a maritime war; greatly reduced expenses; the prospect of advantageous commerce in Africa; and "the glory for France, in propagating civilization, of doing something honorable for herself" (327–28). Note his adherence to a form of Condorcet's vision of pacific, civilizing settlement.

104. Desjobert, *L'Algérie en 1846*, 91.

105. Desjobert's remarks about Abdelkader suggest, nonetheless, a belief in the superiority of European civilization: he writes that Abdelkader "was the progressive man of his times. . . . His organizational genius began by centralizing Arab society, as much as it could be; he wanted to send all of the young people of good families to France to be educated in our civilization, just as the Turks and Egyptians do" (*L'Algérie en 1846*, 114).

106. See, for instance, Desjobert's use of Genty de Bussy, a former civil administrator, who wrote that as the system of extermination was "inadmissible in the current state of our societies, rejected by our mores, and contrary to the sworn faith, to adopt it would make us the bane of Europe and would raise a tide of indignation against us. The French of today would descend from the north, as the Huns and Vandals once did, to massacre several thousand families! No, we could not be cursed enough, if we acted in this way; and if there were not enough room on this land for the natives and for us, it would be wiser to leave it completely to them; our pride might suffer, but our character would be uplifted. . . . We will speak no further of such a system; France can only reject it with scorn" (*L'Algérie en 1846*, 95). Desjobert consistently avoided using such language himself, but he seeded his text liberally with such quotations.

107. *Democracy* I, *OC* 1.1:5, Lawrence, 12.

108. His comments on India are typical of this judgment: "The immense empire of the English in India was established so suddenly and is of such recent date that Europe, struck with astonishment at the sight of such a singular revolution, has had no time to research its causes and study its effects. It did not see and still does not see in this great revolution anything but an inexplicable and almost

marvelous *event*." In the margin he noted, "For those who study the facts attentively, the event remains great, but it ceases to be inexplicable." (*OC* 3.1:443).

109. Scholars have long puzzled over the question why Tocqueville never cited Constant; see Lamberti, "De Constant à Tocqueville." Kelly regards the fact that Tocqueville probably "failed to read [Constant] seriously" as reflective of "a kind of fissure in the culture of liberalism" that was bridged only by later liberals, under the Second Empire and after Tocqueville's death (*The Humane Comedy*, 5–6).

110. On affinities and differences between France's two most prominent nineteenth-century liberals, see Lamberti, "De Constant à Tocqueville"; Holmes, "Constant and Tocqueville"; and Kelly, *The Humane Comedy.*

111. "The liberty of the ancients compared with that of the moderns" (Constant, *Political Writings*, 327).

112. He envisioned modern politics as relegated to representative governments that freed the people from political concerns to pursue their private interests, within nations that eschewed aggression in favor of peaceful, mutually profitable relations with other nations (Constant, *Political Writings*, esp. 318–21).

113. Holmes, "Constant and Tocqueville," 37–38.

114. See Kelly, *The Humane Comedy*, 39–41.

115. He wrote, "I do not wish to speak ill of war: war almost always broadens a people's mental horizons [*pensée*] and elevates its character [*coeur*]. In some cases it alone can prevent the excessive development of certain inclinations naturally produced by equality and must be considered the necessary remedy for certain inveterate diseases to which democratic societies are liable" (*Democracy* II, pt. 3, chap. 22, *OC* 1.2:274; Lawrence, 649).

116. In the early essay, written at J. S. Mill's request, Tocqueville had presented most of the theoretical argument of *The Ancien Régime*; the later work simply filled in the archival details. See "The Social and Political Condition of France," published in the *London and Westminster Review* in April 1836 and translated by Mill (the original essay in French is included in *OC* 2.1).

117. *L'Ancien Régime*, *OC* 2.1: 246; *Old Regime*, 243.

118. August 15, 1840, *OC* 11:89–90.

119. For Tocqueville's indictment (and barbed praise) of Napoleon, see his 1842 induction address to the Académie Française, in *Oeuvres complètes*, ed. Beaumont, vol. 9; also see Richter, "Threats to Liberty" and "Tocqueville, Napoleon, and Bonapartism."

120. See Welch, *De Tocqueville*, chaps. 2–3; and Wolin, *Tocqueville between Two Worlds*, chap. 14.

121. *Democracy* I, pt. 2, chap. 6, *OC* 1.1:245–47; Lawrence, 235–37. Tocqueville fears as well that France does not even have a *tradition* of active citizenship to fall back on during this difficult transition, for the instinctive patriotism of the ancien régime sort, "like all unpondered passions . . . impels men to great ephemeral efforts, but not to continuous endeavour." In the second volume of *Democracy*, Tocqueville similarly identifies the revolutionary instability that follows the transformation of traditional structures of authority between masters and domestic servants: "The lines between authority and tyranny, liberty and license, and right and might seem to them so jumbled and confused that no one knows exactly

what he is, what he can do, and what he should do. Such a condition is revolutionary, not democratic" (*OC* 1.2: 193; Lawrence, 580).

122. *Democracy* I, *OC* 1.1: 246; Lawrence, 236.

123. *Democracy* I, *OC* 1.1: 248; Lawrence, 237.

124. See Tocqueville's 1842 Académie speech, *Oeuvres complètes*, ed. Beaumont, vol. 9.

125. I am grateful to Pratap Mehta for fruitful discussions on this topic.

126. On Tocqueville's belief in the importance of historical memory for national political life, see Smith, *Politics and Remembrance*.

127. As Françoise Mélonio and François Furet have written in their introduction to *The Old Regime*, "For Tocqueville, history was the continuation of politics by other means" (1).

128. From *OC* 15.2: 263. See Boesche, *Strange Liberalism*, 195–96. It is telling that the specific examples Tocqueville provided of such displays of public virtue in France often involved military action rather than domestic political efforts of the kind he applauded in America. The *Souvenirs* are filled with lamentations about the mediocrity of Tocqueville's fellow politicians. Unpracticed in great action, most were, in his view, utterly unprepared to act in the face of the 1848 revolution; "only Lamartine," he wrote, "seemed to have both the standing and the ability to attempt it" (*Recollections*, 49).

129. Tocqueville, *Journey to America*, 217–18. See also the section in *Democracy* I that, not accidentally, follows Tocqueville's discussion of American patriotism: it treats the relationship of virtue and right and claims, "No man can be great without virtue, nor any nation great without respect for rights" (pt. 2, chap. 6, *OC* 1.1: 248; Lawrence, 238). Also see Boesche, *Strange Liberalism*, chap. 11.

130. Like the French nobility as he had described them in 1836, he often seems "more attached to the semblance of power than to power itself" ("Political and Social Condition of France," 142).

131. Tocqueville's ambivalence about the French settlers in Algeria shows, I think, that he did struggle with this question. Having admired the deep engagement in local politics of the American settlers, he clearly hoped that a similar dynamic could be created in Algeria and even that it would stimulate a more engaged politics in France. He found the French settlers he met there selfish and cruel, however, and they only corroborated his early fears that the French national character was unsuited to the creation of stable societies abroad.

132. Constant anticipated this "bread and circuses" argument as well, and he pleaded with national leaders not to bend to the temptation of staging imperial circuses: "When a government lavishes upon us great displays of heroism, of numberless creations and destruction, we are tempted to reply: 'The smallest grain of millet would better suit our business.' The most brilliant feats and their grandiose celebrations are only funeral ceremonies at which we dance upon the graves" (*Political Writings*, 70–71, quoting La Fontaine's "Le Coq et la perle").

133. Letter to Royer-Collard, August 15, 1840, *OC* 11:90; translation from *Selected Letters*, 144.

134. Letter of March 18, 1841, *OC* 6.1: 335; translation modified from *Selected Letters*, 151. This exchange took place in the context of the Eastern Crisis of the early 1840s, a low point in French-British relations, as I discuss in chapter 7.

135. *OC* 6.1: 337–38. Mill himself considered Britain's project of good governance and improvement in India to be a source of national pride for Britain, as I discuss in a later chapter.

136. In a letter of December 23, 1840, to Robert Barclay Fox, *OC* 13:454. Tocqueville's own statement of this view appears in *OC* 6.1: 329–31.

137. *Democracy* I, *OC* 1.1: 331; Lawrence, 316. As Sheldon Wolin has remarked, while in chapter 10 Tocqueville "portrays a society in which violence is deeply woven into its material existence," the rest of the work presents a "sanitized republicanism" (*Tocqueville between Two Worlds*, 266, 271).

138. *Democracy* I, *OC* 1.1: 174, Lawrence, 169; *OC* 5.2: 191. See *Democracy* I, *OC* 1.1: 361–62; Lawrence, 345–46 for Tocqueville's favorable impressions of Ohio industry.

139. Tocqueville wrote the essay "Quinze jours au désert" aboard "the steamboat *The Superior*, begun August 1, 1831" (*Oeuvres*, 1991, 1:360) and in 1840 decided to publish it in the second volume of *Democracy*. When he read it to Beaumont, however, Beaumont predicted that its success would eclipse his own novel, *Marie, ou l'esclavage aux États-Unis*, which drew heavily on the same trip and was published in 1835. According to Beaumont, Tocqueville chose out of loyalty not to publish the manuscript (Pierson, *Tocqueville in America*, 231). The work, which recounts the journey Tocqueville and Beaumont made from Buffalo, through Detroit and Flint, into the newly settled forests of the Michigan Territory, is valuable as a record of Tocqueville's early questions about and reactions to the encounter of expanding Western settlements with vulnerable native peoples. See (*Oeuvres*, 1991, 1:360–413, and, for a translation of the complete text, Pierson, *Tocqueville in America*, 229–89.

140. *Democracy* I, *OC* 1.1: 333–34; Lawrence, 318.

141. See "Quinze jours" (Pierson, *Tocqueville in America*, 234). In the same text Tocqueville quotes one of his American hosts on the Amerindians: "Their race is dying. They are not made for civilization; it kills them" (232). The passivity of this construction—the Indians are killed by "civilization" itself—recurs in Tocqueville's own account.

142. Democracy I, *OC* 1.1: 354; Lawrence, 338 (also see 326).

143. Connolly, *The Ethos of Pluralization*, 171.

144. See *Atala* (first published 1801) and *Les Natchez* in *Oeuvres romanesques et voyages*, and the discussion of Chateaubriand in Thom, *Republics, Nations, and Tribes*, 119ff. Also see Sayre, *Les Sauvages américains*, 125–43, on earlier French contributions to the "noble savage" tradition.

145. See his warnings in the "First Report," *OC* 3.1: 329; *Empire and Slavery*, 147.

146. Tocqueville said of the frontiersmen, "[O]ne read on their lips this half-expressed thought: What is the life of an Indian? That was the general sentiment. In the heart of this society, so *policé*, so prudish, so sententiously moral and virtuous, one encounters a complete insensibility, a sort of cold and implacable egoism when it's a question of the American indigenes. The inhabitants of the United States do not hunt the Indians with hue and cry as did the Spaniards in Mexico. But it's the same pitiless instinct which animates the European race here as every-

where else" ("Quinze jours," translation modified from Pierson, *Tocqueville in America*, 235).

147. *Democracy* I, *OC* 1.1: 355; Lawrence, 339 (translation modified).

148. Democracy I, *OC* 1.1: 352–53; Lawrence, 334–35. He cites the sparse settlement of the state of Georgia, suggesting that in such areas, settlers cannot even take cover behind claims to need the land to sustain themselves.

149. Democracy I, *OC* 1.1: 352; Lawrence, 335.

150. Democracy I, *OC* 1.1: 342; Lawrence, 327. In pointing out similarities between Amerindians and the Germans described by Tacitus, Tocqueville concludes that "amid the diversity of human affairs it is possible to discover a few pregnant facts from which all others derive" (328).

151. Democracy I, *OC* 1.1: 346, 342; Lawrence, 330, 327.

152. Democracy I, *OC* 1.1: 346–47; Lawrence, 330–31. During his visit to Ireland, Tocqueville made a similar observation about the "horrible condition of society" that results from conquest by a "civilized" over a "half barbarous" people. See Hereth, *Alexis de Tocqueville*, 158–59; and Drescher, *Dilemmas of Democracy*, 195.

153. Democracy I, *OC* 1.1: 348; Lawrence, 332; also see Lawrence, 328. It is striking that for his portrait of "savage" life Tocqueville seems to rely heavily on the captivity narrative of (and his own encounter with) John Tanner, a European who lived for thirty years with an indigenous tribe.

154. Democracy I, *OC* 1.1: 342; Lawrence, 326.

155. He notes that the "destructive influence of civilized nations on others less civilized can be observed among the Europeans themselves," citing the impoverishment and subordination of French and Spanish settlers in regions dominated by Anglo-Americans (Lawrence, 333).

156. See Conklin, *A Mission to Civilize*, and Pyenson, *Civilizing Mission*. Although Pyenson's subtitle suggests that the French had undertaken their *mission civilisatrice* with the conquest of Algiers, his argument is largely confined to the later period and also to the sciences rather than to a more general mission of cultural tutelage.

157. "A Few Words on Non-intervention," *CW* 21.119.

158. See chapter 5 above, and Mehta, "Liberalism, Nation, and Empire."

159. *Democracy* I, *OC* 1.1: 339; Lawrence, 324. Later Tocqueville emphasizes that it was precisely the breakdown of communal attachments that led to the barbarization of Amerindians: "In weakening among the North American Indians the sentiment of attachment to their country [*le sentiment de la patrie*], in dispersing their families, in obscuring their traditions, in interrupting the links of memory, in changing all their customs [*habitudes*], and in increasing their needs beyond measure, European tyranny rendered them more disorderly and less civilized than they were before. The moral and physical condition of these peoples continually grew worse, and they became more barbarous as they became more wretched. Nevertheless, the Europeans have not been able completely to change the character of the Indians; and though they have had power to destroy, they have never been able to subdue and civilize [*policer*] them" (*OC* 1.1: 333; Lawrence 318).

160. The French were to use similar arguments in Algeria to declare thousands of hectares of communal grazing land "empty" and legally open for appropriation

by the state (under the "common-law principle that 'les biens sans maître sont à l'état' "), which then sold them to individual colonists. See Ruedy, *Modern Algeria*, 70. In the "Second Letter on Algeria," Tocqueville himself noted without discomfort that because the Arab population in Algeria was sparsely settled, they "sell the land easily and at a low price, and . . . a foreign population can establish itself next to them without trouble and without causing them to suffer" (*OC* 3.1: 151). For the use of Lockean arguments (based on chapter 5 of *Second Treatise*) to justify expropriation of Amerindians see Arneil, *John Locke and America*. William Connolly offers a sophisticated version of the claim that Tocqueville himself accepted expropriation on such grounds; but he does not acknowledge Tocqueville's explicit repudiation of the argument (see Connolly, *The Ethos of Pluralization*, 168–69).

161. Pierson, *Tocqueville in America*, 596. "The world belongs to us," say the "honest citizens" Tocqueville meets in Buffalo, as he recounts in "Quinze jours." "God, in denying its first inhabitants the faculty of civilizing themselves, has predestined them to inevitable destruction. The true proprietors of this continent are those who know how to take advantage of its riches. Satisfied with his reasoning, the American goes to the temple where he hears a minister of the gospel repeat to him that men are brothers" (Pierson, *Tocqueville in America*, 235).

162. *Democracy* I, *OC* 1.1: 350; Lawrence 334–35.

163. *Democracy* I, *OC* 1.1: 350; Lawrence, 334–35, 338, and 339 n. 29

164. *Democracy* I, *OC* 1.1: 354; Lawrence, 338.

165. Connolly, "Pluralism," 56.

166. Also see Welch, "Colonial Violence."

167. Others, too, hoped that Algeria might offer France an opportunity to rival Anglo-American achievements; General Clauzel, given the Algerian command shortly after the July Revolution, declared in an 1835 proclamation, "By force of perseverance, we shall create a new people who will grow even more rapidly than those established on the other side of the Atlantic" (Collingham, *The July Monarchy*, 250).

168. See "Some Ideas about What Prevents the French from Having Good Colonies" (*OC* 3.1: 35–40; *Empire and Slavery*, 1–4; also see *Democracy* I, *OC* 398 n. 19, 345 n. 17; Lawrence, 333 n. 19 and 329 n. 17, where Tocqueville describes the French in America as "the most dangerous denizens of the wilderness"). In this judgment, Tocqueville follows earlier French portraits of the French as hopeless colonizers (see, for instance, Raynal's *Histoire des Deux Indes*, IV.15).

Chapter 7
Tocqueville and the Algeria Question

1. "Debate of 1846," *OC* 3.1: 298; *Empire and Slavery*, 123.

2. See Chevallier and Jardin, introduction, 12–13; the questionnaire is undated, but the editors surmise it dates to around 1833.

3. On Tocqueville's early electoral bids, see Jardin, *Tocqueville*, 279–96. Jardin notes the significance of Tocqueville's choice to write about Algeria as he formally entered elective politics. The letters on Algeria were published in the *Presse Seine*

et Oise, a newspaper he played a small part in running. No copies of the printed articles exist, and so our sources for these pieces are Tocqueville's manuscripts. The articles were anonymous by custom, but their authorship was widely known (Jardin, *Tocqueville*, 320). Also see Jardin, "Tocqueville et l'Algérie."

4. *Le Moniteur universel* announced their arrival in Algiers in May 1841; see *OC* 5.2: 199; and Lawlor, *Tocqueville in Chamber of Deputies*, 133.

5. Tocqueville has been called one of the "artisans of [France's] colonial renaissance" (Valet, *L'Afrique du Nord*, 145).

6. See Lively, *Social and Political Thought*, chap. 7, and especially Tocqueville's remark, "I think that there is no one in France less revolutionary than myself, or anyone who has a deeper hatred for what is called the revolutionary spirit (which spirit, in passing, combines very easily with a lover of absolute government)," quoted by Lively, 204, from a letter to Eugène Stoffels (October 5, 1836). Lively argues that it was one of Tocqueville's "main concern[s] to detach the liberal movement from its revolutionary leanings" (205). It was precisely the belief that good mores could grow out of a new society if it was well organized that lay behind Tocqueville's enthusiasm for these projects: witness his discussion of township government in New England (*Democracy* I, pt. 1, chap. 5).

7. Letter to Francisque (Claude) Corcelle of September 26, 1840, *OC* 15:151.

8. Letter to Corcelle of October 10, 1846, *OC* 6.2: 127; also see Chevallier and Jardin, introduction, 32. Corcelle's own concern about the effects of the conquest on indigenous Algerians seems to have impressed itself upon Tocqueville, for his letters to Corcelle include some of Tocqueville's most thoughtful and ambivalent remarks on the subject. See also his letter from Algiers of December 1, 1846: "Not having you along, I tried at least to make up for your absence by asking a lot of questions to do with that great side of the African affair that occupies you so much, the maintenance of the indigenous race in the face of our own. I brought back this general notion, that, for the rest, I already had: that it is not only cruel, but absurd and impracticable, to try to force back or exterminate the natives; but through what means could the two races really be brought into contact? I confess with sorrow [*chagrin*] that my mind is troubled and hesitates. . . . Whatever happens, we can be sure that our proximity will create a social revolution among the Arabs, with troublesome effects" (*OC* 15:224).

9. See Lively, *Social and Political Thought*, chap. 2, especially 42ff., for a discussion of Tocqueville's beliefs about the moral import of historical and sociological study. "I wanted to discover not only what illness killed the patient, but how the patient could have been cured," Tocqueville wrote in the preface to the *Ancien Régime*. "My purpose has been to paint a picture both accurate and instructive" (*Old Regime*, 86; Lively, 29).

10. "All those who now wish to establish or secure the independence and dignity of their fellow men must show themselves friends of equality; and the only worthy means of appearing such is to be so. . . . Thus, the question is not how to reconstruct an aristocratic society, but how to make liberty proceed out of that democratic state of society in which God has placed us" (*Democracy* II, pt. 4, chap. 7, *OC* 1.2: 328; Lawrence, 695).

11. George Frederickson has argued that Tocqueville believed that the "civilization of Africa and Asia by Europeans was the . . . next great step in the progress

of the human race" (Comparative Imagination, 113). But Tocqueville never shared the unalloyed confidence of his British liberal contemporaries that such a civilizing project was politically possible or even wholly desirable.

12. Tocqueville himself recognized that some of his views would be ascribed to latent sympathy for the old-regime aristocracy, but he denied the bias, perhaps too confident in his intellectual independence: "Democratic or aristocratic prejudices are alternatively attributed to me; I would perhaps have had one or the other had I been born in another century and country. But accident of birth has left me free to defend both. . . . The aristocracy was already dead when I was born, and democracy had not yet come into being. My instincts could not therefore be drawn blindly toward either one or the other," he wrote in a letter to his friend and future translator Henry Reeve (March 22, 1837, OC 6.2: 37–38).

13. Cheryl Welch has offered a psychologically subtle reading of Tocqueville's violations or evasions, in his treatments of Algeria, of many of his own moral commitments and intuitions, and his "efforts to make colonial violence absent to his imagination" ("Colonial Violence," 257). She argues compellingly that his strategies of evasion and modes of self-deception are characteristic of a weakness in liberalism more broadly, in that when liberals experience guilt over the commission of violence, having few means of justifying it explicitly, they resort to "more subtle means of psychic insulation."

14. November 27, 1857, *Oeuvres complètes*, ed. Beaumont, 6:422; *Selected Letters*, 359. Todorov quotes the second sentence of this passage, but in ignoring the rest of the letter, he overstates Tocqueville's belief that European imperialism was a civilizing project, even while he concedes that in the cases Tocqueville knew well, he did not believe that civilization had occurred in practice (Todorov, *On Human Diversity*, 194).

15. He recommended that the British Parliament abolish the East India Company and assume direct administrative responsibility for the country: as his antislavery articles suggest, Tocqueville believed that the greatest problems of colonial government stemmed from a lack of metropolitan interest in the colonies.

16. *Oeuvres complètes*, ed. Beaumont, 6:422–23; *Selected Letters*, 359–60. Tocqueville's letters to English correspondents consistently display a tone rather different from that of all his other writings on empire: these letters treat empire as a *collective* European (or Christian) project and emphasize its civilizing aspect.

17. This last explanation, which I discuss further below, is offered by Todorov in *On Human Diversity*, 202ff., and supported by Dion, "Durham et Tocqueville," 63.

18. "Second Letter," OC 3.1: 151; *Empire and Slavery*, 24.

19. See Tocqueville's letter to Beaumont of August 9, 1840, OC 18:420–21.

20. "First Letter," OC 3.1: 138; *Empire and Slavery*, 12.

21. See Liebersohn, "Discovering Indigenous nobility," and *Aristocratic Encounters*, for compelling treatments of Tocqueville as one of many postrevolutionary Europeans who, in contrast to their prerevolutionary forebears, looked to indigenous societies for examples of nobility and social distinction rather than as models of democracy, equality, or anarchy. The affinity Tocqueville felt for such nobility led, Liebersohn argues, to a greater ambivalence about the losses caused by imperial conquest than were felt by "more unequivocal, 'progressive' writers"

of the time. Liebersohn does not discuss the writings on Algeria, in which Tocqueville also identifies a certain nobility in the indigenous peoples (especially the Kabyles and among the religious aristocracy of the marabouts); here, however, a recognition of nobility did not lead to the lamentations about the ravages of empire that we see in the America writings. Some of these differences can be attributed to Tocqueville's stance: unresponsible observer in America, who could afford a tone of nostalgia or elegy; and government strategist for Algeria, who did not have that luxury.

22. *OC* 3.1: 152–53; *Empire and Slavery*, 26. Throughout this discussion Tocqueville made clear his desire to see the Algerian population protected by law, but he never used the language of justice or of indigenous rights to legal guarantees or political participation.

23. See *Democracy* I, *OC* 1.1: 350–51; Lawrence, 335.

24. See, for instance, notes made probably in 1842, when Tocqueville wrote, "I do not believe that the amalgamation of the two races is possible" (*OC* 3.1: 290). Conklin notes that the initial support among French commentators generally for intermarriage between French and Algerians dissolved in the early decades of the conquest (*Mission to Civilize*, 20–21).

25. "Second Letter," *OC* 3.1: 141; *Empire and Slavery*, 16.

26. See Lorcin, *Imperial Identities*, for a thorough analysis of the "Kabyle myth" in French thought, its role in nineteenth-century French racial theories, and its consequences for both the military and the civilian administration of Algeria. The crux of the myth lay in the binary contrast between Arabs (who were cast as fanatical, nervous, and weak) and Kabyles (seen as secular, vigorous, and honorable, and as appropriate allies for the French). Lorcin argues that by the 1850s what had begun as a rough Arab-Kabyle dichotomy hardened into the Kabyle myth, with a pseudoscientific apparatus and the active participation of ethnological and anthropological societies.

27. *OC* 3.1: 131; *Empire and Slavery*, 6–7.

28. See Tocqueville's "Notes on the Koran," *OC* 3.1: 154–62; *Empire and Slavery*, 27–35, especially his notes on chaps. 8 and 9.

29. "Second Letter," *OC* 3.1: 148; *Empire and Slavery*, 22.

30. "Second Letter," *OC* 3.1: 143–44; *Empire and Slavery*, 17–18. Tocqueville added that "after 300 years [the Arab population] is reawakening and acting under a national leader" (*OC* 3.1: 145; *Empire and Slavery*, 19).

31. "Second Letter," *OC* 3.1: 143; *Empire and Slavery*, 17.

32. On the marabouts' political role during the chaotic period of the French conquest, see Clancy-Smith, *Rebel and Saint*, 65–92.

33. "Essay on Algeria," *OC* 3.1: 220; *Empire and Slavery*, 64.

34. In 1841, Tocqueville recommended the total destruction of any nascent Arab political life, arguing that the French should "destroy everything that resembles a permanent aggregation of population, or, in other words, a town. I think it is of the greatest importance not to let any town remain or rise in Abd-el-Kader's domain" ("Essay on Algeria," *OC* 3.1: 229; *Empire and Slavery*, 72).

35. "Second Letter," *OC* 3.1: 151; *Empire and Slavery*, 24.

36. *OC* 5.2: 192; *Empire and Slavery*, 37; "wilderness" is in English. In a letter to his wife on May 9, quoted by his French editor, Tocqueville wrote, "Beyond

the last outposts, war and desert begin. I say desert in the sense of *wilderness* and not desert." For the complete letter, see OC 14:419.

37. Entry of May 7, 1841, *OC* 5.2: 191; *Empire and Slavery*, 36. Timothy Mitchell argues that Tocqueville, like other European visitors of Middle Eastern societies in his day, too readily took the "visible exterior" of Algiers to be "a representation of the invisible *vie intérieure*" (*Colonising Egypt*, 56–58).

38. *OC* 5.2: 192; *Empire and Slavery*, 37.

39. As Tocqueville was to report in 1847, colonial warfare was more uncertain and thus more vicious than European combat. It was impossible to establish a secure border, so wars at the frontier against an armed populace or colonial rivals were likely to continue indefinitely, with ongoing violence against the population at large. "It is undoubtedly very difficult, we must recognize, to know where to stop in the occupation of a barbarous land. As you ordinarily encounter neither a constituted government nor stable populations, you hardly ever obtain a respected frontier" (*OC* 3.1: 315–16; *Empire and Slavery*, 135).

40. *OC* 3.1: 275; *Empire and Slavery*, 111.

41. *OC* 3.1: 226–27; *Empire and Slavery*, 70.

42. *OC* 3.1: 244; *Empire and Slavery*, 84.

43. *OC* 3.1: 242; *Empire and Slavery*, 83.

44. It has been argued that Tocqueville's experience with West Indian colons during the debates over slavery led him to be wary, when he turned to Algeria, about settlers' "possible excesses . . their independent attitude, and the pressure they would unfailingly place on the government" (Martel, "Tocqueville et les problèmes coloniaux," 382).

45. *OC* 3.1: 274; *Empire and Slavery*, 110.

46. In this preference of property rights to political participation, Tocqueville came far closer to supporting the priorities of the July Monarchy he so disdained than he ever did in debates on domestic politics. For a discussion of the Louis-Philippe's "bourgeois monarchy" and its hostility to extension of suffrage, see Furet, *Revolutionary France*, 340ff.

47. *OC* 3.1: 278; *Empire and Slavery*, 114. Also see Tocqueville's first parliamentary report of 1847, in which Tocqueville draws lessons for Algeria from Lord Durham's report on Canada, which identified as one of the key factors inhibiting settlement in Quebec the difficulty of acquiring property (*OC* 3.1: 333n; *Empire and Slavery*, 148n).

48. "It is clear that social power should be involved in more things, should guide and direct individuals more often in a colony like Algeria than in any other colony I know . . . I only want us not to forget that it should not play a larger part than necessary, and that we must count principally on the free, passionate, and energetic action of individuals for success" (Essay on Algeria, *OC* 3.1: 252; *Empire and Slavery*, 91); also see *Empire and Slavery*, 95–96, for Tocqueville's argument that there is "at once too little and too much centralization" in the administration of Algeria. On James Mill's similar arguments for improving governance by placing responsibility on the shoulders of particular individuals, see Stokes, *English Utilitarians and India*, 73–75.

49. "Notes diverses sur la colonisation de l'Algérie," *OC* 3.1: 291.

50. Under such conditions, he argued, Frenchmen could not be persuaded to colonize even the most fertile provinces of France ("Notes diverses," *OC* 3.1: 291).

51. The Chamber of Deputies followed Beaumont's suggestion to convene a single committee of eighteen (instead of the usual nine) members to consider both questions; Tocqueville was chosen (in preference to Beaumont) to draft both reports. The committee included Beaumont, Corcelle, and Desjobert, among others.

52. "Aujourd'hui, on peut le dire, la société indigène n'a plus pour nous de voile." With the image of the veil, Tocqueville resorts in passing to an orientalist trope more typical of his early writings ("First Report," *OC* 3.1: 309; *Empire and Slavery*, 130). Tocqueville reported that one of the major discoveries of Bugeaud's science was that the indigenous population would continue to be "as hostile to us as they are today," so that "in order for us to remain in such a country, our troops would have be almost as numerous in times of peace as in times of war, for it was less a matter of defeating a government than of subjugating a people" ("First Report," *OC* 3.1: 316–17; *Empire and Slavery*, 135).

53. Because Tocqueville's wife joined him on the second trip and wrote on his behalf to his family, we do not have the rich documentation of his immediate impressions that we do for the first (when Tocqueville himself wrote extensively to his wife as well as to his father and brother Édouard). The most complete account of his tour with Bugeaud was written by a journalist, Bussière, who accompanied them; see "Le Maréchal Bugeaud et la colonisation de l'Algérie," published in the *Revue des deux mondes* in November 1853.

54. "First Report," *OC* 3.1: 322–23; *Empire and Slavery*, 140–41. Tocqueville added, "[W]e can be accused sometimes less of having civilized the indigenous administration than of having lent its barbarity the forms and intelligence of Europe."

55. Indeed, Tocqueville believed it was his role to focus attention on the big questions of imperial conquest, as his colleagues were likely to get lost in the details (*OC* 3.1: 292).

56. "First Report," *OC* 3.1: 323; *Empire and Slavery*, 141). Tocqueville's language echoes earlier French concerns about the counterproductive brutality of the conquest. A royal commission on the condition of the territory, for instance, had in 1834 condemned the destruction of cemeteries, the conversion of mosques into barracks, the seizure of buildings without compensation to their owners, "in contempt . . . of the most fundamental and natural rights of the people. In a word," the commissioners added, "we have outdone in barbarity the barbarians we have come to civilize and complain about our lack of success with them" (cited by Ruedy, *Modern Algeria*, 50).

57. "First Report," *OC* 3.1: 323n; *Empire and Slavery*, 140n.

58. *OC* 3.1: 323; *Empire and Slavery*, 141.

59. See, for instance, his *Correspondence anglaise*, in which he asks his friend Henry Reeve about the effects of warfare with the indigenous people on settlement and wonders whether the state should be involved directly in founding villages for settlers (*OC* 6.1: 93–94). Tocqueville had also learned about indirect governance during his extensive study of the British empire in India, where he believed the British had preserved the most effective elements of the former Mughal adminis-

trative structure (see *OC* 3.1: 456ff.). See Stokes, *English Utilitarians and India*, 310, for the argument that although indirect governance was widespread in the later British colonies in Africa, it was not much practiced in India.

60. "First Report," *OC* 3.1: 319; *Empire and Slavery*, 138.

61. "First Report," *OC* 3.1: 322–24; *Empire and Slavery*, 140–42.

62. Haileybury College, Hertford, founded in 1805 to train civil servants for India, stood at the center of nineteenth-century thinking in Britain about colonial governance as well as at the forefront of utilitarian thought and the new discipline of political economy (T. R. Malthus held the first chair of political economy there, from 1805 to 1834; Sir James Mackintosh also taught at Haileybury). See Stokes, *English Utilitarians and India*, 52 and 87. Also see *CW* 30:64.

63. "First Report," *OC* 3.1: 329–30; *Empire and Slavery*, 146.

64. See Drescher, *Tocqueville and England*, for the most thorough account.

65. He wrote to Henry Reeve, for instance, to ask about the use of indigenous versus European armies; the coordination of colonial governance in the metropole; how land is distributed in settlement colonies such as Australia and New Zealand; and how war against the indigenous people affects the prospects for European settlement (see *OC* 6.1: 92–94). In 1847 as the committee for which he was rapporteur was meeting, Tocqueville wrote to Mill to ask about British methods for gaining adequate information about the colonies, and in particular about the instruction for colonial servants at Haileybury College (see *OC* 6.1: 348, letter of April 23, 1847).

66. "The possession of India is onerous from a financial perspective. It costs more than it brings in and would cost even more if they wanted to govern it in its own interest . . . [yet it] is not always by financial and commercial considerations that a people should judge the worth of a conquest" (*OC* 3.1: 478).

67. This was James Mill's position, for instance, as we saw in chapter 5.

68. "Essay on Algeria," *OC* 3.1: 213; *Empire and Slavery*, 59.

69. On the consequent diplomatic crisis, see Pinkney, *Decisive Years*, 128–38; Collingham, *The July Monarchy*, 221–39.

70. The notes and speeches in *OC* 3.2 frequently mention England's and Russia's "natural interests" as being opposed; see, for instance, 315.

71. As J. S. Mill observed in his own essay entitled "The Spirit of the Age," this phrase "is in some sense a novel expression. . . . The idea of comparing one's own age with former ages, or with our notion of those which are yet to come, had occurred to philosophers; but it never before was itself the dominant idea of any age. It is an idea essentially belonging to an age of change. . . . The present times possess this character" (*CW* 32:228).

72. *OC* 3.2: 290; translation from Drescher, *Tocqueville and England*, 156.

73. *Correspondence and Conversations of Alexis de Tocqueville with Nassau William Senior*, 1:23–24. He also said with considerable smugness, "The Eastern question, which you thought and think so much of, has never elicited with us the least interest, except so far as we have feared that it might bring war. . . . Lord Palmerston as not acquired a grain of popularity by his success" (1:22–23).

74. "Essay on Algeria," *OC* 3.1: 213; *Empire and Slavery*, 59.

75. Drescher, *Tocqueville and England*, 161.

76. As he told Lord Hatherton in his letter of November 27, 1857 (*Oeuvres complètes*, ed. Beaumont, 6:423).

77. Tocqueville drew on the English bishop Reginald Heber, whose journals were translated into French in 1830; he quotes Heber's assessment of the English as a "true caste" (*OC* 3.1: 479–80).

78. *OC* 3.1: 448; also see 541 and, at 507, "Proselytism is born not only from the sincerity of belief, but from the idea of the equality of men and above all the unity of the human race."

79. *OC* 6.1: 254; translation from *Selected Letters*, 363.

80. *OC* 6.1: 254; *Selected Letters*, 363–64.

81. *OC* 6.1: 254; *Selected Letters*, 363.

82. See the 1841 "Essay on Algeria" (*Empire and Slavery*, 81–85) and the "Second Report" (174–98). General Bugeaud and the Arab Bureaus insisted that civilian colonization should be strictly controlled, and confined to a strip along the coast, with the area beyond the coastal mountains restricted to military settlement. See Bugeaud, *De la colonisation de l'Algérie* (1847); and Sullivan, *Thomas-Robert Bugeaud*, 142–54.

83. See the "Second Letter on Algeria," *OC* 3.1: 149 and 151; *Empire and Slavery*, 23 and 25. Tocqueville writes, "It is not enough for the French to place themselves next to the Arabs if they do not manage to establish durable ties with them and finally to form a single people from the two races."

84. November 15, 1857, *OC* 6.2: 206.

85. "It is the status quo that will be the loss of the colonies [*qui perdra les colonies*]; every impartial observer recognizes this without trouble. And if there is a way for France to keep them, it will come only from the abolition of slavery" ("L'Emancipation des esclaves," *OC* 3.1: 81; *Empire and Slavery*, 200). French slave colonies at this time included Guadeloupe and Martinique in the Caribbean, Guyana, and Réunion (the former Bourbon) in the Indian Ocean. For more extensive treatments of Tocqueville's views on slavery, see Drescher, *Dilemmas of Democracy*, chap. 6; Gershman, "Tocqueville and Slavery"; Lawlor, *Tocqueville in Chamber of Deputies*, 100–130; and Martel, "Tocqueville et les problèmes coloniaux."

86. Welch, *De Tocqueville*, 173.

87. Other members of the society were Guizot and Odilon Barrot, and later Victor Hugo, Louis Blanc, Lamartine, and General Cavaignac (Blackburn, *Overthrow of Colonial Slavery*, 485–92).

88. As Drescher notes, "The July Monarchy presented a pattern of continuously reiterated consensus on the necessity of abolition and an equally continuous evasion of implementation," as colonists repeatedly, and successfully, sought delays and postponements (*Dilemmas of Democracy*, 170–71).

89. On Tocqueville's view of race and his exchange with Gobineau, see Richter, "Debate on Race"; Frederickson, *The Comparative Imagination*, chap. 6; Resh, "Tocqueville and the Negro"; and Stokes, "Tocqueville and Racial Inequality." On currents of racism in French thought during this period, see Staum, *Labeling People*.

90. Letter of November 17, 1853, *Correspondance Tocqueville-Gobineau*; translation in *The European Revolution*, 227.

91. Also see Drescher, *Dilemmas of Democracy*, 174, and Jardin, "Tocqueville, Beaumont, et le problème de l'inégalité."

92. Frederickson, *The Comparative Imagination*, 105–7.

93. In *Democracy*, Tocqueville wrote, "I do not think that the white and black races will ever be brought anywhere to live on a footing of equality" (OC 1.1: 372; Lawrence, 356). He added that whether southern whites continued to refuse emancipation, or granted it, "great misfortunes are to be anticipated. If freedom is refused to the Negroes in the South, in the end they will seize it themselves; if it is granted to them, they will not be slow to abuse it" (OC 1.1: 379; Lawrence, 363). Such passages make clear why it was that, as Drescher has noted, Tocqueville's and Beaumont's works on America "furnished ample material for the spokesmen of the anti-abolitionists in France" (*Dilemmas of Democracy*, 177).

94. "I am so convinced that the increasing indifference of the nation for its tropical possessions is now the greatest and so to speak the only obstacle that prevents emancipation from being seriously undertaken that I shall believe the cause of emancipation vindicated the day that the Government and the country are convinced that keeping the colonies is necessary for the strength and greatness of France" (*Siècle* essay, OC 3.1: 84; *Empire and Slavery*, 203).

95. "L'Emancipation des esclaves," OC 3.1: 79; *Empire and Slavery*, 199.

96. "L'Emancipation des esclaves," OC 3.1: 84; *Empire and Slavery*, 203.

97. *Siècle* essay, OC 3.1: 88–89; *Empire and Slavery*, 203

98. *Siècle* essay, OC 3.1: 83, 93–94; *Empire and Slavery*, 202, 211–12.

99. *Siècle* essay, OC 3.1: 84; *Empire and Slavery*, 203.

100. "L'Emancipation des esclaves," OC 3.1: 102–3; *Empire and Slavery*, 219.

101. Tocqueville defended such restrictions on land purchase as beneficial, ultimately, for the freed slaves themselves, since the collapse of the sugar economies of the colonies, he argued, would be disastrous not only for the white planters but for all residents of the colonies. He also argued that these restrictions were justified in that they were simply a means of "placing [freed blacks] artificially in the position in which the European worker finds himself naturally," given the far higher cost of land in Europe.

In 1829, Edward Gibbon Wakefield, an Englishman with family connections to thinkers such as Ricardo and the Mills, had made a similar argument about the need to prevent laborers in the colonies from buying cheap land. He claimed, in *A Letter from Sydney*, that many past efforts at colonization had failed because colonial lands had been so inexpensive that laborers were able to buy their own lands, leaving the owners of capital unable to hire laborers. "The result was disastrous, since the most productive farming required the proper combination of labor and capital," as Bernard Semmel comments. The only alternative to slavery, Wakefield believed, was to set a high price on colonial lands, through "systematic colonization." See Semmel, "Philosophic Radicals and Colonialism," 514. Tocqueville's familiarity with British debates about colonization makes it likely that he had read of this well-known argument.

102. Drescher, *Dilemmas of Democracy*, 181.

103. In the case of abolition, Tocqueville justified unequal legal and political rights as necessary as well for the well-being of the freed slaves, because their lives too ultimately would depend on the health of the colonial economies, because they were still vulnerable to abuse by their former masters, and because the experience of servitude had left them in need of greater guidance and control from the state than white citizens required (*Siècle* essay, *OC* 3.1: 102–4; *Empire and Slavery*, 219–20).

104. As Melvin Richter has written in his excellent article on the subject, "Tocqueville conspicuously failed to apply to the French action in North Africa the sociological insight and ethical awareness he had demonstrated in his study of the United States" ("Tocqueville on Algeria," 363).

105. *Democracy* I, *OC* 1.1: 333; Lawrence, 318.

106. Tocqueville distinguished 1789 from 1793, which he associated with the violent overthrow of social and political order. When he insisted that he was not a revolutionary, he spoke of the latter sense. As we have seen in his slavery articles, Tocqueville believed that one of his most important political tasks was to defend the principles of 1789.

107. *Democracy* II, *OC* 1.2: 298–99; Lawrence, 669.

108. *Democracy* I, *OC* 1.1: 379; Lawrence, 363.

109. *OC* 3.1: 227; *Empire and Slavery*, 71. He went on: "I believe that the right of war authorizes us to ravage the country and that we must do it, either by destroying harvests during the harvest season, or year-round by making those rapid incursions called razzias, whose purpose is to seize men or herds" (228).

110. Tocqueville's ministry was occupied primarily with the unstable politics of Europe, particularly in Italy, where Piedmont and Austria were sparring over Lombardy, and where Rome was in revolution.

111. Tocqueville, *Recollections*, 255.

112. Tocqueville, "The Political and Social Condition of France," (1836), 166 (reprinted in *OC* 2.1).

113. Todorov, *On Human Diversity*, 201. Todorov continues, describing the view he attributes to Tocqueville, "Internal liberalism favors . . . the strong and the rich; external liberalism, transformed into nationalism, does the same. Liberalism seeks to guarantee to each individual the free exercise of his abilities; thus, colonizers have the right to colonize" (202).

114. Richter, "Tocqueville on Algeria," 364.

115. While Jardin writes that Tocqueville "did not question the legitimacy of such a conquest, having none of the bad conscience on this matter that people of the twentieth century have" (*Tocqueville*, 318), criticism of empire on either moral or practical grounds, as we have seen, was by no means a twentieth-century development, nor was it foreign to Tocqueville.

116. Hereth argues that Tocqueville "never applied his knowledge of the evil consequences of foreign rule to Algeria" because in this context he adopted an "exclusively French viewpoint," one that demonstrates the "limits of Tocqueville's understanding of politics and freedom" but that also attests to Tocqueville's belief that politics must appeal to the passions of the people (*Alexis de Tocqueville*, 161–62).

117. Tocqueville cited the British abolition of slavery as one great event of his day that suggested that the decadence of his age was not yet total. "We are often unjust toward our times. Our fathers saw such extraordinary things that in comparison with their accomplishments, all those of our contemporaries seem commonplace. Still, the world today offers some great spectacles that would astonish us if we were not weary and distracted" ("The Emancipation of Slaves," *OC* 3.1: 79; *Empire and Slavery*, 199).

118. See especially the 1847 reports, where Tocqueville argues for capping the number of French soldiers in Algeria at the very high figure of ninety-four thousand (*OC* 3.1: 314ff; *Empire and Slavery*, 133). Tocqueville estimated that the European civilian population was one hundred thousand (*OC* 3.1: 341; *Empire and Slavery*, 156). The native (Arab and Kabyle) population was probably about 2.3 million (Ageron, *Modern Algeria*, 4 and 31).

119. "What has made the European family of nations an improving, instead of a stationary portion of mankind?" he asks. "Not any superior excellence in them, which, when it exists, exists as the effect, not as the cause; but their remarkable diversity of character and culture. Individuals, classes, nations, have been extremely unlike one another: they have struck out a great variety of paths, *each leading to something valuable*" (*On Liberty*, *CW* 18:274). This statement of the value of diversity *among nations* is quite rare in Mill's work.

120. Recall his claims in *Considerations* that the Basques and Bretons should be incorporated into the "French nationality" rather than "sulk on [their] own rocks, the half-savage relic of past times" (*CW* 19:549).

121. As Connolly has noted, "Tocqueville provides the model from which most conventional portraits of pluralism are drawn, particularly in the American setting"; he cites Joseph Schumpeter, Robert Dahl, Paul Ricoeur, Isaiah Berlin, and Michael Walzer as examples ("Pluralism," 54).

122. See Lively, *Social and Political Thought*, 33ff.; and Welch, *De Tocqueville*, 28–31.

123. *Democracy* I, *OC* 1.1: 327; Lawrence, 313. Tocqueville gave a somewhat more romantic tone to a similar claim in *Democracy* II, where he argued: "To force all men to march in step toward the same object—that is a human idea. To introduce an infinite variety into actions but to combine them in such a way that all these actions lead by a thousand different paths toward the accomplishment of one great design—that is a divine idea. The human idea of unity is almost always sterile, but that of God is immensely fruitful" (first appendix to part 4; Lawrence, appendix Y, 735).

124. *Democracy* II, pt. 4, chap. 6, *OC* 1.2: 322–23; Lawrence, 690.

125. "à moitié barbare"—see "Essay on Algeria," *OC* 3.1: 229; *Empire and Slavery*, 72.

126. Françoise Mélonio has argued that even if national glory was the primary purpose of colonization, for Tocqueville, his belief in a *mission civilisatrice* and France's special revolutionary calling in particular constituted an element in his justification; she writes that "the imperialist drift which he does not escape, but whose danger he has the merit of perceiving, demonstrates the ambiguity of his quest for grandeur" ("Nations et nationalismes," 70–72).

127. April 12, 1840, *OC* 6.1: 58; translation quoted from *Selected Letters*, 141–42. Tocqueville is referring to British preparations for the Opium War. In a similar spirit, he wrote to Lady Theresa Lewis in October 1857, "Nothing in the world has occurred to equal the conquest, and still more the government of India by the English. Nothing has done more to fix the eyes of mankind on that small island. Do you believe . . . that a people having filled such a vast place in the imagination of mankind can safely withdraw from it? As for me, I do not" (*Oeuvres complètes*, ed. Beaumont, 6:412–13).

Chapter 8
Conclusion

1. Alan Ryan, a self-described "loyal disciple of Mill," offers a subtle critique of liberal progressivism while asserting a chastened and modest commitment to the Millian conviction in "man as a progressive being" ("A Political Assessment of Progress," 95).

2. Alice Conklin demonstrates the power these views continued to exercise over French imperial policy in the late nineteenth century in *A Mission to Civilize*.

3. See Collini, "Idea of Character," 41; and Hall, "Rethinking Imperial Histories," 7; on ideas of eastern Europe as poised between civilization and barbarism that emerged in the late eighteenth century and "acquired the fixed force of formulas" in the nineteenth, see Wolff, *Inventing Eastern Europe*, 13.

4. On the increasing virulence of racism in mid-nineteenth-century Britain see Stepan, *Idea of Race*; Wheeler, *The Complexion of Race*; and Hall, *Civilising Subjects*, chaps. 6 and 7. On race-based arguments for empire in France, see Staum, *Labeling People*. Partha Chatterjee discusses the late-nineteenth-century waning of liberal reformism and the rise of authoritarian conservatism in British colonial policy in *The Nation and Its Fragments*, chap. 2.

5. Although Mill argued forcefully against racist thinkers such as Carlyle (see chapter 5 above), he believed scientific knowledge was not yet advanced enough to prove definitively that race had no role in the development of human character; thus his statements on the subject are often tentative and qualified. See Varouxakis, "Mill on Race," 29.

6. Sankar Muthu, in *Enlightenment against Empire*, has examined a more resolutely anti-imperialist strain of eighteenth-century thought in the works of Diderot, Kant, and Herder; in chapter 6, he details the philosophical connections between Herder's critique of empire and his commitment to the idea of the nation.

7. On the criticisms of others during this period, including Hume and Blackstone, see Armitage, "British Conception of Empire," 100–103.

8. In his perceptive account of Burke, in *Liberalism and Empire*, Uday Mehta appears to portray Burke as unique among eighteenth-century thinkers, rather than situating him in a broader context of imperial critique among both British and continental political philosophers.

9. "Speech in Reply," May 28, 1794; *WS* 7:264.

10. As Alison Dube has noted, Bentham was critical of "hot-headed innovators, full of their own notions, [who] only pay attention to abstract advantage" ("Tree of Utility," 37, quoting a letter from Bentham to John Quincy Adams, *WJB* 10:555).

11. Bentham, *Colonies, Commerce, and Constitutional Law*, 64. Also see Bentham's observation, sparked by the Hastings trial (and discussed in chapter 3), that "[d]istant mischiefs make little impression on those on whom the remedying of them depends" (*WJB* 2:547–48).

12. Burke, "Letter to the Sheriffs of Bristol," *WS* 3:309. Also see the "Speech at Bristol Previous to Election, September 6, 1780; *WS* 3:659.

13. "Speech in Reply," May 28, 1794, *WS* 7:260; "Ninth Report of Select Committee," *WS* 5:204.

14. As I noted in chapter 3, Provost John Hely-Hutchison had sought to establish a limited number of scholarships contingent on work duties, which Burke argued were merely "fresh insults" because Catholics otherwise continued to be excluded from the university. See page 88 above.

15. See Richter, "Comparative Political Analysis" and "The Uses of Theory."

16. I am grateful to Cheryl Welch for helping to clarify this aspect of my argument.

17. As Mill wrote in *Representative Government*, "[S]uch a thing as government of one people by another, does not and cannot exist. . . . if the good of the governed is the proper business of a government, it is utterly impossible that a people should directly attend to it. The utmost they can do is give some of their best men a commission to look after it; to whom the opinion of their own country can neither be much of a guide in the performance of their duty, nor a competent judge of the mode in which it has been performed" (*CW* 19:569).

18. See Hall, "The Nation Within and Without," and Rendall, "Citizenship, Culture, and Civilization." Also see Mandler, "Race and Nation" on some ways in which Victorian thinkers drew on a civilizational narrative in their conceptions of nation building in Britain.

Miles Taylor has recently demonstrated that colonial considerations played an important but very different role in debates leading up to the passage of the first Reform Act in 1832. What was at issue at that time was not the political incapacity of non-European subjects, but rather the representation of British colonial interests, especially West Indian planters and the British East India Company. Tory opponents of the Reform Bill insisted that in abolishing the small two-member boroughs, the bill would end the "virtual representation" of these colonial interests. As Taylor writes, a number of Tories even argued that the Reform Bill "would create a 'tyrannical assembly' over 120 million in the colonial empire unless small boroughs remained open to men with imperial experience and interests" ("Empire and Parliamentary Reform," 295, citing Sir Richard Vyvyan; see *Hansard's Parliamentary Debates*, vol. 3, cols. 642–43, March 21, 1831).

19. See Collini, "Political Theory," 217, "Idea of Character," and *Public Moralists*, chap. 3; Bellamy, *Liberalism and Modern Society*, chap. 1; Rendall, "Citizenship, Culture, and Civilization"; and Hall, "From Greenland's Icy Mountains," 226ff. and *Civilising Subjects*, chap. 7.

20. As Collini has argued, the case for reform "rested heavily upon distinguishing the sober industrious artisan from the feckless, unreliable residuum of un- and under-employed unskilled labor" ("Political Theory," 217). While those calling for women's suffrage disputed the characterization of women as dependent or incapable, they largely accepted that the debate should be one about the character of the potential voters rather than about the right to vote. See Clark, "Gender, Class, and Nation," 240–41.

21. As Jane Rendall has shown, leading suffragists such as Lydia Becker, Barbara Boudichon, and Mill's step-daughter Helen Taylor "owed much to Millite liberalism" and emphasized the independence, intelligence, industry, and respectability of potential female voters. As she notes, "Many suffragists initially shared Mill's distrust of democracy" and supported limits like those he proposed, such as educational qualifications and plural voting. See Rendall, "Citizenship, Culture, and Civilisation," 136–37 and 144; and Collini, "Idea of Character," 46.

22. Catherine Hall has noted the shifting emphasis among figures of the "other" that helped to define Englishness in the period leading up to the Reform Act: from the figure of the slave in abolition debates of the 1830s, to the Indian "mutineer" after 1857, and, in the mid-1860s, the Jamaican black ("From Greenland's Icy Mountains," 216).

23. Frances Power Cobbe, "Criminals, Idiots, Women, and Minors," published in *Fraser's Magazine* in December 1868, 778. Jane Rendall describes Cobbe as "politically closer to the Conservative than to the Liberal party, [though she] allied herself very clearly with a progressive theology" ("Citizenship, Culture, and Civilisation," 142).

24. Cobbe goes on to single out England as the society most favorable to women's rights ("Criminals, Idiots," 791). She also points to imperial power as emblematic of the highest pleasures of the masculine world (792).

25. "Rationale of Representation" (1835), *CW* 18:31–32. Here he suggests excluding those who have received parish relief within the past year, been convicted of a criminal offense, or "been seen drunk, during the year previous." In "Reform of the Civil Service" (1854), Mill again notes the impossibility of devising a test of morals, but he suggests there that tests of intellect will often capture evidence of many moral virtues (*CW* 18:209). Also see "Thoughts on Parliamentary Reform" (1859) (*CW* 19:323). In *Considerations on Representative Government*, Mill suggests disqualifying paupers and nontaxpayers but drops the objection to public drunkards.

26. Mill went on to mention "the more intrinsically valuable member[s] of society" ("Thoughts on Parliamentary Reform," *CW* 19:324).

27. Debate of May 3, 1865, *Hansard's Parliamentary Debates*, vol. 178, cols. 1424–25. Robert Lowe, Viscount Sherbrooke, had lived in Australia in the 1840s and had been opposed to universal male suffrage there. Though a Liberal, Lowe led opposition to Gladstone's 1866 Reform Bill. See Hall, "Rethinking Imperial Histories," 15–16.

28. As for universal suffrage, Mill himself had disparaged "those in whom an *à priori* theory has silenced common sense," who "maintain, that power over others . . . should be imparted to people who have not acquired the commonest and most essential requisites for . . . pursuing intelligently their own interests"—

at a minimum, reading, writing, and basic arithmetic. *Considerations on Representative Government*, *CW* 19:470.

29. *Hansard's, Parliamentary Debates*, vol. 178, cols. 1424–25.

30. "Parliamentary Reform," *CW* 19:327.

31. "Parliamentary Reform," *CW* 19:335.

32. See "Civilization," *CW* 18:128. The essay was published in April 1836, the same month that Mill's translation of Tocqueville's essay "On the Social and Political Condition of France" was published in the *Westminster Review*, and Tocqueville's influence is evident in the essay's concerns.

33. "Civilization," *CW* 18:135. "This torpidity and cowardice," Mill argued, "is a natural consequence of the progress of civilization, and will continue until met by a system of cultivation adapted to counteract it" ("Civilization," *CW* 18:132). Also see Bellamy, *Liberalism and Modern Society*, 27–29.

34. *On Liberty*, *CW* 18:272. Burrow has observed that "the Country Party language of public virtue and Mill's embattled progressive liberalism have a good deal in common; a strenuous moralism and an acute sociological anxiety" (*Whigs and Liberals*, 84).

35. Mill noted that European conformity would not look exactly like China's: it would be imposed by public opinion rather than state authorities, and it would involve not stationariness but surrender to fashion, whether in aesthetics, politics, or morals. Tastes in such matters would change, even rapidly: but individuals would choose and judge based not on their own ideas of the useful or beautiful, but rather in conformity to public opinion.

36. See Kateb, "Reading of *On Liberty*," 62. Kateb argues that Mill must have assumed that only a minority in western European societies "waste their lives" and that even if Mill would have approved of interfering paternalistically in such lives, he believed that "it is better *for others* that a minority be left alone rather than saved against their will."

37. Richard Bellamy has been particularly critical of Mill's effort to marry the idea of autonomy with that of progress, citing Mill's defense of the Poor Law and of state-mandated birth control in overpopulated countries as examples of the "paternalistic potential of Mill's argument." Bellamy argues that "Mill had identified autonomy with acting in accordance with his ideals. As a result, all actions which did not aim at social improvement of the approved kind became *ipso facto* non-autonomous and hence legitimate bases for paternalistic interference" (*Liberalism and Modern Society*, 31).

38. Charles Taylor ("Dynamics of Democratic Exclusion") argues that pressures to exclude vulnerable groups within Europe may have been integral to the process of democratization. Uday Mehta's compelling account of liberal "strategies of exclusion" identifies related philosophical underpinnings of liberal exclusions of non-Europeans, such as "a tacit allegiance to a particular order of society" that belies its ostensible universalism. Mehta, who regards these strategies as characteristic of liberal thought from Locke through the nineteenth century, does not directly connect the liberal exclusion of the nineteenth century to processes of democratization (*Liberalism and Empire*, 58).

39. On the changing and always somewhat uncomfortable alliance between French republican universalism and the racism of the later nineteenth century, see Conklin, *A Mission to Civilize*, 9.

40. Although he believed it was inadvisable to make the governance of India a matter for parliamentary debate and control, Mill believed that the government in India could continue to serve as a model of good colonial governance if civil servants were well trained and the parliament granted considerable autonomy to the colonial authority (*Considerations on Representative Government*, *CW* 19:574–77).

41. Letter to Henry Samuel Chapman, January 7, 1866, *CW* 16:1135–36.

42. *CW* 18:240. The context is Mill's criticism of Evangelicals and their allies in the Indian administration for attempting to mandate Christian instruction in all Indian schools: Mill's concern is clearly in part about the prospect in Britain of "religious persecution" of "all who do not believe in the divinity of Christ" (241), a danger to which he, religiously so unorthodox, was particularly alert. Mill's later intimations that he was horrified by the British reaction even at the time of the rebellion perhaps suggest he felt an obligation as a Company employee not to comment on it.

43. Letter to David Urquhart, October 4, 1866, *CW* 16:1205–6. Of course, the atrocities Mill mentions in India were primarily perpetrated by East India Company officials, rather than English colonial settlers.

44. In the words of a public statement made by the Jamaica Committee under Mill's chairmanship, in 1868 (*CW* 21:433).

45. On the increasing criticism and marginalization of liberal justifications of empire and liberal ideologies of rule in the latter half of the nineteenth century, the ascendancy of notions of cultural difference, and the replacement of the liberal aspiration to assimilate and civilize colonized peoples with new strategies of imperial rule that emphasized "the rehabilitation of so-called native social and political forms," see Mantena, "Crisis of Liberal Imperialism," chapter 6 of "Alibis of Empire."

Bibliography

Primary Sources

Beaumont, Gustave de. *Marie, Ou l'esclavage aux États-Unis, tableau de moeurs américaines*. 2 vols. Paris, 1835.

Bentham, Jeremy. *A Bentham Reader.* Edited by Mary P. Mack. New York: Pegasus, 1969.

———. *Colonies, Commerce, and Constitutional Law: Rid Yourselves of Ultramaria and Other Writings on Spain and Spanish America*. Edited by Philip Schofield. Oxford: Clarendon Press, 1995.

———. *Correspondence of Jeremy Bentham*. Edited by Timothy L. S. Sprigge. 11 vols. London: Athlone Press, 1968–2000.

———. *Economic Writings*. Edited by W. Stark. 3 vols. London: Allen and Unwin, 1952.

———. *Rights, Representation, and Reform: Nonsense upon Stilts and Other Writings on the French Revolution*. Edited by Philip Schofield, Catherine Pease-Watkin, and Cyprian Blamires. Oxford: Clarendon Press, 2002.

———. *Securities against Misrule and Other Constitutional Writings for Tripoli and Greece*. Edited by Philip Schofield. Oxford: Clarendon Press, 1990.

———. *The Works of Jeremy Bentham*. Edited by John Bowring. 11 vols. Edinburgh: W. Tait, 1843.

Bond, E. A., ed. *Speeches of the Managers and Counsel in the Trial of Warren Hastings*. London: Longman, Brown, Green, Longmans, and Roberts, 1859.

Broome, Ralph. *Letters from Simkin the Second, to His Dear Brother in Wales, Containing an Humble Description of the Trial of Warren Hastings, Esq*. London, 1789.

Bugeaud, Thomas Robert. *De la colonisation de l'Algérie*. Paris: A. Guyot, 1847.

Burke, Edmund. *The Correspondence of Edmund Burke*. Edited by Thomas W. Copeland. 10 vols. Cambridge: Cambridge University Press, 1958–78.

———. *The Speeches of the Right Hon. Edmund Burke, in the House of Commons, and in Westminster Hall*. 4 vols. London: Longman, Hurst, Rees, Orme, and Brown, 1816.

———. *Works*. London: John C. Nimmo, 1887.

———. *Writings and Speeches of Edmund Burke*. General editor, Paul Langford. Textual editor, William B. Todd. 9 vols. Oxford: Oxford University Press, 1981–2000.

Bussière, A. "Le Maréchal Burgeaud et la colonisation de l'Algérie: Souvenirs et récits de la vie coloniale en Afrique." *Revue des deux mondes*, November 1853.

Chateaubriand, François-René. *Oeuvres romanesques et voyages*. Edited by Maurice Regard. Paris: Gallimard, 1969.

Cobbe, Frances Power. "Criminals, Idiots, Women and Minors." *Fraser's Magazine* 78 (1868): 777–94.

Condorcet, Marie Jean Antoine Nicolas Caritat, marquis de. *Esquisse d'un tableau historique des progrès de l'esprit humain*. In *Oeuvres complètes de Condorcet*, vol. 8. Paris, 1804.

———. *Oeuvres complètes de Condorcet*, 21 vols. Paris, 1804.

———. *Sketch for a Historical Picture of the Progress of the Human Mind*. Translated by June Barraclough. New York: Noonday, 1955.

Constant, Benjamin. *Appel aux nations chrétiennes en faveur des Grecs*. Paris, 1825.

———. *Benjamin Constant, Publiciste: 1825–1830*. Edited by Ephraïm Harpaz. Paris: Champion, 1987.

———. *Discours de M. Benjamin Constant à la Chambre des Députés*, 2 vols. Paris: J. Pinard, 1828.

———. *Ecrits littéraires (1800–1813)* vol. 3.2 of *Oeuvres complètes*. Edited by Paul Delbouille and Simone Balayé. Tübingen: M. Niemeyer, 1995.

———. *Mélanges de littérature et de politique*. Paris: Pichon et Didier, 1829.

———. *Oeuvres*. Edited by Alfred Roulin. Paris: Bibliothèque de la Pléiade, 1957.

———. *Political Writings*. Edited by Biancamaria Fontana. Cambridge: Cambridge University Press, 1988.

———. *Positions de combat à la veille de juillet 1830: Articles publiés dans "Le Temps," 1829–1830*. Edited by Ephraïm Harpaz. Paris: Champion-Slatkine, 1989.

Dalrymple, John. *An Essay Towards A General History of Feudal Property in Great Britain*. London: A. Millar, 1957.

Desjobert, Amédée. *L'Algérie en 1846*. Paris: Gillaumin, 1846.

———. *La Question d'Alger: Politique, colonisation, commerce*. Paris: Crapelet, 1837.

Diderot, Denis. *Political Writings*. Edited by John Hope Mason and Robert Wokler. Cambridge: Cambridge University Press, 1992.

Dunbar, James. *Essays on the History of Mankind in Rude and Cultivated Ages*. 2d ed. London: W. Strahan, 1781.

Enfantin, Prosper. *La Colonisation de l'Algérie*. Paris: P. Bertrand, 1843.

Ferguson, Adam. *An Essay on the History of Civil Society*. Edited by Fania Oz-Salzberger. Cambridge: Cambridge University Press, 1995.

Guizot, François. *Histoire de la civilisation d'Europe*. Paris: Pichon et Didier, 1828.

———. *Memoirs to Illustrate the History of My Time*. London: Richard Bentley, 1865.

Hansard's Parliamentary Debates. 3d ser. London: HMSO, 1829–91.

Hazlitt, William. *The Spirit of the Age*. London: Henry Colburn, 1825.

Hume, David. *Essays: Moral, Political, and Literary*. Edited by Eugene F. Miller. Indianapolis: Liberty Fund, 1985.

Kames, Henry Home Lord. *Historical Law-Tracts*. London, 1758.

———. *Sketches of the History of Man*. 3d ed. Dublin, 1774.

Mill, James. "Affairs of India." *Edinburgh Review* 16 (April 1810): 128–57.

———. *The Collected Works of James Mill*. London: Routledge, Thoemmes Press, 1992.

———. "Colony." Reprinted from *Supplement to the Encyclopaedia Britannica*. London: Innes, n.d. [1828].

———. *The History of British India*. London: Baldwin, Cradock, and Joy, 1820.

———. *The History of British India*. Edited by H. H. Wilson. 5th ed. 6 vols. London: James Madden, 1858; reprint New York: Chelsea House, 1968.

———. *Political Writings*. Edited by Terence Ball. Cambridge: Cambridge University Press, 1992.

———. "Review of M. de Guignes. *Voyages à Peking, Manille, et l'Ile de France, faits dans l'intervalle des années 1784 à 1804*." *Edinburgh Review* 14 (July 1809): 407–29.

———. "Review of *Sketch of the Political History of India, from the Introduction of Mr Pitt's Bill in 1784*. By John Malcolm (London, 1811)." *Edinburgh Review* 20 (July 1812): 38–54.

———. "Review of *Voyage aux Indes orientales*, by Le P. Paulin De S. Barthélemy, Missionary." *Edinburgh Review* 15 (1810): 363–84.

Mill, John Stuart. *Collected Works*. Edited by J. M. Robson and R. F. McRae. 33 vols. Toronto: University of Toronto Press, 1963–.

———. *The Correspondence of John Stuart Mill and Auguste Comte*. Edited and translated by Oscar A. Haac. London: Transaction, 1995.

Millar, John. *Observations Concerning the Distinction of Ranks in Society*. 2d ed. London: J. Murray, 1773.

———. *The Origin of the Distinction of Ranks*. 4th ed. Edinburgh: W. Blackwood, 1806.

Montesquieu. *The Spirit of the Laws*. Edited and translated by Anne Cohler, Basia Miller, and Harold Stone. Cambridge: Cambridge University Press, 1989.

Mulligan, Hugh. *Poems Chiefly on Slavery and Oppression*. London: W. Lowndes, 1788.

Paine, Thomas. *Political Writings*. Edited by Bruce Kuklick. Cambridge: Cambridge University Press, 1989.

Raynal, Abbé (Guillaume-Thomas-François). *Histoire philosophique et politique des établissements et du commerce des Européens dans les deux Indes*. 3d ed. Neuchâtel: Libraires associés, 1783.

Ricardo, David. *The Works and Correspondence of David Ricardo*. Edited by Piero Sraffa with the collaboration of M. H. Dobb. 11 vols. Cambridge: Cambridge University Press, 1951–73.

Robertson, William. *An Historical Disquisition Concerning the Knowledge Which the Ancients Had of India*. London, 1791.

———. *History of America*. 2 vols. London, 1803.

———. *The History of the Reign of the Emperor Charles V*. 4 vols. London: A. Strahan for T. Cadell Jun. and W. Davies and E. Balfour, 1802.

Rousseau, Jean-Jacques. *Oeuvres complètes*. Edited by Bernard Gagnebin and Marcel Raymond. 5 vols. Paris: Gallimard, 1959–95.

Simmons, R. C., and P.D.G. Thomas, eds. *Proceedings and Debates of the British Parliaments Respecting North America, 1754–1783*. Vols. 4, January–May 1774, and 5, June 1774–March 1775. White Plains: Kraus International Publications, 1985.

Smith, Adam. *Correspondence of Adam Smith*. Edited by Ernest Campbell Mossner and Ian Simpson Ross. Indianapolis: Liberty Fund, 1987.

———. *Essays on Philosophical Subjects*. Edited by W.P.D. Wightman and J. C. Bryce. Indianapolis: Liberty Fund, 1980.

———. *An Inquiry into the Nature and Causes of the Wealth of Nations*. Edited by R. H. Campbell, Andrew S. Skinner and W. B. Todd. 2 vols. Indianapolis: Liberty Fund, 1976.

———. *Lectures on Jurisprudence*. Edited by R. L. Meek, D. D. Raphael, and P. G. Stein. Indianapolis: Liberty Fund, 1982.

———. *The Theory of Moral Sentiments*. Edited by D. D. Raphael and A. L. Macfie. Indianapolis: Liberty Fund, 1982.

Tocqueville, Alexis de. *Correspondence and Conversations of Alexis de Tocqueville with Nassau William Senior*. London: Henry S. King, 1872; reprint (2 vols. in one) New York: Augustus M. Kelley, 1968.

———. *Democracy in America*. Translated by George Lawrence. Edited by J. P. Mayer. New York: Harper and Row, 1966.

———. *"The European Revolution" and Correspondence with Gobineau*. Edited and translated by John Lukacs. Westport, Conn.: Greenwood Press, 1974.

———. *Journey to America*. Translated by George Lawrence. Edited by J. P. Mayer. New Haven: Yale University Press, 1959.

———. "Letter on American Slavery." In *Letters on American Slavery*. Boston: American Anti-Slavery Society, 1860.

———. *Oeuvres*. Edited by André Jardin. 2 vols. vol. 1 also edited by Françoise Mélonio and Lise Queffélec. Paris: Gallimard, 1991.

———. *Oeuvres complètes*. Edited by Gustave Beaumont. Paris, 1860.

———. *Oeuvres complètes*. Edited by J. P. Mayer. Paris: Gallimard, 1958–98.

———. *The Old Regime and the Revolution*. Edited by François Furet and Françoise Mélonio. Translated by Alan S. Kahan. Chicago: University of Chicago Press, 1998.

———. "Political and Social Condition of France." *London and Westminster Review*, April 1836.

———. *Recollections*. Translated by George Lawrence. Edited by J. P. Mayer and A. P. Kerr. New Brunswick, NJ: Transaction, 1995.

———. *Selected Letters on Politics and Society*. Translated by James Toupin and Roger Boesche. Edited by Roger Boesche. Berkeley and Los Angeles: University of California Press, 1985.

———. *Writings on Empire and Slavery*. Edited and translated by Jennifer Pitts. Baltimore: Johns Hopkins University Press, 2001.

Secondary Sources

Adas, Michael. *Machines as the Measure of Man: Science, Technology, and Ideologies of Western Dominance*. Ithaca, NY: Cornell University Press, 1989.

Ageron, Charles-Robert. *Modern Algeria*. Translated by Michael Brett. Edited by Michael Brett. Trenton: Africa World Press, 1991.

Agnani, Sunil M. "Enlightenment Universalism and Colonial Knowledge: Denis Diderot and Edmund Burke, 1770–1800." Ph. D. diss., Columbia University, 2004.

Ahmad, Siraj. "The Theater of the Civilized Self: Edmund Burke and the East India Trials." *Representations* 78 (2002): 28–55.

Alexandrowicz, C. H. "Empirical and Doctrinal Positivism in International Law." *British Year Book of International Law* 47 (1974–75): 286–89.

———. *An Introduction to the History of the Law of Nations in the East Indies.* Oxford: Clarendon Press, 1967.

Anderson, Brian A. "Mill on Bentham: From Ideology to Humanized Utilitarianism." *History of Political Thought* 4, no. 2 (1983): 341–56.

Andrew, C. M., and A. S. Kanya-Forstner. "Centre and Periphery in the Making of the Second French Colonial Empire, 1815–1920." *Journal of Imperial and Commonwealth History* 16, no. 3 (1988): 9–34.

Anelli, Boris. "Benjamin Constant et la guerre pour l'indépendance de la Grèce." *Annales Benjamin Constant* 23–24 (2000): 195–203.

Armitage, David. "The British Conception of Empire in the Eighteenth Century." In *Imperium/Empire/Reich: Ein Konzept politischer Herrschaft im deutsch-britischen Vergleich*, edited by Franz Bosbach and Hermann Hiery. Munich: Saur, 1999.

———. "Edmund Burke and Reason of State." *Journal of the History of Ideas* 61, no. 4 (2000): 617–34.

———. *The Ideological Origins of the British Empire.* Cambridge: Cambridge University Press, 2000.

Arneil, Barbara. *John Locke and America: The Defence of English Colonialism.* Oxford: Clarendon Press, 1996.

Bain, Alexander. *James Mill: A Biography.* London: Longman, Green, 1882.

Baker, Keith Michael. *Condorcet: From Natural Philosophy to Social Mathematics.* Chicago: University of Chicago Press, 1975.

———. Introduction to *Condorcet: Selected Writings*, edited by Keith Michael Baker. Indianapolis: Bobbs Merrill, 1976.

Ball, Terence. "The Formation of Character: Mill's 'Ethology' Reconsidered." *Polity* 33, no. 1 (2000): 25–48.

———. Introduction to *James Mill: Political Writings*, edited by Terence Ball. Cambridge: Cambridge University Press, 1992.

Bastid, Paul. *Benjamin Constant et sa doctrine.* 2 vols. Paris: Armand Colin, 1966.

Baudet, Henri. "Tocqueville et la pensée coloniale du XIXe siècle." In *Tocqueville, Livre du centenaire 1859–1959*, Paris: Editions du Centre National de la Recherce Scientifique, 1960.

Bayly, C. A. *Imperial Meridian: The British Empire and the World, 1780–1830.* London: Longman, 1989.

———. *Indian Society and the Making of the British Empire.* Cambridge: Cambridge University Press, 1987.

Bayly, Susan. *Caste, Society, and Politics in India from the Eighteenth Century to the Modern Age.* Cambridge: Cambridge University Press, 1999.

Bellamy, Richard. *Liberalism and Modern Society.* Oxford: Polity Press, 1992.

———, ed. *Victorian Liberalism: Nineteenth Century Political Thought and Practice.* London: Routledge, 1990.

Benians, E. A. "Adam Smith's Project of an Empire." *Cambridge Historical Journal* 1 (1925): 249–83.

Benot, Yves. Diderot, *De l'athéisme à l'anticolonialisme.* Paris: Maspero, 1981.

Benot, Yves. *La Révolution française et la fin des colonies*. Paris: Éditions la découverte, 1987.

Berlin, Isaiah. "The Thought of de Tocqueville (Review of *The Social and Political Thought of Alexis de Tocqueville*, by J. Lively)." *History* 50 (1965): 199–206.

Berry, Christopher J. *Social Theory of the Scottish Enlightenment*. Edinburgh: Edinburgh University Press, 1997.

Blackburn, Robin. *The Overthrow of Colonial Slavery: 1776–1848*. London: Verso, 1988.

Boesche, Roger. *The Strange Liberalism of Alexis de Tocqueville*. Ithaca, N.Y.: Cornell University Press, 1987.

Boralevi, Lea Campos. *Bentham and the Oppressed*. New York: Walter de Gruyter, 1984.

Bouche, Denise. *Histoire de la colonisation française*. Vol. 2. Paris: Fayard, 1991.

Bourke, Richard. "Liberty, Authority, and Trust in Burke's Idea of Empire." *Journal of the History of Ideas* 63, no. 1 (2000): 453–71.

Bowen, D. *The Protestant Crusade in Ireland, 1800–70*. Dublin: Gill and Macmillan, 1971.

Bowen, H. V. "British Conceptions of a Global Empire." *Journal of Imperial and Commonwealth History* 26, no. 3 (1998): 1–27.

Bowler, Peter J. *The Invention of Progress: The Victorians and the Past*. Oxford: Basil Blackwell, 1989.

Bowles, Paul. "The Origin of Property and the Development of Scottish Historical Science." *Journal of the History of Ideas* 46, no. 2 (1985): 197–209.

Bromwich, David. *A Choice of Inheritance: Self and Community from Edmund Burke to Robert Frost*. Cambridge: Harvard University Press, 1989.

———. "The Context of Burke's Reflections." *Social Research* 58, no. 2 (1991): 313–54.

———. "Culturalism, the Euthanasia of Liberalism." *Dissent*, winter 1995, 89–106.

———. Introduction to *On Empire, Liberty, and Reform: Speeches and Letters*, by Edmund Burke, edited by David Bromwich. New Haven: Yale University Press, 2000.

Brown, Stewart J., ed. *William Robertson and the Expansion of Empire*. Cambridge: Cambridge University Press, 1997.

Bryson, Gladys. *Man and Society: The Scottish Inquiry of the Eighteenth Century*. Princeton: Princeton University Press, 1945.

Burns, J. H. "The Light of Reason: Philosophical History in the Two Mills." In *James and John Stuart Mill: Papers of the Centenary Conference*, edited by J. M. Robson and Michael Laine. Toronto: University of Toronto Press, 1976.

Burrow, J. W. *Evolution and Society: A Study in Victorian Social Theory*. Cambridge: Cambridge University Press, 1970.

———. *Whigs and Liberals: Continuity and Change in English Political Thought*. Oxford: Clarendon Press, 1988.

Bury, J. B. *The Idea of Progress: An Inquiry into Its Origin and Growth*. London: Macmillan, 1920.

Campbell, T. D. *Adam Smith's Science of Morals*. London: George Allen and Unwin, 1971.

Canny, Nicholas. "The Origins of Empire: An Introduction." In *The Oxford History of the British Empire: The Origins of Empire*, edited by Nicholas Canny. Oxford: Oxford University Press, 1998.

Canter, H. V. "The Impeachments of Verres and Hastings: Cicero and Burke." *The Classical Journal* 9 (1913–14): 199–211.

Carlisle, Janice. *John Stuart Mill and the Writing of Character.* Athens: University of Georgia Press, 1991.

Carnall, Geoffrey. "Burke as Modern Cicero." In *The Impeachment of Warren Hastings*, edited by Geoffrey Carnall and Colin Nicholson. Edinburgh: Edinburgh University Press, 1989.

———. "Robertson and Contemporary Images of India." In *William Robertson and the Expansion of Empire*, edited by Stewart J. Brown. Cambridge: Cambridge University Press, 1997.

Carnall, Geoffrey, and Colin Nicholson, eds. *The Impeachment of Warren Hastings*. Edinburgh: Edinburgh University Press, 1989.

Chatterjee, Partha. *The Nation and Its Fragments: Colonial and Postcolonial Histories*. Princeton: Princeton University Press, 1993.

Chevallier, J.-J., and André Jardin. Introduction to *Écrits et discours politiques*, by Alexis de Tocqueville, edited by J.-J. Chevallier and André Jardin. Paris: Gallimard, 1962.

Clancy-Smith, Julia A. *Rebel and Saint: Muslim Notables, Populist Protest, Colonial Encounters: Algeria and Tunisia, 1800–1904*. Berkeley and Los Angeles: University of California Press, 1994.

Clark, Anna. "Gender, Class, and the Nation." In *Re-reading the Constitution: New Narratives in the Political History of England's Long Nineteenth Century*, edited by James Vernon. Cambridge: Cambridge University Press, 1996.

Coats, A. W. "Adam Smith and the Mercantile System." In *Essays on Adam Smith*, edited by Andrew S. Skinner and Thomas Wilson. Oxford: Clarendon Press, 1975.

Cobban, Alfred. *The Nation State and National Self-Determination*. London: Collins, 1969.

Colley, Linda. *Britons: Forging the Nation, 1707–1837*. London: Pimlico, 1992.

———. "A Magazine of Wisdom." *London Review of Books*, September 4, 1997, 3–5.

Collingham, H.A.C. *The July Monarchy: A Political History of France, 1830–1848*. Edited by R. Alexander. London: Longman, 1988.

Collini, Stefan. "The Idea of 'Character' in Victorian Political Thought." *Transactions of the Royal Historical Society*, 5th ser., 35 (1985): 29–50.

———. "Political Theory and the 'Science of Society' in Victorian Britain." *Historical Journal* 23, no. 1 (1980): 203–31.

———. *Public Moralists: Political Thought and Intellectual Life in Britain, 1850–1930*. Oxford: Oxford University Press, 1991.

Collini, Stefan, Donald Winch, and J. W. Burrow. *That Noble Science of Politics: A Study in Nineteenth-Century Intellectual History.* Cambridge: Cambridge University Press, 1983.

Conklin, Alice. *A Mission to Civilize: The Republican Idea of Empire in France and West Africa, 1895–1930*. Stanford: Stanford University Press, 1997.

Conniff, James. "Burke and India: The Failure of the Theory of Trusteeship." *Political Research Quarterly* 46, no. 2 (1993): 291–310.

———. "Edmund Burke's Reflections on the Coming Revolution in Ireland." *Journal of the History of Ideas* 47, no. 1 (1986): 37–59.

———. *The Useful Cobbler: Edmund Burke and the Politics of Progress*. Albany: State University of New York Press, 1994.

Connolly, William. *The Ethos of Pluralization*. Minneapolis: University of Minnesota Press, 1995.

———. "Pluralism, Multiculturalism, and the Nation-State: Rethinking the Connections." *Journal of Political Ideologies* 1, no. 1 (1996): 53–73.

Conway, Stephen. "Bentham and the Nineteenth-Century Revolution in Government." In *Victorian Liberalism*, edited by Richard Bellamy. New York: Routledge, 1990.

———. "Bentham, Benthamites, and the Nineteenth-Century British Peace Movement." *Utilitas* 2 (1990): 221–43.

———. "Bentham on Peace and War." *Utilitas* 1 (1989): 82–201.

Crimmins, James E. "Bentham's Political Radicalism Reexamined." *Journal of the History of Ideas* 55, no. 2 (1994): 259–81.

Danziger, Raphael. *Abd Al-Qadir and the Algerians: Resistance to the French and Internal Consolidation*. New York: Holmes and Meier, 1977.

De Bruyn, Frans. "Edmund Burke's Gothic Romance: The Portrayal of Warren Hastings in Burke's Writings and Speeches on India." *Criticism* 29, no. 4 (1987): 415–38.

Dinwiddy, John. *Bentham*. Oxford: Oxford University Press, 1989.

Dion, Stéphane. "Durham et Tocqueville sur la colonisation libérale." *Journal of Canadian Studies* 25, no. 1 (1990): 60–78.

Dirks, Nicholas B. *Castes of Mind: Colonialism and the Making of Modern India*. Princeton: Princeton University Press, 2001.

Drescher, Seymour. *Dilemmas of Democracy: Tocqueville and Modernization*. Pittsburgh: University of Pittsburgh Press, 1968.

———. *Tocqueville and England*. Cambridge: Harvard University Press, 1964.

Dube, Allison. "The Tree of Utility in India: Panace or Weed?" In *J. S. Mill's Encounter with India*, edited by Martin I. Moir, Douglas M. Peers, and Lynn Zastoupil. Toronto: University of Toronto Press, 1999.

Duchet, Michèle. *Anthropologie et histoire au siècle des lumières*. Paris: François Maspero, 1971.

Dutton, Geoffrey. *The Hero as Murderer: The Life of Edward John Eyre*. London: Collins, 1967.

Einaudi, M. "The British Background of Burke's Political Philosophy." *Political Science Quarterly* 49, no. 4 (1934): 576–96.

Emerit, Marcel. *L'Algérie à l'époque d'Abd-el-Kader*. Paris: Éditions Larose, 1951.

———. *Les Saint-Simoniens en Algérie*. Paris: Les belles lettres, 1941.

Feuer, L. S. "John Stuart Mill as a Sociologist: The Unwritten Ethology." In *James and John Stuart Mill: Papers of the Centenary Conference*, edited by John M. Robson and Michael Laine. Toronto: University of Toronto Press, 1976.

Finley, M. I. "Colonies—an Attempt at a Typology." *Transactions of the Royal Historical Society* 26 (1976): 167–88.

Fontana, Biancamaria. *Benjamin Constant and the Post-revolutionary Mind.* New Haven: Yale University Press, 1991.

———. Introduction to *Constant: Political Writings*, edited by Biancamaria Fontana. Cambridge: Cambridge University Press, 1988.

Forbes, Ducan. "James Mill and India." *Cambridge Journal* 5 (1951): 19–33.

———. "Sceptical Whiggism, Commerce, and Liberty." In *Essays on Adam Smith*, edited by Andrew S. Skinner and Thomas Wilson. Oxford: Clarendon Press, 1975.

———. " 'Scientific' Whiggism: Adam Smith and John Millar." *Cambridge Journal* 7 (1953–54): 643–70.

Frederickson, George M. *The Comparative Imagination: On the History of Racism, Nationalism, and Social Movements.* Berkeley and Los Angeles: University of California Press, 1997.

Frémeaux, Jacques. *Les Bureaux Arabes dans l'Algérie de la conquête.* Paris: Denoël, 1993.

Fuchs, Michel. *Edmund Burke, Ireland, and the Fashioning of Self. Studies on Voltaire and the Eighteenth Century*, vol. 343. Oxford: Voltaire Foundation, 1996.

Furet, François. *Revolutionary France: 1770–1880.* Oxford: Blackwell, 1992.

Germain, Roger. *La Politique indigène de Bugeaud.* Paris: Larose, 1955.

Gershman, Sally. "Alexis de Tocqueville and Slavery." *French Historical Studies* 9, no. 3 (1976): 467–83.

Ghosh, R. N. "John Stuart Mill on Colonies and Colonisation." In *John Stuart Mill: Critical Assessments*, edited by John Cunningham Wood. London: Croom Helm, 1987.

Gibbins, John. "J. S. Mill, Liberalism, and Progress." In *Victorian Liberalism: Nineteenth Century Political Thought and Practice*, edited by Richard Bellamy. London: Routledge, 1990.

Gibbons, Luke. *Edmund Burke and Ireland.* Cambridge: Cambridge University Press, 2003.

Griswold, Charles L. *Adam Smith and the Virtues of Enlightenment.* Cambridge: Cambridge University Press, 1999.

Haakonssen, Knud. "James Mill and Scottish Moral Philosophy." *Political Studies* 33 (1985): 628–36.

———. *The Science of a Legislator: The Natural Jurisprudence of David Hume and Adam Smith.* Cambridge: Cambridge University Press, 1981.

———, ed. *Traditions of Liberalism: Essays on John Locke, Adam Smith, and John Stuart Mill.* St. Leonards, New South Wales, Australia: Centre for Independent Studies, 1988.

Habibi, Don A. *John Stuart Mill and the Ethic of Human Growth.* Dordrecht: Kluwer, 2001.

Halévy, Elie. *The Growth of Philosophic Radicalism.* Translated by Mary Morris. Boston: Beacon Press, 1955.

Hall, Catherine. *Civilising Subjects: Metropole and Colony in the English Imagination, 1830–1867.* Chicago: University of Chicago Press, 2002.

Hall, Catherine. " 'From Greenland's Icy Mountains . . . to Afric's Gold Sand': Ethnicity, Race, and Nation in Mid-Nineteenth-Century England." *Gender and History* 5, no. 2 (1993): 212–30.

———. "The Nation within and Without." In *Defining the Victorian Nation: Class, Race, Gender, and the Reform Act of 1867*, edited by Catherine Hall, Keith McClelland, and Jane Rendall. Cambridge: Cambridge University Press, 2000.

———. "Rethinking Imperial Histories: The Reform Act of 1867." *New Left Review* 208 (1994): 3–29.

———. *White, Male, and Middle-Class: Explorations in Feminism and History.* New York: Routledge, 1992.

Hamdani, Amar. *La Vérité sur l'expédition d'Alger.* Paris: Balland, 1985.

Hamowy, Ronald. *The Scottish Enlightenment and the Theory of Spontaneous Order.* Carbondale: Southern Illinois University Press, 1987.

Hampsher-Monk, Iain. "Rhetoric and Opinion in the Politics of Edmund Burke." *History of Political Thought* 9, no. 3 (1988): 455–84.

Harlow, Vincent T. *The Founding of the Second British Empire, 1763–1793.* 2 vols. London: Longmans, 1964.

Harrison, Ross. *Bentham.* London: Routledge and Kegan Paul, 1983.

Hart, David M. "The Radical Liberalism of Charles Comte and Charles Dunoyer." Ph.D. diss., King's College, Cambridge, 2003.

Hart, H.L.A. *Essays on Bentham: Studies in Jurisprudence and Political Theory.* Oxford: Clarendon Press, 1982.

———. "The United States of America." *In Essays on Bentham: Studies in Jurisprudence and Political Theory.* Oxford: Clarendon Press, 1982.

Hazareesingh, Sudhir. *From Subject to Citizen: The Second Empire and the Emergence of Modern French Democracy.* Princeton: Princeton University Press, 1998.

Heffernan, Michael. "The Parisian Poor and the Colonization of Algeria during the Second Republic." *French History* 3, no. 4 (1989): 377–403.

Hereth, Michael. *Alexis de Tocqueville: Threats to Freedom in Democracy.* Durham, N.C.: Duke University Press, 1986.

Herzog, Don. "Puzzling through Burke." *Political Theory* 19, no. 3 (1991): 336–63.

Holmes, Stephen. *Benjamin Constant and the Making of Modern Liberalism.* New Haven: Yale University Press, 1984.

———. "Constant and Tocqueville: An Unexplored Relationship." *Annales Benjamin Constant* 12 (1991): 29–41.

Hont, Istvan. "The Language of Sociability and Commerce: Samuel Pufendorf and the Theoretical Foundations of the 'Four-Stages Theory.' " In *The Languages of Political Theory in Early-Modern Europe*, edited by Anthony Pagden. Cambridge: Cambridge University Press, 1987.

———. "The Permanent Crisis of a Divided Mankind: 'Contemporary Crisis of the Nation State' in Historical Perspective." In *The Contemporary Crisis of the Nation State*, edited by John Dunn. Oxford: Blackwell, 1995.

Hoogensen, Gunhild. "Bentham's International Manuscripts versus the Published 'Works.' " *Journal of Bentham Studies* 4 (2001): 1–14.

Höpfl, H. M. "From Savage to Scotsman: Conjectural History in the Scottish Enlightenment." *Journal of British Studies* 17, no. 2 (1978): 19–40.

Hudson, Nicholas. "From 'Nation' to 'Race': The Origin of Racial Classification in Eighteenth-Century Thought." *Eighteenth-Century Studies* 29, no. 3 (1996): 247–64.

Iyer, Raghavan. *Utilitarianism and All That*. London: Concord Grove Press, 1983.

Janes, Regina. "At Home Abroad: Edmund Burke in India." *Bulletin of Research in the Humanities* 82 (1979): 160–74.

Janes, Regina. "High Flying: Edmund Burke's Eire-India." *Bulletin of Research in the Humanities* 82 (1979): 185–89.

Jardin, André. "Alexis de Tocqueville, Gustave de Beaumont et le problème de l'inegalité des races." In *L'Idée de race dans la pensée politique française contemporaine*, edited by P. Guiral and E. Temime. Paris: Editions du CNRS, 1977.

———. *Tocqueville: A Biography*. Translated by Lydia Davis. New York: Farrar Straus and Giroux, 1988.

———. "Tocqueville et l'Algérie." *Revue des travaux de l'Académie des sciences morales et politiques*, 4th ser., no. 1 (1962): 61–74.

Julien, Charles-André. *Histoire de l'Algérie contemporaine. La conquête et les débuts de la colonisation, 1827–1871*. Paris: Presses Universitaires de France, 1964.

Kahan, Alan S. *Aristocratic Liberalism: The Social and Political Thought of Jacob Burckhardt, John Stuart Mill, and Alexis de Tocqueville*. Oxford: Oxford University Press, 1992.

Kateb, George. "A Reading of *On Liberty*." In *On Liberty*, edited by David Bromwich and George Kateb. New Haven: Yale University Press, 2003.

Keene, Edward. *Beyond the Anarchical Society: Grotius, Colonialism, and Order in World Politics*. Cambridge: Cambridge University Press, 2002.

Kelly, George Armstrong. *The Humane Comedy: Constant, Tocqueville, and French Liberalism*. Cambridge: Cambridge University Press, 1992.

Kinzer, Bruce L., Ann P. Robson, and John M. Robson. *A Moralist in and out of Parliament: John Stuart Mill at Westminster, 1865–1868*. Toronto: University of Toronto Press, 1992.

Knox, B. A. "The British Government and the Governor Eyre Controversy." *Historical Journal* 19, no. 4 (1976): 877–900.

Koebner, Richard. *Empire*. Cambridge: Cambridge University Press, 1961.

Koebner, Richard, and Helmut Dan Schmidt. *Imperialism*. Cambridge: Cambridge University Press, 1964.

Kramnick, Isaac. "The Left and Edmund Burke." *Political Theory* 11, no. 2 (1983): 189–214.

———. *The Rage of Edmund Burke: Portrait of an Ambivalent Conservative*. New York: Basic Books, 1977.

Kurer, Oskar. *John Stuart Mill: The Politics of Progress*. New York: Garland, 1991.

Kurfirst, Robert. "J. S. Mill on Oriental Despotism, Including Its British variant." *Utilitas* 8, no. 1 (1996): 73–87.

Lach, Donald. "Leibniz in China." *Journal of the History of Ideas* 6 (1945): 436–55.

Lach, Donald. "The Sinophilism of Christian Wolff (1679–1754)." *Journal of the History of Ideas* 14, no. 4 (1953): 561–74.

Lafleur, Laurence J. "Jeremy Bentham and the *Principles*." In *An Introduction to the Principles of Morals and Legislation*, by Jeremy Bentham edited by Laurence J. Lafleur. New York: Macmillan, 1948.

Laird, M. A. Introduction to *Bishop Heber in Northern India: Selections from Heber's Journal*, edited by M. A. Laird. London: Cambridge University Press, 1971.

Lamberti, Jean-Claude. "De Benjamin Constant à Alexis de Tocqueville." *Revue France-Forum* 203–4 (1983): 19–26.

Langford, Paul. *A Polite and Commercial People*. Oxford: Oxford University Press, 1989.

Laski, Harold. *Edmund Burke*. Dublin: Falconer, 1947.

Lawlor, Mary. *Alexis de Tocqueville in the Chamber of Deputies, His Views on Foreign and Colonial Policy*. Washington, D.C.: Catholic University of America Press, 1959.

Lawson, Philip. *The Imperial Challenge: Quebec and Britain in the Age of the American Revolution*. Montreal: McGill-Queen's University Press, 1989.

Leung, Man To. "Extending Liberalism to Non-European Peoples: A Comparison of John Locke and James Mill." DPhil thesis, Oxford University, 1988.

Liebersohn, Harry. *Aristocratic Encounters: European Travelers and North American Indians*. Cambridge: Cambridge University Press, 1998.

———. "Discovering Indigenous Nobility: Tocqueville, Chamisso, and Romantic Travel Writing." *American Historical Review* 99, no. 3 (1994): 746–66.

Lively, Jack. *The Social and Political Thought of Alexis de Tocqueville*. Oxford: Clarendon Press, 1962.

Lloyd, Trevor. "John Stuart Mill and the East India Company." In *A Cultivated Mind: Essays on J. S. Mill Presented to John M. Robson*, edited by Michael Laine. Toronto: University of Toronto Press, 1991.

Long, Douglas G. *Bentham on Liberty: Jeremy Bentham's Idea of Liberty in Relation to His Utilitarianism*. Toronto: University of Toronto Press, 1977.

Lorcin, Patricia M. E. *Imperial Identities: Stereotyping, Prejudice, and Race in Colonial Algeria*. New York: I. B. Tauris, 1995.

Mack, Mary Peter. *Jeremy Bentham: An Odyssey of Ideas, 1748–1792*. London: Heinemann, 1963.

Mahoney, Thomas H. D. *Edmund Burke and Ireland*. Cambridge: Harvard University Press, 1960.

Majeed, Javed. *Ungoverned Imaginings: James Mill's "The History of British India" and Orientalism*. Oxford: Clarendon Press, 1992.

Makdisi, Saree. *Romantic Imperialism: Universal Empire and the Culture of Modernity*. Cambridge: Cambridge University Press, 1998.

Mandler, Peter. " 'Race' and 'Nation' in Mid-Victorian Thought." In *History, Religion, and Culture: British Intellectual History, 1795–1950*, edited by Stefan Collini, Richard Whatmore, and Brian Young. Cambridge: Cambridge University Press, 2000.

Mantena, Karuna. "Alibis of Empire." Ph.D. diss., Harvard University, 2004.

Marshall, P. J. "Britain and the World in the Eighteenth Century: Reshaping the Empire." *Transactions of the Royal Historical Society*, 6th ser., 8 (1998): 1–18.

———. "Burke and Empire." In *Hanoverian Britain and Empire: Essays in Memory of Philip Lawson*, edited by Stephen Taylor, Richard Connors, and Clyve Jones. Rochester, N.Y.: Boydell Press, 1998.

———. "The Caribbean and India in the Later Eighteenth Century: Two British Empires or One." In *A Free Though Conquering People: Eighteenth-Century Britain and Its Empire*. Burlington, Vt.: Ashgate, 2003.

———. "A Free Though Conquering People': Britain and Asia in the Eighteenth Century." In *A Free Though Conquering People: Eighteenth-Century Britain and Its Empire*. Burlington, Vt.: Ashgate, 2003.

———. *The Impeachment of Warren Hastings*. Oxford: Oxford University Press, 1965.

———. "The Moral Swing to the East: British Humanitarianism, India, and the West Indies." In *East India Company Studies: Papers Presented to Professor Sir Cyril Philips*, edited by Kenneth Ballhatchet and John Harrison. Hong Kong: Asian Research Science, 1986.

———. *Problems of Empire: Britain and India, 1757–1813*. London: Allen and Unwin, 1968.

———. "Warren Hastings as Scholar and Patron." In *Statesmen, Scholars, and Merchants*, edited by Anne Whiteman, J. S. Bromley and P.G.M. Dickson. Oxford: Clarendon Press, 1973.

Marshall, P. J., and Glyndwr Williams. *The Great Map of Mankind: Perceptions of New Worlds in the Age of Enlightenment*. Cambridge: Harvard University Press, 1982.

Martel, André. "Tocqueville et les problèmes coloniaux de la monarchie de juillet." *Revue d'histoire économique et sociale* 32 (1954): 367–88.

Matthewson, Tim. "Jefferson and Haiti." *Journal of Southern History* 61 (1995): 209–48.

Mazlish, Bruce. *James and John Stuart Mill: Father and Son in the Nineteenth Century*. New Brunswick, N.J.: Transaction, 1988.

McCann, Andrew. *Cultural Politics in the 1790s*. London: Macmillan, 1999.

Meek, Ronald L. "New Light on Adam Smith's Glasgow Lectures on Jurisprudence." *History of Political Economy* 8, no. 4 (1976): 439–77.

———. "Smith, Turgot, and the 'Four Stages' Theory." *History of Political Economy* 3, no. 1 (1971): 9–27.

———. *Social Science and the Ignoble Savage*. Cambridge: Cambridge University Press, 1976.

Mehta, Pratap B. "Liberalism, Nation, and Empire: The Case of J. S. Mill." Paper presented at the American Political Science Association, San Francisco, 1996.

Mehta, Uday S. "Liberal Strategies of Exclusion." *Politics and Society* 18, no. 4 (1990): 427–54.

———. *Liberalism and Empire: A Study in Nineteenth-Century British Liberal Thought*. Chicago: University of Chicago Press, 1999.

Mélonio, Françoise. "Nations et nationalismes." *Tocqueville Review* 18, no. 1 (1997): 61–75.

Mélonio, Françoise. *Tocqueville and the French*. Translated by Beth G. Raps. Charlottesville: University Press of Virginia, 1998.

Merle, Marcel, ed. *L'Anticolonialisme européen, de Las Casas à Karl Marx*. Paris: A. Colon, 1969.

Metcalf, Thomas R. *The Aftermath of Revolt: India, 1857–1870*. Princeton: Princeton University Press, 1964.

Mitchell, Timothy. *Colonising Egypt*. Cambridge: Cambridge University Press, 1988.

Moir, Martin I. Introduction to *Writings on India*, by John Stuart Mill, edited by John M. Robson, Martin Moir and Zawahir Moir. Toronto: University of Toronto Press, 1990.

Moir, Martin I., Douglas M. Peers, and Lynn Zastoupil, eds. *J. S. Mill's Encounter with India*. Toronto: University of Toronto Press, 1999.

Moore, Robin. "John Stuart Mill and Royal India." In *J. S. Mill's Encounter with India*, edited Martin I. Moir, Douglas M. Peers, and Lynn Zastoupil. Toronto: University of Toronto Press, 1999.

Mueller, Iris Wessel. *John Stuart Mill and French Thought*. Urbana: University of Illinois Press, 1956.

Mukherjee, S.N. *Sir William Jones: A Study of Eighteenth-Century British Attitudes to India*. Cambridge: Cambridge University Press, 1968.

———. "Sir William Jones and British Attitudes towards India." *Journal of the Royal Asiatic Society* (1964): 37–47.

Musselwhite, David. "The Trial of Warren Hastings." In *Literature, Politics, and Theory*, edited by Francis Barker et al. London: Methuen, 1986.

Muthu, Sankar. *Enlightenment against Empire*. Princeton: Princeton University Press, 2003.

Nisbet, Robert A. *Social Change and History: Aspects of the Western Theory of Development*. Oxford: Oxford University Press, 1969.

Nussbaum, Felicity. *Torrid Zones: Maternity, Sexuality, and Empire in Eighteenth-Century English Narratives*. Baltimore: Johns Hopkins University Press, 1995.

O'Brien, Conor Cruise. *The Great Melody: A Thematic Biography and Commented Anthology of Edmund Burke*. Chicago: University of Chicago Press, 1992.

O'Brien, Karen. *Narratives of Enlightenment: Cosmopolitan History from Voltaire to Gibbon*. Cambridge: Cambridge University Press, 1997.

———. "Protestantism and the Poetry of Empire." In *Culture and Society in Britain, 1660–1800*, edited by Jeremy Black. Manchester: Manchester University Press, 1997.

Pagden, Anthony. *Lords of All the World: Ideologies of Empire in Spain, Britain, and France, 1500–1850*. New Haven: Yale University Press, 1995.

———. "The Struggle for Legitimacy and the Image of Empire in the Atlantic to C.1700." In *The Oxford History of the British Empire: The Origins of Empire*, edited by Nicholas Canny. Oxford: Oxford University Press, 2001.

Parekh, Bhikhu. "Decolonizing Liberalism." In *The End of "Isms"? Reflections on the Fate of Ideological Politics after Communism's Collapse*, edited by Aleksandras Shtromas. Oxford: Blackwell, 1994.

———. "Liberalism and Colonialism: A Critique of Locke and Mill." In *The Decolonization of Imagination: Culture, Knowledge, and Power*, edited by Jan Nederveen Pieterse and Bhikhu Parekh. London: Zed Books, 1995.

———. "Superior People: The Narrowness of Liberalism from Mill to Rawls." *Times Literary Supplement*, February 25, 1994, 11–13.

Peers, Douglas M. "Imperial Epitaph: John Stuart Mill's Defence of the East India Company." In *J. S. Mill's Encounter with India*, edited Martin I. Moir, Douglas M. Peers, and Lynn Zastoupil. Toronto: University of Toronto Press, 1999.

Philips, C. H. *The East India Company, 1784–1834*. Manchester: Manchester University Press, 1961.

Philips, C. H., and Mary Doreen Wainwright, eds. *Indian Society and the Beginnings of Modernization, c.1830–1850*. London: University of London School of Oriental and African Studies, 1976.

Pierson, George Wilson. *Tocqueville in America*. Baltimore: Johns Hopkins University Press, 1996.

Pinkney, David H. *Decisive Years in France, 1840–1847*. Princeton: Princeton University Press, 1986.

Pocock, J.G.A. *Barbarism and Religion*. 3 vols. Cambridge: Cambridge University Press, 1999–2003.

———. *Virtue, Commerce, and History*. Cambridge: Cambridge University Press, 1985.

Pomeranz, Kenneth. *The Great Divergence: Europe, China, and the Making of the Modern World Economy*. Princeton: Princeton University Press, 2000.

Pyenson, Lewis. *Civilizing Mission: Exact Sciences and French Overseas Expansion, 1830–1940*. Baltimore: Johns Hopkins University Press, 1993.

Quinn, Frederick. *The French Overseas Empire*. Westport, Conn.: Praeger, 2000.

Reddy, William M. *The Invisible Code: Honor and Sentiment in Postrevolutionary France, 1814–1848*. Berkeley and Los Angeles: University of California Press, 1997.

Rendall, Jane. "Citizenship, Culture, and Civilisation: The Languages of British Suffragists, 1866–1874." In *Suffrage and Beyond: International Feminist Perspectives*, edited by Caroline Daley and Melanie Nolan. New York: New York University Press, 1994.

———. "Scottish Orientalism: From Robertson to James Mill." *Historical Journal* 25 (1982): 43–69.

Resh, Richard W. "Alexis de Tocqueville and the Negro: *Democracy in America* Reconsidered." *Journal of Negro History* 48 (1963): 251–59.

Rey-Goldzeiguer, Annie. "La France coloniale de 1830–1870." In *Histoire de la France coloniale*, edited by Jean Meyer, Jean Tarrade, Annie Rey-Goldzeiguer, and Jacques Thobie. Paris: Colin, 1991.

Richter, Melvin. "Comparative Political Analysis in Montesquieu and Tocqueville." *Comparative Politics* 1, no. 2 (1969): 129–60.

———. "Debate on Race: Tocqueville-Gobineau Correspondence." *Commentary* 25 (1958): 151–60.

———. "Europe and the Other in Eighteenth-Century Thought." *Politisches Denken* 1997: 25–47.

Richter, Melvin. "Tocqueville, Napoleon, and Bonapartism." In *Reconsidering Tocqueville's Democracy in America*, edited by Abraham Eisenstadt. New Brunswick, N.J.: Rutgers University Press, 1988.

———. "Tocqueville on Algeria." *Review of Politics* 25 (1963): 362–98.

———. "Threats to Liberty: Montesquieu and Tocqueville on New Forms of Illegitimate Domination." In *Alexis de Tocqueville—zur Politik in der Demokratie*, edited by Michael Hereth and Jutta Höffgen. Baden-Baden: Nomosverlagsgesellschaft, 1981.

———. "The Uses of Theory: Tocqueville's Adaptation of Montesquieu." In *Essays in Theory and History*, edited by Melvin Richter. Cambridge: Harvard University Press, 1970.

Riddly, John. "Warren Hastings: Scotland's Benefactor?" In *The Impeachment of Warren Hastings*, edited by Geoffrey Carnall and Colin Nicholson. Edinburgh: Edinburgh University Press, 1989.

Robert, Adolphe. *Dictionnaire des parlementaires français*. Paris, 1889–91.

Robertson, John. "Empire and Union: Two Concepts of the Early Modern European Political Order." In *A Union for Empire: Political Thought and the British Union of 1707*, edited by John Robertson. Cambridge: Cambridge University Press, 1995.

Robinson, Nicholas K. *Edmund Burke: A Life in Caricature*. New Haven: Yale University Press, 1996.

Robson, John M. "Civilization and Culture as Moral Concepts." In *Cambridge Companion to Mill*, edited by John Skorupski. Cambridge: Cambridge University Press, 1998.

———. *The Improvement of Mankind: The Social and Political Thought of John Stuart Mill*. Toronto: University of Toronto Press, 1968.

———. "John Stuart Mill and Jeremy Bentham." In *Essays in English Literature from the Renaissance to the Victorian Age*, edited by Millar MacLure and F. W. Watt. Toronto: University of Toronto Press, 1964.

Rosen, Fred. *Bentham, Byron, and Greece: Constitutionalism, Nationalism, and Early Liberal Political Thought*. Oxford: Clarendon Press, 1992.

———. "Elie Halévy and Bentham's Authoritarian Liberalism." In *Jeremy Bentham: Critical Assessments*, edited by Bhikhu Parekh. London: Routledge, 1993.

———. "Eric Stokes, British Utilitarianism, and India." In *J. S. Mill's Encounter with India*, edited by Martin I. Moir, Douglas M. Peers, and Lynn Zastoupil. Toronto: University of Toronto Press, 1999.

———. *Jeremy Bentham and Representative Democracy*. Oxford: Clarendon Press, 1983.

Rosenthal, Jerome. "Voltaire's Philosophy of History." *Journal of the History of Ideas* 16 (1955): 151–78.

Ross, Ian Simpson. *The Life of Adam Smith*. Oxford: Clarendon Press, 1995.

Rothschild, Emma. *Economic Sentiments : Adam Smith, Condorcet, and the Enlightenment*. Cambridge: Harvard University Press, 2001.

Ruedy, John. *Modern Algeria: The Origins and Development of a Nation*. Bloomington: Indiana University Press, 1992.

Ryan, Alan. "Mill in a Liberal Landscape." In *Cambridge Companion to Mill*, edited by John Skorupski. Cambridge: Cambridge University Press, 1998.

———. "A Political Assessment of Progress." In *Progress: Fact or Illusion?* edited by Bruce Mazlish and Leo Marx. Ann Arbor: University of Michigan Press, 1996.

Sabin, Margery. *Dissenters and Mavericks: Writings about India in English, 1765–2000*. Oxford: Oxford University Press, 2002.

Sack, J. J. "The Memory of Burke and the Memory of Pitt: English Conservatism Confronts Its Past, 1806–1829." *Historical Journal* 30, no. 3 (1987): 623–40.

Said, Edward. *Culture and Imperialism*. New York: Knopf, 1993.

———. *Orientalism*. New York: Vintage, 1979.

Saintoyant, J. *La Colonisation Française pendant la période napoléonienne (1799–1815)*. Paris: La Renaissance du Livre, 1931.

———. *La Colonisation Française pendant la Révolution (1789–1799)*. 2 vols. Paris: La Renaissance du Livre, 1930.

Sayre, Gordon M. *Les Sauvages Américains: Representations of Native Americans in French and English Colonial Literature*. Chapel Hill: University of North Carolina Press, 1997.

Schefer, Christian. *L'Algérie et l'évolution de la colonisation française*. Paris: Librairie de la Société de l'Histoire de France, 1928.

Schofield, Philip. "Jeremy Bentham: Legislator of the World." In *Current Legal Problems*, edited by M.D.A. Freeman. Oxford: Oxford University Press, 1998.

Schuyler, R. L. "The Climax of Anti-imperialism in England." *Political Quarterly* 36, no. 4 (1921): 537–60.

———. "The Rise of Anti-imperialism in England." *Political Quarterly* 37, no. 3 (1922): 440–71.

Schwartzberg, Steven. "The Lion and the Phoenix: British Policy toward the 'Greek Question,' 1821–32." *Middle Eastern Studies* 24, nos. 2–3 (1988): 139–77, 287–311.

Semmel, Bernard. *The Governor Eyre Controversy*. London: MacGibbon and Kee, 1962.

———. "The Philosophic Radicals and Colonialism." *Journal of Economic History* 21, no. 4 (1961): 513–25.

———. *The Rise of Free Trade Imperialism: Classical Political Economy, the Empire of Free Trade, and Imperialism, 1750–1850*. Cambridge: Cambridge University Press, 1970.

Skinner, Andrew S. "Adam Smith: An Economic Interpretation of History." In *Essays on Adam Smith*, edited by Andrew S. Skinner and Thomas Wilson. Oxford: Clarendon Press, 1975.

Sloane, W. M. "Napoleon's Plans for a Colonial System." *American Historical Review* 4, no. 3 (1899): 439–55.

Smart, J.J.C., and Bernard Williams. *Utilitarianism: For and Against*. Cambridge: Cambridge University Press, 1973.

Smith, Bruce James. *Politics and Remembrance: Republican Themes in Machiavelli, Burke, and Tocqueville*. Princeton: Princeton University Press, 1985.

Soltau, Roger Henry. *French Political Thought in the Nineteenth Century*. New York: Russel and Russel, 1931.

Spadafora, David. *The Idea of Progress in Eighteenth-Century Britain.* New Haven: Yale University Press, 1990.

Stanlis, Peter J. "Edmund Burke and the Law of Nations." *American Journal of International Law* 47, no. 3 (1953): 397–413.

———. *Edmund Burke and the Natural Law.* Shreveport, La.: Huntington House, 1986.

Staum, Martin. *Labeling People.* Montreal: McGill-Queen's University Press, 2003.

Steele, E. D. "J. S. Mill and the Irish Question: Reform and the Integrity of the Empire, 1865–1870." *Historical Journal* 13, no. 3 (1970): 419–50.

———. "J. S. Mill and the Irish Question: The Principles of Political Economy, 1848–1865." *Historical Journal* 13, no. 2 (1970): 216–36.

Stein, Peter G. *Legal Evolution: The Story of an Idea.* Cambridge: Cambridge University Press, 1980.

Stepan, Nancy. *The Idea of Race in Science: Great Britain, 1800–1960.* London: Macmillan, 1982.

Stephen, Leslie. *The English Utilitarians.* London: Duckworth, 1900.

Stevens, David. "Adam Smith and the Colonial Disturbances." In *Essays on Adam Smith*, edited by Andrew S. Skinner and Thomas Wilson. Oxford: Clarendon Press, 1975.

Stocking, George W., Jr. "Scotland as the Model of Mankind: Lord Kames' Philosophical View of Civilization." In *Toward a Science of Man: Essays in the History of Anthropology*, edited by Timothy H. H. Thoresen. The Hague: Mouton, 1975.

Stokes, Curtis. "Tocqueville and the Problem of Racial Inequality." *Journal of Negro History* 75, nos. 1–2 (1990): 1–15.

Stokes, Eric. *The English Utilitarians and India.* Oxford: Clarendon Press, 1959.

Stora, Benjamin. *Histoire de l'Algérie coloniale, 1830–1954.* Paris: Éditions la Découverte, 1991.

Suleri, Sara. *The Rhetoric of English India.* Chicago: University of Chicago Press, 1992.

Sullivan, Antony Thrall. *Thomas-Robert Bugeaud, France, and Algeria, 1784–1849: Politics, Power, and the Good Society.* Hamden, Conn.: Archon, 1983.

Sullivan, Eileen. "Liberalism and Imperialism: J. S. Mill's Defense of the British Empire." *Journal of the History of Ideas* 44, no. 4 (1983): 599–617.

Sutherland, Lucy S. *The East India Company in Eighteenth-Century Politics.* Oxford: Clarendon Press, 1952.

Taylor, Charles. "Dynamics of Democratic Exclusion." *Journal of Democracy* 9, no. 4 (1998): 143–56.

Taylor, Miles. "Empire and Parliamentary Reform: The 1832 Reform Act Revisited." In *Rethinking the Age of Reform: Britain, 1780–1850*, edited by Arthur Burns and Joanna Innes. Cambridge: Cambridge University Press, 2003.

Thom, Martin. *Republics, Nations, and Tribes.* London: Verso, 1995.

Thomas, William. *The Philosophic Radicals: Nine Studies in Theory and Practice, 1817–1841.* Oxford: Clarendon Press, 1979.

Todorov, Tzvetan. *On Human Diversity: Nationalism, Racism, and Exoticism in French Thought*. Translated by Catherine Porter. Cambridge: Harvard University Press, 1993.

Tuck, Richard. *The Rights of War and Peace: Political Thought and the International Order from Grotius to Kant*. Oxford: Oxford University Press, 1999.

Twining, William. "Imagining Bentham: A Celebration." *Current Legal Problems* 51 (1998): 1–36.

Valet, René. *L'Afrique du nord devant le parlement au XIXme siècle*. Algiers: Imprimerie "La typo-litho," 1924.

Vanech, William. "Painful Homecoming: Reflections on Burke and India." *Bulletin of Research in the Humanities* 82 (1979): 175–84.

Varouxakis, Georgios. "John Stuart Mill on Race." *Utilitas* 10, no. 1 (1998): 17–32.

———. *Mill on Nationality*. London: Routledge, 2002.

———. "National Character in John Stuart Mill's Thought." *History of European Ideas* 24, no. 6 (1998): 375–91.

Venturi, Franco. "Oriental Despotism." *Journal of the History of Ideas* 24 (1963): 133–42.

Walzer, Michael. *Interpretation and Social Criticism*. Cambridge: Harvard University Press, 1985.

Washbrook, D. A. "India, 1818–1860: The Two Faces of Colonialism." In *The Nineteenth Century*, edited by Andrew Porter. Oxford: Oxford University Press, 1999.

Welch, Cheryl. "Colonial Violence and the Rhetoric of Evasion: Tocqueville on Algeria." *Political Theory* 31, no. 2 (2003): 235–64.

———. *De Tocqueville*. Oxford: Oxford University Press, 2001.

———. *Liberty and Utility: The French Idéologues and the Transformation of Liberalism*. New York: Columbia University Press, 1984.

Welsh, Jennifer M. *Edmund Burke and International Relations: The Commonwealth of Europe and the Crusade against the French Revolution*. London: Macmillan, 1995.

Wheeler, Roxann. *The Complexion of Race: Categories of Difference in Eighteenth-Century British Culture*. Philadelphia: University of Pennsylvania Press, 2000.

Whelan, Frederick G. *Edmund Burke and India: Political Morality and Empire*. Pittsburgh: University of Pittsburgh Press, 1996.

———. "Oriental Despotism: Anquetil-Duperron's Response to Montesquieu." *History of Political Thought* 22, no. 4 (2001): 619–47.

White, Stephen K. *Edmund Burke: Modernity, Politics, and Aesthetics*. Lanham, Md.: Rowman and Littlefield, 2000.

Williford, Miriam. *Jeremy Bentham on Spanish America: An Account of His Letters and Proposals to the New World*. Baton Rouge: Lousiana State University Press, 1980.

Wilson, Kathleen. "Citizenship, Empire, and Modernity in the English Provinces, c. 1720–90." In *Cultures of Empire: Colonizers in Britain and the Empire in the Nineteenth and Twentieth Centuries*, edited by Catherine Hall. New York: Routledge, 2000. 157–86.

Wilson, Kathleen. *The Island Race: Englishness, Empire, and Gender in the Eighteenth Century*. London: Routledge, 2003.

———. *The Sense of the People: Politics, Culture, and Imperialism in England, 1715–1785*. Cambridge: Cambridge University Press, 1995.

Winch, Donald. "Adam Smith's 'Enduring Particular Result': A Political and Cosmopolitan Perspective." In *Wealth and Virtue*, edited by Istvan Hont and Michael Ignatieff. Cambridge: Cambridge University Press, 1983.

———. "Bentham on Colonies and Empire." *Utilitas* 9, no. 1 (1997): 147–54.

———. *Classical Political Economy and Colonies*. Cambridge: Harvard University Press, 1965.

———. *Riches and Poverty: An Intellectual History of Political Economy in Britain, 1750–1834*. Cambridge, 1996.

Wokler, Robert. "Anthropology and Conjectural History in the Enlightenment." In *Inventing Human Science: Eighteenth-Century Domains*, edited by Christopher Fox, Roy Porter, and Robert Wokler. Berkeley and Los Angeles: University of California Press, 1995.

———. "Apes and Races in the Scottish Enlightenment: Monboddo and Kames on the Nature of Man." In *Philosophy and Science in the Scottish Enlightenment*, edited by Peter Jones. Edinburgh: John Donald, 1988.

Wolff, Larry. *Inventing Eastern Europe: The Map of Civilization on the Mind of the Enlightenment*. Stanford: Stanford University Press, 1994.

Wolin, Sheldon. *Tocqueville between Two Worlds*. Princeton: Princeton University Press, 2001.

Wood, Dennis. *Benjamin Constant: A Biography*. New York: Routledge, 1993.

Wood, P. B. "The Natural History of Man in the Scottish Enlightenment." *History of Science* 27 (1989): 89–123.

Woolf, Stuart. "French Civilization and Ethnicity in the Napoleonic Empire." *Past and Present* 124 (1989): 96–120.

Zastoupil, Lynn. "India, J. S. Mill, and 'Western' Culture." In *J.S. Mill's Encounter with India*, edited by Martin I. Moir, Douglas M. Peers, and Lynn Zastoupil. Toronto: University of Toronto Press, 1999.

———. *John Stuart Mill and India*. Stanford: Stanford University Press, 1994.

———. "Moral Government: J. S. Mill on Ireland." *Historical Journal* 26, no. 3 (1983): 707–17.

Index